LIFE AGAINST DEATH

The Psychoanalytical Meaning of History

LIFE
AGAINST
DEATH

The Psychoanalytical Meaning of History

BY

NORMAN O. BROWN

Wesleyan University Press

MIDDLETOWN, CONNECTICUT

Library of Congress Catalog Card Number: 59-5369

ISBN: 0-8195-6010-3

Copyright © 1959 by Wesleyan University
Manufactured in the United States of America
First Wesleyan paperback edition, 1970; fifth printing, 1977

10 9 8 7 6

Contents

Acknowledgments

THE AUTHOR acknowledges with gratitude the help he has had from many quarters in the completion of this volume. First of all are numerous friends, colleagues and students alike, who have assisted through discussion, argument, and sometimes challenge; to most of these I have proffered my personal thanks. The Fund for the Advancement of Education of the Ford Foundation made it possible for me to spend the year 1953–1954 in the psychological and anthropological studies that underlie this book; for this I am indebted. In addition, I am indebted to the Research Fund of Wesleyan University, which assisted financially in the preparation of the manuscript. I am grateful to Professor E. M. Chick, now at the University of California, who made for my benefit the translation of Rilke's "Ueber Kunst" quoted herein. And lastly, I am grateful to the many authors and publishers from whose works brief quotations appear in this text, as specifically acknowledged elsewhere; and particularly to the following, who have kindly granted me permission to use passages of substantial length from the publications specified:

George Allen & Unwin Ltd., London, for Freud's *General Introduction to Psychoanalysis*.

Basic Books, Inc., New York, for Abraham's *Selected Papers on Psychoanalysis*; for Ferenczi's *Further Contributions to the Theory and Technique of Psychoanalysis* and his *Sex in Psychoanalysis*; and for Freud's *Collected Papers* and his *The Origins of Psychoanalysis*.

Harcourt, Brace & Co., Inc., New York, for Keynes' *Essays in Persuasion*.

The Hogarth Press, Ltd., London, for Ferenczi's *Final Con-*

tributions to the Problems and Methods of Psychoanalysis, his *Further Contributions to the Theory and Technique of Psychoanalysis*, and his *Sex in Psychoanalysis*; for Freud's *Beyond the Pleasure Principle*, his *Civilization and Its Discontents*, his *Collected Papers*, his *The Ego and the Id*, his *The Future of an Illusion*, his *Group Psychology and the Analysis of the Ego*, his *Inhibitions, Symptoms and Anxiety*, his *Moses and Monotheism*, his *New Introductory Lectures on Psychoanalysis*, and his *An Outline of Psychoanalysis*; and for Jones' *Papers on Psycho-Analysis*.

Alfred A. Knopf, Inc., New York, for Freud's *Moses and Monotheism;* for Herskovits' *Economic Anthropology;* and for Spengler's *Decline of the West.*

R. F. Kahn, Esq., Cambridge University, representing the Keynes Trustees, for Keynes' *Essays in Persuasion.*

Liveright Publishing Corporation, New York, for Freud's *A General Introduction to Psychoanalysis*, copyright 1935 by Edward L. Bernays.

The Macmillan Company, New York, for Yeats' "Crazy Jane Talks with the Bishop," from his *Collected Poems.*

New Directions, Inc., New York, for Miller's *Sunday After the War.*

Random House, Inc., New York, for Marx' *Capital;* and for Nietzsche's *Philosophy of Friedrich Nietzsche.*

Routledge & Kegan Paul Ltd., London, for Grisar's *Luther.*

Yale University Press, New Haven, for Hartman's *The Unmediated Vision.*

Introduction

IN 1953 I turned to a deep study of Freud, feeling the need to reappraise the nature and destiny of man. Inheriting from the Protestant tradition a conscience which insisted that intellectual work should be directed toward the relief of man's estate, I, like so many of my generation, lived through the superannuation of the political categories which informed liberal thought and action in the 1930's. Those of us who are temperamentally incapable of embracing the politics of sin, cynicism, and despair have been compelled to re-examine the classic assumptions about the nature of politics and about the political character of human nature. But, unless I am mistaken, the feeling that traditional schools of thought have become stereotyped and sterile is not limited to those with my kind of background. This book is addressed to all who are ready to call into question old assumptions and to entertain new possibilities. And since new ideas will not come if their entry into the mind is subject to conformity with our old ones and with what we call common sense, this book demands of the reader— as it demanded of the author—a willing suspension of common sense. The aim is to open up a new point of view. The task of judicious appraisal, confronting theoretical possibility with the stubborn facts of present events and past history, comes later.

But why Freud? It is a shattering experience for anyone seriously committed to the Western traditions of morality and rationality to take a steadfast, unflinching look at what Freud has to say. It is humiliating to be compelled to admit the grossly seamy side of so many grand ideals. It is criminal to violate the civilized taboos which have kept the seamy side concealed. To experience Freud is to partake a second time of the forbidden fruit; and this book cannot without sinning communicate that experience to the reader.

But to what end? When our eyes are opened, and the fig leaf no longer conceals our nakedness, our present situation is experienced in its full concrete actuality as a tragic crisis. To anticipate the direction of this book, it begins to be apparent that mankind, in all its restless striving and progress, has no idea of what it really wants. Freud was right: our real desires are unconscious. It also begins to be apparent that mankind, unconscious of its real desires and therefore unable to obtain satisfaction, is hostile to life and ready to destroy itself. Freud was right in positing a death instinct, and the development of weapons of destruction makes our present dilemma plain: we either come to terms with our unconscious instincts and drives —with life and with death—or else we surely die.

But even Freud is not enough. In the hands of Freud, psychoanalysis was a living organism in constant evolution. Since Freud's death orthodox psychoanalysis has become a closed, almost scholastic system, itself no exception to the general cultural trend toward stereotypy and sterility. Rigorous probing reveals that the entire metapsychological foundations of psychoanalysis need reinterpretation. It is well known that orthodox psychoanalysis has been unable to make much out of Freud's later concept of the death instinct; even the earlier and supposedly better-established concepts of sexuality, repression, and sublimation need reformulation.

In Parts Two to Four, under the headings "Eros," "Death," and "Sublimation," this book offers a systematic statement, critique, and reinterpretation of the crucial concepts in psychoanalytic theory. The difficulty of this enterprise can be seen by the catastrophe of so-called neo-Freudianism. It is easy to take one's stand on the traditional notions of morality and rationality and then amputate Freud till he is reconciled with common sense—except that there is nothing of Freud left. Freud is paradox, or nothing. The hard thing is to follow Freud into that dark underworld which he explored, and stay there; and also to have the courage to let go of his hand when it becomes apparent that his pioneering map needs to be redrawn.

Underlying the crisis in Freudianism is an existential or social ambiguity from which Freud himself was not free. Esoterically, Freud knew that what he had in hand was either nothing at all or a revolution in human thought. Exoterically, he launched the psychoanalytical movement as a method of therapy controlled by professional adepts and available only to a select and wealthy few, individuals moreover whose usefulness to society was already impaired by an "abnormal" degree of frustration or mental disorder. We, however, are concerned with reshaping psychoanalysis into a wider general theory of human nature, culture, and history, to be appropriated by the consciousness of mankind as a whole as a new stage in the historical process of man's coming to know himself.

Freud, with his genius and his humanity, tried to keep in the field of psychoanalytical consciousness not only the problems of the neurotic patient, but also the problems of mankind as a whole, as is shown by his writings on culture, from *Totem and Taboo* (1913) to *Moses and Monotheism* (1937). But Freud never faced fully the existential and theoretical consequences of taking what I call the general neurosis of mankind—the problem defined in Part One of this book—as the central under which mankind would be cured of its general neurosis, as this book attempts to do in Part Six, "The Way Out." Indeed Freud was not fully equipped to make the shift to an anthropological point of view: the primary data are then obtained not from the couch, but by going out into culture and into history—that register, in Gibbon's words, of the vices and follies of mankind. What is needed is a synthesis of psychoanalysis, anthropology, and history; and Géza Róheim's work in this direction is pioneer work of significance second only to Freud's. And again the catastrophe of neo-Freudian psychology should warn us that this synthesis is not to be cheaply won by compromising the differences between psychoanalysis and traditional academic vision. Part Five of this book, "Studies in Anality," explores the revolutionary consequences for the science of human culture of one of the most grotesque of Freudian paradoxes.

A by-product, but an essential one, of this reinterpretation of

xii LIFE AGAINST DEATH

psychoanalysis is a reinterpretation of Freud's own position in intellectual history. As long as he is regarded simply as the founder of a method of individual therapy, it is enough to see him as part of medical history, as the heir of Charcot and Breuer. But if psychoanalysis represents a new stage in the general evolution of human self-consciousness, then it is part of the diagnosis of our present situation to unearth and appraise the more obscure connections between Freud and other trends in modern thought. The unpremeditated affinity between Freud and Nietzsche is well known; and Freud himself acknowledged that the poets had anticipated him in the discovery of the unconscious.

It was a surprise to perceive, in the course of this study, other affinities not generally recognized: first, Freud's methodological affinity with the heretical tradition in logic that can be labeled dialectical; second, his doctrinal affinity with a certain tradition of mystic heresy of which the most important modern representative is Jacob Boehme. More generally, the last chapter, "The Resurrection of the Body," outlines my view of psychoanalysis as the missing link between a variety of movements in modern thought—in poetry, in politics, in philosophy—all of them profoundly critical of the inhuman character of modern civilization, all of them unwilling to abandon hope of better things.

The outcome of this effort to renew psychoanalysis, and through psychoanalysis to renew thought on the nature and destiny of man, is a rather eccentric book. Eccentricity is unlikely to be "right"; but neither is this book trying to be "right." It is trying merely to introduce some new possibilities and new problems into the public consciousness. Hence the style of the book: paradox is not diluted with the rhetoric of sober qualification. I have not hesitated to pursue new ideas to their ultimate "mad" consequences, knowing that Freud too seemed mad. Actually there are some signs that my direction may not be quite so eccentric as it seemed when it was being thought out (1953–1956). Among these welcome signs is Herbert Marcuse's *Eros and Civilization* (1955), the first book, after Wilhelm Reich's ill-fated adventures, to reopen the possibility of the abolition of repression.

Part One

THE PROBLEM

The entry into Freud cannot avoid being a plunge into a strange world and a strange language—a world of sick men, a diagnostic language of formidable technicality. But this strange world is the world we all of us actually live in.

I

The Disease Called Man

THERE IS one word which, if we only understand it, is the key to Freud's thought. That word is "repression." The whole edifice of psychoanalysis, Freud said, is based upon the theory of repression.[1] Freud's entire life was devoted to the study of the phenomenon he called repression. The Freudian revolution is that radical revision of traditional theories of human nature and human society which becomes necessary if repression is recognized as a fact. In the new Freudian perspective, the essence of society is repression of the individual, and the essence of the individual is repression of himself.

The best way to explore the notion of repression is to review the path which led Freud to his hypothesis. Freud's breakthrough was the discovery of meaningfulness in a set of phenomena theretofore regarded, at least in scientific circles, as meaningless: first, the "mad" symptoms of the mentally deranged; second, dreams; and third, the various phenomena gathered together under the title of the psychopathology of everyday life, including slips of the tongue, errors, and random thoughts.

Now in what sense does Freud find meaningfulness in neurotic symptoms, dreams, and errors? He means, of course, that these phenomena are determined and can be given a causal explanation. He is rigorously insisting on unequivocal allegiance to the principle of psychic determinism; but he means much more than that. For if it were possible to explain these phenomena on behavioristic principles, as the result of superficial associations of ideas, then they would have a cause but no meaning. Meaningfulness means expression of a purpose or an

intention. The crux of Freud's discovery is that neurotic symptoms, as well as the dreams and errors of everyday life, do have
meaning, and that the meaning of "meaning" has to be radically
revised because they have meaning. Since the purport of these
purposive expressions is generally unknown to the person
whose purpose they express, Freud is driven to embrace the
paradox that there are in a human being purposes of which he
knows nothing, involuntary purposes,[2] or, in more technical
Freudian language, "unconscious ideas." From this point of
view a new world of psychic reality is opened up, of whose
inner nature we are every bit as ignorant as we are of the
reality of the external world, and of which our ordinary conscious observation tells us no more than our sense organs are
able to report to us of the external world.[3] Freud can thus define psychoanalysis as "nothing more than the discovery of the
unconscious in mental life." [4]

But the Freudian revolution is not limited to the hypothesis
of an unconscious psychic life in the human being in addition
to his conscious life. The other crucial hypothesis is that some
unconscious ideas in a human being are incapable of becoming
conscious to him in the ordinary way, because they are strenu-
ously disowned and resisted by the conscious self. From this
point of view Freud can say that "the whole of psychoanalytic
theory is in fact built up on the perception of the resistance
exerted by the patient when we try to make him conscious of
his unconscious." [5] The dynamic relation between the unconscious and the conscious life is one of conflict, and psychoanalysis is from top to bottom a science of mental conflict.

The realm of the unconscious is established in the individual when he refuses to admit into his conscious life a purpose
or desire which he has, and in doing so establishes in himself a
psychic force opposed to his own idea. This rejection by the
individual of a purpose or idea, which nevertheless remains his,
is repression. "The essence of repression lies simply in the function of rejecting or keeping something out of consciousness." [6]
Stated in more general terms, the essence of repression lies in
the refusal of the human being to recognize the realities of his
human nature. The fact that the repressed purposes nevertheless remain his is shown by dreams and neurotic symptoms,

which represent an irruption of the unconscious into consciousness, producing not indeed a pure image of the unconscious, but a compromise between the two conflicting systems, and thus exhibiting the reality of the conflict.

Thus the notion of the unconscious remains an enigma without the theory of repression; or, as Freud says, "We obtain our theory of the unconscious from the theory of repression." [7] To put it another way, the unconscious *is* "the dynamically unconscious repressed." [8] Repression is the key word in the whole system; the word is chosen to indicate a structure dynamically based on psychic conflict. Freud illustrates the nature of psychic repression by a series of metaphors and analogies drawn from the social phenomena of war, civil war, and police action. [9]

From neurotic symptoms, dreams, and errors to a general theory of human nature may seem like a long step. Granting that it is a long step, Freud could argue that he is entitled to explore the widest possible application of a hypothesis derived from a narrow field. He could take the offensive and claim that traditional theories of human nature must be regarded as unsatisfactory because they have nothing to say about these peripheral phenomena. What theory of human nature, except Freud's, does have anything significant to say about dreams or insanity? And are dreams and insanity really negligible factors on the periphery of human life?

But the truth of the matter is that Freud maintains that to go from neurotic symptoms, dreams, and errors, to a new theory of human nature in general involves no further step at all. For the evidence on which the hypothesis of the repressed unconscious is based entails the conclusion that it is a phenomenon present in all human beings. The psychopathological phenomena of everyday life, although trivial from a practical point of view, are theoretically important because they show the intrusion of unconscious intentions into our everyday and supposedly normal behavior.

Even more theoretically important are dreams. For dreams, also "normal" phenomena, exhibit in detail not only the existence of the unconscious but also the dynamics of its repression (the dream-censorship). But since the same dynamics of re-

pression explained neurotic symptoms, and since the dreams of
neurotics, which are a clue to the meaning of their symptoms,
differ neither in structure nor in content from the dreams of
normal people, the conclusion is that a dream is itself a neurotic
symptom.[10] We are all therefore neurotic. At least dreams show
that the difference between neurosis and health prevails only
by day; and since the psychopathology of everyday life exhibits the same dynamics, even the waking life of the "healthy"
man is pervaded by innumerable symptom-formations. Between
"normality" and "abnormality" there is no qualitative but only
a quantitative difference, based largely on the practical question of whether our neurosis is serious enough to incapacitate
us for work.[11]

Or perhaps we are closer to the Freudian point of view if
we give a more paradoxical formulation; the difference between
"neurotic" and "healthy" is only that the "healthy" have a
socially usual form of neurosis. At any rate, to quote a more
technical and cautious formulation of the same theorem, Freud
says that from the study of dreams we learn that the neuroses
make use of a mechanism already in existence as a normal part
of our psychic structure, not of one that is newly created by
some morbid disturbance or other.[12]

Thus Freud's first paradox, the existence of a repressed unconscious, necessarily implies the second and even more significant paradox, the universal neurosis of mankind. Here is the
pons asinorum of psychoanalysis. Neurosis is not an occasional
aberration; it is not just in other people; it is in us, and in us
all the time. It is in the psychoanalyst: Freud discovered the
Oedipus complex, which he regarded as the root of all neurosis,
by self-analysis. *The Interpretation of Dreams* is one of the
great applications and extensions of the Socratic maxim, "Know
thyself." Or, to put it another way, the doctrine of the universal neurosis of mankind is the psychoanalytical analogue of the
theological doctrine of original sin.

The crucial point in Freud's basic hypothesis is the existence
of psychic conflict; the hypothesis cannot be meaningfully formulated without some further specification of the nature of
the conflict and the conflicting forces. Now Freud made repeated analyses of the fundamental psychic conflict, at several

different levels and from several points of view. Let us at this point try to abstract the common core from these various accounts.

In our first description of Freud's theory of repression we used the word "purpose" to designate that which is repressed into the unconscious. This excessively vague word conceals a fundamental Freudian axiom. The psychic conflict which produces dreams and neuroses is not generated by intellectual problems but by purposes, wishes, desires. Freud's frequent use of the term "unconscious idea" can be misleading here. But as Freud says, "We remain on the surface so long as we treat only of memories and ideas. The only valuable things in psychic life are, rather, the emotions. All psychic forces are significant only through their aptitude to arouse emotions. Ideas are repressed only because they are bound up with releases of emotions, which are not to come about; it would be more correct to say that repression deals with the emotions, but these are comprehensible to us only in their tie-up with ideas." [18] Freud is never tired of insisting that dreams are in essence wish-fulfillments, expressions of repressed unconscious wishes, and neurotic symptoms likewise.

Now if we take "desire" as the most suitably abstract of this series of terms, it is a Freudian axiom that the essence of man consists, not, as Descartes maintained, in thinking, but in desiring. Plato (and, *mutatis mutandis*, Aristotle) identified the *summum bonum* for man with contemplation; since the *telos* or end is the basic element in definition, this amounts to saying that the essence of man is contemplation. But ambiguously juxtaposed with this doctrine of man as contemplator is the Platonic doctrine of Eros, which, as elaborated by Plato in the *Symposium* and the *Phaedrus*, suggests that the fundamental quest of man is to find a satisfactory object for his love. A similar ambiguity between man as contemplator and man as lover is to be found in Spinoza and Hegel. The turning point in the Western tradition comes in the reaction to Hegel. Feuerbach, followed by Marx, calls for the abandonment of the contemplative tradition in favor of what he calls "practical-sensuous activity"; the meaning of this concept, and its relation to Freud, would take us far afield. But Schopenhauer, in his notion of the primacy of will—however much he may undo his own notion by his search for an escape from the primacy of the will—is a landmark, seceding from the great, and really rather insane, Western tradition that the goal of mankind is to become as contemplative as possible. Freudian psychology eliminates the category of pure contemplation as nonexistent. Only a wish, says Freud, can possibly set our psychic apparatus in motion.[14]

With this notion of desire as the essence of man is joined a definition of desire as energy directed toward the procurement of pleasure and avoidance of pain. Hence Freud can say, "Our entire psychical activity is bent upon procuring pleasure and avoiding pain, is automatically regulated by the pleasure-principle." [15] Or, "It is simply the pleasure-principle which draws up the programme of life's purpose." [16] At this level of analysis, the pleasure-principle implies no complicated hedonistic theory nor any particular theory as to the sources of pleasure. It is an assumption taken from common sense, and means much the same as Aristotle's dictum that all men seek happiness: Freud says that the goal of the pleasure-principle is happiness.[17]

But man's desire for happiness is in conflict with the whole world. Reality imposes on human beings the necessity of renunciation of pleasures; reality frustrates desire. The pleasure-principle is in conflict with the reality-principle, and this conflict is the cause of repression.[18] Under the conditions of repression the essence of our being lies in the unconscious, and only in the unconscious does the pleasure-principle reign supreme. Dreams and neurotic symptoms show that the frustrations of reality cannot destroy the desires which are the essence of our being: the unconscious is the unsubdued and indestructible element in the human soul. The whole world may be against it, but still man holds fast to the deep-rooted, passionate striving for a positive fulfillment of happiness.[19]

The conscious self, on the other hand, which by refusing to admit a desire into consciousness institutes the process of repression, is, so to speak, the surface of ourselves mediating between our inner real being and external reality. The nucleus of the conscious self is that part of the mind or system in the mind which receives perceptions from the external world. This nucleus acquires a new dimension through the power of speech, which makes it accessible to the process of education and acculturation. The conscious self is the organ of adaptation to the environment and to the culture. The conscious self, therefore, is governed not by the pleasure-principle but by the principle of adjustment to reality, the reality-principle.

From this point of view dreams and neurotic symptoms, which we previously analyzed as produced by the conflict between the conscious and unconscious systems, can also be analyzed as produced by the conflict between the pleasure-principle and the reality-principle.[20] On the one hand, dreams, neurotic symptoms, and all other manifestations of the unconscious, such as fantasy, represent in some degree or other a flight or alienation from a reality which is found unbearable.[21] On the other hand, they represent a return to the pleasure-principle; they are substitutes for pleasures denied by reality.[22] In this compromise between the two conflicting systems, the pleasure desired is reduced or distorted or even transformed to pain. Under the conditions of repression, under the domination of the reality-principle, the pursuit of pleasure is degraded to the status of a symptom.[23]

But to say that reality or the reality-principle causes repression defines the problem rather than solves it. Freud sometimes identifies the reality-principle with the "struggle for existence," as if repression could be ultimately explained by some objective economic necessity to work.[24] But man makes his own reality and various kinds of reality (and various compulsions to work) through the medium of culture or society. It is therefore more adequate to say that society imposes repression, though even this formula in Freud's early writings is connected with the inadequate idea that society, in imposing repression, is simply legislating the demands of objective economic necessity. This naïve and rationalistic sociology stands, or rather falls, with Freud's earlier version of psychoanalysis. The later Freud, as we shall see, in his doctrine of anxiety is moving toward the position that man is the animal which represses himself and which creates culture or society in order to repress himself. Even the formula that society imposes repression poses a problem rather than solves it; but the problem it poses is large. For if society imposes repression, and repression causes the universal neurosis of mankind, it follows that there is an intrinsic connection between social organization and neurosis. Man the social animal is by the same token the neurotic animal. Or, as Freud puts it, man's superiority over the other animals is his capacity for neurosis, and his capacity for neurosis is merely the obverse of his capacity for cultural development.[25]

Freud therefore arrives at the same conclusion as Nietzsche ("the disease called man"[26]), but by a scientific route, by a study of the neuroses. Neurosis is an essential consequence of civilization or culture. Here again is a harsh lesson in humility, which tender-minded critics and apostles of Freud evade or suppress. We must be prepared to analyze clinically as a neurosis not only the foreign culture we dislike, but also our own.

Neurosis and History

THE DOCTRINE that all men are mad appears to conflict with a historical perspective on the nature and destiny of man: it appears to swallow all cultural variety, all historical change, into a darkness in which all cats are gray. But this objection neglects the richness and complexity of the Freudian theory of neurosis.

In the first place there are several distinct kinds of neurosis, each with a different set of symptoms, a different structure in the relations between the repressed, the ego, and reality. We are therefore in a position to return to the varieties and complexities of individual cultures if we entertain, as Freud does in *Civilization and Its Discontents,* the hypothesis that the varieties of culture can be correlated with the varieties of neurosis: "If the evolution of civilization has such a far-reaching similarity with the development of an individual, and if the same methods are employed in both, would not the diagnosis be justified that many systems of civilization—or epochs of it—possibly even the whole of humanity—have become 'neurotic' under the pressure of civilizing trends? To analytic dissection of these neuroses therapeutic recommendations might follow which could claim a great practical interest." [1]

And furthermore, it is a Freudian theorem that each individual neurosis is not static but dynamic. It is a historical process with its own internal logic. Because of the basically unsatisfactory nature of the neurotic compromise, tension between the repressed and repressing factors persists and produces a constant series of new symptom-formations. And the series of symptom-formations is not a shapeless series of mere changes; it exhibits a regressive pattern, which Freud calls the slow return of the repressed. It is a law of neurotic diseases, he says, that these obsessive acts increasingly come closer to the original impulse and to the original forbidden act itself.[2] The doctrine of the universal neurosis of mankind, if we take it seriously, therefore compels us to entertain the hypothesis that the pattern of history exhibits a dialectic not hitherto recognized by historians, the dialectic of neurosis.

A reinterpretation of human history is not an appendage to psychoanalysis but an integral part of it. The empirical fact which compelled Freud to comprehend the whole of human history in the area of psychoanalysis is the appearance in dreams and in neurotic symptoms of themes substantially identical with major themes—both ritualistic and mythical—in the religious history of mankind. The link between the theory of neurosis and the theory of history is the theory of religion, as is made perfectly clear in *Totem and Taboo* and *Moses and Monotheism.*

And the link affects both ends linked. Freud not only maintains that human history can be understood only as a neurosis but also that the neuroses of individuals can be understood only in the context of human history as a whole. From the time when he wrote *Totem and Taboo* (1913), Freud says in *Moses and Monotheism* (1937), "I have never doubted that religious phenomena are to be understood only on the model of the neurotic symptoms of the individual."[3] According to the analogy elaborated in *Moses and Monotheism,* "In the history of the species something happened similar to the events in the life of the individual. That is to say, mankind as a whole passed through conflicts of a sexual-aggressive nature, which left permanent traces, but which were for the most part warded off and forgotten; later, after a long period of latency, they came to life again and created phenomena similar in structure and tendency to neurotic symptoms."[4]

This analogy supplies Freud with his notion of the "archaic heritage"; mankind is a prisoner of the past in the same sense as "our hysterical patients are suffering from reminiscences" and neurotics "cannot escape from the past."[5] Thus the bondage of all cultures to their cultural heritage is a neurotic constriction. And conversely, Freud came to recognize that the core of the neuroses of individuals lay in the same "archaic heritage," "memory-traces of the experiences of former generations," which "can only be understood phylogenetically." [6] The repressed unconscious which produces neurosis is not an individual unconscious but a collective one. Freud abstains from adopting Jung's term but says, "The content of the unconscious is collective anyhow." [7] Ontogeny recapitulates phylogeny (each individual recapitulates the history of the race): in the few years of childhood "we have to cover the enormous distance of development from primitive man of the Stone Age to civilized man of today." [8] From this it follows that the theory of neurosis must embrace a theory of history; and conversely a theory of history must embrace a theory of neurosis.

Psychoanalysis must view religion both as neurosis and as that attempt to become conscious and to cure, inside the neurosis itself, on which Freud came at the end of his life to pin his hopes for therapy. Psychoanalysis is vulgarly interpreted as dismissing religion as an erroneous system of wishful thinking. In *The Future of an Illusion*, Freud does speak of religion as a "substitute-gratification"—the Freudian analogue to the Marxian formula, "opiate of the people." But according to the whole doctrine of repression, "substitute-gratifications"—a term which applies not only to poetry and religion but also to dreams and neurotic symptoms—contain truth: they are expressions, distorted by repression, of the immortal desires of the human heart.

The proper psychoanalytical perspective on religion is that taken in *Moses and Monotheism*, where Freud set out to find the fragment of historic and psychological truth in Judaism and Christianity. Even Marx—in the same passage in which the notorious formula "opiate of the people" occurs—speaks of religion as "the sigh of the oppressed creature, the heart of a heartless world." [9] But Marx, lacking the concept of repression and the unconscious—that is to say, not being prepared to recognize the mystery of the human heart—could not pursue the line of thought implied in his own epigram. Psychoanalysis is equipped to study the mystery of the human heart, and must recognize religion to be the heart of the mystery. But psychoanalysis can go beyond religion only if it sees itself as completing what religion tries to do, namely, make the unconscious conscious; then psychoanalysis would be the science of original sin. Psychoanalysis is in a position to define the error in religion only after it has recognized the truth.

It is not to be denied that Freud's earlier writings, especially *Totem and Taboo*, contain, besides much that looks forward to *Moses and Monotheism*, another line of thought on the relation between psychoanalysis and history. This other line of thought works out the notion that ontogeny recapitulates phylogeny in a different way. The psychoanalytical model for understanding history is not neurosis but the process of growing up; or rather, maturity is envisaged not as a return of the repressed infantile neurosis but as the overcoming of it. In effect, Freud correlates his own psycho-sexual stages of the individual with the stages of the history postulated by nineteenth-century evolutionary-minded thinkers of the type of Comte and Frazer. Thus in *Totem and Taboo* he says that the animistic phase corresponds to narcissism, in both time and substance; the religious phase corresponds to the stage of object-finding in which dependence on the parents is paramount; while the scientific phase corresponds to maturity, in which the individual, who by now has renounced the pleasure-principle and has accepted reality, seeks his object in the outer world.[10]

This line of thought is a residue of eighteenth-century optimism and rationalism in Freud; in it history is not a process of becoming sicker but a process of becoming wiser. The early Freud—if we forget the later Freud—thus justifies the quite naïve and traditionalist view of history held by most psychoanalysts. But this line of thought is not simply inadequate as history; it is inadequate as psychoanalysis. It belongs with Freud's early system of psychoanalysis, with his early theory of the instincts, and with his early (and traditionalist) theory of the human ego.

It is true that the implementation of the approach to history adumbrated in Freud's later writings involves great difficulties. Freud himself, in the passage suggesting a correlation between cultures and neurosis, put his finger on the heart of the problem when he pointed out the need to develop a concept of a "normal" or healthy culture by which to measure the neurotic cultures recorded by history.[11] From the point of view taken in this book, the development of such a concept is the central problem confronting both psychoanalysis and history. And the lack of such a concept explains the failure of both historians and psychoanalysts (with the exception of Róheim) to pursue Freud's pioneering efforts.

But if historians have failed to follow Freud, poets have characteristically anticipated him. Is there not, for example, a still unexplored truth in the statement of the German poet Hebbel: "Is it so hard to recognize that the German nation has up till now no life history to show for itself, but only the history of a disease (*Krankheitsgeschichte*)?" [12] And not just the German nation—which is or used to be the scapegoat carrying all the sins of the Western world. According to James Joyce, "History is a nightmare from which I am trying to awaken." [13] The poets, and Nietzsche—Nietzsche's *Genealogy of Morals* is the first attempt to grasp world history as the history of an ever increasing neurosis. And both Nietzsche and Freud find the same dynamic in the neurosis of history, an ever increasing sense of guilt caused by repression. Nietzsche's climax—"Too long has the world been a madhouse" [14]—compares with the dark conclusion of *Civilization and Its Discontents:* "If civilization is an inevitable course of development from the group of the family to the group of humanity as a whole, then an intensification of the sense of guilt . . . will be inextricably bound up with it, until perhaps the sense of guilt may swell to a magnitude that individuals can hardly support." [15]

The necessity of a psychoanalytical approach to history is pressed upon the historian by one question: Why does man, alone of all animals, have a history? For man is distinguished from animals not simply by the possession and transmission from generation to generation of that suprabiological apparatus which is culture, but also, if history and changes in time are essential characteristics of human culture and therefore of man, by a desire to change his culture and so to change himself. In making history "man makes himself," to use the suggestive title of Gordon Childe's book. Then the historical process is sustained by man's desire to become other than what he is. And man's desire to become something different is essentially an unconscious desire. The actual changes in history neither result from nor correspond to the conscious desires of the human agents who bring them about. Every historian knows this, and the philosopher of history, Hegel, in his doctrine of the "cunning of Reason," made it a fundamental point in his structural analysis of history. Mankind today is still making history without having any conscious idea of what it really wants or under what conditions it would stop being unhappy; in fact what it is doing seems to be making itself more unhappy and calling that unhappiness progress.

Christian theology, or at least Augustinian theology, recognizes human restlessness and discontent, the *cor irrequietum,* as the psychological source of the historical process. But Christian theology, to account for the origin of human discontent and to indicate a solution, has to take man out of this real world, out of the animal kingdom, and inculcate into him delusions of grandeur. And thus Christian theology commits its own worst sin, the sin of pride.

Freud's real critique of religion in *The Future of an Illusion* is the contention (also Spinoza's) that true humility lies in science. True humility, he says, requires that we learn from Copernicus that the human world is not the purpose or the center of the universe; that we learn from Darwin that man is a member of the animal kingdom; and that we learn from Freud that the human ego is not even master in its own house.[16] Apart from psychoanalysis there are no secular or scientific theories as to why man is the restless and discontented animal. The discontented animal is the neurotic animal, the animal with desires given in his nature which are not satisfied by culture. From the psychoanalytical point of view, these unsatisfied and repressed but immortal desires sustain the historical process. History is shaped, beyond our conscious wills, not by the cunning of Reason but by the cunning of Desire.

The riddle of history is not in Reason but in Desire; not in labor, but in love. A confrontation with Marx will clarify Freud. It is axiomatic in Marxism to define the essence of man as labor. Freud has no quarrel with the Marxist emphasis on the importance of the "economic factor" in history: he formally praises Marxism for "its clear insight into the determining influence which is exerted by the economic conditions of man upon his intellectual, ethical, and artistic reactions." [17] For Freud, work and economic necessity are the essence of the reality-principle: but the essence of man lies not in the reality-principle but in repressed unconscious desires. No matter how stringently economic necessities press down on him, he is not in his essence *Homo economicus* or *Homo laborans;* no matter how bitter the struggle for bread, man does not live by bread alone.

Thus Freud becomes relevant when history raises this question: What does man want over and beyond "economic welfare" and "mastery over nature"? Marx defines the essence of man as labor and traces the dialectic of labor in history till labor abolishes itself. There is then a vacuum in the Marxist utopia. Unless there is no utopia, unless history is never abolished, unless labor continues to be, like Faust, driven to ever greater achievements, some other and truer definition of the essence of man must be found. Freud suggests that beyond labor there is love. And if beyond labor at the end of history there is love, love must have always been there from the beginning of history, and it must have been the hidden force supplying the energy devoted to labor and to making history. From this point of view, repressed Eros is the energy of history and labor must be seen as sublimated Eros. In this way a problem not faced by Marx can be faced with the aid of Freud.

Marxism is a system of sociology; the importance of the "economic factor" is a sociological question to be settled by sociologists; Freud himself, speaking as a sociologist, can say that in imposing repression "at bottom society's motive is economic." [18] The quarrel between psychoanalysis and "economic determinism" arises in the tacit psychological assumptions behind economic determinism, and therefore arises only when we pass from sociology to psychology, from the abstraction of "society" to the concrete human individual. The issue is not the importance of economics but its psychology. Marx himself, though always complicated, is not free from the tacit assumption, held generally by economic determinists, that the concrete human needs and drives sustaining economic activity are just what they appear to be and are fully in consciousness: "self-preservation" and "pleasure," as understood by the utilitarians, summarize the psychological theory implied by the ingenuous invocation of categories like "economic necessity" and "human needs."

But the proof that human needs are not what they seem to be lies precisely in the fact of human history. The Faustian restlessness of man in history shows that men are not satisfied by the satisfaction of their conscious desires; men are unconscious of their real desires. Thus a psychology of history must be psychoanalytical.

In so far as Marx faced this question at all, lacking the concept of repressed unconscious desires he could only come up with a psychology of history which condemns man to be eternally Faustian and precludes any possibility of happiness. Marx needs a psychological premise to explain the unceasing bent for technological progress sustaining the dialectic of labor in history. Lacking the doctrine of repression—or rather not being able to see man as a psychological riddle—Marx, as a sympathetic critic has shown, turns to biology and postulates an absolute law of human biology that the satisfaction of human needs always generates new needs.[19] If human discontent is thus biologically given, it is incurable. Quite specifically, not only "the abolition of history" but also an "economy of abundance," as envisioned in Marx's utopian phase, are out of the question. Hence the dark clouds of pessimism in the third volume of *Capital,* where he says: [20]

> Just as the savage must wrestle with nature, in order to satisfy his wants, in order to maintain his life and to reproduce it, so the civilized man has to do it in all forms of society and under all modes of production. With his development the realm of natural necessity expands, because his wants increase; but at the same time the forces of production increase, by which these wants are satisfied.

But Marx's assumption of a biological basis for "progress" in history really amounts to a confession that he is unable to explain it psychologically.

Psychoanalysis can provide a theory of "progress," but only by viewing history as a neurosis. By defining man as the neurotic animal, psychoanalysis not merely assumes man's Faustian character but also explains why man is so. To quote Freud: [21]

> What appears . . . as an untiring impulsion toward further perfection can easily be understood as a result of the instinctual repression upon which is based all that is most precious in human civilization. The repressed instinct never ceases to strive for complete satisfaction, which would consist in the repetition of a primary experience of satisfaction. No substitutive or reactive formations and no sublimations will suffice to remove the repressed instinct's persisting tension.

By the same token, psychoanalysis offers a theoretical framework for exploring the possibility of a way out of the nightmare of endless "progress" and endless Faustian discontent, a way out of the human neurosis, a way out of history. In the case of the neurotic individual, the goal of psychoanalytical therapy is to free him from the burden of his past, from the burden of his history, the burden which compels him to go on having (and being) a case history. And the method of psychoanalytical therapy is to deepen the historical consciousness of the individual ("fill up the memory-gaps") till he awakens from his own history as from a nightmare. Psychoanalytical consciousness, as a higher stage in the general consciousness of mankind, may be likewise the fulfillment of the historical consciousness, that ever widening and deepening search for origins which has obsessed Western thought ever since the Renaissance. If historical consciousness is finally transformed into psychoanalytical consciousness, the grip of the dead hand of the past on life in the present would be loosened, and man would be ready to live instead of making history, to enjoy instead of paying back old scores and debts, and to enter that state of Being which was the goal of his Becoming.

Part Two

EROS

Freud's two instincts—Eros and Death—are fundamental hypotheses as to the general character of the repressed forces inherent in human nature by virtue of its connection with a body. Though repressed and unrecognized, these are the energies which create human culture, and to recognize their existence is to reinterpret human culture. Human culture is then reconnected with the human body. Eros creates culture, and Eros is the bodily sexual instinct.

Sexuality and Childhood

As we saw in the first chapter, it is in our unconscious repressed desires that we shall find the essence of our being, the clue to our neurosis (as long as reality is repressive), and the clue to what we might become if reality ceased to repress. The results of Freud's exploration of the unconscious can be summarized in two formulae: Our repressed desires are the desires we had, unrepressed, in childhood; and they are sexual desires.

In analyzing neurotic symptoms and dreams, Freud found that they invariably contained a nucleus representing a return or regression to the experiences of early childhood. But, according to the whole hypothesis of repression, the consciousness which comes into conflict with the unconscious is the product of education. It follows that children are in some sense unrepressed. Or, to put it another way, in the child the conscious and the unconscious are not yet separated. It was therefore natural to infer that the adult, in flight from repressive reality in dreams and neurosis, regresses to his own childhood because it represents a period of happier days before repression took place.[1] Furthermore, Freud found that the analysis of neurotic symptoms invariably led not only to the patient's childhood but also to his sexual life. The symptom is not merely a substitute for a pleasure denied by reality, but more specifically a substitute for sexual satisfaction denied by reality. But the repressed sexual desires whose presence was indicated were for the most part of the kind labeled "abnormal" or "perverse." Thus the analysis of neurosis required the construction of a theory of sexuality which would account for perverted as well as normal sexuality and would trace both to their origins in childhood.[2]

The axiom on which Freud constructed this extension of his basic hypothesis is that the pattern of normal adult sexuality is not a natural (biological) necessity but a cultural phenomenon. The pattern of normal adult sexuality—the mutual love of man and woman and all the variations of the pattern—represents a particular organization of certain possibilities given in the human organism. This sexual organization is made possible by the social organization which marks the transition from ape to man, and simultaneously it makes that social organization possible. Man's sexual organization and his social organization are so deeply interconnected that we cannot say which came first, but can only assume a simultaneous evolution (whether sudden or gradual) of both.

The critical institution in the transition from ape to man, the link between man's sexual and social organization, is parenthood, with the prolonged maintenance of children in a condition of helpless dependence.[3] That parenthood implies family organization of some sort or another, and that family organization is the nucleus of all social organization, are anthropological axioms which Freud accepted and built into his structure. Freud's originality consists in drawing attention to the consequences of prolonged parenthood and prolonged infantile dependence on the sexual life of both parents and children. As far as the parents are concerned, it is clear that while adult sexuality serves the socially useful purpose of breeding children, it is for the individual in some sense an end in itself as a source of pleasure—according to Freud, the highest pleasure. Adult sexuality, in so far as it is restricted by rules designed to maintain the institution of the family and in so far as the desire for sexual satisfaction is diverted and exploited for the purpose of maintaining a socially useful institution, is a clear instance of that subordination of the pleasure-principle to the reality-principle which is repression; as such it is rejected by the unconscious essence of the human being and therefore leads to neurosis.[4]

Prolonged infancy has even more far-reaching consequences. On the one hand, infancy is protected from the harshness of reality by parental care; it represents a period of privileged irresponsibility and freedom from the domination of the reality-principle. This privileged irresponsibility permits and promotes an early blossoming of the essential desires of the human being, without repression and under the sign of the pleasure-principle.[5] On the other hand, the infant's objective dependence on parental, especially maternal, care promotes a dependent attitude toward reality and inculcates a passive (dependent) need to be loved, which colors all subsequent interpersonal relationships.[6] This psychological vulnerability is subsequently exploited to extract submission to social authority and to the reality-principle in general.

Thus prolonged infancy shapes human desires in two contradictory directions: on the one hand, on the subjective side, toward omnipotent indulgence in pleasure freed from the limitations of reality; on the other hand, on the objective side, toward powerless dependence on other people. The two tendencies come into conflict because the early experience of freedom and absorption in pleasure must succumb to the recognition of the reality-principle, in a capitulation enforced by parental authority under the threat of loss of parental love. And since the pleasure-principle is forced to capitulate against its will and for reasons which the child does not understand, under circumstances which reproduce its primal experiences of helpless dependence (anxiety), the capitulation can be accomplished only by repression. Hence it constitutes a trauma from which the individual never recovers psychologically. But in the unconscious the repressed dreams of omnipotent indulgence in pleasure persist, as the nucleus of man's universal neurosis and his restless discontent, the *cor irrequietum* of St. Augustine. The infantile conflict between actual impotence and dreams of omnipotence is also the basic theme of the universal history of mankind. And in both conflicts—in the history of the individual and the history of the race—the stakes are the meaning of love.

With his rude, persistent demand for the bodily origin of spiritual things, Freud starts not with love but with sexuality. But the man who discussed what he called the sexual life of children, and who insisted on the sexual character of thumbsucking, must have had a special definition of sexuality. In fact, Freud's definition of the sexual instinct shows that he means something very general. It is the energy or desire with which the human being pursues pleasure, with the further specification that the pleasure sought is the pleasurable activity of an organ of the human body. He attributed the capacity of yielding such pleasure (an erotogenic quality, he calls it) to all parts of the surface of the human body and also to the internal organs. The organ in question may be the genital, or it may be the mouth, as in thumb-sucking, or it may be the eyes, as in the delight of seeing.[7] If sex is so defined, there will surely be little disposition to deny that infants do have a sexual life, or even that sex in this sense is their chief aim. Infants are naturally absorbed in themselves and in their own bodies: they are in love with themselves; in Freudian terminology, their orientation is narcissistic. Infants are ignorant of the serious business of life (the reality-principle) and therefore know no guide except the pleasure-principle, making pleasurable activity of their own body their sole aim. And since childhood is a period of real immunity from the serious business of life, children are really in a position to obtain pleasure from the activity of their bodies to an extent which the adult is not. So Freud's definition of sexuality entails the proposition that infants have a richer sexual life than adults.

If we grant that children pursue pleasurable activity of their bodies, we ask why this must be called sexual. The answer is that Freud is offering a genetic, historical explanation of adult sexuality, tracing it to its origin in childhood. On general grounds, because of his general notion of the individual psyche as a historically evolving and historically determined organization, Freud could only reject the idea that the powerful adult sexual drive appeared suddenly from nowhere at the age of puberty. And the evidence of dreams and neurotic symptoms pointed unmistakably to the childhood origin of the repressed sexuality of the adult. Now to say that the infantile pattern of seeking pleasurable activity of the body is sexual is equivalent to saying that this is the infantile pattern which develops into adult sexuality. Freud then found that this hypothesis not only explained the prominence of sexual themes in the repressed unconscious (in dreams and symptoms) but also accounted for the adult sexual perversions, thus satisfying the basic desiderata for an adequate theory of sexuality.

If normal adult sexuality is a pattern which has grown out

of the infantile delight in the pleasurable activity of all parts of the human body, then what was originally a much wider capacity for pleasure in the body has been narrowed in range, concentrated on one particular (the genital) organ, and subordinated to an aim derived not from the pleasure-principle but from the reality-principle, namely, propagation (in Freudian terminology, the genital function). Then the pattern of normal adult sexuality (in Freud's terminology, genital organization) is a tyranny of one component in infantile sexuality, a tyranny which suppresses some of the other components altogether and subordinates the rest to itself.[8] (We shall see later that genital organization is constructed not by the sexual instinct but by the death instinct.) But the pattern of normal adult sexuality can exist only on condition that the discarded pattern of infantile sexuality continues to exist side by side with it, and in conflict with it, in the repressed unconscious.

The discarded elements of infantile sexuality are, judged by the standard of normal adult sexuality, perverse. The adult sexual perversions, like normal adult sexuality, are well-organized tyrannies: they too represent an exaggerated concentration on one of the many erotic potentialities present in the human body, which are all actively explored in infancy. The manner of this tyranny, as well as the close connection between normal and perverted sexuality, is illustrated by the fact that various erotic activities, which are called perversions if they are pursued as substitutes for the normal sexual act, are called legitimate if they are subordinated as preliminaries to the normal sexual aim. Children, on the other hand, explore in indiscriminate and anarchistic fashion all the erotic potentialities of the human body.[9] In Freudian terms, children are polymorphously perverse. But if infantile sexuality, judged by the standard of normal adult sexuality, is perverse, by the same token normal adult sexuality, judged by the standard of infantile sexuality, is an unnatural restriction of the erotic potentialities of the human body.

Freud's notion of normal adult sexuality (genital organization) as an unnatural tyranny is so contrary to our usual way of thinking that it needs to be elaborated. We usually think of the pattern of normal adult sexuality as given by nature, as a

biological necessity. In other words, we accept the subordination of sexual activity to the purpose of reproduction as a natural state of affairs. In what sense, then, does Freud call it
unnatural? Is not subordination to the reproductive function
characteristic of sexuality wherever it appears, not only in
human beings but also in animals and even plants? Adult animals seem to have what Freud calls genital organization. Will
Freud say that in their case genital organization is an unnatural
tyranny?

These objections take us to the root problem of the distinction between men and animals. Psychoanalysis must maintain
that there is a qualitative distinction between men and animals;
but the distinction is based on what is perhaps only a quantitative phenomenon, namely, the peculiar prolongation of infancy
in the human species. In the case of man, the prolongation of
infancy and the postponement of puberty give infantile sexuality a longer period in which to mature, and at the same time
parental care shelters it from the reality-principle. Under these
conditions infantile sexuality achieves a full bloom to which
there can be no parallel in other species of animals. Hence there
is a conflict in the sexual life of man, as there is not in other
animals. In man infantile sexuality is repressed and never out-
grown; repression (and consequently neurosis) distinguishes
man from the other animals. The result is that genital organization is a tyranny in man because his peculiar infancy has left
him with a lifelong allegiance (i.e., fixation) to the pattern of
infantile sexuality.

Thus Freud's theory of infantile sexuality is an essential part
of his theory of neurosis, so that he puts this concept on the
same level of importance as his concept of repression and the
unconscious, and says that psychoanalysis stands or falls by the
expansion of the idea of the "sexual function" as opposed to the
narrower one of a "genital function." [10] The therapeutic value
of the concept of infantile sexuality as an aid in the psychiatric
treatment of those individuals whose neurosis has reached the
point of incapacitating them for practical living is not the issue
here. What matters is the flood of light which the concept of
infantile sexuality throws on the universal neurosis of mankind
and on his ultimate nature and destiny.

In Freud's theory of infantile sexuality there is first of all a critique of the genital function and an implied rejection of genital intercourse—"free love" and the orgasm—as a solution to the sexual problem. Not only is there an implied critique of D. H. Lawrence; there is an implied critique of superficial followers of Freud himself, and even some great ones (Abraham, Reich, Fenichel), who have idealized the "genital character" as a way out of the human neurosis. Thus Fenichel: "The ability to obtain full satisfaction through genital orgasm makes the physiological regulation of sexuality possible and thus puts an end to the damming up of instinctual energies, with its unfortunate effects on the person's behavior." [11] This appearance of finding the solution to the world's problems in the genital has done much to discredit psychoanalysis: mankind, from history and from personal experience, knows better. How perilous the pitfalls are that lie on both sides of the psychoanalytical path can be seen in the sad career of Wilhelm Reich. A man with keen insight into the sociological implications of psychoanalysis, he foundered on the theory of infantile sexuality (as do the neo-Freudians) and ended up in a glorification of the orgasm as the solution to all social and bodily ailments.

Freud sees conflict—in his earlier theory, between the pleasure-principle and the reality-principle; in his later theory, between Eros and Death—in the genital act itself. He distinguishes fore-pleasure and end-pleasure in sexual intercourse. The fore-pleasure is the preliminary play with all parts of the body, and represents a perpetuation of the pure polymorphous perverse play of infantile sexuality. The end-pleasure in the orgasm is purely genital and post-pubertal.

From the Freudian point of view the subordination of fore-pleasure to end-pleasure in sexual intercourse is a compromise concealing a conflict between the desire of the immortal child in us for pure polymorphous play and the reality-principle which imposes genital organization on us. This conflict explains the fact that while it is not true, as the Church father said, that *post coitum omne animal triste*, it is true of the human animal: the immortal child in us is frustrated, even in the sexual act, by the tyranny of genital organization. Hence the attempt to overthrow genital organization in certain practices of mysticism—mysticism being able, as Freud said, "to grasp certain relations in the deeper layers of the ego and the id which would otherwise be inaccessible." [12] The heretical Christian sect known as Adamites, who sought to recapture in this life the innocent eroticism of Adam before the Fall, practiced *coitus reservatus,* intercourse without orgasm, that is to say, pure forepleasure.[13] If he knew psychoanalysis, Needham would not be so puzzled that in Taoist mysticism *"coitus reservatus* should have been considered so valuable for mental health." [14]

For Freud, the clue not only to normal adult sexuality but to our whole repressed and hidden ultimate essence lies in infantile sexuality. This is not a proposition to which we take kindly. Ignorance and fear, both of them the results of repression, together with the noble illusion, fostered by our higher aspirations, that we are all soul and no body, set in motion one or another of a number of mechanisms of intellectual flight whenever the topic of sexuality is taken seriously. If deference to the scientific attitude has induced a certain broad- or openmindedness toward the general topic, the specific details are more than we can take, and we slip into the evasion of abhorrence or amusement. We are likely to withdraw our willingness to listen when we are told that infantile sexuality is polymorphously perverse. And Freud must mean that polymorphous perversity is the pattern of our deepest desires. How can this proposition be taken seriously?

If we divest ourselves of the prejudice surrounding the "perverse," if we try to be objective and analyze what infantile sexuality is in itself, we must return again to the definition. Infantile sexuality is the pursuit of pleasure obtained through the activity of any and all organs of the human body. So defined, the ultimate essence of our desires and our being is nothing more or less than delight in the active life of all the human body. That this is Freud's notion becomes abundantly clear if we examine the specific nature of the "perverse" components in infantile sexuality. They include the pleasure of touching, of seeing, of muscular activity, and even the passion for pain.[15] It is therefore perfectly consistent, and implies no change of view, when in his later writings Freud added the term "life instinct" as synonymous with what he in other contexts called "the sexual instinct," "Eros," or "libido." And there is no difference between Freud's notion of the ultimate essence of the human being and William Blake's when he said, "Energy is the only life, and is from the Body. . . . Energy is Eternal Delight." [16] As with the concept of repression and the unconscious, so in his concept of the libido Freud appears less as an inventor of unheard-of novelties than as one who grasped in rational and scientific form intuitions which have haunted the imagination of poets and philosophers throughout the modern or Romantic period of our intellectual history.

Freud and Blake are asserting that the ultimate essence of our being remains in our unconscious secretly faithful to the principle of pleasure, or, as Blake calls it, delight. To say this is to call in question the psychological assumptions upon which our Western morality has been built. For two thousand years or more man has been subjected to a systematic effort to transform him into an ascetic animal. He remains a pleasure-seeking animal. Parental discipline, religious denunciation of bodily pleasure, and philosophic exaltation of the life of reason have all left man overtly docile, but secretly in his unconscious unconvinced, and therefore neurotic. Man remains unconvinced because in infancy he tasted the fruit of the tree of life, and knows that it is good, and never forgets.

Freud is also asserting that in spite of two thousand years of higher education based on the notion that man is essentially a soul for mysterious accidental reasons imprisoned in a body, man remains incurably obtuse and still secretly thinks of himself as first and foremost a body. Our repressed desires are not just for delight, but specifically for delight in the fulfillment of the life of our own bodies. Children, at the stage of early infancy which Freud thinks critical, are unable to distinguish between their souls and their bodies; in Freudian terminology, they are their own ideal.[17] Children are also unable to make the distinction—fundamental for culture, the reality-principle, and the serious business of life—between higher and lower functions and parts of the body. They have not acquired that sense of shame which, according to the Biblical story, expelled mankind from Paradise, and which, presumably, would be discarded if Paradise were regained.[18] Neurotic symptoms, with their fixation on perversions and obscenities, demonstrate the refusal of the unconscious essence of our being to acquiesce in the dualism of flesh and spirit, higher and lower.

Thus Freud's doctrine of infantile sexuality, rightly understood, is essentially a scientific reformulation and reaffirmation of the religious and poetical theme of the innocence of childhood. Freud of course neither advocates nor thinks possible a return to a state of innocence; he is simply saying that childhood remains man's indestructible goal. His pessimism is ultimately based on his inability to see how this goal is reconcilable with man's equally deep commitment to culture and cultural progress. With this qualification, it is true to say that Freud takes with absolute seriousness the proposition of Jesus: "Except ye become as little children, ye can in no wise enter the kingdom of heaven." As a religious ideal, the innocence of childhood has turned out to resist assimilation into the rational-theological tradition. Only mystics and heretics like St. Francis and Jacob Boehme have made Christ's ideal their own. Poets like Blake and Rilke have affirmed its secular validity. Rousseau attempted to grasp it in philosophic-rational terms. Freud formulated it as an indispensable axiom of scientific psychology.

This concept of childhood enables Freud to grasp a fundamental form of human activity in the world over and beyond the economic activity and struggle for existence dictated by the reality-principle. For children on the one hand pursue pleasure: on the other hand they are active; their pleasure is in the active life of the human body. Then what is the pattern of activity, free from work, the serious business of life, and the reality-principle, which is adumbrated in the life of children? The answer is that children play.[19]

Freud is not merely referring to all the activities conventionally recognized as children's play; he is also making a structural analysis of the infantile activities which he insisted were sexual and perverse, of which thumb-sucking is the prototype. In early infancy the child, according to Freud, inevitably takes his own body as his sexual object; in doing so, he plays with it. Play is the essential character of activity governed by the pleasure-principle rather than the reality-principle. Play is "purposeless yet in some sense meaningful." [20] It is the same thing if we say that play is the erotic mode of activity. Play is that activity which, in the delight of life, unites man with the objects of his love, as is indeed evident from the role of play in normal adult genital activity. But according to Freud, the ultimate essence of our being is erotic and demands activity according to the pleasure-principle.

Freud has thus put into his science the famous conclusion of Schiller's *Letters on the Aesthetic Education of Man:* "Man only plays when in the full meaning of the word he is a man, and he is only completely a man when he plays." And, from another point of view, Sartre says: "As soon as a man apprehends himself as free and wishes to use his freedom . . . then his activity is play." [21] Sartre appreciates the concept of play because of his concern with the problem of existential freedom: Schiller appreciated it because of his concern with the aesthetic nature of man. But the same notion of play can be and has been reached by minds operating within the Christian religious tradition, and taking the Christian notion of redemption and regeneration of the flesh seriously: for example, the fountainhead of Protestant mystical theology, Jacob Boehme. I quote from H. H. Brinton: [22]

> In giving the will primacy over the intellect Boehme's system makes it supremely difficult to define the nature of the *summum bonum*, which is the end of all action. The essence of will is purposeful activity yet such activity is generated by want. How then can we have activity as a final goal? Boehme answers by calling the perfect state "play." In "play" life expresses itself in its fullness; therefore play as an end means that life itself has intrinsic value. . . . When Boehme is speaking of God's life as it is in itself he refers to it as "play." . . . Adam ought to have been content to play with nature in Paradise. "As God plays with the time of this outward world, so also should the inward divine man play with the outward in the revealed wonders of God in this world, and open the Divine Wisdom in all creatures, each according to its property." Adam fell when this play became serious business.

Boehme had the divine naïveté to take the Christian promise of the regeneration of the flesh, the perfection of man in the flesh, seriously. As Brinton says, "Boehme hears the divine melody, not from a choir of Protestant angels, nor in the Gregorian chant of the Church. It is for him *'das Freudenspiel der ewigen Gebärung'*—'the joyful play of eternal generation.' " [23] In other words, Boehme placed man's perfection and bliss not in a Protestant future life nor in Catholic sacraments, but in the transformation of this bodily life into joyful play.

Heretical mystics of the type of Jacob Boehme deserve more honor than they have received from secular humanists. For modern secular humanist intellectuals have in the main followed Plato and Descartes over the abyss into the insane delusion that the true essence of man lies in disembodied mental activity. The philosophers' efforts to overcome the mind-body dualism in theory are betrayed by the philosophers' own practical commitment to the pure life of the mind. The rationalism of the philosophers has only led them further astray, and the irrationality of the mystics has enabled them to hold fast to a truth for which the time was not ripe. Perhaps the time is now ripe when the mystic can break the glass through which he sees all things darkly, and the rationalist can break the glass through which he sees all things clearly, and both together can enter the kingdom of psychological reality.

The doctrine that play is the essential mode of activity of a free or of a perfected or of a satisfied humanity has obvious implications for social reform. Over a hundred years ago the utopian socialist Fourier tried to work out the structure of a society in which work had been transformed into play; his influence can be seen in some of the early writings of Marx, which call for the abolition of labor as a necessary precondition for the emancipation of genuinely free and genuinely human self-activity. These utopian speculations have been laughed out of serious consideration by the realists, who apparently are made happy if they can prove, by their special interpretation of the doctrine of original sin, that their children and their children's children are condemned to be as unhappy as they are. But history is transforming the question of reorganizing human society and human nature in the spirit of play from a speculative possibility to a realistic necessity. The most realistic observers are emphasizing man's increasing alienation from his work; the possibility of mass unemployment—i.e., liberation from work—given by modern technology; and the utter incapacity of human nature as it is today to make genuinely free use of leisure—to play.

The crisis of our time was diagnosed by one of the greatest and most realistic of twentieth-century economists, John Maynard Keynes, in an essay written in 1930 and called "Economic Possibilities for Our Grandchildren." Keynes takes as his premise the proposition that, because of modern technological advances, mankind is solving the economic problem, which "always has been hitherto the primary, most pressing problem of the human race—not only of the human race, but of the whole of the biological kingdom from the beginnings of life in its most primitive forms." [24] Keynes' reflections on this situation are as follows:

> Thus we have been expressly evolved by nature—with all our impulses and deepest instincts—for the purpose of solving the economic problem. If the economic problem is solved, mankind will be deprived of its traditional purpose.
>
> Will this be a benefit? If one believes at all in the real values of life, the prospect at least opens up the possibility of benefit. Yet I think with dread of the readjustment of the habits and instincts of the ordinary man, bred into him for countless generations, which he may be asked to discard within a few decades.
>
> To use the language of today—must we not expect a general "nervous breakdown"? We already have a little experience of what I mean—a nervous breakdown of the sort which is already common enough in England and the United States amongst the wives of the well-to-do classes, unfortunate women, many of them, who have been deprived by their wealth of their traditional tasks and occupations—who cannot find it sufficiently amusing, when deprived of the spur of economic necessity, to cook and clean and mend, yet are quite unable to find anything more amusing.
>
> To those who sweat for their daily bread leisure is a longed-for sweet—until they get it.
>
> There is the traditional epitaph written for herself by the old charwoman:
>
> Don't mourn for me, friends, don't weep for me never,
> For I'm going to do nothing for ever and ever.

This was her heaven. Like others who look forward to leisure, she conceived how nice it would be to spend her time listening-in—for there was another couplet which occurred in her poem:

> With psalms and sweet music the heavens'll be ringing,
> But I shall have nothing to do with the singing.

Yet it will only be for those who have to do with the singing that life will be tolerable—and how few of us can sing!

These reflections generate in Keynes a mood of anxious foreboding. "There is no country and no people," he writes, "who can look forward to the age of leisure and abundance without a dread."

From the Freudian point of view the necessary readjustment of the habits and instincts of the ordinary man appears no less formidable, but there are grounds for optimism not accessible to Keynes. For Keynes the art of life itself, which in an age of abundance and leisure will have to replace the art of accumulating the means of life, is a difficult art requiring refined sensitivity of the kind possessed by the Bloomsbury group and immortalized in the work of Virginia Woolf. So Keynes looks with dread at the prospect of the ordinary man's emancipation from work. But from the Freudian point of view, every ordinary man has tasted the paradise of play in his own childhood. Underneath the habits of work in every man lies the immortal instinct for play. The foundation on which the man of the future will be built is already there, in the repressed unconscious; the foundation does not have to be created out of nothing, but recovered. Nature—or history—is not setting us a goal without endowing us with the equipment to reach it.

But the concept of play is not simply a tool for eschatological prophecy and social criticism; it has, like all valuable eschatological concepts, analytical applications to history and anthropology. Huizinga in *Homo Ludens* elaborated Frobenius' definition of human culture as *eines aus dem natürlichen Sein aufgestiegenen Spieles*. He shows the presence of an irreducible nonfunctional element of play in all the basic categories of human cultural activity—religion, art, war, law, economics. Huizinga suggests that the advance of civilization has repressed the play element in culture; the implication is that, since play is the distinctively human mode of activity, the advance of civilization has dehumanized culture.

Take, for example, economic behavior. The element of play in primitive economics—in potlatch contests of prestige, in the merry-go-round circuits of gift-exchange—is obvious. Perhaps primitive economics can be distinguished from civilized economics as that pattern of economic behavior in which play and the pleasure-principle have primacy over the ostensibly rational calculus of maximum gains—that is to say, over the reality-principle. Perhaps, more generally, the two levels of culture which sociology has distinguished under various labels—primitive and civilized, *Gemeinschaft* and *Gesellschaft*, folk and urban—can be distinguished psychoanalytically. Primitive is that level of culture in which the rhythm of what Freud calls the primary process—the rhythm of dreams and childhood play —is predominant. Civilized is that level of culture which effectively represses the rhythm of the primary process in favor of rationality and the reality-principle. The exploration of this hypothesis is part of a psychoanalytical anthropology.

And is there no element of play in that triumph of utilitarian rationalism and the reality-principle, modern economic behavior? Fifty years ago Thorstein Veblen, in *The Theory of the Leisure Class*, exposed the irrational psychological springs of pecuniary emulation and showed that economic competition, not the theory but the practice, psychologically considered, is a "game of ownership" lineally descended from the barbarian game of predatory war.[25] Quite recently economic theorists, abandoning the notion that the model of a rational-utilitarian man can explain the actualities of economic behavior, have found their most fruitful alternative model in the theory of gambling and games.[26]

What then does psychoanalysis have to add to Huizinga and Veblen? The play element in culture provides a prima facie justification for the psychoanalytical doctrine of sublimation, which views "higher" cultural activities as substitutes for lost infantile pleasures. Thus Ferenczi's psychoanalytical study of money as a sublimation concludes with the proposition that the pursuit of money is governed not only by the reality-principle but also by the pleasure-principle;[27] Ferenczi is vindicated by the *Theory of Games and Economic Behavior.*

Furthermore, the psychoanalytical notion of the repressed unconscious seems necessary in order to define the play element in culture. It seems to be an essential feature of the play element in culture, for example the "game of ownership," that it must not be perceived or enjoyed as such, it is unconscious play, and at the same time it is never pure play. In other words, it has the same psychic structure as a neurotic symptom. According to basic Freudian theory, a repressed instinct is bound to return in the form of neurotic symptoms, compromises between the pleasure-principle and the reality-principle which are not recognized as such. And the neurotic symptoms are "substitute-gratifications"; they provide pleasure, but only neurotic pleasure. Further psychoanalytical light on culture as neurotic play depends on the difficult and paradoxical concept of sublimation, to which we shall return later in this book. In the meantime, we should also warn the reader that to analyze culture or economic activity or even games as play, as a manifestation of Eros, without also taking account of Freud's aggressive instinct (Veblen's "predatory instinct"), is, to put it mildly, one-sided.

Our indestructible unconscious desire for a return to childhood, our deep childhood-fixation, is a desire for a return to the pleasure-principle, for a recovery of the body from which culture alienates us, and for play instead of work. And yet, on the other hand, childhood cannot be recovered and paradise cannot be regained. For the infantile experience of freedom and absorption in pleasure has a fatal flaw. It has not come to terms with the reality-principle. (Later in this book we shall see that death is the reality with which human beings, infants and adults, cannot come to terms.) The infant's world of pleasure and play is built out of wishes uninhibited by the reality-principle and satisfied by unreal, hallucinatory fulfillment. Through an elementary mechanism, wish-fulfillment thinking, which survives also in the daydreaming and fantasy of adults, the child is able to create a world where dreams come true and wishes are omnipotent. And by the same token this early blossoming of the erotic life of man remains basically subjective.

It fails to reach the objective world; the child takes himself and his own body as the object of his love. In Freudian terminology, infantile sexuality is fundamentally autoerotic or narcissistic. Freud is too realistic to follow the mystics or romantics who wish to ignore the demands of the reality-principle. Infantilism, however glorified, is no solution.

Hence there is for Freud a final contradiction between the reality-principle and our unconscious desires. Here is the source of Freud's pessimism, and the central problem for anyone who takes Freud seriously. Hence anyone who takes Freud seriously must follow him into the closest anatomy of the desires of childhood—in his terminology, infantile sexuality. Even in childhood, according to Freud, human love can be seen going out beyond itself and finding its first object in the world, the mother. Our analysis of Eros, even infantile Eros, is incomplete until we have analyzed this love of objects in the world, how it originates, and what its aim is.

The Self and the Other:
Narcissus

THE HUMAN FAMILY is distinguished from the animal family by a prolongation of the period in which the infant is protected from the harsh realities of life by parental care. In this sheltered situation, the erotic potentialities of human nature blossom, but blossom in an unearthly atmosphere divorced from the realities of human life. Hence this early blossoming of the erotic life must succumb to repression when it finally confronts the reality-principle. But though it is repressed, or rather because it is repressed, this early experience of love stays with us as the immortal dream of love, as an indestructible demand of human nature, as the source of our restless discontent. The infantile experience to which our dreams return is an experience of pleasure, so that a return to the pleasure-principle is an indestructible demand of human nature. But is a return to the pleasure-principle all that human nature demands? From the Freudian point of view this question is the same as to ask whether infantile sexuality involves anything over and beyond pleasure.

Normal adult genital sexuality, both at the sensual level of physical intercourse and at the sublimated level of being in love, indicates that the sexual instinct seeks, over and beyond bodily pleasure, some appropriate form of union with objects in the world. But the pattern of normal adult sexuality, as we have seen, can be no clue to the essential nature of the erotic desires of mankind. If we ask what relation to objects in the world is contained in the pattern of infantile sexuality, then we must take as our point of departure Freud's repeated assertions that infantile sexuality follows two paths of finding objects in the world, exhibits two modes of relating itself or binding itself to objects in the world.

The terms he uses most frequently to designate these two relations are "identification" and "object-choice." He defines identification as the desire to be like another object, and object-choice as the desire to possess another object; he usually writes as if identification is the mode in which children love their fathers, while object-choice is the mode in which they love their mothers.[1] It is through its natural propensity to make identifications and object-choices that Eros constructs the family, which in turn is the model for all social organization. And it is by making identifications with his parents that the child absorbs and makes his own their moral standards (the super-ego), so that through its propensity for identification Eros is the fountainhead of morality.

To understand the Freudian categories of identification and object-choice, we must go behind them and call for an explanation of why love of objects in the world takes these two forms and only these two. After all, it is not self-evident that love should turn out to be on the one hand a desire to be like, and on the other hand a desire to possess.

Starting from the axiom that the love of objects in the world is modeled on the primal love of the child for the mother, Freud claims that the child's relation to the mother is first and foremost a relation of dependence on the mother for survival; the path to the mother is established first of all by elementary economic needs. In the terminology of Freud's earliest pair of basic instincts, the sexual instinct follows a path to an object marked out for it by the self-preservation instinct. Freud therefore calls object-choice, modeled on this primal pattern of love of the mother, anaclitic, i.e., "leaning up against" the non-sexual instinct of self-preservation. This anaclitic character of object-choice—its connection with self-preservation, economic need, and dependence—explains why its characteristic aim is to possess its object. Quite distinct from anaclitic object-choice, and distinctly traceable not only in the neuroses and in the sexual perversions but also in the normal erotic attitudes of woman, Freud finds another pattern of choice in which the infantile model of the object is not the mother but the subject himself. The subject wants to love himself and satisfies his self-love circuitously either by loving an object like himself or by finding an object which loves him as he loves himself. Relating this second type of love to the child's general love of himself and his own body, Freud calls this second relation to objects narcissistic. Thus in some of his writings he uses the terms "narcissistic object-choice" and "anaclitic object-choice," corresponding to his later terminology of "identification" and "true object-choice" (or "object-cathexis"). Summarizing the distinction, Freud says that the human being has originally two sexual objects: himself and the woman who tends him.[2]

Freud's distinction between identification and object-choice, or between narcissistic and anaclitic object-choices, does not survive close examination. He is unable to maintain consistently the correlation of identification with love of the father and object-choice with love of the mother, and has to speak of anaclitic relations with the father and identifications with the mother.[8] But the fundamental issue is not confusion in the application of these categories, but confusion in the categories themselves. Close examination of Freud's own premises and arguments suggests that there is only one loving relationship to objects in the world, a relation of being-one-with-the-world which, though closer to Freud's narcissistic relation (identification), is also at the root of his other category of possessive love (object-choice).

If love seeks only identification with objects in the world, then possessiveness is not an essential feature of love. Our criticism is directed against Freud's notion of "true object-cathexis" as an irreducible desire to possess the beloved. The very fact that "true object-cathexis" is fundamentally anaclitic should make us suspicious of its integrity as a mode of loving. For to be anaclitic means that love follows not its own path but one marked out for it by economic needs, the fact of dependence, and the reality-principle in general. Hence, as Freud himself always insisted, it is a pattern established by a fusion of the sexual instinct and the non-sexual instinct. In the phase when he assumed the two instincts to be sex and self-preservation, Freud spoke of object-choice as a manifestation of the sexual instincts leaning on the self-preservation instincts. In the phase when he assumed the two instincts to be Eros and aggression, he spoke of the inevitable aggressive component in object-choice if it is to possess its object.[4]

Furthermore, Freud's own analysis of possessive love (object-choice) and its primal model, love of the mother, shows that its erotic aim is not possession but union with the object, a union which is hardly distinguishable from his own category of identification. He derives identification from the desire for union with the world in the form of incorporation, after the primal model of the relation of the child to the mother's breast.[5] At the same time he says that incorporation of the object is the aim of normal adult loving, i.e., of object-choice.[6] Thus the distinction between object-choice and identification breaks down, both of them meeting in a project of incorporation or being-one-with-the-world, modeled on the primal relation of the child to the mother's breast. Hence Freud says that "at the very beginning, in the primitive oral phase of the individual's existence, object-cathexis and identification are hardly distinguished from each other."[7] And consistently with this, he asserts that the aim of normal adult loving is the restoration of this "primal condition in which object-libido [i.e., anaclitic object-choice] and ego-libido [i.e., narcissistic object-choice] cannot be distinguished."[8]

In Freud's later writings the importance of the early phase of dependence on the mother is increasingly emphasized, and in that context he finds it necessary to conclude that the essence of love of the mother is the need to be loved;[9] but if so, then love of the mother is essentially narcissistic, since he says that "to be loved is the aim and the satisfaction of the narcissistic object-choice."[10] One more passage from Freud's later writings shows both the breakdown of the whole distinction between anaclitic and narcissistic object-choice, and also Freud's failure explicitly to withdraw the distinction: "You remember the object-choice after the anaclitic type, which psychoanalysis talks about? The libido follows the path of the narcissistic needs, and attaches itself to the objects that ensure their satisfaction."[11]

The collapse of the distinction between identification and

object-choice leaves love with one essential aim over and above pleasure, which is to become one with objects in the world. Freud himself repeatedly drew attention to the interchangeability of identification and object-choice; to explain the self-punishment in melancholia and also the self-punishing institution of the super-ego he postulated that we give up a loved object (object-choice) only on condition of making an identification with the lost object.[12] This process, which replaces an object-choice with an identification, is easier to comprehend if we abandon the notion that the two are an irreducible duality. For, as Freud says, we make the identification with the lost object by introjecting or incorporating it into the self, not really incorporating it, but incorporating it passively by making ourselves like it.

But since real incorporation of the object can be said to be the aim of object-love, the choice now appears to be not between identification and object-choice, but between active identification with the object and passive remodeling of the self so as to erect in the self a substitute for the object lost. The choice is between erotic action on the outside world (Ferenczi's "alloplastic adaptation") and passive alteration of the subject's own body and psyche as a substitute for erotic action denied (Ferenczi's "autoplastic adaptation").[13] This distinction is, I think, what Freud is driving at in the following obscure formula: "The return of the libido from the object to the ego and its transformation into narcissism makes a representation of a happy love, and conversely, an actual happy love corresponds to the primal condition in which object-libido and ego-libido cannot be distinguished." [14]

Thus Freud's clinical analysis, corrected, points to the conclusion that Eros is fundamentally a desire for union (being one) with objects in the world. But then the clinical formulations are brought in line with the more philosophical formulations in Freud's later writings, when he assumed the existence of two basic instincts, Eros and Death. From the time that he wrote *Beyond the Pleasure Principle*, he preferred to define the aim of Eros as unification or seeking union.[15] There is an obvious affinity between this doctrine of Eros and certain intuitions adumbrated in the philosophic, poetic, and religious tradition; but as a result of his failure to discard the distinction between identification and object-choice, Freud left his doctrine of Eros as seeking union hanging in metaphysical air, divorced from his deepest analyses of concrete psychological realities. Our reinterpretation is intended to open the way for an analysis of the concrete psychological realities in terms of a desire for union.

The aim of Eros is union with objects outside the self; and at the same time Eros is fundamentally narcissistic, self-loving. How can a fundamentally narcissistic orientation lead to union with objects in the world? The abstract antinomy of Self and Other in love can be overcome if we return to the concrete reality of pleasure and to the fundamental definition of sexuality as the pleasurable activity of the body, and think of loving as the relation of the ego to its sources of pleasure. Narcissistic love is fundamentally a desire for pleasurable activity of one's own body. Our problem then is: How does the desire for pleasurable activity of one's own body lead to other bodies?

The answer is contained in Freud's doctrine of the peculiar ego-structure, the sense of one's relation to the outside world, which is developed in infancy and which, like the rest of infantile sexuality, is repressed but never abandoned in the adult. In the unreal, protected situation of human infancy, the infant develops an unreal sense of reality. Reality is his mother, that is to say, love and pleasure; infantile sexuality affirms the union of the self with a whole world of love and pleasure.

In technical Freudian terminology, the infant develops a pure pleasure-ego instead of a reality-ego, a pure pleasure-ego which absorbs into identity with itself the sources of its pleasure, its world, its mother.[16] Hence "the ego-feeling we are aware of now is thus only a shrunken vestige of a far more extensive feeling—a feeling which embraced the universe and expressed an inseparable connection of the ego with the external world."[17] But the primal experience of union of the self with a world of love and pleasure sets the pattern for all human love, so that "when later on an object manifests itself as a source of pleasure, it becomes loved, but also incorporated into the ego."[18] Hence "an actual happy love corresponds to the primal condition in which object-libido and ego-libido cannot be distinguished." Freud summarizes the development of love thus: "Love originates in the capacity of the ego to satisfy some of its instincts autoerotically through the obtaining of organ-pleasure. It is primarily narcissistic, is then transferred to those objects which have been incorporated in the ego, now much extended, and expresses the motor striving of the ego after these objects as sources of pleasure." [19] Thus the human libido is essentially narcissistic, but it seeks a world to love as it loves itself.

It is the human ego that carries the search for a world to love: or rather this project, in the unconscious stratum of the ego, guides human consciousness in its restless search for an object that can satisfy its love, as in St. Augustine: "I did not yet love, and I loved to love; I sought what I might love, in love with loving." Freud says not only that the human ego-feeling once embraced the whole world, but also that Eros drives the ego to recover that feeling: "The development of the ego consists in a departure from primal narcissism and results in a vigorous attempt to recover it." [20] In primal narcissism the self is at one with a world of love and pleasure; hence the ultimate aim of the human ego is to reinstate what Freud calls "limitless narcissism" [21] and find itself once more at one with the whole world in love and pleasure. The erotic energy in the ego is in the (unconscious) pure pleasure-ego project; and hence the pure pleasure-ego is in conflict with the reality-ego, until reality and pleasure can really meet and create what Ferenczi called "the erotic sense of reality." Eros, as a force in the human ego, seeks to *affirm* a world of love and pleasure: "Affirmation, as being a substitute for union, belongs to Eros." [22]

The ultimate aim of the Freudian Eros—to affirm union with the world in pleasure—is substantially the same as Spinoza's formula for the ultimate aim of human desire—the intellectual love of God. God, in Spinoza's system, is the totality of Nature (*Deus sive Natura*). He defines love as pleasure (*laetitia*) together with the idea of an external cause (the source of the pleasure), adding that it is a property of love to will a union with the beloved object, in the sense that satisfaction lies in the presence of the beloved object. Hence for Spinoza the ultimate aim of human desire is to unite with the world in pleasure; and, as in Freud, this is the ultimate aim of an energy (desire) which is in essence narcissistic. For Spinoza the energy of the individual is essentially directed at self-maintenance, self-activity, self-perfection (*conatus in suo esse perseverandi*), which is also self-enjoyment (*laetitia*). Thus for Spinoza, as for Freud, the self-perfection (narcissism) of the human individual is fulfilled in union with the world in pleasure.[23]

There are important differences between Freud and Spinoza —differences not recognized, for example, in Stuart Hampshire's acute comparison of the two.[24] Above all, Freud has two instincts at war with each other, in place of Spinoza's single *conatus*, and thus can grasp human bondage (Spinoza's term) as internal conflict and not simply as ignorance. And, as we shall see later, Freud's final notion of Death as the antagonist of Eros is incompatible with Spinoza's notion of eternity. Nevertheless, on essential points they are allied, and both are at odds with the Western tradition. Like Freud, Spinoza is at war with the illusion of free will; and, as in Freud, the commitment to the principle of psychological determinism results in the "hideous hypothesis" that the basis of our ordinary morality is irrational and superstitious. Spinoza is thus also driven to a gloomy picture of our present state of human bondage as a sick state in which we are determined by unconscious determinations: "It is plain that we are disturbed by external causes in a number of ways, and that, like the waves of the sea agitated by contrary winds, we fluctuate and are unconscious of the issue and our fate." [25] Hence Spinoza, like Freud, replaces moralism by clinical understanding, and prescribes a radical psychoanalysis to make us conscious of the causes which have determined our nature and, by making us conscious of our determinism, to make us free.

On the problem of human happiness, what distinguishes Spinoza from the Western philosophic tradition and aligns him with Freud is his allegiance to the pleasure-principle and his rejection of mind-body dualism. His allegiance to the pleasure-principle brings him to recognize the narcissistic, self-enjoying character of human desire, and hence to recognize that human perfection consists in an expansion of the self until it enjoys the world as it enjoys itself. And with his rejection of mind-body dualism, Spinoza never forgets that man's desire is for the active life of his own body. From his notion of mind and body as two attributes of one substance, it follows that the power and perfection of the human intellect is at the same time the power and perfection of the human body. "If anything increases, diminishes, helps, or limits our body's power of action, the idea of that thing increases, diminishes, helps, or limits our mind's power of thought." [26]

Hence the expansion of the self, in which human perfection consists, is at the same time the expansion of the active life of the human body, unifying our body with other bodies in the world in active interaction: "That which so disposes the human body that it can be affected in many ways, is profitable to man, and is more profitable in proportion as by its means the body becomes better fitted to be affected in many ways and to affect other bodies." [27] Spinoza sees the inadequacy of the human body as currently structured to sustain the project of human Eros: "In this life, therefore, it is our chief endeavour to change the body of infancy, so far as its nature permits and is conducive thereto, into another body which is fitted for many things." [28]

What Spinoza cannot see, without becoming Freud, is that the endeavor to acquire "a body which is fitted for many things" is the endeavor to recover the body of infancy. Spinoza's "body fitted for many things" is structurally identical with the polymorphously perverse body of infantile sexuality in Freud, the body delighting in the activity of all of its organs. But Spinoza recognizes the "body fitted for many things" as the bodily counterpart of the intellectual love of God: "He who possesses a body fitted for doing many things, possesses the power of causing all the modifications of the body to be related to the idea of God, in consequence of which he is affected with a love of God which must occupy or form the greatest part of his mind, and therefore he possesses a mind of which the greatest part is eternal." [29] Spinoza's intellectual love of God is identical with Freud's polymorphous perversity of children.

If Freud's (and Spinoza's) Eros is essentially narcissistic, it can and should be distinguished—in spite of the fact that Freud did not care to distinguish it [30]—both from the Platonic Eros and the Christian Agape. The Platonic Eros is the child of defect or want. Its direction is away from the insufficient self; its aim is to possess the object which completes it (there is a Platonic residue in Freud's inadequate notion of object-choice). The Christian Agape, with its self-sacrificial structure, has the same basis in the insufficiency of the self, but in it the self can be completed by no object and therefore must be extinguished. In the words of Luther, "To love is the same as to hate oneself"; [31] in the words of St. Augustine, "Love slays what we have been that we may be what we were not." [32]

From the psychoanalytical point of view, Platonic Eros is inseparable from an aggressive component, Christian Agape inseparable from a masochistic component. Freud's doctrine of the narcissistic essence of love seems to lay the groundwork for transcending the by now exhausted debate between Eros and Agape and to pose the proper question, at least for our time, which is to develop a love based neither on self-hatred nor the need to appropriate, but on self-acceptance, self-activity, self-enjoyment. And the Freudian (and Spinozistic) recognition of the bodily nature of all self-enjoyment indicates the obstacle that prevents both Platonist and Christian from accepting the self—the human body.

On the other hand, both the Platonic Eros and the Christian Agape, at their highest point of mystic exaltation, transcend their own limitations and their mutual differences and become a positive challenge requiring an extension and development of the Freudian doctrine of narcissism. In Plato's *Symposium*, after Eros has satisfied its own want by coming to possess the essence of Beauty, it passes on to a further stage, not grounded in the original definition, which Plato calls "giving birth in beauty"—as if the satisfied Eros must overflow, out of its own abundance, into creativity. And in Luther, the perfect Agape of God is a *quellende Liebe*, a love overflowing into creativity.[33] These images suggest that the self-activity and self-enjoyment of the narcissistic Eros must consist in an overflow outward into the world. And the poetic mysticism of Blake has the same intuition: "Exuberance is Beauty. . . . The cistern contains, the fountain overflows." [34]

The principle of erotic exuberance needs to be incorporated into Freud's doctrine of the narcissistic Eros. In technical psychoanalytical terms, Freud recognizes that libido goes out to objects from what he calls a "narcissistic reservoir," [35] but is not clear why that reservoir must overflow. The nearest Freud comes to answering this question is in the essay "On Narcissism" (1914): [36]

> Whence does that necessity arise that urges our mental life to pass on beyond the limits of narcissism and to attach the libido to objects? The answer which would follow from our line of thought would once more be that we are so impelled when the cathexis of the ego with libido exceeds a certain degree. A strong egoism is a protection against disease, but in the last resort we must begin to love in order that we may not fall ill, and must fall ill if, in consequence of frustration, we cannot love. Somewhat after this fashion does Heine conceive of the psychogenesis of the Creation.

But later writings show Freud's feeling that he does not fully comprehend the attachment of libido to objects. In the essay "On Transience" (1915), speaking of mourning, he says: "But why it is that this detachment of libido from its objects should be such a painful process is a mystery to us and we have not hitherto been able to frame any hypothesis to account for it." [37] And in a footnote in *Civilization and Its Discontents* (1930)— omitted in the English translation—Freud poses the limits of narcissism as a still unsolved problem: "A consideration of the possibilities of human happiness should not neglect to take into account the relative proportions of narcissism and object-libido. One would like to know what it means for the economy of the libido to be essentially dependent on oneself." [38]

One can see Freud's thought inhibited by a conception of Self and Other as mutually exclusive alternatives. The image of Narcissus in myth and poetry points in another direction: Narcissus needs a pool, a mirror, in which to see himself. And, in the mysticism of Boehme, the psychogenesis of Creation is God's need for "self-reflection" (*Selbstabbildung*) and for a mirror (*Spiegel*) in which to see himself. [39] Along these lines Freud's narcissism would have the need for the Other more deeply grounded: narcissism, like Narcissus, would be a fountain of play and of erotic exuberance. Nietzsche's Zarathustra says, "I love him whose soul is overfull so that he forgets himself and all things are in him"; and also, "His word pronounced *selfishness* blessed, the wholesome healthy selfishness that wells from a powerful soul—from a powerful soul to which belongs the high body, beautiful, triumphant, refreshing, around which everything becomes a mirror—the supple, persuasive body, the dancer whose parable and epitome is the self-enjoying soul." [40]

The psychoanalytical method seeks to connect the dreams of metaphysics with the physiology of dreams; the physiological basis of the narcissistic Eros and of the pure pleasure-ego project is the relation of the infant to the mother's breast. All love relationships, Freud said, repeat the pattern of this primordial model. Every object-finding is in reality a refinding. [41] "The state of being in love results from the fulfillment of infantile conditions of love . . . whatever fulfils this condition of love becomes idealized." [42] "The desire to suck includes within it the desire for the mother's breast, which is therefore the first object of sexual desire; I cannot convey to you any adequate idea of the importance of this first object in determining every later object adopted, of the profound influence it exerts, through transformation and substitution, upon the most distant fields of mental life." [43]

Here again Freud is only seeing face to face what religious and poetic mysticism has divined darkly and expressed symbolically in the cult of the Madonna and Child. Evelyn Underhill's book on mysticism is prefaced by this quotation from Coventry Patmore: "The Babe sucking its mother's breast, and the Lover returning, after twenty years' separation, to his home and food in the same bosom, are the types and princes of Mystics." *Das ewig weibliche* draws us on: Faust, the incarnation of our restless discontent, achieves final salvation, which is also the end of restlessly striving Faustian man, in his reunion with *das ewig weibliche* in a cloud of mother-figures led by the Mater Gloriosa who is Virgin, Mother, and Queen, so that "Eros may rule, for he began all." [44]

At the mother's breast, in Freudian language, the child experiences that primal condition, forever after idealized, "in which object-libido and ego-libido cannot be distinguished"; [45]

in philosophic language, the subject-object dualism does not corrupt the blissful experience of the child at the mother's breast. But the subject-object dualism is not the only dualism which besets our adult interaction with the world; and conversely, the primal childhood experience, according to Freud, is idealized because it is free from all dualisms. If therefore we think of man as that species of animal which has the historical project of recovering his own childhood, psychoanalysis suggests the eschatological proposition that mankind will not put aside its sickness and its discontent until it is able to abolish every dualism.

In psychoanalytical theory, the dualisms besetting human interaction with the world stem not from the subject-object relation but from the dualism of instincts inside the subject. Throughout the evolution of Freud's thought, Eros always has an antagonist. In his earlier theory the antagonist is self-preservation, or the ego-instinct (more colloquially, hunger); in his later theory the antagonist is the death or aggressive instinct. The whole theory of Eros therefore must hang somewhat in the air until we have examined Eros' antagonist. But we can introduce in advance the Freudian theorem that the instinctual life of man starts from a primitive undifferentiated fusion of the two instincts—a fusion in which they are not mutually antagonistic—and, in so far as it is fixated to childhood, seeks to restore the instinctual fusion. The relation of the child to the mother's breast remains our ideal because it represents such an instinctual fusion. When Freud was thinking of the dualism of the sexual and self-preservation instincts (love and hunger), he coined the term "anaclitic" (i.e., "leaning up against") to describe the relation between the two instincts in the child at the breast, where the first satisfaction of the sexual instinct is simultaneously the first satisfaction of the self-preservation instinct (or ego instinct): "The first auto-erotic sexual gratifications are experienced in connection with vital functions in the service of self-preservation. The sexual instincts are at the outset supported upon the ego-instincts." [46] We have already argued that Freud was wrong in trying to present anaclitic love as a second mode of loving, distinct from narcissistic love; the primal anaclitic situation, which, according to Freud, remains our ideal of love, does not represent a distinct mode of loving but a fusion of the erotic with the nonerotic, specifically economic (self-preservation, hunger) needs and satisfactions.

But according to psychoanalysis this state of instinctual fusion remains our unconscious ideal; and on the other hand civilization makes antagonistic opposites out of economics and love, work and play. Psychoanalysis thus suggests that mankind will not cease from discontent and sickness until the antinomy of economics and love, work and play, is overcome. We are back once more to the utopian dreams of Fourier and to his serious exploration of the possibility of realizing the goal of *travail attrayant*, pleasurable work.

In Freud's writings after 1920 the antithesis of the sexual and self-preservation instincts is replaced by the antithesis of Eros and what Freud called either the aggressive or the destructive or the death instinct. The fundamental polarity in human nature, in Freud's later writings, is not hunger and love, but love and hate, love and aggression, love and the will to power. But the primal experience of satisfaction, which retains humanity's unconscious allegiance, is free not only from the antinomy of work and play but also from the ambivalence of love and hate. Freud, misled by his metaphysical bias toward dualism—a bias which we shall criticize in detail when we consider his instinct theory—often speaks as if the ambivalence of love and hate were a fundamental fact of human nature, present in the child from the start.[47] But when he is not theorizing but simply analyzing the facts, he says that in the earliest phase "there is no ambivalence in the relation to the object, i.e., the mother's breast." [48]

There is a technical point at issue here in the psychoanalytical theory of the stages through which infantile sexuality passes on the way to genital organization. The first stage, the oral stage—the stage in which the child's chief zone of pleasure is the mouth at the mother's breast—is subdivided into a first oral phase distinct from a second phase, the second phase being "distinguished by the onset of biting activities," and therefore being called "the oral-sadistic phase." [49] The appearance of aggressive biting activities marks the first emergence of the ambivalence of love and hate: hence Abraham calls the first oral stage "pre-ambivalent." [50]

Thus the ambivalence of love and hate is not an innate datum of human nature (and one of the grounds for Freud's pessimism disappears). Or rather, Freud's own doctrine that man in his unconscious keeps his allegiance to the primal experience of satisfaction at the mother's breast requires us to say that man unconsciously seeks to abolish the ambivalence of love and hate. And in fact Freud's later writings attribute to the human ego a basic tendency to "reconcile," "synthesize," "unify" the dualisms and conflicts with which the human being is beset; [51] Abraham sets the goal of achieving a "post-ambivalent" stage; Ferenczi calls for a "fresh instinctual fusion." [52] But the possibility of post-ambivalent instinctual refusion must remain hypothetical until we have examined the cause of the ambivalence and the nature of Eros' instinctual antagonist.

V

Art and Eros

PSYCHOANALYSIS has not developed an adequate theory of art. That psychoanalysis has made fundamental contributions to the study of art is a proposition denied only by the willfully ignorant. Psychoanalysis has introduced revolutionary new ideas as to the nature of the thematic content of art. The thematic content of art is always in some sense man; the psychoanalytical contribution to the content-analysis of art is no more than, and no less than, its contribution to the understanding of human nature. Psychoanalysis has introduced equally important, though less generally recognized, ideas as to the technique of art. The technique of art, so radically different from the technique of science and rational discourse, is rooted in what Freud called the primary process—the procedures of the unconscious which, Freud insists, are radically different from the logical procedures of the conscious system, and which, though in this sense illogical, are nevertheless in their own way meaningful and purposive. Trilling is justified in saying, "Freud discovered in the very organization of the mind those mechanisms by which art makes its effects, such devices as the condensations of meanings and the displacement of accent." [1]

Freud thus opened new possibilities with regard to both content-analysis and technique-analysis in art. But the exploitation of these new possibilities has been hampered by the absence of a general psychoanalytical theory of art. Without such a theory, there is no way of estimating the importance of the discovery of the themes and techniques of the unconscious in art. Trilling's essay "Freud and Literature" illustrates how a good critic can recognize Freud's contribution to content- and technique-analysis in literature and still remain an orthodox critic. The discovery of psychoanalytic themes in art is put in proper perspective, as we academics say, by the doctrine that "there is no single meaning to any work of art." By means of this cliché the house that Freud built is absorbed into the stately mansion of traditional criticism. We are free to recognize a psychoanalytic theme in art, but we are not compelled to; and if we do recognize a psychoanalytic theme, we need not be disturbed, because we are free to drown it in a rich orchestration of multiple meanings. Similarly, the possibilities opened up by the analogues between artistic technique and the processes of the unconscious are put in proper perspective by the traditional tribute to "the formal control of the conscious mind." Thus no Copernican revolution takes place in the mind of Lionel Trilling, and business can go on as usual for professional critics. The ego remains the master in the house of art.[2]

Psychoanalysis will continue to be no more than a tantalizing or disturbing possibility on the fringes of artistic criticism as long as it has no adequate general theory of art and of the place of art in life. Freud's own statements on this subject are unsatisfactory. Not without justification does Trilling conclude that Freud's general statements bespeak a contempt for art; not without justification does he maintain that Freud's notion of art as a "substitute-gratification" and as an "illusion in contrast to reality" suggests that art is essentially an opiate of the people, an escape into an unreal world of fantasy indistinguishable from a full-blown neurosis, both art and neurosis having the basic dynamic of a flight from reality.

Now neither the doctrine that art provides pleasures which compensate for the harshness of life, nor the doctrine that art has affinity with madness, can be ruled out as false or insignificant. But anyone who has had experience of art knows that this is not the whole story. It is clear that Freud himself knows that this is not the whole story: hence the vacillations in his statements about art. Thus in some passages he gives a general theory of art; in other passages he implies that the secret of art is impervious to psychoanalytical investigation.[3] In some passages art is assimilated to dreams and madness; in other passages all the recognition that Trilling demands is given to the "social intention and the formal control of the conscious mind" as differentiating art from dreams and madness.

Freud's vacillations cannot be discarded by a simple option between the more "moderate" and the more "extreme" position. To do so would be simply to choose sides in the sterile debate which goes on between professional psychoanalysts and professional critics—a debate which perpetuates Freud's own vacillations but fails to perpetuate his capacity to see both sides of the question. Freud's vacillations must be understood as the reflection of a deeper ambiguity at the heart of psychoanalytical theory—the question whether man's ultimate allegiance is to the reality-principle or to the pleasure-principle. The issue here is not a technical or factual question as to the relative weight of these two principles in the dynamics of the human psyche. It is rather a practical one of individual or social therapy; or, to use another terminology, the issue is eschatological. The question is: What shall man do to be saved?

Freud's writings, taken as a whole, vacillate between two opposite answers to this perpetual question of unhappy humanity. Sometimes the counsel is instinctual renunciation: Grow up and give up your infantile dreams of pleasure, recognize reality for what it is. And sometimes the counsel is instinctual liberation: Change this harsh reality so that you may recover lost sources of pleasure. And sometimes, of course, Freud attempts a compromise between the two attitudes. Thus for example the reality-principle, which he first defined nakedly as an allegiance to "that which is real, even if it should be unpleasant," is later softened into that "which at bottom also seeks pleasure—although a delayed and diminished pleasure, one which is assured by its realization of fact, its relation to reality." [4] This dilemma explains Freud's drift to pessimism.

The basic dialectic in Freud is the tension between his deep humanitarian desire to help mankind and his intellectual realism, which refused to accept a cheap and easy solution. His realism and his humanitarianism could come together only on the platform of instinctual liberation. All Freud's work demonstrates that the allegiance of the human psyche to the pleasure-principle is indestructible and that the path of instinctual renunciation is the path of sickness and self-destruction. When, therefore, in his later writings he counsels instinctual renunciation, it is a counsel of despair; and a careful reading of his later writings shows Freud still trying to find a way out of the prison.

But art is inseparably wedded to the pleasure-principle, and is in fact the most powerful evidence in support of Freud's doctrine of man's indestructible allegiance to the pleasure-principle:

> A thing of beauty is a joy for ever:
> Its loveliness increases; it will never
> Pass into nothingness; but still will keep
> A bower quiet for us, and a sleep
> Full of sweet dreams, and health, and quiet breathing.
> Therefore, on every morrow, are we wreathing
> A flowery band to bind us to the earth,
> Spite of despondence, of the inhuman dearth
> Of noble natures, of the gloomy days,
> Of all the unhealthy and o'er-darkened ways
> Made for our searching: yes, in spite of all,
> Some shape of beauty moves away the pall
> From our dark spirits.[5]

This is the truth contained in Freud's formula of art as substitute-gratification. Compare Nietzsche's doctrine of the necessary connection between suffering and art: "What must this people have suffered, that they might become thus beautiful."[6]

If man's salvation lies in instinctual renunciation laid at the feet of the reality-principle, then Freud is being characteristically consistent and courageous when he offends Trilling and betrays contempt for art, which he loved. Judged at the bar of the reality-principle, the consolations of art are childish, and they reinforce mankind's willful refusal to put away childish things. But if man's destiny is to change reality until it conforms to the pleasure-principle, and if man's fate is to fight for instinctual liberation, then art appears, in the words of Rilke, as the *Weltanschauung* of the last goal.[7] Its contradiction of the reality-principle is its social function, as a constant reinforcement of the struggle for instinctual liberation; its childishness is to the professional critic a stumbling block, but to the artist its glory.

Freud's evaluation of art shifts with his shifting mood as to the possibility of making room for the pleasure-principle in the

real world. At the outset of his career, when he was still under
the spell of Charcot's famous diagnosis ("*C'est toujours la chose
génitale, toujours—toujours—toujours*"),[8] he tended to identify
instinctual liberation and a recovery of sanity with a relaxation
of Victorian sexual morality, with sexual liberation in the ordinary sense of the term—a point of view which can be best
studied in Wilhelm Reich,[9] who essentially remained with
it and who broke with Freud in order to remain with it. This
oversimplified view of the problem naturally engendered an
oversimplified optimism with regard to its solution. At this
stage, Freud's realism and his humanitarianism could come together on a program of oversimplified sexual liberation.

With this tentative theoretical synthesis—perhaps also in-
fluenced by the political upheavals of 1903–1905—Freud wrote
his most socially critical, even rebellious, book, *Wit and the Unconscious*. But *Wit and the Unconscious* is also his most significant contribution to the theory of art, although it has not been
exploited as such. It is true that Freud disclaims any intention of
offering a general theory of art, limits himself strictly to the
problem of wit, and even denies that humor and comedy in
general involve that contribution from the sphere of the unconscious which he claims to be essential in wit.[10] But like all of
Freud, this is a pioneer work which invites, even requires, extension and modification. It is also Freud's earliest work in applied psychoanalysis, and it is written with a cautiousness which
the later Freud would not have felt necessary. It is doubtful
if the later Freud would have maintained that humor and comedy involve no contribution from the unconscious; a quite different analysis of the psychogenesis of humor is offered in an
essay written in 1928.[11] If we take courage and explore *Wit and
the Unconscious* for suggestions as to the general nature of art,
we get a quite different picture from that which emerges from
those later passages, written by a more pessimistic Freud, in
which art seems to be regarded as childishness and as a narcotic.

In *Wit and the Unconscious* Freud affirms the connection
between art and the pleasure-principle, but the pursuit, through
art, of pleasure incompatible with the reality-principle is not
despised but glorified. When the psychic apparatus is not used
to satisfy one of our indispensable instinctual gratifications, he

says, we let it work for pleasure; we even try to derive pleasure from its very activity. Herein, he suspects, is the true basis of all aesthetic thinking.[12]

Freud also affirms the connection between art and childishness; however childishness is not a reproach, but the ideal kingdom of pleasure which art knows how to recover. What we are striving to obtain, he says, is a sort of euphoria—a return to the bygone state in which we were accustomed to satisfy our psychic needs with scant effort. This was the state of childhood, when we needed neither wit nor humor to make us happy, and indeed we knew nothing about them.[13] The function of art—Freud says "wit"—is to help us find our way back to sources of pleasure that have been rendered inaccessible by the capitulation to the reality-principle which we call education or maturity—in other words, to regain the lost laughter of infancy.[14]

This notion of art as driving at a recovery of childhood needs philosophical elaboration. It opens the way for a psychoanalytical reformulation of the truth contained in the Platonic doctrine of *anamnesis*. Plato in the *Phaedrus*—one of the greatest explorations of the psychology of beauty—not only gives full recognition to the affinity between the love of beauty and madness, but also sees in the fevered pursuit of beauty a struggle to recover a lost vision of perfection. Those who do not join in the conclusion that

> . . . trailing clouds of glory do we come
> From God, who is our home

have been haunted by the force of the Platonic notion of *anamnesis*, and at a loss how to explain it. Hence the persuasiveness of mystical formulations ultimately rooted in Platonism, such as the following from Poe: "Inspired by an ecstatic prescience of the glories beyond the grave, we struggle, by multiform combinations among the things and thoughts of Time, to attain a portion of that Loveliness whose very elements, perhaps, appertain to eternity alone."[15] The Freudian doctrine of the archetypal status of childhood can put the Platonic doctrine of *anamnesis* on a naturalistic basis. Max Scheler has noted that the Freudian emphasis on childhood opened up a way to resolve the old philosophic controversy between empiricism and the doctrine of innate ideas.[16]

In *Wit and the Unconscious* Freud also suggests that art, both as a return to the pleasure-principle and as a return to childhood, must be essentially a play activity. He uses the category of play to establish a connection between the techniques of art and the techniques of the primary process, the infantile and the unconscious. Play on words—the technique of wit—is recovered when thought is allowed to sink into the unconscious. In returning to the unconscious in the quest for the materials of wit, our thoughts are only revisiting the old home where in infancy word play reigned.[17] It takes only the reflection that metaphor, which is the building block of all poetry, is nothing but a playing with words, to see how readily Freud's analysis of wit invites extension to the whole domain of art.

Freud does not merely connect art with the unconscious and the infantile; he also distinguishes it from other manifestations of the unconscious and the infantile, such as dreams and neurosis. He distinguishes art from dreams by insisting that art has a social reference and an element of conscious control:

> The dream is a completely asocial psychical product . . . it remains unintelligible to the person himself and therefore completely without interest to anyone else. . . . Wit, on the other hand, is the most social of all pleasure-seeking psychic functions. . . . It must therefore bind itself to the condition of intelligibility; it may utilize the distortion that is possible in the unconscious by means of condensation and displacement, but not to the point that the intelligence of the third person cannot still detect the meaning.[18]

Thus Freud here takes the same position as Charles Lamb, quoted by Trilling as a contradiction of Freud: "The poet dreams being awake. He is not possessed by his subject but he has dominion over it." [19] With the reference to the indispensable third person (an audience), Freud relates the demand for intelligibility to the demand for communication. The implication is that art has the function of making public the contents of the unconscious. In another passage Freud says that the indispensable third person must be suffering from the same repressions which the creative artist has overcome by finding a way of expressing the repressed unconscious.[20] And in his essay on Jensen's novella, also written in the same early phase of his thought, Freud says that the author "directs his attention to the unconscious in his own psyche, is alive to its possibilities of development and grants them artistic expression." [21] Thus art, like psychoanalysis itself, appears to be a way of making the unconscious conscious. Freud many times quotes the artists in support of his psychoanalytical discoveries. At his seventieth birthday celebration he disclaimed the title of "discoverer of the unconscious," saying that "the poets and philosophers before me discovered the unconscious; what I discovered was the scientific method by which the unconscious can be studied." [22] But while psychoanalysis tries to reach the unconscious by extending the conscious, art represents an irruption from the unconscious into the conscious. Art has to assert itself against the hostility of the reality-principle and of reason, which is enslaved to the reality-principle. Hence its aim, in Freud's words, is the veiled presentation of deeper truth; hence it wears a mask, a disguise which confuses and fascinates our reason.[23] The mask which seduces us is derived from the play of the primary process.

It is the tension between the unconscious and the conscious which differentiates the play of the primary process in art from the play of the primary process in dreams. Freud does not confine himself to general statements about the conscious element as distinguishing art from dreams; he analyzes the difference between the technique of wit and the technique of dreams in a way that should interest any critic who concedes that "Freud discovered in the very organization of the mind those mechanisms by which art makes its effects." [24] Thus the ambiguity in wit—and the ambiguity of art in general is a leading theme of modern criticism—is both related to and distinguished from the compromise character of symbol-formation in dreams and neurotic symptoms.

> Wit does not make compromises as the dream does, it does not yield to the inhibition, but insists on retaining unchanged the play with words or nonsense. It limits itself, however, to

a selection of situations in which this play or this nonsense may also appear permissible (the joke) or meaningful (wit), thanks to the ambiguity of words and the multiplicity of thought-relationships. Nothing better distinguishes wit from all other psychic phenomena than this two-faced, two-tongued quality. . . .[25]

Art differs from dreaming not only because it makes the unconscious conscious—a purely cognitive relation—but also because it liberates repressed instincts—a libidinal relation. Because of the repression that arises from civilized life, we have lost many of the primary pleasures of which the censorship disapproves. But we find renunciation extremely difficult; hence we discover that wit enables us to make our renunciation regressive and thus to regain what we have lost. Its object from the beginning is the same: to rid us of our inhibitions, and thereby to make those sources of pleasure that have long been blocked once more accessible for our gratification. As such, art struggles against repressive reason and the reality-principle in an effort to regain lost liberties.[26] A special pleasure in wit is derived from an *"economy in the expenditure of inhibitions or suppressions."* Our normal orderly responsible selves, dominated by the reality-principle, are sustained by a constant expenditure in psychic energy devoted to the maintenance of the repression of our fundamental desires. Art, by overcoming the inhibition and by activating the playful primary process, which is intrinsically easier and more enjoyable than the procedures of normal responsible thought, on both counts effects a saving in psychic expenditure and provides relief from the pressures of reason.[27]

Art, if its object is to undo repressions, and if civilization is essentially repressive, is in this sense subversive of civilization. Some of Freud's formulations on the role of the indispensable third person suggest that the function of art is to form a subversive group, the opposite of that authoritarian group the structure of which Freud analyzed in *Group Psychology and the Analysis of the Ego.* The indispensable third person must be suffering from the same repressions as the creative artist. The relation between the artist and the third person is one of identification, and identification is the relation which. according to

Group Psychology, binds together the members of an authoritarian group.[28] In contrast with the repressive structure of the authoritarian group, the aim of the partnership between the artist and the audience is instinctual liberation.

Freud works out the relation between the element of pure play and the element of instinctual liberation in wit by means of the analogy of the distinction between fore-pleasure and end-pleasure in sexual intercourse. In sexual intercourse the fore-pleasure is in the preliminary play with all parts of the body, and it represents a perpetuation of the pure polymorphous perverse play of infantile sexuality; the end-pleasure in the orgasm is purely genital and post-pubertal. Freud says that the element of pure play in wit serves as an "alluring premium" which makes possible the much greater pleasure of liberating repressed desires. It seems to me that the word "art" can be substituted for the word "wit" in the following passage, allowing for a few minor changes:

> It begins as play, in order to derive pleasure from the free use of words and ideas. As soon as the strengthening reason forbids this play with words as senseless and with ideas as foolish, it turns to the joke in order to retain these sources of pleasure and to be able to gain new pleasure from the liberation of the nonsensical. As real but non-tendentious wit it assists ideas and strengthens them against the assault of the critical judgment, utilizing in this process the principle of interchange of pleasure-sources; and finally it joins with the major tendencies struggling against repression, in order to remove inner inhibitions according to the principle of fore-pleasure.[29]

Art seduces us into the struggle against repression.

This notion of art as a mode of instinctual liberation suggests a further distinction between art on the one hand and dreams and neurosis on the other. Dreams and neurosis give expression to the repressed unconscious, but they do not liberate it. The distinction between giving expression to the unconscious and liberating the unconscious is difficult. Perhaps we should say that neurosis and dreams are the determinate outcome of the unconscious, while art is its conscious articulation. For the liberation in art is connected with the element of consciousness in it. Freud compares humor to psychoneurotic defense mechanisms inaugurated, like humor, to protect from pain; but at the same time he distinguishes humor from the neurotic defense mechanism. Indeed he calls it the highest of all defense functions; quite unlike repression, humor openly confronts ideas that are in themselves painful or are connected with painful images, and thus it is instrumental in overcoming the automatic machinery of defense.[30]

The neurotic mechanism involves repression and a shutting of the eye of consciousness, and a resultant psychic automatism. Art does not withdraw the eye of consciousness, does not repress, and attains some freedom. And by liberating the instincts, art attains a positive pleasure denied to dreams and neurosis. Dreams are wish-fulfillment fantasies; neurotic symptoms are substitutes for forbidden pleasures, but as compromises they never satisfy. Art, on the other hand, not being a compromise with the unconscious either in the cognitive or in the libidinal sense, affords positive satisfaction, and cannot be simply classed, as in Freud's later formulations, with dreams and neurosis as a "substitute-gratification." This I take to the meaning of the contrast between dream and wit stated in *Wit and the Unconscious:* that the one primarily guards against pain, while the other seeks pleasure.[31] This formulation must be understood in the light of the distinction which Freud drew between avoidance of pain and positive happiness, the distinction which made him say love is not "content to strive for avoidance of pain—that goal of weary resignation; rather it passes that by heedlessly and holds fast to the deep-rooted passionate striving for a positive fulfillment of happiness." [32] Art gives us this positive pleasure in so far as it attains that goal which must always remain the goal of humanity—conscious play. Freud has seen that the category of conscious play gives the final distinction between dreams and neurosis and art; the dream is always a wish, but wit is actualized play.[33]

The conception of art derived from what Freud says about wit is substantial enough to constitute at least the outline of a psychoanalytical theory of art. Art as pleasure, art as play, art as the recovery of childhood, art as making conscious the unconscious, art as a mode of instinctual liberation, art as the fellowship of men struggling for instinctual liberation—these ideas plainly fit into the system of psychoanalysis. How do they fit art? Detached from the specific psychoanalytical context, these ideas are not new: they wear the stigmata of the romantic movement, or as Mario Praz calls it, the Romantic Agony. Freud takes his place in European intellectual history if we place him at the meeting point between nineteenth-century science and what Whitehead called the Romantic Reaction.

How close the romantic artist gets to the psychoanalytical point of view can be seen in Rilke's essay "Ueber Kunst," [34] first published in 1899, the year before Freud's *Interpretation of Dreams*. Rilke presents art as a way of life, "like religion, science, or even socialism," "distinguished from other interpretations of life by the fact that it is not a product of the times, and appears, so to speak, as the *Weltanschauung* of the ultimate goal," and as "the sensuous possibility of new worlds and times." The work of art is "always in response to a present time," but "the times are resistance"; "it is only from this tension between contemporary currents and the artist's untimely conception of life that there arises a series of small discharges [*Befreiungen*], which are the work of art."

Thus the dialectic between art and society derives from the artist's contact with the ultimate essence of humanity, which is also humanity's ultimate goal: "History is the index of men born too soon." And as for the artist, "Again and again someone in the crowd wakes up, he has no ground in the crowd, and he emerges according to much broader laws. He carries strange customs with him and demands room for bold gestures. The future speaks ruthlessly through him." But as spokesmen for the essence and for the future, artists are the spokesmen for what is repressed in the present: "Their winged heart everywhere beats against the walls of their time; their work was that which was not resolved in the lives they lived."

The artist is compared by Rilke to "a dancer whose movements are broken by the constraint of his cell. That which finds no expression in his steps and the limited swing of his arms, comes in exhaustion from his lips, or else he has to scratch the unlived lines of his body into the walls with his wounded fingers." Art is a way of life faithful to the natural instincts, and therefore faithful to childhood: "Not any self-control or self-limitation for the sake of specific ends, but rather a carefree letting go of oneself: not caution, but rather a wise blindness; not working to acquire silent, slowly increasing possessions, but rather a continuous squandering of all perishable values. This way of being has something naïve and instinctive [*Unwillkürliches*] about it, and resembles that period of the unconscious [*des Unbewussten*] best characterized by a joyous confidence, namely the period of childhood." The child "has no anxiety about losing things." Everything the child has sensed passes through his love, and is illuminated by it: "And whatever has once been lit up in love remains as an image, never more to be lost, and the image is possession; that is why children are so rich." (Rilke's thought is complemented by Freud's remark on happiness: "Happiness is the deferred fulfillment of a prehistoric wish. That is why wealth brings so little happiness; money is not an infantile wish." [35]) The artist is the man who refuses initiation through education into the existing order, remains faithful to his own childhood being, and thus becomes "a human being in the spirit of all times, an artist." Hence the artist tree is distinguished by profounder roots in the dark unconscious: "Artists extend much farther down into the warmth of all Becoming; in them other juices rise into fruit."

Perhaps Rilke needs to be supplemented by psychoanalysis. It is certain, on the other hand, that psychoanalytical formulations seem like a scrannel pipe of wretched straw when set beside Rilke. Psychoanalysts should, like Freud, envy the capacity of poets, "with hardly an effort to salve from the whirlpool of their own emotions the deepest truths, to which we others have to force our way, ceaselessly groping amid torturing uncertainties." [36]

Language and Eros

I F PSYCHOANALYSIS represents any advance in the general
theory of human nature, it must be able to advance the
theory of language; and conversely, symptoms are so close
to symbols that psychoanalysis cannot state its theory of neurosis without having a general theory of what Cassirer called the
animal symbolicum. Language, like art, is one of those problems
the solution of which requires a synthesis of psychoanalysis
with non-psychoanalytical disciplines, a synthesis aimed at a
general theory of human nature and based on a resolute commitment to the vision of culture as neurosis. Hence Freud (apart
from one inadequate paragraph to be considered later) has no
general theory of language; and the most significant attempt at
synthesis is that of the psychoanalytically minded anthropologist Weston LaBarre.[1]

The essential paradox in the psychoanalytical approach to
language is to see it as sublimated sexuality and as a crucial
instrument in that general deflection of libido from sexual to
social aims which, according to psychoanalytical theory, is
sublimation and is culture. Hence Freud, in his nearest approach
to a general theory of language, tentatively adopted Sperber's
theory of the derivation of language from the mating calls of
animals, language being constituted by establishing a connection
between the mating calls and work processes. "Primitive man
thus made his work agreeable, so to speak, by treating it as the
equivalent of and substitute for sexual activities." [2]

Sublimation is perhaps the most difficult concept in psychoanalysis, and only later in this book shall we be prepared to
understand it. Above all, sublimation is a process involving not
just the sexual instinct but also its antagonist, and therefore it

cannot be understood before we understand Eros' antagonist. Quite specifically, in Freud's later theory, negation, a fundamental principle in language, is regarded as a derivative of the death instinct.[3] We do not at this point have a theory of sublimation, and therefore do not offer a theory of language. And yet it may be worth while to make a preliminary assessment of the psychoanalytic point of view.

If language is made out of love, we must transcend the economic-rational, or operational, notion of "the origin of language from and in the process of human labor" (Engel's phrase).[4] From the psychoanalytical point of view language is indeed inseparable from human labor; its function, in Freud's comment on Sperber, is to make work possible. But work is made possible by being made agreeable, and it is made agreeable by becoming a substitute for repressed sexuality. Over and beyond labor there is love, and labor is sustained by the energy of repressed love.

But if language is made out of (sublimated) sexuality, it can hardly be genital sexuality (the mating calls of animals), as supposed in Sperber's theory. Such a hypothesis is at odds with the psychoanalytical emphasis on infantile, pregenital sexuality as the great reservoir of Eros from which sublimations (and culture) are drawn. It is also at odds with the fact that the acquisition of the power of speech by the human child occurs during the early blossoming of infantile sexuality and as an inseparable part of it. It takes no psychoanalytical finesse, but only simple observation of childhood, to recognize that in the history of every human being language originates in the infantile life of play, pleasure, and love which centers round the mother; over this primary function is built the secondary function of organizing human energy in socially productive work. In the ontogenetic development of every human being, it is the language of love and the pleasure-principle before it becomes the language of work and the reality-principle; language is an operational superstructure on an erotic base.

Freud says that ideas are libidinal cathexes, that is to say, acts of love; that conscious attention is no mere act of perception but also a libidinal hypercathexis; and that "affirmation, as being a substitute for union, belongs to Eros."[5] Psychoanalysis then would have to ally itself with the theory of Rousseau and

Herder, restated by the modern authority on comparative linguistics, Jespersen: "Men sang out their feelings long before they were able to speak their thoughts." [6] Susanne Langer, following Jespersen, says of language, "Its beginnings are not natural adjustments, ways to means; they are purposeless lalling-instincts, primitive aesthetic reactions, and dream-like associations of ideas." [7] And if language has an infantile erotic base, it must be basically a playful activity. Observation of children shows that learning to speak is for them in itself play and then serves to enrich their life of play. And the analysis of language, not a particular language but language generally, reveals its essentially playful structure. In the words of Cassirer, "Language is, by its very nature and essence, metaphorical"; and every metaphor is a play upon words.[8] Jespersen also concludes that "language originated as play." [9] The element of play in language is the erotic element; and this erotic element is in essence not genital, but polymorphously perverse.

If, in the history of every child, language is first of all a mode of erotic expression and then later succumbs to the domination of the reality-principle, it follows, or perhaps we should say mirrors, the path taken by the human psyche and must share the ultimate fate of the human psyche, namely neurosis. Language will then have to be analyzed as compromise-formation, produced by the conflict of the pleasure-principle and the reality-principle, like any neurotic symptom. To regard human speech, the self-evident sign of our superiority over animals, as a disease or at least as essentially diseased, is for common sense, and for the philosopher Cassirer, a monstrous hypothesis.[10] Yet psychoanalysis, which insists on the necessary connection between cultural achievement and neurosis and between social organization and neurosis, and which therefore defines man as the neurotic animal, can hardly take any other position. On this point Freud was not aware of the implications of the line of thought he started; nineteenth-century science, with which he identified himself, was not critical of its own instruments. But if psychoanalysis is carried to the logical conclusion that language is neurotic, it can join hands with the twentieth-century school of linguistic analysis—a depth analysis of language—inspired by that man with a real genius for the psychopathology of language, Wittgenstein. He said, "Philosophy is a battle against the bewitchment [*Verhexung*] of our intelligence by means of language." [11]

Some of these linguistic analysts have had the project of getting rid of the disease in language by reducing language to purely operational terms. From the psychoanalytic point of view, a purely operational language would be a language without a libidinal (erotic) component; and psychoanalysis would suggest that such a project is impossible because language, like man, has an erotic base, and also useless because man cannot be persuaded to operate (work) for operation's sake. Wittgenstein, if I understand him correctly, has a position much closer to that of psychoanalysis; he limits the task of philosophy to that of recognizing the inevitable insanity of language. "My aim is," he says, "to teach you to pass from a piece of disguised nonsense to something that is patent nonsense." "He who understands me finally recognizes [my propositions] as senseless." [12] Psychoanalysis begins where Wittgenstein ends. The problem is not the disease of language, but the disease called man.

Language as disease and language as play—the two meet in the concept of neurotic play, that is to say, magic (Wittgenstein's "bewitchment"). In his essay on "Animism, Magic and Omnipotence of Thought," [13] Freud goes beyond Frazer's notion that primitive magic is simply a system of erroneous thinking which, lacking a true ("scientific") understanding of the connections between things, posited causal interrelation on the basis of superficial association of ideas. Freud looks for a dynamic psychological factor which would explain the positive commitment to magic, and he finds it in the belief in the omnipotence of thoughts and wishes. But since the belief in the omnipotence of thoughts is also to be found in children and in adult civilized neurotics, Freud is able to make a psychoanalytic explanation of it. It is a characteristic feature in the narcissistic phase of infantile sexual development; primitive adults preserve a high degree of the narcissistic orientation, while adult civilized neurotics regress to it.

Now if we can say that language is diseased in so far as it contains magical qualities, in so far as it reflects a belief in the reality of thoughts and wishes, we are able to trace the magi-

cal quality of language to its organic connection with the narcissistic phase of infantile sexual development, the phase in
which the child develops the pure pleasure-ego. For the world
of the pure pleasure-ego is a dream world, a world constructed
out of "neurotic currency" in which wishes are true—though
for the child this currency is not neurotic, since he knows nothing of the conflict of the pleasure-principle and the reality-
principle and his unreal world is his real world. And by the
same token it is a world of play, in which the representation
of the gratified wish is accepted as real. And in effect, says Freud,
it *is* real; the child and the primitive man are satisfied with play
and imitative representation not because they realize their impotence and are resigned to these substitutes, but because they
so obviously place an excessive valuation on their wishes.[14]
Language as play and language as disease are the two sides of
language as wish-fulfillment thinking, and wish-fulfillment
thinking is a legacy of childhood indelible in our minds, carrying the secret project of the pure pleasure-ego, the search for
an erotic sense of reality.

The mystical tradition long ago recognized the neurotic
character of language. Jacob Boehme speaks of the language of
Adam—different from all languages as we know them—as the
only natural language, the only language free from distortion
and illusion, the language which man will recover when he recovers paradise. According to Boehme, Adam's language was
an unclouded mirror of the senses, so that he calls this ideal
language "sensual speech"—*die sensualische Sprache*. It is the
language appropriate to a species that is actualizing the true
potentialities of its sensuous or sensual nature, and as such is in
unity with all of sensuous nature and all life. Hence Boehme
says that animals enjoy true self-expression, while men do not:

> No people understands any more the sensual language, and
> the birds in the air and the beasts in the forest do understand
> it according to their species. Therefore man may reflect what
> he has been robbed of, and what he is to recover in the second
> birth. For in the sensual language all spirits speak with each
> other, they need no other language, for it is the language of
> nature.[15]

Hence that heir of the mystics and ally of psychoanalysis in the task of making the unconscious conscious, modern poetry, has envisaged the necessity of transcending language. Valéry defines the goal of art as the recovery of our sensuous and sensual nature: "The art of the superior artist is to restore by means of conscious operations the integrity [*valeur*] of sensuality and the emotional power of things." [16] But if language is essentially a neurotic compromise between the erotic (pleasure) and operational (reality) principles, it follows that the consciousness, in the artistic use of language, is subversive of its own instrument and seeks to pass beyond it. Language is, in Valéry's words, "the beautiful chains which entangle the distracted god in the flesh"—

> Belles chaînes en qui s'engage
> Le dieu dans la chair égaré.[17]

And the goal of poetry is an experience essentially ineffable: "The Beautiful implies effects of unspeakableness, indescribableness, ineffability. . . . Now if it is desired to produce such an effect by means of things said, by language—or if such an effect is felt as a result of the use of language—it follows that language is being employed in order to make mute, is expressing muteness." [18]

Similarly Rilke sets the goal of mute speech, "essentially natural speech by means of the body" [19]—in Boehme's terms, sensual speech. The ineffability of beauty, and the connection between beauty and what Valéry calls the integrity of sensuality, together constitute a measure of the repression of Eros in civilization, as well as a measure of the difference between men as they are today, with their neurotic addiction to their neurotic speech, and men as they might be if they attained their proper perfection as an animal species and recovered the power of sensual speech.

Part Three
DEATH

*Freud finally came to identify the instinctual dualism under-
lying the conflicts in human life as the dualism of Life (Eros)
and Death. Psychoanalytical therapists after Freud (and even
Freud himself) have seen in the death instinct an irreducible
obstacle in the way of therapy. Lacking Freud's stoical courage,
the Epigoni have dropped the death instinct without putting
any other hypothesis in its place. But the possibility of therapy
will not be reopened by shutting one's eyes to the grounds of
Freud's pessimism.*

VII

Instinctual Dualism
and Instinctual Dialectics

THE THEORY of the instincts is psychoanalysis in its most opaque and most unsympathetic form. We are suspicious of the very word "instinct": it suggests an unalterable biological datum, and therefore seems to deny man the power to alter himself, and simultaneously to deny the environment the power to alter him, leaving him with a fixed nature irreconcilable with the actual variety in human character and conduct. Or, starting from the methodological principle that theories of human nature must be derived from the observation of human behavior, we fail to see how from the observation of human behavior we can derive anything except a classification of the varieties of human behavior; and we fail to see anything gained, except mystification, by calling such classifications instincts.

This initial lack of sympathy turns into outright rejection when we find that Freud steadily insists that the instincts are two and only two; at this point psychoanalysis seems quite arbitrary and therefore unscientific. Then finally we find that Freud changes his mind quite radically as to the nature of the two instincts in the middle of his psychoanalytical career. And his argumentation is a jungle of technical psychoanalytical considerations mixed with biological speculations. Having lost all sense of direction, we happily pounce on the passage where Freud says, "The instincts are mythical beings, superb in their indefiniteness," [1] and interpret it as justification for forgetting the whole subject. But the next sentence in the same passage reads, "In our work we cannot for a moment overlook them, and yet we are never certain that we are seeing them clearly."

First, therefore, we must clarify the scientific status of these instincts which are "mythical beings." Freud regards them as the basal concepts of psychoanalysis, having a status comparable to such concepts as matter and energy in physics. But, he says, in truly empirical sciences these basal concepts are not the foundation stone but the coping stone of the whole structure. And he argues that while a speculative theory must be based on sharply defined concepts, an empirical science will be "gladly content with nebulous, scarcely imaginable conceptions, which it hopes to apprehend more clearly in the course of its development, or which it is even prepared to replace by others." [2] (Freud said this long before he decided to abandon his earlier instinct theory.) In another passage Freud argues that such basal concepts, in the beginning stages of a science, must have some measure of uncertainty, and strictly speaking must be in the nature of conventions, "although everything depends on their being chosen in no arbitrary manner, but determined by important relations they have to the empirical material—relations that we seem to divine before we can clearly recognize and demonstrate them." [3] To all but extreme positivists Freud's defense of the scientific status of the "mythical" instincts will, I think, be acceptable. Basal concepts such as instincts are groping attempts to answer the fundamental problem which any given science is trying to solve, and at the same time they must spring out of the empirical material which is the real foundation for the science.

The light which shows a path through the complications of the Freudian theory of instincts is a clear perception of the problem he is trying to answer and of the facts from which the answer is to be derived. We must return to the fundamental concept of psychoanalysis, the pillar on which the whole edifice rests—repression. The empirical material on which psychoanalysis rests is the observation of repression, resistance, and conflict in human life. And the goal of psychoanalysis is to create a theory of human nature which explains why there is repression.

This goal immediately explains two formal characteristics of the theory of instincts. The Freudian theory of the instincts is persistently dualistic because it starts from the fact of conflict in mental life and aims at explaining that fact. Hence the Freudian critique of Jung's monistic theory of the libido centers on the argument that it undermines the theory of repression.[4] Secondly, the Freudian "instinct" is a borderland concept between the mental and the biological, because Freud is seeking an explanation of man as neurotic or repressed in terms which would relate man's specifically human characteristic (repression) to his animal (bodily) nature. Hence he defines an instinct as "both the mental representative of the stimuli emanating from within the organism and penetrating to the mind, and at the same time a measure of the demand made upon the energy of the latter in consequence of its connection with the body." [5]

As a borderland concept between the human and the animal, the instinct theory inevitably takes Freud into biological as well as psychological considerations. Thus his general approach to the problem of repression gave his instincts two formal characteristics. On the one hand, they must be common to all animals, or even all life; on the other hand, they must be a mutually antagonistic pair. These formal characteristics hold true for both the earlier and the later theories of the instincts. For whether the antagonism, or as Freud calls it the ambivalence, is between sex and self-preservation, or between sex and aggression, or between life and death, in every case Freud postulates an ultimate duality grounded in the very nature of life itself.

Freud began by borrowing from the romantic poets the antithesis of hunger and love, which, translated into scientific terminology, gave him the antithesis of the sexual and self-preservation instincts. The antithesis of the sexual and self-preservation instincts corresponds to the antithesis of the pleasure-principle and the reality-principle, which is, in Freud's earlier theory, the cause of repression. At the same time they can plausibly be regarded as present in all organisms or at least all animals, the sexual instinct working to preserve the species and the self-preservation instinct working to preserve the individual member of the species. This first theory of repression was upset by developments in the exploration of the sexual instinct (libido). The antithesis of sex and self-preservation was undermined when empirical facts forced on psychoanalysis the recognition of the narcissistic character of the sexual instinct; for narcissistic libido cathects the self, and there was no way of distinguishing narcissistic libido from the self-preservation instinct. The only duality which the narcissistic libido suggested was the duality of ego-libido and object-libido; but since the facts which forced on psychoanalysis the concept of the narcissistic libido showed the convertibility of ego-libido into object-libido and vice versa, this duality was not firm enough.

Hence, again looking for a dualism, Freud turned to the ambivalence of love and hate, an ambivalence prominent, like hunger and love, in romantic philosophy and poetry, and also prominent in the clinical picture of psychopathological case histories. He thus obtained a fresh start with the antithesis of the sexual and aggressive instincts. But again the empirical facts which suggested the antithesis showed that sexual and aggressive instincts were not an ultimate duality. No one has shown more clearly than Freud himself how love can turn into hate, and the fusion of both in the phenomenon of sadism. So, to obtain a firm enough duality, Freud turns for inspiration to the biological antithesis of life and death, and links the hypothesis of a universal biological death instinct with the psychological phenomenon of masochism.

Now he is able to postulate an irreconcilable conflict between Eros, seeking to preserve and enrich life, and the death instinct, seeking to return life to the peace of death. Now ambivalent fusions, such as that of sadism, no longer threaten to undermine the basic dualism. Such ambivalent fusions are secondary fusions, compromises generated in the eternal struggle of life and death. Sadism represents an extroversion of the innate death instinct, a transformation of the desire to die into the desire to kill, a transformation achieved by Eros so as to reduce the innate self-destructive tendency in the organism and turn it into a useful ally in the erotic task of maintaining and enriching life.[6]

If a psychoanalytic theory of the instincts must have the formal characteristics Freud demanded, if it is to trace the conflicts in mental life to basic conflicts in "the demands made upon the mind in consequence of its connection with the body," it is difficult to see any way of avoiding Freud's final duality of the life and death instincts. Assuming we have to have a duality, the technical arguments which forced Freud from one duality to another till he reached this final hypothesis are both logically coherent and strongly based on empirical data. Psychoanalysts after Freud, who have not accepted the life-and-death duality, have not been able to produce any alternative. They content themselves with rejecting the death instinct, and thus drift into instinctual monism, as Jung did, or into that general theoretical skepticism or indifference which is so congenial to the practitioner-technician.

The psychoanalytical practitioners have good reason to draw back from Freud's final instinct theory. The theory, as he left it, results in complete therapeutic pessimism, and is therefore worse than useless for therapists. Freud himself was unable to use the death instinct in his own later clinical writings, with one significant exception, namely the essay "Analysis Terminable and Interminable." This essay analyzes the factors preventing complete cure. Freud's therapeutic pessimism is grounded in his hypothesis of the eternal and irreconcilable struggle of life and death in every organism, producing in every human being the "spontaneous tendency to conflict" and manifesting itself in neurotic patients as an unconscious resistance to cure, a kind of "psychical entropy." [7]

Quite apart from the specific character of the death instinct —the subject of the next chapter—Freud's system as a whole is given a metaphysical tendency toward pessimism by the formal prerequisite that conflicts in mental life are to be traced to instincts. The aim of the theory of instincts is to build a bridge between mental conflict (neurosis) and human biology, and, at least as Freud handled it, it ends by finding the causes of conflict in the biological domain. But if the causes are biological data, the hope of cure is groundless. It is true that Freud more than once disavows the propriety of giving a biological, as opposed to a psychological, explanation of repression.[8] But when, for example in *Civilization and Its Discontents*, he invokes the "primal," "innate" conflict of ambivalence between Eros and Death as the ultimate explanation of the human neurosis, we must assume he means "innate," i.e., biologically given.[9] And the vision of Life and Death in *Beyond the Pleasure*

Principle completes the picture by seeing all organic life caught in the conflict of ambivalence.

All organic life is then sick; we humans must abandon hope of cure, but we can take comfort in the conclusion that our sickness is part of some universal sickness in nature. The metaphysical courage, even grandeur, of *Beyond the Pleasure Principle* should not blind us to the fact that it is metaphysics (Freud calls it speculation); it is true religion, in the Spinozistic sense; it is Freud's attempt to see all things in God and *sub specie aeternitatis.* To argue *ad hominem* against a metaphysical system is easy, and psychoanalysis equips us to do so. It is easy to argue that Freud has projected the neurosis of mankind onto the whole organic world, with the effect of exhibiting the inevitability and permanence of the human neurosis. It is easy to argue that this is a rationalization really expressing that unconscious resistance to cure which, according to Freud, makes patients cling tenaciously to illness and suffering and which is a manifestation of the wish to die.[10] It is less easy to see how the psychoanalytical exploration of the human neurosis leads to any other theoretical conclusion or any other instinctual resolution.

A psychoanalysis which remains psychoanalysis must keep the theory of instincts. In it is contained the commitment to restore to man his animal nature and to eliminate the mystery of the soul. Hence the instincts must be universal biological principles. The question is: What had to happen to an animal in order to make him into a man-animal? And a psychoanalysis which remains psychoanalysis must keep the duality of instincts. The essence of the man-animal is neurosis, and the essence of neurosis is mental conflict. The human neurosis must be traced to an instinctual ambivalence, a conflict between forces inherent in all organic life, unless we are to return to the traditional and stale notion that the psychic conflict in man is due to the ambivalence between his superorganic soul and his animal body.

If, on the other hand, psychoanalysis is to retain hope and keep open the possibility of therapy, it must find a way to avoid Freud's metaphysical vision of all life sick with the struggle between Life and Death. It must hold fast to the vision that man is distinguished from other animals by the privilege of being sick; that there is an essential connection between being sick and being civilized; in other words, that neurosis is the privilege of the uniquely social animal. It must therefore maintain that instinctual ambivalence is a human prerogative.

We need, in fine, a metaphysic which recognizes both the continuity between man and animals and also the discontinuity. We need, instead of an instinctual dualism, an instinctual dialectic. We shall have to say that whatever the basic polarity in human life may be—whether it is the polarity of hunger and love, or love and hate, or life and death—this polarity exists in animals but does not exist in a condition of ambivalence. Man is distinguished from animals by having separated, ultimately into a state of mutual conflict, aspects of life (instincts) which in animals exist in some condition of undifferentiated unity or harmony. Psychoanalysis must find the basis of human neurosis in the animal, and at the same time must recognize that the animal is not neurotic (except when it is brought into contagious contact with man). Since the basis of human neurosis is conflict, the polarities which develop into conflict at the human level must exist, but not as conflict, and therefore somehow undifferentiated, at the animal level.

This dialectical metaphysics is no less metaphysical than the metaphysics of *Beyond the Pleasure Principle*. The difference between the two can be best seen if we relate them to their proper models in pure philosophical speculation. Freud correctly found a model for his own view in the pre-Socratic philosopher Empedocles, who found the ultimate principle of the universe to be the eternal conflict between love and strife.[11] Our speculation has a similar analogy to the philosophy of Empedocles' predecessors—Anaximander, who said that the strife of opposites is produced by the separating of opposites out of a primal state of undifferentiated unity, and Heraclitus, who asserted the ultimate unity of opposites, including life and death.

The difference between a dualism of the instincts and a dialectical unity of the instincts is small and elusive; but slight shades of difference at this fundamental level can have large consequences. Freud's dualism undermines the distinction between different levels in what is nevertheless the continuous hierarchy of organisms; the shift from the logic of Empedocles to the logic of Anaximander makes it possible to formulate both the continuity and the discontinuity between man and animals. Freud's dualism also leads to suicidal therapeutic pessimism, because it results in representing conflict not as a human aberration but as a universal biological necessity; our modification of Freud's ontology restores the possibility of salvation. It is the distinctive achievement of man to break apart the undifferentiated or dialectical unity of the instincts at the animal level. Man separates the opposites, turns them against each other, and, in Nietzsche's phrase, sets life cutting into life. It is the privilege of man to revolt against nature and make himself sick. But if man has revolted from nature, it is possible for him to return to nature and heal himself. Then man's sickness may be, again in Nietzsche's phrase, a sickness in the sense that pregnancy is a sickness, and it may end in a birth and a rebirth.[12] The Freudian dualism prevents us from positing any break with nature, and consequently precludes the notion of a return to nature; and since the failure to posit a break with nature entails the necessity of projecting man's sickness back into nature, a return to nature, even if it were possible, would not be a return to health.

Dialectics rather than dualism is the metaphysic of hope rather than despair. There is no way of eliminating questions of faith from human life as long as human life is subject to general conditions of repression. Or rather—since, as Freud said, faith is a derivative of love—dialectics is the metaphysic of Eros, hoping all things according to St. Paul and seeking reunification according to Freud.

Actually the dialectical metaphysic of hope does not lack empirical grounds, grounds established by psychoanalysis itself. The only grounds for hope for humanity are in the facts of human childhood; and psychoanalysis is nothing without the doctrine that mankind is that species of animal which has the immortal project of recovering its own childhood. But childhood is the state of nature. The notion of man's revolt from nature and return to nature, though incompatible with Freud's instinct ontology, is required by his theory of childhood. Quite specifically, Freud's ontological postulate of the innate ambivalence of instincts, as we have seen, is contradicted by the empirical theorem of a first, pre-ambivalent stage in infancy. And the fixation to that first pre-ambivalent experience commits mankind to the unconscious project of overcoming the instinctual ambivalence which is his actual condition and of restoring the unity of opposites that existed in childhood and exists in animals.

It is characteristic both of the complications in Freud's thought, and also of his capacity to surpass himself, that although his basic ontology should preclude the possibility of any reconciliation between the two antagonistic instincts, he nevertheless formulates such a goal when he speaks of their possible fusion. He furthermore assigns the task of working toward such a fusion to the ego, that is to say to the conscious self, attributing to it a tendency to "synthesize," "harmonize," "reconcile," "organize" the conflicts and divisions in mental life.[13] From Freud's point of view this unifying tendency in the ego must be a manifestation of the erotic or life instinct, to which he attributed the function of seeking ever wider unification. This is a remarkably optimistic analysis of the ego, implying as it does a predominance of Eros in its instinctual constitution, and implying that the victory of the ego is a victory of Eros or Life over Death. One wonders how the ego escapes so lightly from the death instinct.

But if in man the instincts have departed from a primal state of undifferentiated unity, then, just as Freud said object-finding was refinding, we may add that the fusion sought by the ego is refusion. If so, then we may question Freud's statement that the tendency to synthesis and unity is entirely absent from the id (the instinctual reservoir).[14] Then his picture of the weak but coherent ego seeking to tame the strong chaos in the id has to be modified. Fusion may be a goal sought by the body and the unconscious instincts themselves as much as by the ego. If, therefore, Freud in these passages permits himself to be too optimistic about the ego, he is perhaps too pessimistic about the id.

If psychoanalysis must say that instincts, which at the level of animality are in a harmonious unity, are separated at the level of humanity and set into conflict with each other, and that mankind will not rest content until it is able to abolish these conflicts and restore harmony, but at the higher level of consciousness, then once again it appears that psychoanalysis completes the romantic movement and is understood only if interpreted in that light. It is one of the great romantic visions, clearly formulated by Schiller and Herder as early as 1793 and still vital in the systems of Hegel and Marx, that the history of mankind consists in a departure from a condition of undifferentiated primal unity with himself and with nature, an intermediate period in which man's powers are developed through differentiation and antagonism (alienation) with himself and with nature, and a final return to a unity on a higher level or harmony.[15] But these categories—primal unity, differentiation through antagonism, final harmony—remain in the romantics arbitrary and mystical because they lack a foundation in psychology. The psychoanalytical theory of childhood completes the romantic movement by filling this gap.

But at the same time, to make conscious the unconscious connection between psychoanalysis and the romantic movement is to give psychoanalysis a philosophy of history. Primal unity, differentiation through antagonism, and final harmony constitute for the romantics the historical path and destiny of the human species as a whole. The pessimism of Freud's final position and his failure to develop a philosophy of history are intimately connected. For the therapist and humanitarian, a philosophy of history has to take the form of an eschatology, declaring the conditions under which redemption from the human neurosis is possible.

The possibility of redemption lies in the reunification of the instinctual opposites. But Freud finally came to see the instinctual opposites as Life (Eros) and Death. How can Life and Death be unified? We must turn to an examination of the death instinct.

Death, Time, and Eternity

THE PSYCHOANALYTICAL theory of neurosis requires us to postulate a real instinctual ambivalence in man. The possibility of therapy depends on recognizing that instinctual ambivalence is a human prerogative, absent at the animal level and correlative with repression at the human level, and therefore in principle surpassable, if repression can be surpassed. And Freud had good reasons for moving from his earlier formulations of the duality to his final formulation, Life and Death. But if the instinctual duality is Life and Death, our modification of Freud's ontology entails the hypothesis that Life and Death coexist in some undifferentiated unity at the animal level and that they could be reunified into some higher harmony in man. But in every human ideology, and in the experience of every human individual, Death is the great adversary. How can Death be unified with Life? If we want to cure, we had better follow Freud and study Death.

Under the general heading of the death instinct Freud groups three distinct sets of phenomena. First of all, biological and psychological considerations suggested that the activity of all organisms and also of the human mind was directed at getting rid of tensions and attaining inactivity. (I believe the term preferred in modern biological theory is "homeostasis.") In this light the pleasure-principle, which Freud from the first had seized upon as the guiding principle of mental life, appeared as a Nirvana-principle, aiming at inactivity, rest, or sleep, the twin brother of death. Second, Freud, assuming a connection between Eros and the pleasure-principle, contrasted with the pleasure-principle that compulsion to repeat which in many cases produces fixations to traumatic experiences in the past and a daemonic compulsion to bring suffering on oneself. Freud therefore argued that the compulsion to repeat was a tendency independent of and more elemental than the pleasure-principle. He then brought the compulsion to repeat into relation with the conservative character of the instincts in all organic life, and put forward the idea that there was a general instinctual tendency to restore an earlier state of things, ultimately derived from a tendency in all organisms to return to the inorganic or dead level out of which life arose. And finally Freud referred to the psychoanalytic analysis of the sado-masochistic complex. He now modified his earlier view that masochism represented an introversion of what was originally a sadistic drive, and took the reverse position that there was a primary masochism directed against the self and that sadism was an extroversion of this primary masochism, which he identified with the death instinct.[1]

Clarity requires that we distinguish these three elements in Freud's death instinct. Nirvana, the repetition-compulsion, and masochism may all represent death, but if they do, they represent different aspects of death. Freud's equivocation may contain a real truth; these three forms of "death" may turn out to be really three forms of one death; but first we must grasp them separately. And in our analysis, carrying forward our modification of Freud's ontology, we must press always for clarification of the relation between the biological and human levels—the crucial question of what happened when animals became men.

Assuming that the Nirvana-principle, or homeostasis, is a fundamental principle of organic life, how does it operate in the mental life of human beings? Freud in his earlier writings said that the pleasure-principle expressed the fundamental aim of human desire and had the negative goal of reduction of tension (unpleasure). He thus identified the pleasure-principle at the human level with homeostasis in all organic life, implicitly obliterating any distinction in this respect between the human and animal levels.

One of the advances opened up in *Beyond the Pleasure Principle,* but developed only later, was the discrimination between homeostasis and the pleasure-principle. Freud was forced in this direction by his assimilation of homeostasis and the death instinct, since the connection between the pleasure-principle and the libido, that is to say the sexual or erotic or life instinct, seemed obvious. He therefore abandoned the notion that the goal of the pleasure-principle was a quantitative reduction of tension, and proposed that the essence of pleasure should be found in a certain quality rather than quantity, but he was unable to specify the nature of this quality.[2] Pursuing this new line of thought, Freud detected in the operations of the libido, in sexual relations, in social relations, and in the relations between the conflicting factors in the human psyche (the ego, the super-ego, and the id), a tendency to seek ever greater unification—a tendency, therefore, which went beyond the purely negative goal of release of tension.[3] Consequently Eros, and by implication the pleasure-principle, appeared not to seek the negative goal of reducing unpleasure, but to represent a "deep-rooted, passionate striving for a positive fulfilment of happiness"[4]—a happiness which lay in some form of ever wider unification. Freud therefore withdrew the identification of the pleasure-principle and Nirvana (homeostasis) still assumed in *Beyond the Pleasure Principle*, and advanced the idea that "the *Nirvana*-principle expresses the tendency of the death-instincts, the *pleasure*-principle represents the claim of the libido."[5]

This new idea fits badly with all the previous arguments pointing toward a connection between the pleasure-principle and Nirvana, between the libido and the goal of reducing tension. Therefore Freud, not unaware of this other side of the picture, in the same passage postulates a transformation of the Nirvana-principle through which it became the pleasure-principle: "We must perceive that the Nirvana-principle, which belongs to the death-instincts, underwent a modification in the living organism through which it became the pleasure-principle, and henceforth we shall avoid regarding the two principles as one."[6] But such a transformation implies in this context a transformation of the death instinct into the life instinct incompatible with the Freudian dualistic ontology.

Freud's dualistic ontology has confused an important issue. Let us postulate, as biology seems to do, that homeostasis expresses the tendency of all organic life to seek a state of equilibrium. Let us accept from Freud's later writings the idea that the pleasure-principle at the human level is not reducible or equivalent to homeostasis. Then Freud's own analysis suggests that what at the biological level appears as the static Nirvana-principle, at the human level appears as a dynamic pleasure-principle.

This reformulation preserves the element of continuity between men and animals, but at the same time it recognizes the necessary element of discontinuity. To identify the pleasure-principle with man and the Nirvana-principle with life in general is only another way of saying that man, and only man, is the neurotic animal. The neurotic animal is the discontented animal; man's discontent implies the disruption of the balanced equilibrium between tension and release of tension which governs the activity of animals. Instinctual repression transforms the static homeostasis principle in animals into the dynamic pleasure-principle in man; homeostasis can exist only under conditions of instinctual satisfaction. It is the search for instinctual satisfaction under conditions of instinctual repression that produces in man the restless quest of the pleasure-principle for a quality of experience denied to it under conditions of repression. The restless pleasure-principle is the search for psychic health under conditions of psychic disease, and therefore is itself a symptom of the disease, just as Freud said the progress of psychic disease may also be regarded as an attempt to cure.[7]

By the same token, if man could put an end to repression and obtain instinctual satisfaction, the restless pleasure-principle would return to the Nirvana-principle, that is to say, a balanced equilibrium between tension and tension release. If therefore the Nirvana-principle "belongs to the death-instincts" and the pleasure-principle belongs to Eros, their reunification would be the condition of equilibrium or rest of life that is a full life, unrepressed, and therefore satisfied with itself and affirming itself rather than changing itself. Thus interpreted, psychoanalysis reaffirms ageless religious aspirations. For Nirvana, if it expresses the rhythm of the lowest form of organic life, also expresses the highest aspirations of Buddhism. And how Nirvana differs from that eternal rest not only of the spirit but also of the body which St. Augustine promises as man's ultimate felicity,[8] is a distinction which I leave to theologians.

The reunification of Life and Death—accepting for the moment Freud's equation of Death and Nirvana—can be envisioned only as the end of the historical process. Freud's pessimism, his preference for dualism rather than dialectics, and his failure to develop a historical eschatology are all of a piece. To see how man separated from nature, and separated out the instincts, is to see history as neurosis; and also to see history, as neurosis, pressing restlessly and unconsciously toward the abolition of history and the attainment of a state of rest which is also a re-unification with nature. It comes to the same thing to say that the consequence of the disruption of the unity of Life and Death in man is to make man the historical animal. For the restless pleasure-principle—which is the morbid manifestation of the Nirvana-principle—is what makes man Faustian, and Faustian man is history-making man. If repression were overcome, the restless career of Faustian man would come to an end, because he would be satisfied and could say, "*Verweile doch, du bist so schön.*" [9]

Let us now turn to the repetition-compulsion and attempt in the same way to discriminate its mode of functioning at the animal level from its mode of functioning at the human level. The difficulty with Freud's notion of the repetition-compulsion as a factor in all organic life is that he sees a connection between two distinct phenomena—the fact that all organisms die, and the fact that biological instincts are fundamentally conservative (he instances the migration of birds and fishes and the laws of heredity and embryology).[10] If we postpone till we come to the sado-masochistic complex consideration of Freud's notion of an internal drive to die, we are left with the repetition-compulsion as a principle of instinctual conservatism. In *Beyond the Pleasure Principle* Freud correctly saw that the problem was to relate the human phenomenon of "progress," "perfectionism," to the conservatism of instincts at the organic level, and (if we ignore some hesitations) he correctly saw that these apparent opposites are the same thing:

> It may be difficult . . . to abandon the belief that there is an instinct toward perfection at work in human beings. . . .

I have no faith, however, in the existence of any such internal instinct and I cannot see how this benevolent illusion is to be preserved. The present development of human beings requires, as it seems to me, no different explanation from that of animals. What appears in a minority of human individuals as an untiring impulse to further perfection can easily be understood as a result of instinctual repression. The repressed instinct never ceases to strive for complete satisfaction, which would consist in the repetition of a primary experience of satisfaction. No substitute or reactive formations and no sublimations will suffice to remove the repressed instinct's persisting tension.[11]

The difference between men and animals is repression. Under conditions of repression, the repetition-compulsion establishes a fixation to the past, which alienates the neurotic from the present and commits him to the unconscious quest for the past in the future. Thus neurosis exhibits the quest for novelty, but underlying it, at the level of the instincts, is the compulsion to repeat. In man, the neurotic animal, the instinctual compulsion to repeat turns into its opposite, the quest for novelty, and the unconscious aim of the quest for novelty is repetition.

Furthermore, it is repression which turns the repetition-compulsion into an antagonist of the pleasure-principle. Freud had to recognize that the repetition-compulsion could be a principle of pleasure as well as a principle of traumatic daemonic compulsion, thus running into the same confusion that made him formulate the Nirvana-principle first as Eros, then as Death. "Children," he observes, "cannot have their *pleasurable* experiences repeated often enough, and they are inexorable in their insistence that the repetition shall be an identical one"; in contrast, in the adult "novelty is always the condition of enjoyment." [12] Childhood is, psychologically speaking, the state of nature; at the animal level there is no antagonism between the pleasure-principle and the repetition-compulsion. The repetition-compulsion—the conservative tendency of instincts—seems to be a biological principle imposing the limitations of a species-essence on each individual member of a species and directing the individual to enjoy the life proper to his species. In the discontented animal, man, it is transformed into a regressive fixation to the past, with the effect of unconsciously compelling him to change himself, to become, to find the life proper to his species. But if repression were overcome and man could enjoy the life proper to his species, the regressive fixation to the past would dissolve; the restless quest for novelty would be reabsorbed into the desire for pleasurable repetition; the desire to Become would be reabsorbed into the desire to Be.

Man, the discontented animal, unconsciously seeking the life proper to his species, is man in history: repression and the repetition-compulsion generate historical time. Repression transforms the timeless instinctual compulsion to repeat into the forward-moving dialectic of neurosis which is history; history is a forward-moving *recherche du temps perdu*, with the repetition-compulsion guaranteeing the historical law of the slow return of the repressed.[13] And conversely, life not repressed—organic life below man and human life if repression were overcome—is not in historical time. If we connect—as Freud did not—the repetition-compulsion with Freud's reiterated theorem that the instinctual processes in the id are timeless,[14] then only repressed life is in time, and unrepressed life would be timeless or in eternity. Thus again psychoanalysis, carried to its logical conclusion and transformed into a theory of history, gathers to itself ageless religious aspirations. The Sabbath of Eternity, that time when time no more shall be, is an image of that state which is the ultimate goal of the repetition-compulsion in the timeless id. The romantics inherited and secularized the mystic aspiration for Eternity: Hegel envisioned the end of the dialectic of history, and humanity's final entry into the eternal realm of "Absolute (perfected) Spirit" (*Absolute Geist*). Psychoanalysis comes to remind us that we are bodies, that repression is of the body, and that perfection would be the realm of Absolute Body; eternity is the mode of unrepressed bodies.

The repetition-compulsion, willy-nilly, involves us in the theory of time; and here, as elsewhere, psychoanalysis is, or ought to be, paradox. The notion of the abolition of time will seem to many, including the orthodox psychoanalysts, not paradox but nonsense. Is not time of the essence of things, and are we gods so that we can abolish it? But time is not of the essence of things. The psychoanalytical theory of time, as Freud saw,[15] must take as its point of departure Kant's doctrine that time does not pertain to things in themselves out there but is a form of perception of the human mind. This Copernican revolution makes time a psychological, not an ontological, problem, and therefore a problem for psychoanalysis. It also, as Schopenhauer saw,[16] opens up the possibility of man's emancipation from the tyranny of time. It suggests that if the human mind were to break through the veil of phenomena and reach "noumenal" reality, it would find no time. It is true that Kant himself firmly shut the door on any such possibility, not only by denying the possibility of reaching "noumenal" reality, but also by asserting the immutability of the forms (including time) through which the human mind perceives reality, and by equating these immutable forms with rationality.

Psychoanalysis, on the other hand, claims to be a break through phenomena to the hidden "noumenal" reality, at least with regard to knowledge of ourselves. And if, as I think we can, we equate Freud's Unconscious with the "noumenal" reality of ourselves, we find Freud positively asserting the discovery that at least in that "noumenal" reality there is no time: "Unconscious mental processes are in themselves timeless"; "In the id there is nothing corresponding to the idea of time." [17] If, therefore, we go beyond Freud, and speculate seriously on the possibility of a consciousness not based on repression but conscious of what is now unconscious, then it follows a priori that such a consciousness would be not in time but in eternity. And in fact eternity seems to be the time in which childhood lives. The poets have said so, and the psychoanalyst Marie Bonaparte expresses it this way:

> The days of the child seem to unfold in some sense outside of our time. These days of childhood—let us each recall them—seem to the child as if they were eternal. . . . Of course the important persons who bring up the child strictly impose the scheme of their time on him . . . but he feels the imposition of adult time by adults as an alien intrusion into his own time, which is essentially in some sense infinite.[18]

Not only does Freud represent a breakthrough to the "noumenal" self, but he also lays the basis for an attack on the Kantian equation of the time-schema with rationality. There are psychoanalytical theorems, which we can discuss only in a later chapter, anatomizing time-consciousness as a diseased consciousness and tending toward the conclusion that what Kant took to be the schemata of rationality are really the schemata of repression.[19] It is true that Freud fails to gather the insights of psychoanalysis together to make a frontal assault on the concept of time: in fact, he recognizes his failure when toward the end of his life he writes, "It is constantly being borne in upon us that we have made far too little use for our theory of the indubitable fact that the repressed remains unaltered by time. This seems to offer us the possibility of an approach to some really profound truths. But I myself have made no further progress here." [20] In particular, Freud does not seem to have envisaged the mutability of the time-schema, much less its abolition (along with the abolition of repression).

On the other hand, recent developments in physics, biology, and anthropology are tending to establish the relativity of time-schemata to variable biological and cultural needs.[21] In other words, the twentieth century has seen the disintegration of the universality and, with the universality, the rationality also, of the time-schema. Postponing further discussion of the problem until we are in a position to exploit the psychoanalytical theory of the mechanisms of repression ("defense mechanisms"), we may, I think, envisage the Sabbath of Eternity, without being mystical except in the sense in which all hope of better things is mystical.

And yet would perfection and happiness be in eternity? Does not such a notion face emotional objections over and above the theoretical objections? Faustian characters as we are, we cannot imagine "rest," "Nirvana," "eternity" except as a cessation of all activity—in other words, as death. What our argument is reaching for is not death rather than life but a reconciliation of life and death. We have therefore to sustain the possibility of activity (life) which is also at rest.

The notion of activity or life which is also at rest is plainly contained in the Christian notion of heaven; and I suspect that the Buddhist Nirvana is not as inert and negative as Christian polemics make it out to be. But the Christian heaven exists to solve problems not soluble on earth; and, since it postulates immortality in heaven, its hidden psychological premise is the im-

possibility of reconciling life and death, either on earth or in
heaven. We can find, as F. C. S. Schiller has shown,[22] a more
satisfactory model of perfection conceived as activity without
motion in Aristotle.

Aristotle's fundamental notion is activity (*energeia*). Motion (*kinesis*) is a special kind of activity, namely imperfect activity; it is the movement of the imperfect toward perfection.
Perfect activity is activity without motion or change or passivity, and therefore, since time is correlative with motion, an
activity not in time. And Aristotle recognizes pleasurable activity of the bodily senses, provided there is no "impediment" (in
Freudian terms, frustration), as an activity without motion or
change, and therefore not in time: "Seeing seems to be at any
moment complete, for it does not lack anything which coming
into being later will complete its form; and pleasure also seems
to be of this nature. For it is a whole, and at no time can one
find a pleasure whose form will be completed if the pleasure
lasts longer. For this reason too, it is not a movement." [23] Pleasure is the measure of perfection in activity. Hence Aristotle's
model of perfect activity: "God always enjoys a single and
simple pleasure; for there is not only an activity of motion, but
also one of motionlessness, and pleasure is rather in rest than
in motion." [24] We can add that activity not generated by want
or defect is purposeless, and therefore play; hence Boehme conceived of God's life as it is in itself as play. Eternity is the
mode of play.

Thus Aristotle succeeds in formulating philosophically the
notion which also underlies the Christian theology of time—
that time is relative to Becoming rather than Being, and Becoming is relative to imperfection or evil. In F. C. S. Schiller's formula, unsatisfactoriness is the cause of impermanence, not vice
versa. We do not have to accept Aristotle's ideas on the nature
of human perfection and imperfection (he has no notion of repression); his notion of activity that is motionless and in eternity
may nevertheless formulate the abstract formal characteristics
of perfection, and therefore may be, in F. C. S. Schiller's words,
"a *scientific* formulation of the popular theological conceptions
of Heaven and Eternity." As to whether perfection is attain-

able, or worth discussing, I can do no better than quote the final words of F. C. S. Schiller's discussion:

> Whether of course there is any possibility of actually realizing any such ideal is quite another question, and no one could be more keenly conscious than myself of the bitter contrast between such dreams of metaphysics and the stern facts of our daily life. But once upon a time our fairest facts, our most uncontroverted truths, were but the visions of a dream, divined by a prescience that slowly hardened into science; and so perchance even dreams like these may come true, or rather be made to come true, if we try. It is, moreover, certain that if we dismiss such thoughts as idle dreams, dreams they will remain, and no end will ever come to the conflict and the friction that wear out our world; whereas, if we consent to look for possibilities of harmony, our willingness may be the first condition of success. And even for the proximate purposes of ordinary life, there is perhaps some practical value in the contemplation of a metaphysical ideal which can stimulate us to be active, while at the same time warning us that such self-realization must assume the form, not of a hideous, barbarous, and neurotic restlessness, nor of an infinite (and therefore futile) struggle, but of an activity which, transcending change and time, preserves itself in an harmonious equipoise.[25]

It is now evident that Freud's equivocation with different forms of "death" was meaningful equivocation. The repetition-compulsion and the Nirvana-principle appear to be two interconnected aspects of the instinctual demand for complete satisfaction and the abolition of repression. The abolition of history, or the Sabbath of Eternity, which is the ultimate aim of the repetition-compulsion, is also the attainment of Nirvana, which is the ultimate aim of the pleasure-principle. But we still see no reason why Freud insists on the term "death." We see no connection between the Nirvana-principle, or the repetition-compulsion, and the state of being dead. Unless there is some real connection, Freud's death instinct is not only a mere metaphor but also a confusing metaphor. It is only the third element in Freud's death instinct, the sado-masochistic complex, which introduces death in the real and literal sense into the death instinct.

The theory of the sado-masochistic complex starts from the

observation of man's peculiar ambivalent capacity for love and
hate, his capacity to love and to destroy others, his capacity to
love and to destroy himself. In traditional ethical terms, identifying love with good and hate with evil, Freud's fundamental
perspective is that the evil in man is not to be explained away
as a superficial excrescence on a basically good human nature,
but is rooted in a deep conflict in human nature itself. Although
his first instinct theory does suggest that man is basically a loving animal, forced by the reality-principle to unloving behavior,
Freud finally rejects the liberal optimist position—tacitly held
by most social scientists and by psychoanalysts of the neo-
Freudian type—that man is inherently good and peaceful and
that his aggressive behavior is simply the result of environmental frustrations or ignorance and poor education. Freud recognized the factor of environmental frustration (in fact he gave us
the concept), but he insists the trouble goes deeper.

For Freud as for St. Augustine, mankind's destiny is a departure from, and an effort to regain, paradise; but in between
these two terms man is at war with himself—driven, says St.
Augustine, by two loves, true love on the one hand and the lust
for power (*libido dominandi*) on the other.[26] In psychoanalytical terms, the conflict inside human nature is at the instinctual
level; hence Freud's dualism of Eros and the aggressive instinct.
As the neo-Freudians have pointed out, Freud has so formulated the conflict between Eros and the aggressive instinct as
to preclude the possibility of salvation or cure. Freud speaks
emphatically of the innate tendency to aggression; with an innate tendency to aggression mankind's only alternative is to
turn it outward and destroy others or turn it inward and destroy himself.

This unpleasant picture of the human situation is developed
by Freud to all its logical consequences in *Civilization and Its
Discontents.* It takes only the capacity to endure unpleasant
truth to prefer the bleak pessimism of *Civilization and Its Discontents* to the lullabies of sweetness and light which the neo-
Freudians serve up as psychoanalysis. It still remains true that if
aggressiveness is innate and accumulates with the growth of
civilization, then psychoanalysis may, like Freud, hope for a
rebirth of Eros, but rationally it can only predict the self-de-

struction of the human race. It is one of the sad ironies of contemporary intellectual life that Freud's hypothesis of an innate death instinct, which has been received with horror as the acme of pessimism, actually offers the only way out of the really pessimistic hypothesis of an innate aggressive instinct.

Freud arrived at the hypothesis of a death instinct when, having in mind the instinctual ambivalence between Eros and aggression at the human level, he pressed, as the psychoanalytical theory of instincts must, the question of what corresponds to it at the level of all organic life. The evolution of his libido theory had already destroyed his earlier distinction between the sexual and self-preservation instincts, transforming the human libido into a general life instinct, seeking to preserve and enrich life. The evolution of the libido theory therefore suggested that the fundamental polarity was life and death. Thus equipped with the hypothesis of a psychological life instinct and death instinct, Freud went on to consider the relation of life and death in biology.

His idea—which, he argues, is not contradicted by biological theory—is that organisms die for internal reasons; death is no external accident; death is an intrinsic part of life. In Freud's words, "The goal of all life is death." [27] Now Freud returns to the sado-masochistic complex. Psychoanalysis had already shown the interchangeability of aggression turned outward and aggression turned inward (masochism), and raised the question as to which of these two is the original form. But aggression turned inward on the self in the form of self-destruction would be a death instinct. Freud therefore supplied his life instinct with its logical opposite by making the assumption that extroverted aggression (sadism) in human beings is derived from a "primary masochism," and by identifying this primary masochism with a death instinct. [28]

Freud never saw that the hypothesis that aggression is extroverted death opened up the possibility of a solution to the problem of aggression. To the end of his life he continued to speak of innate aggressiveness and the destructive instinct as if these were the same as a death instinct. Everything depends on establishing the difference, as well as the continuity, between man and the rest of organic life. Freud's static dualistic ontology made him interpret the unity of life and death in all organisms as an eternal conflict of two distinct and completely opposed forces, one seeking to preserve and extend life, the other seeking to reduce life to the inorganic state out of which it arose. But Freud's own interpretation of the psychoanalytical data suggests that extroversion outward of the death instinct in the form of a drive to mastery or a will to power is a distinctively human phenomenon. And conversely Freud's own formula— "The goal of all life is death"—suggests that at the biological level life and death are not in conflict, but are somehow the same. That is to say, they are some sort of dialectical unity, as Heraclitus said they were: "It is the same thing in us that is alive and dead, awake and asleep, young and old: by a reversal the former are the latter and the latter in turn are the former." We thus arrive at the idea that life and death are in some sort of unity at the organic level, that at the human level they are separated into conflicting opposites, and that at the human level the extroversion of the death instinct is the mode of resolving a conflict that does not exist at the organic level. Then neurosis remains, as it should be, a human privilege; life-and-death does not make nature sick.

If death is a part of life, there is a peculiar morbidity in the human attitude toward death—a morbidity which Freud recognized [29] but did not connect with his theory of the death instinct. "What distinguishes man from other animals," says Unamuno, "is that in one form or another, he guards his dead. And from what does he so futilely protect them? The wretched consciousness shrinks from its own annihilation. . . . The gorilla, the chimpanzee, the orang-outang, and their kind, must look upon man as a feeble and infirm animal, whose strange custom it is to store up his dead." [30] It is not the consciousness of death but the flight from death that distinguishes men from animals. From the times of the earliest cave men, who kept their dead alive by dyeing the bones red and burying them near the family hearth, down to the Hollywood funeral cult, the flight from death has been, as Unamuno said, the heart of all religion. Pyramids and skyscrapers—monuments more lasting than bronze—suggest how much of the world's "economic" activity also is really a flight from death. If death is a part of life, if there is a death instinct as well as a life (or sexual) instinct, man is in flight from his own death just as he is in flight from his own sexuality. If death is a part of life, man represses his own death just as he represses his own life.

According to Freud, aggressiveness represents a fusion of the life instinct with the death instinct, a fusion which saves the organism from the innate self-destructive tendency of the death instinct by extroverting it, a desire to kill replacing the desire to die.[31] As against Freud, we suggest that this extroversion of the death instinct is the peculiar human solution to a peculiar human problem. It is the flight from death that leaves mankind with the problem of what to do with its own innate biological dying, what to do with its own repressed death. Animals let death be a part of life, and use the death instinct to die: man aggressively builds immortal cultures and makes history in order to fight death. Thus Freud's death instinct, if we interpret it dialectically and keep the distinction between men and animals, like the Nirvana-principle and the repetition-compulsion, becomes crucial in the psychology of history, and in fact establishes another crucial link between Freud and the philosopher of history, Hegel.

Existentialist scholarship is discovering a more human Hegel, Hegel the psychologist, Hegel trying to transcend the traditional paranoia of philosophers and find the essence of man not in thinking but in human desires and human suffering. Of Hegel's two systematic attempts to grasp the essence of man, the first identified man with love, and the second identified man with death. Hegel's thought thus passed from Eros to Death, the pair which together form the essence of human nature according to Freud's latest instinct theory. And it was only in his second attempt, through his identification of man with death, that Hegel was able to grasp man as essentially a history-making creature.

At the beginning of his career Hegel shared the sentimental romanticism of the *Sturm und Drang* period, and found the reality of human desire and human action in the microcosm of love. Later, evolving in the same direction as Goethe when he added *Faust* Part II to *Faust* Part I, he found the reality of human action in the macrocosm of human history: man is that unique species of animal which has a history, that is to say, that animal whose essence is not united with his existence as with other animals, but is developed in the dialectic of historical time. In developing his philosophy of man as the animal with a history, Hegel found that his former identification of man with love was inadequate. Love is a little moment in the life of lovers; and love remains an inner subjective experience leaving the macrocosm of history untouched. Human history cannot be grasped as the unfolding of human love.

Hegel was able to develop a philosophy of history only by making a fresh start and identifying man with death. And he develops the paradox that history is what man does with death, along lines almost identical with Freud's. Freud suggests that the aggression in human nature—the drive to master nature as well as the drive to master man—is the result of an extroversion of the death instinct, the desire to die being tranformed into the desire to kill, destroy, or dominate. Hegel postulates a transformation of the consciousness of death into a struggle to appropriate the life of another human being at the risk of one's own life: history as class struggle (the dialectic of Master and Slave, in Hegel's terminology) is based on an extroversion of death. And similarly Hegel's other fundamental category of history, human work or labor, is a transformation of the negativity or nothingness of death into the extroverted action of negating or changing nature. More generally, according to Hegel, time is what man makes out of death: the dialectic of history is the dialectic of time, and "time is the negative element in the sensuous world"; time is negativity, and negativity is extroverted death.[32]

Freud does not have that concept of historicity which is Hegel's strength: Hegel, although trying to grasp the psychological premises of man's historicity, has only an intuitive psychology. And yet Hegel may help us understand death. Hegel needs reformulation in the light of the psychoanalytical doctrine of repression and the unconscious. It is not the consciousness of death that is transformed into aggression, but the unconscious death instinct; the unconscious death instinct is that negativity or nothingness which is extroverted into the action of negating nature and other men. Freud himself, in his most important addition to the theory of the death instinct after *Beyond the Pleasure Principle,* derived affirmation from Eros and negation from its instinctual opposite.[33] On the other hand, Hegel's doctrine of the connection between negation and time is essential if psychoanalysis is to make the breakthrough, which Freud did not make, to a psychoanalytical theory of time.

The relation of the pleasure-principle to the Nirvana-principle suggests that man has a history because the balanced equilibrium between tension and release of tension at the animal level has been disrupted and replaced by a dynamic restless striving. The study of the repetition-compulsion suggests that repression generates historical time by generating an instinct-determined fixation to the repressed past, and thus setting in motion a forward-moving dialectic which is at the same time an effort to recover the past. In that perspective on man's historicity the crucial psychoanalytical concept is fixation to the past. In our new perspective the crucial psychoanalytical concept is the repression of death.

What is the relation between fixation to the past and repression of death? The intermediate term is obvious—the refusal to grow old. At the biological level, organisms live their lives and have no history because living and dying, that is to say growing older, is in them an inseparable unity. With them, in Shakespeare's beautiful phrase, ripeness is all. At the human level, repression produces the unconscious fixation to the infantile past, the instinctual unity of living and dying is disrupted, and both the life instinct and the death instinct are forced into repression. At the biological level, the death instinct, in affirming the road to death, affirms at the same time the road of life: ripeness is all. At the human level, the repressed death instinct cannot affirm life by affirming death; life, being repressed, cannot affirm death and therefore must fly from death; death can only affirm itself (and life) by transforming itself into the force which always denies life, the spirit of Goethe's Mephistopheles.

Then Freud's equivocation with three forms of death—the Nirvana-principle, the repetition-compulsion, and the sado-masochistic complex—turns out to be profoundly suggestive.

Man is the animal which has separated into conflicting opposites the biological unity of life and death, and has then subjected the conflicting opposites to repression. The destruction of the biological unity of life and death transforms the Nirvana-principle into the pleasure-principle, transforms the repetition-compulsion into a fixation to the infantile past, and transforms the death instinct into an aggressive principle of negativity. And all three of these specifically human characteristics—the pleasure-principle, the fixation to the past, and the aggressive negativism—are aspects of the characteristically human mode of being, historical time.

The elucidation of Freud's vision of organic life as a dialectical unity of life and death is hampered by the inadequacies in the current philosophy of organism. Psychoanalysis would like to start with a clear idea of the role of death at the organic level. But the great philosopher of organism, Whitehead, has no chapter on death or on the relation between life and death; it seems as if even he bears unconscious witness to the repression of death in the human consciousness. Psychoanalysis therefore cannot proceed without going beyond Whitehead. Not Whitehead but Hegel puts forward the idea that there is an intrinsic connection between death and that essence of true life, individuality: "The nature of finite things as such is to have the seed of passing away as their essential being: the hour of their birth is the hour of their death." [34] The precious ontological uniqueness which the human individual claims is conferred on him not by possession of an immortal soul but by possession of a mortal body. Without death, Hegel argues, individuals are reduced to the status of mere modes in the one infinite and eternal substance of Spinoza.[35] Whitehead's organisms also, without death, have no individuality: at the simplest organic level, any particular animal or plant has uniqueness and individuality because it lives its own life and no other—that is to say, because it dies.

The intrinsic connection between death and individuality is also suggested by hints contained in Freud's instinct theory. His identification of the life instinct with sexuality identifies it with the force that preserves the immortality of the species. By implication, therefore, it is the death instinct which constitutes the mortal individuality of the particular member of the species. Furthermore, Freud's theorem that Eros or the life instinct, as it operates in the human libido and in the lowest cells, aims to preserve and enrich life by seeking unification implicitly contains the theorem that the aim of the death instinct is separation; and explicitly Freud's theory of anxiety brings birth and death together as separation crises.[36] Freud is thus moving toward a structural analysis of organic life as being constituted by a dialectic between unification or interdependence and separation or independence. The principle of unification or interdependence sustains the immortal life of the species and the mortal life of the individual; the principle of separation or independence gives the individual his individuality and ensures his death.

If death gives life individuality and if man is the organism which represses death, then man is the organism which represses his own individuality. Then our proud views of humanity as a species endowed with an individuality denied to lower animals turns out to be wrong. The lilies of the field have it because they take no thought of the morrow, and we do not. Lower organisms live the life proper to their species; their individuality consists in their being concrete embodiments of the essence of their species in a particular life which ends in death.

But if the psychoanalytical doctrine of repression means anything, man never unfolds the mode of being which is proper to his species and given in his body. Repression generates the instinctual compulsion to change the internal nature of man and the external world in which he lives, thus giving man a history and subordinating the life of the individual to the historical quest of the species. History is made not by individuals but by groups; and the cliché-mongers repeat *ad nauseam* that man is by nature a social animal. It is intrinsic to the psychoanalytical point of view to assert the morbidity of human sociability, not just "civilized" as opposed to "primitive" sociability or "class society" as opposed to "primitive communism," but all of human sociability as we have known it. Freud's formulations of the Primal Father and the Primal Horde (in *Group Psychology and the Analysis of the Ego*) may or may not be adequate explanations of the morbidity in group-formation.

What is essential is the clinical pronouncement that sociability is a sickness.

The essential point in the Freudian diagnosis of human sociability was seen by Róheim: men huddle into hordes as a substitute for parents, to save themselves from independence, from "being left alone in the dark." [87] Society was not constructed, as Aristotle says, for the sake of life and more life, but from defect, from death and the flight from death, from fear of separation and fear of individuality. Thus Freud derives fear of "separation and expulsion from the horde" from castration anxiety, and castration anxiety from the fear of separation from the mother and the fear of death.[88] Hence there are no social groups without a religion of their own immortality, and history-making is always the quest for group-immortality. Only an·unrepressed humanity, strong enough to live-and-die, could let Eros seek union and let death keep separateness.

The unrepressed animal carries no instinctual project to change his own nature; mankind must pass beyond repression if it is to find a life not governed by the unconscious project of finding another kind of life, one not governed by unconscious negativity. After man's unconscious search for his proper mode of being has ended—after history has ended—particular members of the human species can lead a life which, like the lives of lower organisms, individually embodies the nature of the species. But only an individual life in this sense can be satisfactory to the individual who lives it. The attainment of individuality by the human species would therefore mean the return of the restless pleasure-principle to the peace of the Nirvana-principle. The Nirvana-principle regulates an individual life which enjoys full satisfaction and concretely embodies the full essence of the species, and in which life and death are simultaneously affirmed, because life and death together constitute individuality, and ripeness is all. An individual life so regulated is possessed by all organisms below man. Because he too has a body, is an organism, must die, man has also instincts which will not let him rest till he attains individuality.

It is hard, under conditions of general repression, to affirm the death instinct without becoming an enemy of life. For under conditions of general repression the death instinct operates malignantly. In dialectical fusion with the life instinct it is a principle of restless negativity (like Goethe's Mephistopheles); but given the basic unsatisfactoriness of life under conditions of general repression, a defusion into a simple wish to die is always lurking in the background. Thus Schopenhauer seems to affirm death and Nirvana, but because he cannot affirm life, his affirmation of death is spurious. Schopenhauer's hostility to the *principium individuationis* is a hostility to death as well as to life; only he who can affirm birth can affirm death, since birth and death are one. Under conditions of general repression, as long as life is unsatisfactory, death can be affirmed only by those whose life instinct is strong enough to envisage the reconciliation of life and death as a future state of perfection toward which the life instinct strives. Schopenhauer's incapacity to affirm life or death turns on his conviction that "men are so constituted that they could not be happy in whatever kind of world they might be placed"; hence all he can say to the dying individual is, "Thou ceasest to be something which thou hadst done better never to become." [39]

In contrast with Schopenhauer, Nietzsche, because he envisages the possibility of Superman, can affirm life and therefore death: "What has become perfect, all that is ripe—wants to die." Nietzsche's explanation shows how instinctual repression generates the flight from death, how the flight from death underlies both the religion of immortality and the economic institution of hereditary property: "All that is unripe wants to live. All that suffers wants to live, that it may become ripe and joyous and longing—longing for what is farther, higher, brighter. 'I want heirs'—thus speaks all that suffers; 'I want children, I do not want *myself*.'" [40] Those prejudiced against Nietzsche might compare his concept of "wanting heirs" to John Maynard Keynes' critique of purposiveness: [41]

> Purposiveness means that we are more concerned with the remote future results of our actions than with their own quality or their immediate effects on our own environment. The "purposive" man is always trying to secure a spurious and delusive immortality for his acts by pushing his interest in them forward into time. He does not love his cat, but his cat's kittens; nor, in truth, the kittens, but only the kittens' kittens, and so on for-

ward for ever to the end of cat-dom. For him jam is not jam
unless it is a case of jam to-morrow and never jam to-day. Thus
by pushing his jam always forward into the future, he strives to
secure for his act of boiling it an immortality.

In contrast with the neurotic time obsession of repressed humanity, Nietzsche affirms the eternity of repetition: "Joy, however, does not want heirs, or children—joy wants itself, wants
eternity, wants recurrence, wants everything eternally the
same."

Nietzsche's perfection, which is unrepressed life (joy),
wants eternity, but it also wants to die. Eternity is therefore a
way of envisaging mankind's liberation from the neurotic obsession with the past and the future; it is a way of living in
the present, but also a way of dying. Hence the ultimate defect of all heavens with immortality beyond the grave is that in
them there is no death; by this token such visions betray their
connection with repression of life. Anxiety about death does
not have ontological status, as existentialist theologians claim.
It has historical status only, and is relative to the repression of
the human body; the horror of death is the horror of dying
with what Rilke called unlived lines in our bodies. That perfect, resurrected body which the Christian creed promises
would want to die because it was perfect: "All that is perfect
wants to die." It takes the greatest strength to accept death,
says Hegel.[42] Following Hegel, the existentialist philosophers
have returned to the wisdom of Montaigne, that to learn philosophy is to learn how to die. Lacking Freud's concept of Eros,
these philosophers may exhibit the unconscious wish to die,
from which even Freud, with his concept of Eros, was not free.
Nevertheless, in facing death they are serving the cause of life.

The construction of a human consciousness strong enough
to accept death is a task in which philosophy and psychoanalysis can join hands—and also art. It was the poet Rilke who
said it was the poet's mission to bind life and death together,
and who said, "Whoever rightly understands and celebrates
death, at the same time magnifies life."[43] But the hard truth
which psychoanalysis must insist upon is that the acceptance
of death, its reunification in consciousness with life, cannot be

accomplished by the discipline of philosophy or the seduction of art, but only by the abolition of repression. Man, who is born of woman and destined to die, is a body, with bodily instincts. Only if Eros—the life instinct—can affirm the life of the body can the death instinct affirm death, and in affirming death magnify life.

If the repression of death and the repression of individuality have this importance in human history, psychoanalysis ought to be able to detect their role in the formation of neurosis in individual lives. Freud, however, perhaps because he lacked the concept of the repression of death, did not make use of his hypothesis of a death instinct (as distinct from an aggressive instinct) in his clinical writings. But if death is the aspect of life which confers on life individuality, independence, and separateness, then a priori the repression of death should produce symptoms which exhibit on the one hand a flight from independence and separateness and on the other hand the compulsive return of the repressed instinct. But such an ambivalent attitude toward independence and separateness is at the heart of all neurosis, according to Freud's later clinical writings. The ultimate cause of repression and neurosis is anxiety, and anxiety is "the anxiety of separation from the protecting mother." One of the hallmarks of the neurotic personality is a lifelong fixation to the infantile pattern of dependence on other people.[44]

Although Freud does not make the necessary theoretical links between anxiety and his death instinct, he does say that what the ego fears in anxiety "is in the nature of an overthrow or an extinction." [45] It looks therefore as if the specifically human capacity for anxiety does reflect a revolt against death and individuality, or at least some deep disturbance in the organic unity of life and death. And if there is a connection between the human sense of time and the human use of death, there is also good reason to suspect a connection between time and anxiety. Kierkegaard speaks like a psychoanalyst when he says, "Time does not really exist without unrest; it does not exist for dumb animals who are absolutely without anxiety." [46]

Death and Childhood

According to psychoanalytical theory, childhood bequeaths to mankind not only the project of transcending the human neurosis, but also the neurosis itself; not only the erotic possibilities of human nature, but also the self-defeating mechanisms which keep those erotic possibilities unfulfilled. Wisdom directs us to childhood—not only to the immortal wishes of childhood for the substance of things hoped for, but also to the failure of childhood for the cause of our disease.

The neurotic element in infantile sexuality is centered in the so-called infantile organizations of the libido (oral, anal, phallic). In our earlier chapter on infantile sexuality we drew out of Freud the theorem that the final adult disposition of sexual energy (genital organization, or concentration of libido in the genital) is a tyranny at war with the natural tendency of the human body, which is anarchistic and polymorphously perverse. We left hanging in the air the question of how the tyranny of genital organization is established. Genital organization is not the result of puberty but is the outcome of developments in infantile sexuality, specifically the Oedipus complex and castration complex (normally occurring about the age of five); and the Oedipal phase of infantile sexuality, which presupposes a concentration of libido in the genital organs, was preceded by earlier phases in which libido was concentrated in the anal and oral zones. Hence the ideal of polymorphous perversity (or play), rooted in our childhood fixation, has to be measured against a countertendency also rooted in childhood. According to psychoanalysis, it is this countertendency in infancy which establishes the pattern of the human neurosis. Neuroses are classified by their "predispositional point" in infancy, by whether the adult neurotic is unconsciously striving to achieve infantile oral, anal, or genital (Oedipal) ambitions. Character types are similarly classified; and all cultural achievements, viewed as sublimations, are sublimations of infantile sexuality, not adult sexuality, and of infantile sexuality as concentrated in the infantile organizations, not as polymorphously perverse.

The infantile organizations of the libido, pregenital and genital, sustain the human neurosis; they are the bodily counterpart of the disorder in the human mind. It is part of Freud's pessimism that he accepts them as immutable data and can envision their abolition as little as he could the abolition of repression. Optimism, of course, can be recovered cheaply if, with the neo-Freudians, we drop the whole theory of infantile sexuality.[1] We propose to explore another way. Freud's theory of the stages of infantile sexuality (oral, anal, phallic) was formulated very early in his career, and not reformulated in terms of his later theory; but developments in his later theory materially alter the picture.

In the early *Three Contributions to the Theory of Sex* Freud treated the stages of infantile sexuality simply as stages in the maturation of the sexual instinct, and therefore as stages in a biological process, having as its natural goal the Oedipal project. This natural efflorescence of infantile sexuality was viewed as being subjected to disturbance from the outside when the Oedipal project succumbs to the castration complex. The confrontation of the Oedipal project with the threat of castration was represented as the fateful collision between the demands of infantile sexuality and the reality-principle and as the cause of repression.

In Freud's later discussions, however, infantile sexuality is seen as disturbed from a very early stage by the relations between the child and the mother on whom he depends. Freud had regarded the threat of castration as issuing from the father figure; he now discovers that the complicated ambivalences of love and hate which he had envisaged as corrupting the erotic relation between child and father are anticipated in the relations of the child to what he called the pre-Oedipal mother, even as early as the so-called oral stage.[2] But then it follows that infantile sexuality is disturbed by instinctual ambivalence from a very early stage, and therefore its characteristic manifestations (oral, anal, phallic) must be regarded not as creations of Eros alone, but also of Eros' instinctual antagonist. Freud in his later writings introduces a second new perspective on the disturbance of infantile sexuality, without coherently unifying it with the analysis of instinctual ambivalence, in his concept of anxiety. Just as he now sees the castration complex as the climax in a history of an instinctual ambivalence which goes back to a very early stage, so he also sees the castration complex as the climax in the history of infantile anxiety, going back to the birth-trauma.

The effect of Freud's new formulations about instinctual ambivalence and anxiety, as he himself saw—without, I think, drawing the full consequences—is to alter decisively the theory of repression. In Freud's words, "It was anxiety which produces repression and not, as I formerly believed, repression which produces anxiety"; [3] similarly he invokes instinctual ambivalence as the cause of repression. [4] The old formula postulates as the cause of repression the ill-defined "reality-principle." The new formula shifts the cause of repression from the external world to the internal world, and puts the cause of repression inside the child himself, making repression essentially self-repression.

Freud never rewrote the theory of the infantile organizations of the libido in the light of his later formulations about instinctual ambivalence and anxiety. But if, as he said, the theory of repression is the foundation stone of all psychoanalysis, [5] then the new notion of self-repression must be explored. Anxiety and instinctual ambivalence must be explored as the cause of repression. And, in the light of our preceding chapter, anxiety and instinctual ambivalence must be related to the death instinct. If anxiety and instinctual ambivalence run throughout the entirety of infantile sexuality, then the infantile organizations of the libido must be seen as infantile sexuality disturbed by the morbidity of the human death instinct. And since, in Freud's words, "the ego is the only seat of anxiety," [6] and likewise of instinctual ambivalence, the infantile organizations of the libido are ego organizations and not just libidinal organizations. Perhaps then we should regard the sexual organizations as the effect on the body of anxiety in the ego. Then, since, as we saw in the last chapter, anxiety is the ego's incapacity to accept death, the sexual organizations were perhaps constructed by the ego in its flight from death, and could be abolished by an ego strong enough to die.

When Freud speaks of instinctual ambivalence in the infant, he has in mind love and hate; but, as we have seen, his death instinct must be taken more seriously than he took it, and systematically applied to the analysis of infancy. In man the dialectical unity between union and separateness, between interdependence and independence, between species and individual—in short, between life and death—is broken. The break occurs in infancy, and it is the consequence of the institution of the human family. The institution of the family means the prolonged maintenance of human children in a condition of helpless dependence. Parental care makes childhood a period of privileged freedom from the domination of the reality-principle, thus permitting and promoting the early blossoming, in an unreal atmosphere, of infantile sexuality and the pleasure-principle. Thus sheltered from reality by parental care, infantile sexuality —Eros or the life instinct—conceives the dream of narcissistic omnipotence in a world of love and pleasure.

But if the institution of the family gives the human infant a subjective experience of freedom unknown to any other species of animal, it does so by holding the human infant in condition of objective dependence on parental care to a degree unknown to any other species of animal. Objective dependence on parental care creates in the child a passive, dependent need to be loved, which is just the opposite of his dream of narcissistic omnipotence. Thus the institution of the family shapes human desire in two contradictory directions, and it is the dialectic generated by this contradiction which produces what Freud calls the conflict of ambivalence.

But the contradiction in the human psyche established by the family is the contradiction between the life and death instincts as previously defined. The contradiction between the subjective dream of loving union with the world and the objective fact of dependence, with its libidinal correlate the passive need to be loved, means antagonism in the dialectic of union and separateness, independence and dependence, species and individual—the dialectic of life and death. The antagonism is generated not by the intrusion of some new factor, but, as it were, by a hypertrophy of the same instincts which are harmoniously unified at the biological level. The same instincts which constitute all life generate also the human family. The parent-child relation, which is the nucleus of the family, constitutes a new mode of that interdependent union which is the essence of life, and at the same time it generates a new mode of individual independence which is the essence of death. The human family is created by an intenser mode of love and creates an intenser mode of death.

The reaction of the human child to the contradictions in his own psyche developed by his position in the family is anxiety; and anxiety is both a flight from death and a death experience. Infantile anxiety has, according to psychoanalysis, a long history reaching as far back as the act of birth. The anxiety of the infant at birth, when life and death are struggling with each other, is the model for the syndrome of physical sensations and innervations which accompany later outbreaks of anxiety. Otto Rank went so far as to claim that the traumatic experience of birth is the cause of neurosis. Freud attributed the peculiar human capacity for anxiety and neurosis not to the birth trauma, but to the fact that the child nurtured in the human family suffers psychic traumas which are for him as traumatic as the trauma of birth and which therefore re-create the anxiety syndrome in situations where it is not biologically functional as it is at birth.[7]

The purely biological act of birth, which not only destines the organism to death but is in itself the death of a fetus as well as the birth of a baby, is also a biological separation from the mother conferring biological individuality on the child. The prototype of psychic traumas, the experience of wanting but not being able to find the mother, is an experience of psychic separation, and its anxiety is, in Freud's own words, "the anxiety of separation from the protecting mother." [8] And the climactic psychic trauma, castration anxiety, is, according to Freud, also a fear of separation from the mother, or rather a fear of losing the instrument for reuniting with a mother-substitute in the act of copulation.[9] Furthermore all these separations are experienced as a threat of death: again in Freud's own words, what the ego fears in anxiety "is in the nature of an overthrow or extinction." [10]

Thus Freud's own analysis of anxiety shows, although Freud himself never said so, that there is a close and deep connection between anxiety and the death instinct. Anxiety is a response to experiences of separateness, individuality, and death. The human child, which at the mother's breast experiences a new and intense mode of union, of living, and of loving, must also experience a new and intenser mode of separation, individuality, and death; in the dry language of Freud, a trauma is constituted when the ego comes into contact with an excessive demand of its own libido.[11] In the human family the expansion of Eros onto a new and higher level entails the expansion of death onto a new and higher level. It is because the child loves the mother so much that it feels separation from the mother as death. As a result, birth and death, which at the biological level are experienced once only, are at the human psychic level experienced constantly; the child can say with St. Paul, "I die daily."

One effect of the incapacity to accept separation, individuality, and death is to erotize death—to activate a morbid wish to die, a wish to regress to the prenatal state before life (and separation) began, to the mother's womb. Freud analyzed the castration complex as the fear of losing the instrument for reuniting with (a substitute for) the mother's womb. The implication is not only that the morbid or regressive death wish underlies the Oedipal project in infancy, but also that it underlies the adult genital arrangements which fall heir to the destruction of the Oedipus complex—the human family and the genital organization of the human body. Hence, as Freud so often said, in choosing a wife we still seek our mother, and in the genital act "the vagina comes into the inheritance of the mother's womb." [12]

Ferenczi, in *Thalassa*, has amply developed the analysis of sexual intercourse as an aiming at "the genital re-establishment of the intra-uterine situation," without, however, being clear on the morbidity of this "regressive uterine tendency," and therefore, in my opinion, illegitimately projecting the same tendency onto all organic life, just as Freud did.[13] In human beings at any rate, the special concentration of libido in the genital region, in the infantile phallic phase and in the adult genital organization, is engineered by the regressive death instinct, and represents the residue of the human incapacity to accept death, separation, and individuality. And in the same essay Ferenczi, going beyond Freud, showed how the earlier phases of infantile sexuality, the oral and anal, are also dominated by the same regressive trend.[14] The special concentration of libido in the mouth in earliest infancy, the hypercathexis of the act of suckling, results from the inability to accept separation from the mother and is sustained by fantasies of uterine regression. The anal stage (the most fantastic psychoanalytical paradox, of which more later) involves symbolic manipulation of feces as a magic instrument for restoring communion with the mother. Altogether, therefore, the sexual organizations, pregenital as well as genital, appear to be constructed by anxiety, by the flight from death and the wish to die; the distribution of libido in a life not at war with death is polymorphous perversity.

Not only does the incapacity to accept death activate a regressive death wish; it also contaminates Eros and burdens the projects of infantile narcissism with the flight from death. As a result of instinctual ambivalence, the history of childhood is the history of an organism caught in an ever widening sequence of dualisms which it vainly seeks to overcome, till in the end, after a final climactic struggle, it acknowledges defeat and acquiesces in its own permanent impairment. In this sequence of dualisms we can trace the steps by which the death instinct is transformed into a principle of active negativity.

The first stage, the oral stage, is not simply the stage at which erotic activity of the mouth at the mother's breast is the most important activity; it is also the stage which discovers the anxiety of wanting, but not being able to find, the mother's breast. Therefore, says Freud, it is the stage which discovers the dualism of subject and object.[15] It is the stage at which the child formulates the grandiose project of the pure pleasure-ego, the dream of union with the world in love and pleasure. But the construction of the pure pleasure-ego is achieved by inaugurating the first repression, which takes the form of repudiating the external world and projecting out into the repudiated ex-

ternal world anything painful—that is to say, denying its existence.[16] Thus the first affirmation (the pure pleasure-ego project) is accompanied by the first negation. This negation is a
prototype of repression; but negation is also, according to Freud
(and Hegel), a manifestation of the death instinct.[17] At this
stage, then, the incapacity of the ego to accept separation results in a transformation of the instinctual force working for
separation and individual life into a mental force which separates the ego from reality, denies reality, represses reality. And
the effect is to burden the narcissistic project of loving union
with the world with the unreal project of becoming oneself
one's whole world (the solipsism to which the philosophers
regress).

In Freud's second stage, the anal stage, the dualism of subject and object is transformed into that of activity and passivity.
Infantile narcissism carries on from the previous stage the project of denying its own dependence, but now experiences its
dependence on the plane of action, as passivity, and therefore
asserts its independence by rebellious action, by seeking to
transform passivity into activity, as in the game, "Now let's
play that I am the mother and you are the child." [18]

But this obsessional commitment to transform passivity into
activity is aggressiveness. Freud always recognized that aggressiveness originated at this stage (hence the label, anal-sadistic).
He comes close to recognizing that it is at this stage, by the
transformation of passivity into activity, that the fateful extroversion of the death instinct outward onto the world in the
form of aggression takes place.[19] At this point Eros, through
the project of becoming both mother and child, in flight from
death transforms death, already transformed into a principle
of negation, into a principle of negative activity or aggression.
(This stage in the development of the infantile ego is attached
to the anal region, because, as we shall see later, the project of
becoming both mother and child is carried out not in reality,
but in fantasy: the fantasies must have some bodily base, and
attach themselves to a part of the body which can be magically,
fantastically, manipulated as a fantastic double of the self.)

In the final phallic or Oedipal phase, the polarity of activity
and passivity is transformed into the polarity of masculinity and

its opposite, castration.[20] Here infantile narcissism carries over from the preceding stage the rebellion against passivity, but it experiences that passivity on the plane of biological reproduction, as the fact of having been born from the mother. Hence it seeks to transform passivity into activity with the Oedipal project of having a child by the mother; that is to say, by becoming father of oneself. Since Freud himself did not always stick to this interpretation of the Oedipus complex, we quote Freud: "All the instincts, the loving, the grateful, the sensual, the defiant, the self-assertive and independent—all are gratified in the wish to be the *father of himself.*" [21]

The Oedipal project is not, as Freud's earlier formulations suggest, a natural love of the mother, but as his later writings recognize, a product of the conflict of ambivalence and an attempt to overcome that conflict by narcissistic inflation.[22] The essence of the Oedipal complex is the project of becoming God —in Spinoza's formula, *causa sui;* in Sartre's, *être-en-soi-pour-soi.* By the same token, it plainly exhibits infantile narcissism perverted by the flight from death. At this stage (and in adult genital organization) masculinity is equated with activity; the fantasy of becoming father of oneself is attached to the penis, thus establishing a concentration of narcissistic libido in the genital.[23] There it remains, even after the destruction of the Oedipus complex, burdening with fantasies of possession not only the sexual relations of men to women, but also the relations of fathers to sons: sons, as the father's heirs, perpetuate the father. To quote Freud, "At the weakest point of all in the narcissistic position, the immortality of the ego, security is achieved by fleeing to the child. Parental love is nothing but parental narcissism born again." [24] Thus again it appears that the sexual organizations, pregenital and genital, do not correspond to the natural distribution of Eros in the human body: they represent a hypercathexis, a supercharge, of particular bodily functions and zones, a hypercathexis induced by the fantasies of human narcissism in flight from death.

All the problems of infantile sexuality come to a head in the castration complex, which is the link between infantile sexuality and adult behavior. According to the Freudian formula, the Oedipus complex, and with it the whole of infantile sexuality, succumbs to the castration complex. Through the cástration complex infantile sexuality becomes transformed into normal adult sexuality; it is therefore the key to the psychology of adult genital sexuality and more generally the psychology of the two sexes. At the same time the castration complex establishes that reservoir of sexual energy which cannot achieve expression in normal adult sexual activity, and which, through sublimation, creates culture. And finally, it is the mechanism which transforms the infant's dependent love of his parents into the adult's dependent love of social, religious, and moral authority. In general, inasmuch as neurosis is caused by the repression of infantile sexuality, the castration complex is the key to the human neurosis.

How far psychoanalysis is from being a finished system is nowhere better illustrated than in the theory of the castration complex. Freud moved ever forward, introducing modifications in line with his later discoveries of anxiety, instinctual ambivalence, and the pre-Oedipal mother, without, however, reconsidering the whole, and without abandoning earlier formulations inconsistent with the later; but Freud at least knew he had not found an adequate solution. The Epigoni, when they do not abandon the problem altogether, attempt to combine Freud, early and late, into a closed system, with results which the public has rightly chosen to ignore. A reformulation is needed, a reformulation which takes account of the forward movement in Freud's thought.

One of the relics of Freud's earlier theories, not consistently abandoned in his later formulations and still littering the textbook expositions of psychoanalysis, is the notion that the essence of the phallic stage of infantile sexuality is masturbation, and the essence of the castration complex is the repression of masturbation by the parental (usually paternal) threat to punish by castration. Also connected here is the explanation of penis-envy in women (a theorem inseparable from the castration complex) as due to the little girl's apprehension that the female clitoris is inferior to the male penis for purposes of masturbation.

In so far as psychoanalysts talk this way, they justify the quite widespread illusion that if parents would only abstain from repressing masturbation, at least by threats of castration, the children would grow up unscathed by the castration complex. There is similarly a search, involving also the psychoanalytically minded anthropologists, for the right kind of toilet training, as if parental behavior were the cause of anal traumata and subsequent anal character. This whole notion is structured along the lines of Freud's early theory. Its fundamental assumptions are, first, that what is repressed is autoerotic bodily organ pleasure; and second, that repression intervenes from outside. But the concentration of libido in the genital is not a simple manifestation of organ pleasure, but is constructed by the regressive fantasies of infantile narcissism distorted by the flight from death—that is to say, the Oedipal project.

The whole notion is overthrown by Freud's own formula that "masturbation is only the discharge in the genital of the excitation belonging to the [Oedipus] complex." [25] The Oedipal project, as we saw, is the quest to conquer death by becoming father of oneself. It never made sense to suppose that the abandonment of a piece of organ pleasure should be such a trauma and lead to such far-reaching consequences as postulated by the castration complex; but what the castration complex shatters is the infantile solution to the problem of death. Since, as we have seen, the human family must produce a human child incapable of accepting death, it follows that the Oedipal project is inevitably self-generated in the child and is directed against the parents, irrespective of how the parents behave. Hence Freud recognized that there is no way for parents, either lenient or strict, to avoid provoking infantile aggressiveness. Hence in a sublime formula he says, "It is not really a decisive matter whether one has killed one's father or abstained from the deed; one must feel guilty in either case, for guilt is the expression of the conflict of ambivalence, the eternal struggle between Eros and the destructive or death instinct." [26]

The same applies, *mutatis mutandis*, to the anal phase; to state it paradoxically, children toilet train themselves. Psychoanalysis must always take the position that the Child is Father to the Man. Freud said, but did not always abide by his dictum, that "analytic experience has convinced us of the complete truth of the common assertion that the child is psychologically father of the man." [27] The origin of the adult promotion of toilet training lies in an infantile predisposition. Infantile anality is not anal erotism or "playing with feces"; it is not a simple manifestation of the erotic search for organ pleasure and play, rudely repressed by parental toilet training from the outside. It is an ambivalent mixture of Eros and death, involving attachment to the anal zone of regressive fantasies of union with the mother and narcissistic fantasies of being both Self and Other; hence the "playing with feces" contains its own internal drive to master and control them.

Not only does Freud's early theory assume that what is repressed is simply Eros (or play); it also assumes that repression comes from the outside—from the threatening father in the castration complex, from the toilet-training parents in the analogous anal trauma. But the tendency of Freud's later theory is toward a conception of repression as essentially self-repression, the inevitable result of the anxiety and instinctual ambivalence inside the child himself. In the new perspective, the castration complex is the climax in the long history of ambivalence in the relations between the child and the mother, and it represents a definitive victory for the aggressive component over the love component. This perspective is tentatively reached by Freud himself in one of his later writings:

> One might even believe that this first love relation of the child is doomed to extinction for the very reason that it is the first, for these early object-cathexes are always ambivalent to a very high degree; alongside of the child's intense love there is always a strong aggressive tendency present, and the more passionately a child loves an object, the more sensitive it will be to disappointments and frustrations. In the end, the love is bound to capitulate to the accumulated hostility.[28]

Similarly, in the toilet-training analogy, as Abraham pointed out,[29] the disgust at feces emerges in the child not because he assimilates parental indoctrination, but for internal reasons. Before going on to the narcissistic project of the anal phase (symbolic retention, mastery, possession of the world), the infantile ego turns against the narcissistic project of the oral phase (symbolic incorporation, swallowing of the world).

But if the castration complex is the climax to the long his-

tory of instinctual ambivalence, it must be the climax to the
long history of the child's relation to his mother; and then the
role of the father must be quite secondary. In the later phase
of his theory, and in the study of the psychology of women,
Freud uncovered a deeper layer underlying the Oedipus and
castration complexes, the core of which consists in the attachment to what Freud calls the pre-Oedipal mother. It came to
him as a surprise, he says, comparable to the effect in another
field of the discovery of Minoan-Mycenaean civilization behind
that of Greece.[30] The pre-Oedipal mother is the mother who,
in consequence of the biological basis of the family, must become the whole world of the child.

In this general sense, of course, Freud knew all about the
primal or pre-Oedipal mother from the very start of his career.
What he discovered only late in his career was the necessity
of linking his analysis of the Oedipus and castration complexes
to the notion of the primal mother—that is to say, the necessity
of apprehending the Oedipal relation to the father as a superstructure on top of a substructure of Oedipal relations to the
mother. The new point of view revealed that the Oedipus and
castration complexes can be generated in principle without any
reference to the father-figure. The analysis of the little girl
showed that her relations with her mother, by the principle of
transforming passivity into activity, generated the desire to get
the mother with child.[31] Freud calls this project of having a
child by the mother pre-Oedipal; but the Oedipal intent is
plain: what Freud means by calling it pre-Oedipal is that the
project dates to the period before the girl turns to her father.

It is therefore an integral part of Freud's psychology of
women to suppose that the girl conceives the Oedipal project
without reference to the father-figure. And in the same context, Freud describes the castration complex in girls as a revulsion against the mother induced by the discovery of sexual
differentiation, a revulsion against the fact that she is born a
woman, i.e., of the same sex as her mother.[32] Thus, at least for
the girl, the castration complex revolves around the relation to
the mother, and needs no father; in the Freudian psychology
of women the girl turns to the father only after and as a result
of the castration complex. And furthermore it becomes clear

that the preformed preference for masculinity which the whole theory of the castration complex (and penis-envy in women) assumes represents a continuance of the Oedipal *causa sui* project. The revolt against biological dependence on the mother is transposed, by collision with the fact of sexual differentiation, into the desire to be of the opposite sex to the mother.

And what about the boy? Contrary to the usual opinion, Freud's psychology of women is more mature than his psychology of men, because it belongs entirely to his later phase. He himself recognized the need for a comprehensive re-examination of the male castration complex in the light of the pre-Oedipus phase.[33] Actually, however, Freud's revisions of his own formulations show him steadily moving toward the position that the male castration complex can be generated in principle without reference to a father-figure. The first step in this direction was made when Freud saw that the motive power which generated the castration complex was not the father's threat to castrate but the discovery of the sexual organs of the female sex (as in the case of the girl, the castration complex is the reaction to the recognition of the fact of sexual differentiation). He took the next step when he recognized that the discovery of sexual differentiation becomes a traumatic crisis only when the mother is seen in this light. In earlier writings he had spoken of the castration complex being activated by the apprehension of sexual differentiation in relation to a brother or sister. The final step was to see that the essence of the castration complex was to perceive, not the image of the castrating father, but the image of the castrated mother: in Freud's blunt style, the perception of the mother's genitals as devoid of a penis.[34]

Confrontation with the fact of sexual differentiation, for boys as well as girls, transposes the opposition to the mother into a preference for the sex opposite to the mother's, a preference for masculinity in terms of which the opposite of masculinity is castration. Thus the apprehension of the mother in terms of sexual differentiation, as castrated, automatically and without any reference to a father-figure, turns both boy and girl away from the mother and generates horror, terror, contempt.[35] Freud explicitly derives from this horror not only the male contempt for women as the inferior sex and the penis-envy of women, but also the horror of incest which Freud always regarded as the primal taboo, the fundamental moral law, and which he always connected with the first formation of the con-science or super-ego.

A transitional stage in Freud's evolution in this direction is his theory in *The Ego and the Id* (1923) of the twofold nature of the Oedipus complex, in which he recognizes that all the ambivalent relations toward the father, which he had postulated to be the origin of the super-ego, can also develop in relation to the mother.[36] We may therefore conclude that in principle the castration complex and all the far-reaching consequences attributed to it by psychoanalysis rest ultimately on the child's relation to the mother. And, of course, the child's peculiar re-action to the fact of sexual differentiation from the mother— "horror at the mutilated creature"—which is the castration com-plex, is his own invention; it is a tissue of fantasy inseparable from his own fantastic project of becoming father of himself (and, as fantasy, only remotely connected with actual sight of the female genitalia). Hence, just as you are bound to feel guilty whether you have killed your father or not, so Freud says that it is not primarily a question of whether castration is really performed; what is important is that the boy believes in it.[37]

In spite of his discovery of the pre-Oedipal or primal mother, Freud returns in *Group Psychology and Analysis of the Ego* (1921), and in *Moses and Monotheism* (1937), to what he calls his scientific myth of the Primal Father who castrated his sons; and since in these same writings he stresses the impor-tance of the phylogenetic or archaic heritage in the formation of the individual neurosis, he is, I think, involved in formal self-contradiction, the explanation of which may lie in his own Oedipus complex. What the myth of the Primal Father amounts to is a postulation of male superiority and aggressiveness as an immutable fact of nature (the Primal Father, while the cause of culture, is in the state of nature) and the use of this assump-tion to explain the psychology of the human family.

But even granting that male superiority and aggressiveness are universal facts, the question is: Why are they facts? Since the Freudian anthropology is basically a deduction from psychoanalysis, it cannot legitimately be invoked to cover a gap in psychoanalysis itself. If the burden of proof rests on the Freudian anthropology, then the whole notion of the castration complex is open to all the attacks which have been directed against the Freudian anthropology. We are left free to argue, for example, that the castration complex is not a universal phenomenon but exists only in patriarchal cultures. If the invocation of anthropology is not allowed, Freud fails to give an explanation of what has to be explained.

To explain the child's equation of active aggressiveness with the male sex by reference to the brute external fact that the father is the aggressively dominant factor in the family is to assume as given precisely what has to be explained. Psychoanalysis must derive adult male aggression from childhood. Here, and everywhere, psychoanalysis must take the paradoxical position that the Child is Father to the Man; that Primal Father was once a boy, and, if there is anything to psychoanalysis, owes his disposition to his boyhood. A crucial issue in methodology is involved. In the myth of the Primal Father Freud abandons psychological explanation and invokes the category of brute natural force to cover the gap. In the state of nature, force is supreme, and the human family is constituted by the monopoly of force in the hands of the Primal Father, who monopolizes the women and castrates the sons when they threaten his monopoly.

Freud thus is pushed back to the position of Hegel and Nietzsche. Hegel assumed the antinomy of Master and Slave as given by nature; and Nietzsche, offering, like Freud, an explanation of guilt as internalized aggression, invoked the sudden appearance of a "master race" to establish repression and the state, and thus cause the internalization of aggressiveness.[38] It is true that Freud goes beyond Nietzsche and Hegel by attributing the internalization of aggressiveness, and indeed the whole human propensity to aggression, to the institution of the human family; for whereas neither the state nor the antinomy of Master and Slave can be granted to be given by nature, the institution of the family can. Freud reaches down to the level where social and natural institutions are truly joined, and opens up the question of how the psychic dynamism inherent in the human family might, in the fullness of time, produce the antinomy between Master and Slave and the institution of the state. On the other hand, Freud carried into his analysis of the family the presupposition that the antinomy of Master and Slave is given by nature. Freud's primal despotic father simply transposes into the family, and assumes as given the domination which Hegel and Nietzsche conceived in terms of the state.

The proper starting point for a Freudian anthropology is the pre-Oedipal mother. What is given by nature, in the family, is the dependence of the child on the mother. Male domination must be grasped as a secondary formation, the product of the child's revolt against the primal mother, bequeathed to adulthood and culture by the castration complex. Freudian anthropology must therefore turn from Freud's preoccupation with patriarchal monotheism; it must take out of the hands of Jungian *Schwärmerei* the exploitation of Bachofen's great discovery of the religion of the Great Mother, a substratum underlying the religion of the Father—the anthropological analogue to Freud's discovery of the Oedipal mother underlying the Oedipal father, and comparable, like Freud's, to the discovery of Minoan-Mycenaean civilization underlying Greek civilization.

Starting from this basis, a Freudian anthropology would have to work out a theory of the dynamic interrelations between family structure, religion, and material culture (sublimation)—a theory which would have to solve a number of still unsolved problems. It is, for example, by no means obvious that, as assumed by Bachofen (and following Bachofen, such unlikely bedfellows as the Marxists and Robert Graves), a matriarchal religion presupposes a matriarchal family. According to psychoanalytical theory, fantasy is not so crassly tied to reality. What does seem certain is that, as Freud divined and the anthropologists are coming to see, the incest taboo is the mainspring of the dynamic in archaic kinship systems; that the incest taboo is directed against the mother; and that the incest taboo is not to be explained sociologically, by the abstract need for social organization, but by the psychology of guilt and the castration complex. It is not sufficient to say (as anthropologists are now willing to say) that the incest taboo is the foundation of familial organization. We must return to Freud and say that incest guilt (the Oedipal project) created the incest taboo. And if the incest taboo involves a preference for masculinity so strong as to see femininity as castration, it would seem likely that a tendency toward patriarchy is intrinsic to the human family.

According to basic psychoanalytic theory, the castration complex establishes the peculiar capacity of human bodies to devise nonbodily activities (sublimations) and the peculiar capacity of the human self for self-denial (the super-ego). We can begin, I think, to make sense of these paradoxes if we think of the Oedipal project as the *causa sui* (father-of-oneself) project, and therefore in essence a revolt against death generally, and specifically against the biological principle separating mother and child. The castration complex is the consequence of the collision between this project and the perception of the fact of sexual differentiation separating mother and son. The whole question is: What happens to the Oedipal project when it collides with the castration complex? There is a strange contradiction in Freud here. In spite of a lifetime of insisting that the Oedipus complex was the answer to the riddle of the Sphinx and the clue to all neurosis, in an essay entitled "The Passing of the Oedipus-Complex" (1924), he says that the effect of the castration complex on the Oedipus "is more than a repression; when carried out in the ideal way it is equivalent to a destruction and abrogation of the complex"; in the *New Introductory Lectures* he repeats that "in the most normal cases" the complex is "entirely destroyed." [39]

Freud never elucidated these formulae, and he did not cease to describe the all-pervasive effects of the Oedipus complex, not only in neurotics but also in the normal psychology of the two sexes. Apparently his final position is that the Oedipus complex both is and is not retained. Let us attempt to elucidate. The adult flight from death—the immortality promised in all religions, the immortality of familial corporations, the immortality of cultural achievements—perpetuates the Oedipal project of becoming father of oneself: adult sublimation continues the Oedipal project. On the other hand, the confrontation with the fact of sexual differentiation from the mother destroys the bodily-sexual character of the infantile Oedipal project. Hence the outcome is the etherealization—in Freud's terminology, de-sexualization—of the Oedipal project: all sublimations are desex-ualizations. Thus man acquires a soul distinct from his body, and a superorganic culture which perpetuates the revolt against organic dependence on the mother. The soul and the super-organic culture perpetuate both the Oedipal *causa sui* project and that horror of biological fact which is the essence of the castration complex.

Man acquires a soul, but remains only a body. What corre-sponds to the soul in the body is that concentration of libido in the genital which is genital organization. In the Oedipal or phallic phase the morbid death wish and the flight from death have fused with and distorted infantile narcissism so as to pro-duce a concentration of libido in the genital, attaching to it fantasies of reunion with the mother. The castration complex puts an end to the possibility of bodily fulfillment but does not put an end to the fantasies. In the words of one of Freud's last formulations: "As a result of the threat he has given up mas-turbation, but not the activities of his imagination accompany-ing it. . . . Derivatives and modified products of these early masturbatory phantasies usually make their way into his later ego, and play a part in the formation of his character." [40]

Thus the Oedipus complex both survives and is destroyed. The outcome is the desexualized penis, that is to say, a penis burdened by Oedipal fantasies denied bodily fulfillment. In the essay on "The Passing of the Oedipus-Complex" Freud has a formulation that can hardly be improved: "The libidinal trends belonging to the Oedipus-complex are in part desexual-ized and sublimated . . . in part they are inhibited in their aim and changed into affectionate feelings. The whole process, on the one hand, preserves the genital organ, wards off the danger of losing it; on the other hand, it paralyses it, takes away its function from it." [41] And just as the genital and pregenital or-ganizations distort the body of infantile narcissism, so they rep-resent distortions of the ego. The natural function of the ego, as Freud says in *The Ego and the Id*, is to be the sensitive sur-face of the entire body; but the survival of *causa sui* fantasies attached to the genital establishes in the unconscious, as Ferenczi said, the phallus as a miniature of the total ego.[42]

The inevitable legacy of the Oedipal project is the radical deformation of the human ego and the human body. The castration complex finally enforces the separation of the child's body from the mother's body, but traumatically, so that individuality, a true synthesis of Eros and Death, is never attained. Human narcissism, still burdened with the *causa sui* project, still seeks an unreal independence and thus gets morbidly involuted. The castration complex establishes as absolute the dualism of the self and the other, the dualism which infantile narcissism had sought to overcome. The child has to make a choice between love of self and love of the other: according to Freud, the boy's self-love or narcissism turns him away from his mother.[43] But the self so loved is fraudulent: self-love replaces parental love, but, according to Freud, only at the cost of splitting the ego into parent and child.[44] Through the institution of the super-ego the parents are internalized and man finally succeeds in becoming father of himself, but at the cost of becoming his own child and keeping his ego infantile.

At the same time human aggression, inseparable from the *causa sui* project, is likewise internalized, not only in the mutual warfare between ego and super-ego, which must perpetuate the war between parent and child, but also in that general war between the ego and the body which is repression and which sustains the desexualization of the Oedipal project. The morbid death instinct, already transformed into a principle of denial, blossoms after the castration complex into a principle of self-denial and denial of one's own body. Involuted Eros and involuted aggression constitute the "autonomous self" or what passes for individuality in the human species. "The process of individualization," says Róheim, "is naturally built up by or based on hostile trends directed against the mother. . . . However, just because of the dual-unity matrix from which the differentiation takes its starting point, these aggressions are followed by guilt, by reparations, or reidentification and then again by renewed aggression."[45]

Once again it appears that psychoanalysis' closest allies are in the religious tradition. The same harsh judgment on human individuality is contained in the doctrine of original sin.

Boehme, the most psychoanalytical of theologians, develops the doctrine that the primal sin is selfishness, or a vain project of the part to become independent of the totality conceived as a mother-principle, in words which can stand beside Freud's:

> Every will which enters into self-hood and seeks the ground of its life-form (sc. in itself) breaks itself off from the mystery and enters into a capriciousness. It cannot do otherwise for its fellow members stir up dying and death. It lies, and denies union with the Will of God and sets self-hood in its place, so that it goes out from unity into a desire for self. If it knew that all things have brought it forth and are its mothers, and if it did not hold its mother's substance for its own, but in common, then greed, envy, strife and a contrary will would not arise.[46]

According to Boehme, this fall into selfhood, Adam's fall, is a fall from eternity into time, and therefore the beginning of human history; it is also the moment when Adam ceased to play and started to work. In Freudian terminology, the castration complex represses infantile sexuality and inaugurates sublimation.

The special contribution of psychoanalysis is to trace religious and philosophic problems to their roots in the concrete human body. The central paradox in the theory of the castration complex is that confrontation with the fact of sexual differentiation produces in the child and bequeaths to the unconscious of the adult the image of the female as the castrated sex. One of the advantages of eliminating the threatening father from the theoretical picture is that it makes clear that there is no way of keeping the castration complex for the psychology of males without admitting at the same time the theorem which appears to have raised much stiffer opposition, penis-envy in women. Critics have accused Freud of accepting as inevitable and natural nineteenth-century notions of male superiority, and are afraid of any implication that women are by nature and by biology the inferior sex. It is true that Freud confuses the issue by sometimes assuming male social domination as given eternally by nature, and by sometimes attempting to derive penis-envy from the organic biological inferiority of the clitoris to the penis. The assumption of male domination suggests that penis-envy is not absolute or universal, and merely expresses female revolt against social domination by the male; the comparison of the clitoris with the penis on the other hand does make the inferiority of women absolute and biological.

Freud's unsatisfactory oscillation between a social and a biological determinism is transcended if we follow Freud (not the critics) to the concept of the primal mother and the inevitable and universal consequences of being a human child in the human family. The origin of the castration complex in men and penis-envy in women lies neither in society nor in biology but in the secret projects of infantile sexuality. The neo-Freudian critics say, on the one hand, that "Freud's basic attitude is patriarchal," and, on the other, that he "explains psychic differences between the two sexes as the result of anatomical differences." [47] But the real point of the Freudian paradox is that, despite the social order and despite anatomical fact, the immortal wish of both sexes is the same. Penis-envy in women is the residue of the *causa sui* project in women, corresponding to the phallic ego in men. As long as mankind and culture are in flight from death, so long will penis fantasies confuse the erotic, familial, and social life of women, as they do for men.

What underlies both penis-envy in women and the castration complex in men is the immortal allegiance in the unconscious of both sexes to that flagrant contradiction of both the social order and the anatomical facts—what Freud calls the bisexuality of childhood. Infantile sexuality (before the castration complex), just because it is infantile, must be sexually undifferentiated; and since the structure of infancy is the same for both sexes, the basic demands of the libido are the same for both sexes.[48] Hence it is part of Freud's later position to stress the bisexual character of the Oedipal project itself:

> Closer study usually discloses the more complete Oedipus-complex, which is twofold, positive and negative, and is due to the bisexuality originally present in children: that is to say, a boy has not merely an ambivalent attitude toward his father and an affectionate object-relation toward his mother, but at the same time he also behaves like a girl and displays an affectionate feminine attitude to his father and a corresponding hostility and jealousy toward his mother.[49]

Hence, measured by the standard of the unconscious and of childhood, the sexual differentiation of the adult libido, as presupposed in genital organization and the human family—masculine aggressiveness and feminine passivity—is a loss of sexual completeness; hence the fact of sexual differentiation is regarded with horror. In each sex, says Freud, it is the attitude belonging to the opposite sex which succumbs to repression. In each sex the unconscious does not accept the repression but wants to recover the bisexuality of childhood. Corresponding to penis-envy in women, there is in men "a struggle against their passive or feminine attitude toward other men." [50] In his last clinical essay Freud pointed to this fundamental rejection of sexual differentiation as the deepest and most stubborn cause of the neurotic conflict between the libido and reality: [51] and, with Freud's view of genital organization as a biological datum, it follows that neurosis is incurable.

Even if we take the position that genital organization is a formation of the ego not yet strong enough to die, the conflict between the libido and all forms of culture recorded in history remains. For if mankind is unalterably, in the unconscious, in revolt against sexual differentiation and genital organization, genital organization and the castration complex have been the psychosomatic base for all known forms of the human family. In postulating a deep conflict between the erotic aspirations of mankind and the institution of the family, psychoanalysis connects again with the religious tradition. According to a Bible text which mystical theologians love to elaborate, and also according to the myths of very primitive peoples, [52] in heaven none marry and none are given in marriage; and yet in heaven all for the first time truly love.

At the deepest level the androgynous or hermaphroditic ideal of the unconscious reflects the aspiration of the human body to overcome the dualisms which are its neurosis, ultimately to reunify Eros and the death instinct. The dualism of masculine-feminine is merely the transposition into genital terms of the dualism of activity and passivity; and activity and passivity represent unstable fusions of Eros and Death at war with each other. Thus Freud identifies masculinity with aggressiveness and femininity with masochism. [53] In Freud's earlier writings, before he discovered the bisexual disposition in the Oedipus complex, and in line with his early notion that love is essentially possessive ("object-choice"), the libido is assumed to be essentially active and masculine. In his later writings the libido is viewed as essentially bisexual, "a single libido, though its aims, i.e., its modes of gratification, are both active and passive." [54] But activity and passivity are also derivatives of the death instinct. Thus Eros contains in itself the possibility of reunification with its instinctual opposite, and it strives toward that goal. Freud, in *Beyond the Pleasure Principle*, used the myth of the formation of mankind by bisection of an originally bisexual creature to suggest that Eros, in seeking ever wider unification, might be seeking to reinstate a lost condition of primal unity. [55] But with his view of the instincts as a radically discrete pair, he could envisage this primal unity only as a primal conglomerate of all life before it was shattered by the intrusion of some separating force. In a more dialectical view, the primal unity Eros seeks to reinstate is its unity with its own opposite, the death instinct.

As Freud's exploitation of the myth of the primal hermaphrodite or androgyne shows, psychoanalysis, interpreted as a phenomenon in the history of human thought, is only an interpretation of the dreams of mysticism. In the West, cabalistic mysticism has interpreted Genesis 1:27—"God created man in his own image . . . male and female created he them"—as implying the androgynous nature of God and of human perfection before the Fall. [56] From cabalism this notion passed into the Christian mysticism of Boehme, where it is fused with the Pauline mysticism of Galatians 3:28—"There can be no male and female; for ye are all one man in Christ Jesus." [57] In neglecting Boehme, or this side of Boehme, later Protestantism only keeps its head in the sand; for, as Berdyaev writes:

> The great anthropological myth which alone can be the basis of an anthropological metaphysic is the myth about the androgyne. . . . According to his Idea, to God's conception of him, man is a complete, masculinely feminine being, solar and telluric, logoic and cosmic at the same time. . . . Original sin is connected in the first instance with division into two sexes and the Fall of the androgyne, i.e., of man as a complete being. [58]

In the East, Taoist mysticism, as Needham shows, seeks to recover the androgynous self: one of the famous texts of the Tao Te Ching says:

> He who knows the male, yet cleaves to what is female
> Becomes like a ravine, receiving all things under heaven
> (Thence) the eternal virtue never leaks away.
> This is returning to the state of infancy.[59]

And since poetry, as well as psychoanalysis, is the modern heir of the mystical tradition, the hermaphroditic ideal is central, for example, in the message of Rilke. In *Letters to a Young Poet* he writes: "And perhaps the sexes are more related than we think, and the great renewal of the world will perhaps consist in this, that man and maid, freed from all false feeling and aversion, will seek each other not as opposites, but as brother and sister, as neighbours, and will come together as *human beings.*" But deeper than the problem of the relation between the sexes is the problem of the reunification of the sexes in the self. In Rilke as artist, according to his friend Lou Andreas Salome, "both sexes unite into an entity." And Rilke, in his call to God to perfect him as an artist, calls on God to make him a hermaphrodite:

> Mach Einen herrlich, Herr, mach Einen gross,
> bau seinem Leben einen schönen Schooss,
> und seine Scham errichte wie ein Tor
> in einem blonden Wald von jungen Haaren.[60]

Part Four

SUBLIMATION

The link between psychoanalysis and the science of human culture is the concept of sublimation. If psychoanalysis is right, virtually the totality of what anthropologists call culture consists of sublimations. Freud not only regards "higher mental operations, scientific, artistic, ideological activities" as sublimations of sexual energy, but also the less high but more fundamental cultural activity of work. The emotional ties which bind the individual members of a particular culture into a unity, as well as individual and social character structures, are also said to be effects of sublimation. And yet the theory of sublimation is far from clear. This strategic concept reflects all the ambiguities in the relation between psychoanalysis and society.

The Ambiguities of Sublimation

IF PSYCHOANALYSIS is right, we must radically change our attitude toward human culture. The concept of sublimation includes the most outrageous paradoxes, all of them asserting a connection between higher cultural activities and lower bodily regions, between adult "rational" procedures and infantile irrational prototypes, between "pure" mental constructs and sexuality.[1] Conversely, if the psychoanalytical theory of sublimation is rejected, psychoanalysis has nothing much to offer to the science of culture. That is why the neo-Freudians, who abandon the concept of sublimation, have been so easily absorbed into the structure of orthodox anthropology: they no longer have anything shocking or paradoxical to say. Orthodox anthropology, given classic expression in Kroeber's essay on "The Superorganic," defines its own subject matter by making an absolute distinction between nature and culture (biological and cultural evolution, animal and human levels) and between the individual and the social.[2] The whole point of psychoanalysis is its refusal to acquiesce in this mysterious dichotomy. The concept of sublimation is essentially an attempt to relate the organic and superorganic levels, as part of the general effort of psychoanalysis to rediscover the animal in man and to heal the war between body and soul.

What happens to the human body when the human animal becomes more than an animal and acquires that new plane of activity which Kroeber calls the superorganic? The concept of sublimation, in itself, merely states an old problem—the relation of the organic to the superorganic—in a new way, by introducing the concept of infantile sexuality; and thus it raises new problems. Psychoanalysis had to proceed on the one hand with empirical a posteriori correlations between aspects of infantile sexuality and aspects of culture (for example, the correlation between anal erotism and the love of money), and on the other hand with theoretical elaboration so as to make the postulated connection intelligible. A posteriori correlations have been copiously gathered; but the theoretical problem remains unsolved. The beginning of wisdom (not granted in the psychoanalytical textbooks) is to recognize the theoretical difficulty, as Freud did. In the article in which he asserts the paradox that love of money is a sublimation of anal erotism, he confesses his own perplexity: "The inherent necessity of this relationship is naturally not clear even to myself." In one of his later writings he expresses the hope that one day psychoanalysis will understand sublimation. In his last essay on culture he has a long section which explores the drive for "progress in spirituality" (i.e., higher sublimation) and which leaves the question open.[3]

Freud does have lucid definitions of sublimation, but on examination they turn out to be descriptive rather than explanatory. Sublimation changes both the aim and the object of the instinct, so that "what was originally a sexual instinct finds some achievement which is no longer sexual but has a higher social or ethical valuation"; with his scientific integrity, he immediately adds, "These different features do not as yet combine to form an integral picture."[4] He here and elsewhere stresses that sublimation involves on the one hand the desexualization of the aims of the sexual instinct and on the other hand their socialization. But it is not clear how desexualization and socialization take place, or even what these terms mean. The connection between infantile sexuality and culture is postulated, not explained. Attacking the problem from the side of culture, Freud asserts that the survival of culture depends on the sublimation of infantile sexuality:

> Civilization has been built up, under the pressure of the struggle for existence, by sacrifices in gratification of the primitive impulses, and it is to a great extent forever being recreated, as each individual, successively joining the community, repeats the sacrifice of his instinctive pleasures for the common good. The sexual are amongst the most important of the instinctive

forces thus utilized; they are in this way sublimated, that is to say, their energy is turned aside from its sexual goal and diverted towards other ends, no longer sexual and socially more valuable.[5]

The formulation shows that the concept of sublimation is an attempt to relate not only body and spirit, but also individual and society; but again it raises problems which it does not solve. If sublimations are imposed by society on the individual, then sublimation is the result of repression. In other passages Freud doubts whether the situation is so simple: "Sometimes one perceives that it is not only the oppression of culture, but something in the nature of the function itself, that denies us full satisfaction and urges us in other directions."[6] And in many passages Freud presents sublimation as a "way out": "Sublimation is a way out, a way by which the claims of the ego can be met without involving repression."[7] He even describes sublimation not as a sacrifice of pleasure imposed by a hostile reality, but as a source of stable pleasure won from a hostile reality: "The task is then one of transferring the instinctual aims into such directions that they cannot be frustrated by the outer world. Sublimation of the instincts lends an aid in this."[8]

The context of these contradictory passages shows that Freud sometimes attempts to distinguish two kinds of sublimation. Nonrepressive sublimation is exemplified in "higher" mental work, such as science and art, and is accessible only to the elite. The masses on the other hand "are lazy and unintelligent, they have no love for instinctual renunciation" and must be coerced to the necessary sublimation of manual work.[9] If we remove the sociological naïveté or bias from these formulations, we are left with the distinction between mental and manual labor, and with the suggestion that manual labor is in some special sense repressive. But this suggestion is in itself controversial, and is specifically contradicted by other lines of thought in Freud himself. In one passage he suggests that primitive man "made his work agreeable, so to speak, by treating it as the equivalent of and substitute for sexual activities"; in another passage he suggests that in modern society work can be a source of libidinal satisfaction under certain circumstances, "when it has been selected by free choice, i.e., when through sublimation it enables use to be made of existing inclinations." [10]

And conversely, with regard to the highest kind of sublimations—for example the intellectual curiosity of a Leonardo da Vinci—Freud formulates the relation between repression and sublimation extremely ambiguously. He relates desexualized intellectual curiosity to the sexual curiosity of childhood, which he says can be disposed of in three different ways: (1) it can be simply repressed, resulting in a general intellectual inhibition and lack of curiosity; (2) it can be replaced by intellectual investigation, which is then sexualized by association with the repressed sexual investigation impulse, with the result that the intellectual investigation is compulsive; (3) there is perfect sublimation. But honesty compels Freud to admit that even in so-called pure intellectual curiosity there is some sexual repression; that intellectual investigation is partly compulsive; and that the avoidance of sexual themes is itself an evidence of the repression which deflected the libido toward sublimation. [11] The essay on Leonardo is Freud's most elaborate study of sublimation, and the outcome of it is that the highest sublimations, even for the few who are capable of them, are not really a "way out" from repression.

Freud's notion of sublimation as a "way out," as a way of satisfying the instincts in a manner satisfactory to the ego, shows the intimate connection between sublimation and therapy. If the repression of sexuality is the cause of neurosis, what alternative to neurosis does mankind possess? Psychoanalytical therapy is supposed to undo repressions and bring the hitherto repressed sexual energy under the control of the patient's ego. But what is the patient's ego going to do with his own sexuality, now brought under his conscious control?

Clear perception of this problem made Wilhelm Reich see that the outcome of therapy could only be a more erotic mode of behavior in the real world. But for Reich the problem was simplified and distorted by his assumption that the sexuality which culture represses is normal adult genital sexuality. And since Reich maintained that the repression of normal adult sexuality is not necessary for the existence of culture as such, but is required only by those specific cultures which are based on patriarchal domination, it follows that for him the abolition of repression would not threaten culture as such, but only patriarchal domination.[12]

Freud agrees with Reich that modern civilization does repress normal adult genital sexuality: "There is no longer any place in present-day civilized life for a simple natural love between two human beings." [13] And Freud agrees with Reich that society exacts unnecessary amounts of instinctual renunciation: "Psychoanalysis . . . proposes that there should be a reduction in the strictness with which instincts are repressed." [14] But where Freud differs from Reich is in facing the question whether, quite apart from this surplus-repression (Marcuse's term [15]) connected with patriarchal domination, all culture as such involves repression.

The crux of the problem is not the repression of normal adult genital sexuality, but what to do with infantile perverse pregenital sexuality. For Reich, on the one hand, the pregenital stages would simply disappear if full genitality were established; and, on the other hand, the whole notion of sublimation is dropped, its place being taken by a vague doctrine of "work" and "knowledge" as natural manifestations of the unrepressed forces of life.[16] But if the theory of infantile sexuality is retained, the abolition of patriarchal domination, or even the abolition of restrictions on genital sexuality, will not solve the problem. In fact Freud always assumes that one of the chief aims of psychoanalytical therapy is to replace repressions by sublimations; [17] and his therapeutic pessimism is confirmed by his pessimistic appraisal of the possibilities of finding complete satisfaction in sublimation. In the first place, he says, not all of the libido can be sublimated.[18] In the second place, only a minority of men are capable of extensive sublimation.[19] And in the third place, sublimations, by virtue of their intrinsic nature, are "not capable of really complete satisfaction." [20] Sublimations, as the study of Leonardo showed, do not really avoid the curse of repression. And the later doctrine of the death instinct contains a deeper critique: the desexualization intrinsic to all sublimation cannot be the work of the sexual instinct, involves a necessary component of dying to the life of the body, and therefore cannot ever satisfy the life instinct.[21]

The reason why the concept of sublimation remains obscure in psychoanalytical theory is that it lays bare the antagonism between man and culture which Freud was not able to solve. Reich was right in arguing that to fulfill its own therapeutic promise, psychoanalysis has to envisage a social transformation. Reich was wrong in limiting the social transformation involved to the liberation of adult genital sexuality. The therapeutic task is far larger; how large, only a resolute facing of the problem of sublimation can tell. Freud, having no solution to the general problem, and as a therapist handling patients who had to live in the world as it was, could only continue to recommend sublimation. And, since he did not shut his eyes to the limitations of sublimation, he could only envisage the continuation of the warfare between ego and id, and therefore had to make even the psychoanalytically reconstructed ego continue the function of instinctual repression, in the form of stoic self-control and stoic renunciation. But no psychoanalytical reason is given or can be given for believing that "ego-syntonic controls," as Freud calls them, can succeed where old-fashioned repression failed; or, to follow Freud's language in another passage, that secular motives for civilized behavior will succeed where religious motives have failed.[22] The festering antagonism between man and culture remains.

Intimately connected with the problem of therapy, and also involved in the theory of sublimation, is the problem of rationality. For just as sublimation has an ambiguous relation to repression, so it has also an equally ambiguous relation to neurosis. The problem was opened up by one of the most famous formulations in *Totem and Taboo:* [23]

> The neuroses exhibit on the one hand striking and far-reaching points of agreement with . . . art, religion and philosophy. But on the other hand they seem like distortions of them. It might be maintained that a case of hysteria is a caricature of a work of art, that an obsessional neurosis is a caricature of religion and that a paranoic delusion is a caricature of a philosophical system.

Although Freud was personally most interested in developing the relation between religion and neurosis, consistency requires us to say that psychoanalysis postulates a far-reaching connection between all sublimation and neurosis—between culture as such and neurosis: [24]

> A little reflection was bound to show that it would be impossible to restrict to the provinces of dreams and nervous disorders a view such as this of the life of the mind. If that view has hit upon a truth, it must apply equally to normal mental events, and even the highest achievements of the human spirit must bear a demonstrable relation to the factors found in pathology—to repression, to the efforts at mastering the unconscious and to the possibilities of satisfying the primitive instincts.

What distinction, then, if any, can be drawn between neurosis and culture? In these formulations Freud does not equate the two. He makes three distinctions between them: in a cultural formation the activity, though sexual in origin, is desexualized, socialized, and directed at reality in the form of work; in a neurosis the activity is resexualized, withdrawn from the social, and involves a flight from reality.[25] While the criterion of desexualization is obscure, the other two—sociality and reality-reference—provide a useful guide which psychoanalysis has adopted. Thus Róheim: "The difference between a neurosis and a sublimation is evidently in the social aspect of the phenomenon. A neurosis isolates; a sublimation unites. In a sublimation something new is created—a house, or a community, or a tool—and it is created in a group or for the use of a group." [26]

But this rough-and-ready distinction between culture and neurosis was undermined by other lines of thought in Freud himself. Freud was always torn between two aims, individual therapy and general theory. To distinguish between neurosis and culture by taking as the criterion the integration of the activity in the social labor process is to adopt the standpoint of individual therapy. A neurotic individual is distinguished by his alienation from a useful role in society, and the function of individual therapy is to restore the individual to society. Individual therapy must be culture-bound, and its motto must be adjustment. But while cultural activities may be distinguished from individual neurosis by their social character, it does not follow that all socially integrated activity is non-neurotic. For Freud as theoretician recognized that the distinction between "normal" and "neurotic" as applied in individual therapy had no theoretical validity; [27] and as social critic he proceeded to psychoanalyze the irrationality of such universal cultural sublimations as devotion to the church, the army and the state.[28]

Freud thus advances to the hypothesis that "many systems of civilization—or epochs of it—possibly even the whole of humanity—have become 'neurotic' under the pressure of the civilizing trends." [29] Hence Róheim, who follows the complexity of the master even when it leads to self-contradiction, asserts the "structural and fundamental identity of neurosis and civilization." [30] And in Freud's concept of the universal, or social, as distinct from the individual neurosis, the two are so intimately related that participation in the social neurosis spares the individual from the necessity of creating his own private neurosis; the religious believer "by accepting the universal neurosis is spared the task of forming a personal neurosis." [31]

Still sublimation remains the link between psychoanalysis and culture analysis. One can sympathize with the neo-Freudians' desire to formulate psychoanalysis as a social science; in view of Freud's ambiguities, one can sympathize with their abandonment of the concept of sublimation. But the concept of sublimation is a command to relate the human spirit (and its creations) to the human body. In abandoning the concept, the neo-Freudians abandon the body, and then inevitably have to return to autonomous spiritual concepts and norms traditional in Western culture and challenged by Freud. The concept of sublimation commands us to grasp social phenomena as pathological, in medical and scientific terms. When the neo-Freudians lose sight of the body, they abandon the scientific criticism of society, and either preach social adjustment or else fall back on their own private prejudices in favor of the "democratic personality" or the "self-actualizing personality" or whatever.

Couch and Culture

THE PSYCHOANALYTICAL theory of therapy has to be a theory of culture, not only because it has to find outlets in culture for the libido, but also because the becoming conscious of the unconscious, in which therapy consists, is itself a libidinal phenomenon, and therefore also a cultural phenomenon. As long as psychoanalysis retains the traditional notion of consciousness as something the nature of which is self-evident and self-evidently good, it has no difficulty in formulating its therapeutic goal—"Making conscious the unconscious," or "Where id was there shall ego be." [1] It is when asked to explain the process of making conscious the unconscious in terms of its own libido theory—that is, when asked to give a psychoanalytical theory of psychoanalysis itself—that the difficulties arise.

Psychoanalysis was forced to take account of the libidinal aspects of consciousness by the phenomenon of transference in the therapeutic situation. It became apparent that therapy by making conscious the unconscious could be attained only on the condition that the patient re-enact his repressed instinctual life during the analysis itself, giving expression to repressed emotions of love or hate by directing them against the real person of the analyst. The theoretical implications of this fact are twofold, and both are fully recognized by Freud himself. In the first place, repetition in real life is the precondition for reestablishing contact between consciousness and the unconscious: "This revision of the process of repression can only partially be effected by means of the memory-traces of the processes which led up to repression. The decisive part of the work is carried through by creating—in the relationship to the physi-

cian, in the 'transference'—new editions of those early conflicts." [2] And in the second place, the coming into consciousness
of the unconscious is itself a libidinal process, an act of love
directed at the real person of the physician: "The outcome in
this struggle is not decided by his intellectual insight—it is
neither strong enough nor free enough to accomplish such a
thing—but solely by his relationship to the physician. In so far
as his transference bears the positive sign, it clothes the physician with authority, transforms itself into faith in his findings
and in his views. . . . Faith repeats the history of its own origin; it is a derivative of love and at first needed no arguments." [3]

If psychoanalytical consciousness presupposes re-enactment
of the repressed past and is itself an act of love dependent on
the acquisition of a new love object in the real world, then the
possibility of attaining the classic therapeutic goal on the classic
therapeutic couch becomes inexplicable. For, in the first place,
if recollection depends on repetition, the therapeutic situation,
which necessarily limits the possibilities of repetition, limits the
possibilities of recollection and therefore of therapy.[4] And, in
the second place, the role of love for the physician in analytic
therapy makes it questionable whether there is any real distinction between analytic therapy and the earlier therapy by hyp-
notic suggestion, or for that matter between both of these and
religious techniques of shamanistic exorcism as old as humanity
itself. Freud himself said that faith was involved, and that the
analyst inherited the *numen* of the father-figure.

Freud first attempted a solution by laying down the prin-
cie that in psychoanalysis the transference itself should be regarded as a "new artificially acquired neurosis" and that therapy comes to an end with the dissolution of the transference
and the release of the patient from a state of tutelage.[5] But
common sense tells us, and Freud admits, that the transference
is not wholly dissolved.[6] The best evidence is in the physicians
themselves, in the feuds and loyalties inside the psychoanalytical movement. Glover in his polemics against Klein lets the cat
out of the bag: "The transferences and counter-transferences
developing during training analysis tend to give rise in the
candidate to an emotional conviction of the soundness of the
training analyst's theories. This means that many candidates

trained at the present time will for the next twenty-five years practise themselves and propagate the Kleinian precepts." [7]

And furthermore, if the transference is a "new edition of early conflicts," therapy must consist not in mere consciousness but in an inner change manifested in changed behavior.[8] But what kind of change can be regarded as cure? Therapeutic hacks can nonchalantly equate cure with "adjustment" to reality; but for Freud, the critic of reality, there was a problem.

Faced with these practical dilemmas, Freud in his later phase tended to restrict the role of therapist by restricting the transference. He tacitly withdrew the proposition that psychoanalytical consciousness presupposes re-enactment, and instead advanced the notion that the function of analysis was to substitute recollection ("historical truth") for repetition in the present: "The work of analysis progresses best when the patient's pathogenic experiences belong to the past so that the ego can stand at a distance from them." [9] In other words, historical consciousness of the past is no longer made dependent on changing history in the present, but is a substitute for it. Freud thus returns to the traditional notion of pure theory divorced from practice, not only implying its possibility but recommending it as therapy—that is to say, as practice. He is driven back to the traditional theory of pure consciousness, because he wants to avoid repetition and real discharge in the transference situation. Hence he has to invoke a consciousness that is above the instincts: "This struggle between physician and patient, between intellect and the forces of instinct, between recognition and the striving for discharge, is fought out almost entirely over the transference-manifestations." [10] Hence in his last work he says that therapy depends on the patient's "capacity for rising superior to the crude life of the instincts." [11]

Thus, in spite of disclaimers, Freud as therapist did not avoid sponsoring a *Weltanschauung*, and in fact sponsored his own personal solution to life's problems—the life of pure intellect. This return to traditional mind-body dualism is of course inconsistent with basic psychoanalytical theory. It is inconsistent with the basic theorem that the libido seeks objects in the external world, so that loss of objects in the outside world (narcissistic withdrawal) can be said to be a general precondition of all psychoneurotic disturbance. It is inconsistent with the theorem that consciousness is itself a creation of the instincts, mediating between them and the outside world and seeking instinctual gratification in the outside world.

The theory of therapy, especially the transference, requires a psychoanalytical theory of knowledge, or at least of psychoanalytical knowledge. If we retain the original insight that reenactment is a prerequisite for gaining consciousness of the repressed unconscious, we must suppose that there is no direct channel of communication between consciousness and the repressed unconscious, with the result that the repressed unconscious energies must go out into external reality before they can be perceived by consciousness. This conclusion is logical anyhow, if the hypothesis of the existence of a repressed unconscious is combined with the common-sense assumption that consciousness is oriented toward external reality. And in fact Freud develops this doctrine explicitly in *The Ego and the Id.* Defining consciousness as the superficies of the mental apparatus, forming a distinct system functioning nearest to the external world, he goes on to ask, "What does it mean when we say 'making the unconscious conscious'?" He excludes the possibility that unconscious ideas advance from within directly to consciousness, and advances the solution that "anything arising from within that seeks to become conscious must try to transform itself into external perceptions." He concludes by saying that by this assumption, and only by this assumption, can psychoanalysis and its knowledge be reconciled with "the theorem that all knowledge has its origin in external perception." [12]

How then does the unconscious "transform itself into an external perception" in order to become conscious? If this theorem is interpreted in the light of the transference phenomenon, then it follows that the repressed impulses must first find real objects in the external world and attach themselves to those real objects before their nature can become manifest to the subject. To put it crudely, the act of love (or hate) must accompany knowledge of repressed love (or hate). Freud, with his misgivings on the whole subject of transference, did not interpret his own theorem that the unconscious, in order to become conscious, must transform itself into external perceptions, as we have done, in the light of the transference. Instead, he says that the unconscious becomes conscious by getting connected with words—"the verbal images which correspond to it"; these verbal images are memory-residues of external perceptions; the work of analysis supplies verbal images of this kind which act as connecting links between the unconscious and consciousness.[13] If this complicated phraseology is reduced to its crude essence, it means that talk can cure, at least that talk can make the unconscious conscious. While one can appreciate the reasons why Freud, as therapist and as a man for whom pure theory made life worth living, would want to exalt the power of the word—his god Logos, as he says [14]—it is easy to demonstrate, with the aid of Freud, that words have no such power.

The notion of therapy by words does not do justice to the peculiar nature of the "dynamically unconscious repressed," which is "not capable of becoming conscious in the ordinary way," [15] but only through the special procedure of analysis, including transference. Granting that the ideas in the unconscious are "cathexes of memory-traces," [16] the memories referred to are distinctly not the ordinary kind of memory that can be revived through word associations. These memories belonged to the primary process in the id, and never were in consciousness; hence they never were "forgotten."

As will become clearer in the next chapter, the infantile sexual life which Freud discovered as the content of the dynamically unconscious repressed was not a real but a fantasy sexual life. It was a turning point in Freud's career when he was forced to the conclusion that hysterical patients' (psychoanalytically restored) memories were false, and "hysterical symptoms spring from phantasies and not from real events." [17] These "memory-traces" never were "forgotten," for the good and sufficient reason that they never happened. Such memories can hardly become conscious "by coming into connection with the verbal images that correspond to them," but only as a result of enactment. To quote Freud: "We may say that here the patient *remembers* nothing of what is forgotten and repressed, but that he expresses it in *action*. He reproduces it not in his memory but in his behaviour; he *repeats* it, without of course knowing that he is repeating it." [18]

Nor is the notion of making the unconscious conscious by the interposition of words compatible with what Freud says elsewhere about words. In his essay "The Unconscious," taking as his point of departure certain speech disorders in schizophrenia, he makes the distinction between "the *idea of the word* (verbal idea) and the *idea of the thing* (concrete idea)." [19] He goes on to say that "the conscious idea comprises both the concrete idea plus the verbal idea corresponding to it." If we apply this formula to the problem of making the unconscious conscious, it immediately becomes clear that words are not enough. The "thing" is also needed; but what is this "thing"? Freud says it is in the unconscious, as some kind of memory-trace; but above all he stresses that it is an energetic wish reaching to the external world: "The system Ucs [Unconscious] contains the thing—cathexes of objects, the first and true object-cathexes." The speech disorders of schizophrenia which provided his original point of departure show that it is not enough simply to have the words, for the distinctive feature of schizophrenia is precisely that "the object-cathexes are relinquished," while "the cathexis of the ideas of the words corresponding to the objects is retained." Word-consciousness is here presented not as cure, not as true consciousness, but as an intensification of the sickness which is also a halfway house to cure, or true consciousness:

> The cathexis of the verbal idea is not part of the act of repression, but represents the first of the attempts at recovery or cure which so conspicuously dominate the clinical picture of schizophrenia. These endeavors are directed toward regaining the lost objects, and it may well be that to achieve this purpose their path to the object must be by way of the word belonging to it; they then have, however, to content themselves with words in the place of things. [20]

Words, says Freud, are a halfway house to lost things; and words are only one class of the sets of symbols that make up human culture. "If we could not have schizophrenics we also could not have cultures," says LaBarre. [21] Freud's analysis of word-consciousness deepens our understanding not only of language as neurosis, but also of culture as neurosis and of culture as a "substitute-gratification," a provisional arrangement in the quest for real enjoyment.

This fuller appreciation of the true dimensions of real therapy defines the limitations of orthodox psychoanalytical therapy. Orthodox psychoanalytical therapy, with its emphasis on the role of verbalization in consciousness and its de-emphasis of the relation of consciousness to external reality, cultivates word-consciousness and calls it true consciousness. Freud recognized the limitations of analysis and knew how far he himself was from perfect knowledge. Of the effect of orthodox analysis on patients I do not attempt to judge. But the effect of orthodox analysis on the analysts themselves is there for all to judge in their official periodicals. The proportion of mere chatter—verbal gymnastics with Freudian terms with only fugitive relation to reality—bears comparison with the narcissistic overvaluation of words in schizophrenia. Nor does the relation between psychoanalysis and schizophrenia deprive it entirely of therapeutic value. Freud himself says that the overvaluation of words in schizophrenia "represents the first of the attempts at recovery or cure." If ultimate cure consists in finding real objects in external reality corresponding to the lost objects of childhood, then what psychoanalysis does is to effect an immense withdrawal of libido from the macrocosm of the external world, which Freud (and modern man in general) rightly could not love, and to direct it to the microcosm of the internal world. Such narcissistic withdrawal from the outside world is of course the characteristic posture of the libido in schizophrenia. In so far as this libidinal posture goes with a recognition of the unloveliness of the external world, it represents an advance in reality thinking. But in so far as psychoanalysis deflects attention from a further advance, to make external reality such that it can be loved, it can be an obstacle in the way of a final attainment of truth. For psychoanalysis—and before it the mystics—has taught that only when we can love the world can we have true knowledge of ourselves.[22]

The possibility of such a true knowledge of oneself, based not on alienation from oneself and from the world but on internal and external harmony, is examined by Freud in his essay on that social dreamer Josef Popper-Lynkeus. Freud recognizes that the truths which he himself discovered through "moral courage"—i.e., by courageous recognition of the contradictions between the libido and reality—could be absorbed into a higher level of knowledge in a utopia based on love. And then Freud rejects the utopian orientation as incompatible with "the processes of Nature" and "the aims of human society." [23] The rejection of the utopian perspective means that the libido so courageously, and narcissistically, withdrawn from the external world cannot return to the external world in the form of a project to transform it. Freud is left in alienation from reality and in pessimism.

Orthodox psychoanalytical therapy fails to direct the libido back to the external world in the form of a project to change the world; by the same token it fails to provide a solution to the problem of aggression. Psychoanalytical consciousness, by returning to the microcosm of the inner world, puts at the disposal of the ego large quantities of libido that were previously in a state of repression. The result—in so far as psychoanalytical consciousness gets through words to reality—is to make us aware for the first time of the scope and nature of our real desires—in Rilke's beautiful phrase, the unlived lines of our body. And then what is the psychoanalytically conscious ego going to do with its newly discovered desires? Once the limitations of sublimation and the impossibility of "rising above the crude life of the instincts" are recognized,[24] orthodox psychoanalysis, as a result of its inability to transform itself into social criticism, has to send human desire back into repression again. Freud's earlier optimistic hopes of precluding repression through psychoanalytical consciousness are replaced by the theorem that psychoanalytical consciousness "reconstructs the repressions from more solid material." [25] In other words psychoanalysis, after showing us the unlived lines of our body, tells us to forget them, presumably because they are not compatible with "the processes of Nature" or "the aims of human society." And of course the institution of these new "ego-sytonic controls," if we take Freud's theory of aggression seriously, means the internalization of the aggression released by all instinctual renunciation.[26]

Thus Freud found no way of avoiding the internalization of

aggression, the accumulation of guilt, which he himself showed to be a prime factor in the individual and in the social neurosis of mankind. These sad consequences for therapy follow because Freud accepted the inevitability of culture as it is, with its two characteristics—"a strengthening of the intellect, which is beginning to govern instinctual life, and an internalization of the aggressive impulses, with all its consequent advantages and perils." [27]

The only alternative, the only way of avoiding "the intensification of the sense of guilt . . . until perhaps . . . it may swell to a magnitude that individuals can hardly support," [28] is to turn the aggression outward to the external world, as the energy working to change the world. Therapy is war: the question is only which side to choose and which enemy to make. Freud envisioned therapy as based on an alliance between the ego and the reality-principle against the id:

> The position is like a civil war which can only be decided with the help of an ally from without. The analytical physician and the weakened ego of the patient, basing themselves on the real external world, are to combine against the enemies, the instinctual demands of the id and the moral demands of the super-ego. [29]

But there is an alternative—to ally the ego and the id against reality. Apart from certain emotional attitudes—his resignation before the inevitable frustrations of culture, his hostility to the "crude life of the instincts" which he courageously explored—Freud was prevented from envisaging this alternative by theoretical ambiguities in his formulation of the reality-principle. He tells that the mature and rational ego must accept the reality-principle, must substitute the reality-principle for the pleasure-principle which reigns supreme in the id. [30] Of course the rational ego must accept facts as facts, and avoid wishful thinking. But recognition of the world as it is by no means excludes desire or activity to change it, in order to bring reality into conformity with the pleasure-principle. [31] In fact, if we hold fast to the Freudian insight into the immortal strength of our repressed desires, changing reality can be the only rational response of the ego to the contradiction between reality and the

pleasure-principle which reigns supreme in the id. In the conflict between the ego, the id, and reality, something has to give.
In a neurosis, according to Freud, the ego accepts reality and
its energy is directed against the id, but to maintain the repression it must ignore the part of reality associated with the
repressed wishes. In a psychosis the ego is overwhelmed by the
id, severs its connection with reality, and proceeds to create for
itself a new outer and inner world. The healthy reaction, according to Freud, like a neurosis, does not ignore reality; like
a psychosis it creates a new world, but, unlike psychosis, it
creates a new world in the real world; that is, it changes reality.

> Neurosis does not deny the existence of reality, it merely
> tries to ignore it; psychosis denies it and tries to substitute
> something else for it. A reaction which combines features of
> both of these is the one we call normal or "healthy"; it denies
> reality as little as neurosis, but then, like psychosis, is concerned
> with effecting a change in it. This expedient normal attitude
> leads naturally to some achievement in the outer world and
> is not content, like a psychosis, with establishing the alteration
> within itself; it is no longer *auto-plastic* but *allo-plastic*.[32]

Psychoanalysis, unless it is transformed into a critique of
reality, resembles a psychosis in being autoplastic in its aim as
well as in its faith in the magic word.

The transformation of psychoanalysis into a project to
change human culture is the solution to the unsolved problem
of the transference. The transference was necessary because
the unconscious can become conscious only if it is transformed
into an external perception, and the external perception had to
be based on enactment and on actual love (or hate). In more
technical terms, the unconscious can become conscious only
through projection onto the external world. But, as we shall see
in the next chapter, human culture is a set of projections of the
repressed unconscious. Like the transference, human culture is
created by the repetition compulsion and constantly produces
new editions of the infantile conflicts. Like the transference,
human culture exists in order to project the infantile complexes
into concrete reality, where they can be seen and mastered.
The essence of totemism, which Freud regarded as the primal

model of human culture, is the projection of the Oedipus complex onto a real (animal) substitute-object in the external world, and the establishment of the social group by complicity in this symbolic solution to the Oedipal problem.

Human history, as neurosis subject to the law of the increasing return of the repressed, through its long evolution from totemism to monotheism on the one hand and the modern state on the other, has projected more and more of the Oedipus complex into the external world, where it can be seen and mastered. Human culture is thus one vast arena in which the logic of the transference works itself out; the infantile fantasies which create the universal human neurosis cannot themselves be directly apprehended or mastered, but their derivatives in human culture can. Human consciousness can be liberated from the parental (Oedipal) complex only by being liberated from its cultural derivatives, the paternalistic state and the patriarchal God. Thus culture actually does for all mankind what the transference phenomena were supposed to do for the individual. In Freud's words, "They and only they render the invaluable service of making the patient's buried and forgotten love-emotions actual and manifest; for in the last resort no one can be slain *in absentia* or *in effigie*." [33] In the last resort, no one exists *in absentia* or *in effigie*; in the last resort the Oedipus complex exists only in its cultural derivatives; it exists only as long as the life in culture in the present perpetuates the infantile flight from death.

Psychoanalysis thus transformed into a science of culture would, of course, be able to dispense with its mysterious rites of individual initiation. The necessity, on which Freud insisted, of undergoing individual analysis in order to understand what psychoanalysis is talking about would be eliminated: the problem and the data would no longer be individual but social. I am not criticizing psychoanalytical therapy as a technique for restoring broken-down individuals to a useful role in society. Such a technique can be judged only pragmatically. Anything goes if it works, and, as Freud himself admitted, "getting religion" may serve better than psychoanalysis.

But psychoanalysis, thanks to the humanity of Freud, has also within it the possibility of being a new and higher stage in human consciousness as a whole, and a solution to the universal human neurosis. As such, psychoanalytical consciousness can only be the vision of the possibility of human living not based on repression. Itself a part of culture, psychoanalysis can have only the effect of withdrawing libido from culture and reality based on repression, and the only solution to the problem it thus creates is to mobilize libido and consciousness for the transformation of reality. But if psychoanalysis sets itself apart from or above culture, in withdrawing from the mechanism for changing reality it withdraws from reality altogether. If psychoanalysis believes that with magic words and autoplastic ego-modifications it can escape the universal neurosis, it develops a private psychosis instead. It then falls under what Freud called the curse of isolation. The essence of neuroses, as distinguished from culture, is, according to Freud, "that the neuroses are asocial structures; they endeavour to achieve by private means what is effected in society by collective effort." [34]

Apollo and Dionysus

A SOUND instinct made Freud keep the term "sublimation," with its age-old religious and poetical connotations. Sublimation is the use made of bodily energy by a soul which sets itself apart from the body; it is a "lifting up of the soul or its Faculties above Matter" (Swift's definition of religious enthusiasm).[1] "Writing poetry," says Spender, "is a spiritual activity which makes one completely forget, for the time being, that one has a body. It is a disturbance of the balance of body and mind."[2] "Mathematics," says Bertrand Russell, "rightly viewed, possesses not only truth, but supreme beauty— a beauty cold and austere, like that of sculpture, without any appeal to our weaker nature. . . . The true spirit of delight, the exaltation, the sense of being more than man, which is the touchstone of the highest excellence, is to be found in mathematics as surely as in poetry."[3] And, like the doctrine of a soul distinct from the body, sublimation, as an attempt to be more than man, aims at immortality. "I shall not altogether die," says Horace; "my sublimations will exalt me to the stars (*sublimi feriam sidera vertice*)."

Sublimation thus rests upon mind-body dualism, not as a philosophical doctrine but as a psychic fact implicit in the behavior of sublimators, no matter what their conscious philosophy may be. Hence Plato remains the truest philosopher, since he defined philosophy as sublimation and correctly articulated as its goal the elevation of Spirit above Matter. But, as Frazer showed, the doctrine of the external or separable soul is as old as humanity itself.[4]

The original sublimator, the historical ancestor of philosopher and prophet and poet, is the primitive shaman, with his techniques for ecstatic departure from the body, soul-levitation, soul-transmigration, and celestial navigation. The history of sublimation has yet to be written, but from Cornford's pioneering work it is evident that Platonism, and hence all Western philosophy, is civilized shamanism—a continuation of the shamanistic quest for a higher mode of being—by new methods adapted to the requirements of urban life. The intermediate links are Pythagoras, with his soul-transmigrations, and Parmenides, the great rationalist whose rationalistic vision was vouchsafed to him by the goddess after a ride through the sky to the Palace of Night.[5] The discovery of the shamanistic origins connects the historical investigation of Western philosophy with the psychoanalytical investigation. The shaman is far enough from us so that we can recognize that he is, to put it mildly, a little mad; and, as we have seen, psychoanalysis discerns an intrinsic insanity in sublimation. "Pure intelligence," says Ferenczi, "is in principle madness." [6]

The aim of psychoanalysis—still unfulfilled, and still only half-conscious—is to return our souls to our bodies, to return ourselves to ourselves, and thus to overcome the human state of self-alienation. Hence, since sublimation is the essential activity of soul divorced from body, psychoanalysis must return our sublimations to our bodies; and conversely, sublimation cannot be understood unless we understand the nature of the soul—in psychoanalytical terminology, the nature of the ego. Sublimation is the "ego-sytonic" way of disposing of libido. The deflection of libido from its original aim in sublimation is a deflection caused by the influence of the ego; the desexualization is the consequence of passing through the crucible of the ego. Sexual energy is bodily energy, and the desexualized is disembodied energy, or energy made soulful. Technically, therefore, we can ascribe the backwardness of the theory of sublimation to the backwardness of the psychoanalytical theory of the ego; but the backwardness of the psychoanalytical theory of the ego is really due to an existential factor—a hesitation to break with the great Western tradition of sublimation and the soul-body dualism on which it is based.

What orthodox psychoanalysis has in fact done is to reintroduce the soul-body dualism in its own new lingo, by hypostatizing the "ego" into a substantial essence which by means of "defense mechanisms" continues to do battle against the "id." Sublimation is disposed of by listing it as a "successful" defense mechanism.[7] In substantializing the ego, orthodox psychoanalysis follows the authority of Freud, who compared the relation of the ego to the id to that of a rider to his horse [8]—a metaphor going back to Plato's *Phaedrus* and perpetuating the Platonic dualism. But Freud's genius always somewhere transcends itself. The proper starting point is his formula in *The Ego and the Id:* "The ego is first and foremost a body-ego," "the mental projection of the surface of the body," [9] originating in the perceptual system, and, like the perceptual system, having the function of mediating between the body and other bodies in the environment. If we can come to understand how that body-ego becomes a soul distinct from a body, we shall understand sublimation; and, by the same token, we shall understand the conditions under which the soul can recover its natural function and be again a body-ego.

At the beginning of *The Ego and the Id* Freud says, "The ego has the task of bringing the external world to bear upon the id and its tendencies, and endeavours to substitute the reality-principle for the pleasure-principle which reigns supreme in the id. . . . The ego represents what we call reason and sanity, in contrast to the id which contains the passions." [10] The passage suggests that the force which constitutes the essence of the ego, and which it applies when it influences the id, is simply the reality-principle. In other words, the ego is simply a transparent medium between the id and the environment, and the force which causes repression and sublimation is out there in the environment.

This naïve equation of the ego and the reality-principle (and of repression and external reality) disappears from Freud's later writings, but not from the textbooks of psychoanalysis. Thus Fenichel: "The origin of the ego and the origin of the sense of reality are but two aspects of one developmental step." [11] The truth of the matter, according to Freud's later theory, is that the peculiar structure of the human ego results from its incapacity to accept reality, specifically the supreme reality of death and separation. The real achievement of *The Ego and the*

Id is the pioneering effort to make an instinctual analysis of the ego, to see what the ego does with Eros and Death. And in that analysis the point of departure for the human ego is death not accepted, or separation (from the environment, i.e., the mother) not accepted, or, in Freud's preferred terminology, object-loss not accepted.

The ego, to be sure, must always mediate between external reality and the id; but the human ego, not strong enough to accept the reality of death, can perform this mediating function only on condition of developing a certain opacity protecting the organism from reality. The way the human organism protects itself from the reality of living-and-dying is, ironically, by initiating a more active form of dying, and this more active form of dying is negation. The primal act of the human ego is a negative one—not to accept reality, specifically the separation of the child's body from the mother's body. As we saw in a previous chapter, this negative posture blossoms into negation of self (repression) and negation of the environment (aggression). But negation, as the dialectical logicians recognize, and as Freud himself came to recognize when he wrote the essay "On Negation," is a dialectical or ambivalent phenomenon, containing always a distorted affirmation of what is officially denied. To quote Freud: [12]

> Thus the subject-matter of a repressed image or thought can make its way into consciousness on condition that it is *denied*. Negation is a way of taking account of what is repressed; indeed, it is actually a removal of the repression, though not, of course, an acceptance of what is repressed. . . . Negation only assists in undoing *one* of the consequences of repression—namely the fact that the subject-matter of the image in question is unable to enter consciousness. The result is a kind of intellectual acceptance of what is repressed, though in all essentials the repression persists.

It is thus a general law of the ego not strong enough to die, and therefore not strong enough to live, that its consciousness of both its own inner world and the external world is sealed with the sign of negation; [13] and through negation life and death are diluted to the point that we can bear them. "The result is a kind of intellectual acceptance of what is repressed, though in all essentials the repression persists." This dilution of life is desexualization. In other words, sublimation must be understood in the light of Freud's essay "On Negation." Sublimations, as desexualizations, are not really deflections (changes of aim) of bodily Eros, but negations. Here again it becomes apparent that psychoanalysis, if it is to break through the barrier of repression, must break through the logic of simple negation, which is the logic of repression, and adopt a dialectical logic. The mode in which higher sublimations are connected with the lower regions of the body (as postulated by psychoanalytical theory) is the dialectical affirmation-by-negation. It is by being the negation of excrement that money is excrement; and it is by being the negation of the body (the soul) that the ego remains a body-ego.

The negative orientation of the human ego is inseparable from its involuted narcissism; both are consequences of separation not accepted. The point of departure for the human ego is object-loss: in fact, Freud once defined "the process of repression proper" as consisting in "a detachment of the libido from people—and things—that were previously loved." [14] But the object-loss is not accepted. To quote from *The Ego and the Id* again: "When it happens that a person has to give up a sexual object, there quite often ensues a modification in his ego which can only be described as a reinstatement of the object within the ego." [15] That is to say, the object is not "lost," but has to be actively negated, and, by the dialectical principle of affirmation-by-negation, the object is still affirmed (the identification). Thus, as a result of object-loss not accepted, the natural self-love of the organism is transformed into the vain project of being both Self and Other, and this project supplies the human ego with its essential energy. When the beloved (parental) object is lost, the love that went out to it is redirected to the self; but since the loss of the beloved object is not accepted, the human ego is able to redirect the human libido to itself only by deluding the libido by representing itself as identical with the lost object. In Freud's words, "When the ego assumes the features of the object, it forces itself, so to speak, upon the id as a love-object and tries to make good the loss of that object by saying, 'Look, I am so like the object, you can as well love me.' " [16] In technical Freudian terms, an identification replaces object-love, and by means of such identifications object-libido is transformed into narcissistic libido.

According to *The Ego and the Id,* the reservoir of narcissistic libido thus formed constitutes a store of "desexualized, neutral, displaceable energy" at the disposal of the ego, and it is this energy which is redirected outward to reality again in the form of sublimations.[17] Thus desexualization is an intrinsic character not just of sublimations, but of the energy constituting the ego, and this desexualization is the consequence of substituting for bodily erotic union with the world the vain, shadowy project of having the world within the self. To quote Freud, "The transformation of object-libido into narcissistic libido which thus takes place obviously implies an abandonment of sexual aims, a process of desexualization; it is consequently a kind of sublimation." [18] Thus the soul is the shadowy substitute for a bodily relation to other bodies.

The lost objects reinstated in the human ego are past objects; the narcissistic orientation of the human ego is inseparable from its regressive orientation, and both are produced by the dialectic of negation. The separation in the present is denied by reactivating fantasies of past union, and thus the ego interposes the shadow of the past between itself and the full reality of life and death in the present. What we call "character" is this shell imprisoning the ego in the past: "The character of the ego is a precipitate of abandoned object-cathexes." [19] What we call "conscience" perpetuates inside of us our bondage to past objects now part of ourselves: the super-ego "unites in itself the influences of the present and of the past. In the emergence of the super-ego we have before us, as it were, an example of the way in which the present is changed into the past." [20]

The regressive orientation keeps not only our moral personality (character, conscience) in bondage to the past, but also our cognitive faculty—in Freudian terminology, the ego's function of testing reality. The human ego, in its cognitive function, is no transparent mirror transmitting the reality-principle to the id; it has a more active, and distorting, role consequent upon its incapacity to bear the reality of life in the present. The starting point for the human form of cognitive activity is loss of a loved reality: "The essential precondition for the institution of the function of testing reality is that objects shall have been lost which have formerly afforded real satisfaction." [21] But the lost objects are retained and are what the cognitive ego is looking for, so that human consciousness has essentially an anamnestic aim. To quote again the essay "On Negation": [22]

> It is now no longer a question of whether something perceived (a thing) shall be taken into the ego or not, but of whether something which is present in the ego as an image can also be rediscovered in perception (that is, reality). . . . Thus the first and immediate aim of the process of testing reality is not to discover an object in real perception corresponding to what is imagined, but to *rediscover* such an object.

More generally, as stated in *The Interpretation of Dreams:* All thinking is nothing but a detour, departing from the memory of a gratification and following byways till it reaches the cathexis (Freud's word) of the identical memory, now reached by the path of motor action.[23] Despite Freud's formula about substituting the reality-principle for the pleasure-principle of the id, the ego does not abolish the pleasure-principle, but derives from it the energy sustaining its exploration of reality. Thus his fundamental theorem about the human libido—every object-finding is in reality a refinding [24]—is true of consciousness as well. Hence also human consciousness is inseparable from an active attempt to alter reality, so as to "regain the lost objects." [25] The reality which the ego thus constructs and perceives is culture; and culture, like sublimation (or neurosis) has the essential quality of being a "substitute-gratification," a pale imitation of past pleasure substituting for present pleasure, and thus essentially desexualized.

The more specific and concrete mechanism whereby the body-ego becomes a soul is fantasy. Fantasy may be defined as a hallucination which cathects the memory of gratification; [20] it is of the same structure as the dream, and has the same relation to the id and to instinctual reality as the dream. Fantasy and dreaming do not present, much less satisfy, the instinctual demands of the id, which is of the body and seeks bodily erotic union with the world; they are essentially, like neurosis, "substitute-gratifications."

Fantasy is essentially regressive; it is not just a memory, but the hallucinatory reanimation of memory, a mode of self-delusion substituting the past for the present—or rather, by negation identifying past and present. In fact, this "hallucinatory cathexis of the memory of a gratification" alone makes possible the primal act of negation, and constitutes the hidden affirmative content behind every formal negation (including repression). It is through fantasy that the ego introjects lost objects and makes identifications. Identifications, as modes of preserving past object-cathexes and thus darkening life in the present with the shadow of the past, are fantasies. Identifications as modes of installing the Other inside the Self are fantasies. Identifications, as masks worn by the ego to substitute itself for reality and endear itself to the id, are fantasies. By the same token, fantasies are those images already present in the ego which the ego in its cognitive function is seeking to rediscover in reality.

Fantasy, according to *The Interpretation of Dreams,* is the product of the primary process, the human organism's first solution to the problem of frustration, and the raw material for the secondary process in which the exitation arising from the need-stimulus is led through a detour, ending in voluntary motor action so as to change the real world and produce in it the real perception of the gratifying object.[27] Isaacs, who is one of the heretics in British psychoanalysis, is, despite the opposition of that stalwart defender of orthodoxy, Edward Glover, only carrying forward the thought of the later Freud when she says that "reality-thinking cannot operate without concurrent and supporting unconscious phantasies."[28] Fantasy is also the mechanism whereby the ego constructs the pregenital and genital sexual organizations. Again we follow Isaacs, who says that fantasy has the power to alter the body.[29] Perhaps we can say that since life is of the body, fantasy as the negation of life must negate specific bodily organs, so that there can be no fantasy without negation-alteration of the body.

As we saw in a previous chapter, the pregenital and genital organizations are constituted by regressive fantasies of union with the mother, attached to the specific organs where the infantile drama of separation is enacted. For example, the prototype of all "transformation of object-libido into narcissistic libido," and therefore the prototype of all sublimation (and probably the most satisfactory of all sublimations), is infantile thumb-sucking, in which, with the aid of a fantasy or dream of union with the mother, the child makes himself into both himself and his mother's breast. Altogether, therefore, the world of fantasy is that opaque shield with which the ego protects himself from reality and through which the ego sees reality; it is by living in a world of fantasy that we lead a desexualized life. In sublimation the erotic component, what is projected is these infantile fantasies, not the reality of the id. Sublimation is the continuation not of infantile sexuality but of infantile dreaming; it comes to the same thing to say that what is sublimated is infantile sexuality not as polymorphously perverse, but as organized by fantasies into the sexual organizations. "As long as man is suckled at a woman's breast," says Anatole France, "he will be consecrated in the temple and initiated into some mystery of the divine. He will have his dream." [30] Culture, therefore, the product of sublimation, is, in Plato's words, the imitation of an imitation; in Pindar's words, the shadow of a dream.

Fantasy is the clue to the human neurosis and a crux in psychoanalytical theory. Freud himself was somewhat equivocal on the question whether the ultimate pathogenic material in the human psyche was actual experience or fantasy. As late as 1918 he said that "this is the most ticklish question in the whole domain of psychoanalysis." [31] But it was a turning point in Freud's early career when he discovered that the buried cause of neurosis was not an actual event (for example, seduction in childhood) but fantasies: [32]

> One must never allow oneself to be misled into applying to the repressed creations of the mind the standards of reality; this might result in undervaluing the importance of phantasies in symptom-formation on the ground that they are not actualities; or in deriving a neurotic sense of guilt from another source because there is no proof of actual committal of any crime.

One is bound to employ the currency that prevails in the country one is exploring; in our case it is the neurotic currency.

The neurotic currency is wishes and thoughts, given reality in magic and in neurosis by the narcissistic principle of the omnipotence of thought. Hence Freud can say, "It is not really a decisive matter whether one has killed one's father or abstained from the deed; one must feel guilty in either case"; and "It is not primarily a matter of whether castration is really performed: what is important is that the boy believes in it." [33] Hence more generally neurotic symptoms derive not from the facts of infantile sexual life but from the fantastic theories of sexuality developed by children, and expressing the narcissistic wish to be the father of oneself. In fact it is the efflorescence of fantasy in infantile sexuality that necessitates the final catastrophic repression. Infantile sexuality is doomed because "its wishes are incompatible with reality" and it "has no real aim." [34]

Self-styled materialists argue that Freud, in turning from the memory of a real event to fantasy as the cause of neurosis, made a fatal "repudiation of life-experience" and "transition to unabashed idealism." [35] The "repudiation of life experience" and "unabashed idealism" is not Freud's, but humanity's. The recognition that we are all in practice idealists, alienated from our bodies and pursuing, like infantile sexuality itself, "no real aim," is the precondition for overcoming, in reality as well as in theory, the mind-body dualism. The real nature of the primal fantasies is revealed by the fact that they cannot be remembered, but only re-enacted. They exist only as a neurotic way of acting in the present, and only as long as the ego perpetuates the infantile flight from life-and-death and the infantile fantasy-substitutes for the reality of living-and-dying. Or to put it another way, they do not exist in memory or in the past, but only as hallucinations in the present, which have no meaning except as negations of the present.

In his later writings Freud repeats that "hysterical symptoms spring from phantasies, and not from real events," [36] but his interpretation of the "phylogenetic factor" or the "archaic heritage"—i.e., the factor not traceable to individual experience —in the etiology of neurosis causes fresh difficulties. He says that "all we can find in the prehistory of neurosis is that a child catches hold of this phylogenetic experience where his own experience fails him. He fills in gaps in individual truth with prehistoric truth." [37] It is plain from the quotation that the "phylogenetic" element is the same as the element of fantasy; the term "phylogenetic experience" really means that Freud is deriving the element in fantasy not derivable from real events in the history of the individual from real events in the history of the human race. Thus Freud's concept of the "archaic heritage" makes fantasy a real memory once more, only now it is "memory-traces of the experiences of former generations." [38]

This line of thought makes the Primal Father and the Primal Crime real historical events—real historical events which constitute the ultimate pathogenic material in the human psyche. But in an earlier chapter we argued that psychoanalysis breaks down if it has to explain neurosis by invoking history instead of explaining history as neurosis, and that the Primal Crime is a myth, a fantasy. It still remains true that each one of us is suffering from the trauma of becoming human, a trauma first enacted in the Ice Age and re-enacted in every individual born in the human family. But the legacy of the trauma is not an objective burden of guilt transmitted by an objective inheritance of acquired characteristics—as Freud actually postulated [39] —and imposing repression on the organism from outside and from the past, but a fantasy of guilt perpetually reproduced by the ego so that the organism can repress itself. Freud's myth of the Primal Crime still asserts the reality of the fantasy, and still maintains the repression; but an ego strong enough to live would no longer need to hallucinate its way out of life, would need no fantasies, and would have no guilt.

Fantasy, as a hallucination of what is not there dialectically negating what is there, confers on reality a hidden level of meaning, and lends a symbolical quality to all experience. The *animal symbolicum* (Cassirer's definition of man) is *animal sublimans*, committed to substitute symbolical gratification of instincts for real gratification, the desexualized animal. By the same token the *animal symbolicum* is the animal which has lost its world and life, and which preserves in its symbol systems a map of the lost reality, guiding the search to recover it. Thus, as Ferenczi said, the tendency to rediscover what is loved in all the things of the hostile outer world is the primitive source of symbolism. And Freud's analysis of words as a halfway house on the road back to things discloses the substitutive and provisional status of the life of symbolic satisfactions. Sublimations satisfy the instincts to the same degree as maps satisfy the desire to travel.[40] The *animal symbolicum* is man enacting fantasies, man still unable to find a path to real instinctual gratification, and therefore still caught in the dream solution discovered in infancy. Already in the construction of the infantile sexual organizations fantasy confers symbolical meaning on particular parts of the child's own body. In the oral phase the dream of union with the mother is supported by thumb-sucking, and in thumb-sucking the thumb is a symbolic breast. Similarly the anal organization involves the symbolic manipulation of feces. When infantile sexuality comes to its catastrophic end with the castration complex, the child, as Freud says, gives up the body but not the fantasies.[41] Nonbodily cultural objects (sublimations) inherit the fantasies, and thus man in culture, *Homo sublimans*, is man dreaming while awake (Charles Lamb's definition of the poet).[42] LaBarre's epigram expresses the literal truth: "A dollar is a solemn Sir Roger de Coverley dance, a codified psychosis normal in one sub-species of this animal, an institutionalized dream that everyone is having at once." [43]

Sublimation perpetuates the negative, narcissistic, and regressive solution of the infantile ego to the problem of disposing of life and death—in a word, it perpetuates the infantile dream —and yet there is a difference between sublimations and the infantile sexual organizations out of which they arise and which they perpetuate. After the castration complex the ego loses the body but keeps the fantasies. But in losing the body, the ego must in some sense lose the fantasies too (hence Freud speaks of the total abrogation of the Oedipus complex). Fantasies, like everything else, exist only in the present, as hallucinations in the present, and must be attached to objects in the present. According to psychoanalytical theory, after their detachment from the body (in Freud's blunt style, after masturbation is given up) they are projected into reality, forming that opaque medium called culture, through which we apprehend and manipulate reality.

How is this projection effected, and what is its significance? The answer is contained in Freud's late studies of denial, specifically fetishism as the result of denial. Starting from the castration complex, Freud shows that the fact of sexual differentiation both is and is not accepted, or rather that the fact of sexual differentiation from the mother is accepted only at the cost of finding in some other external object a symbolic substitute for the penis, "a compromise formed with the aid of displacement, such as we have been familiar with in dreams." [44] Sublimations are formed out of infantile sexuality by the mechanism of fetishism; sublimations are denials or negations of the fantasies of infantile sexuality, and affirm them in the mode of affirmation by negation. The original fantasies are negations; sublimations are negations of negations. The original activity of the infantile sexual organizations was symbolic; sublimations are symbols of symbols. Thus sublimation is a second and higher level of desexualization; the life in culture is the shadow of a dream.

It is this second level of desexualization or negation that gives us a soul distinct from the body. Freud points out that the simultaneous acceptance and denial in fetishism involves a split in the ego.[45] Of course there is a split inherent in the ego from the start by virtue of its origin in a trauma of separation not accepted and denied by fantasy. As Ferenczi says, "There is neither shock nor fright without some trace of splitting of personality . . . part of the person regresses into a state of happiness that existed prior to the trauma—a trauma which it endeavours to annul." [46] But while the infantile body-ego works out compromises between its soul (i.e., fantasies) and its body (the infantile sexual organizations), and, as Freud said, the child remains his own ideal,[47] the adult body-ego, as structured by the castration complex, has to break itself in two because it is called upon to choose between body and soul; it cannot abandon the body, and is not strong enough to give up the soul. By a process of "narcissistic self-splitting" the ego is divorced from the super-ego: the whole stratum of abandoned object-cathexes (identifications) which form its own character becomes uncon-

scious; and, in Schilder's terminology, the intellectual ego is split
from the body-ego.[48]

But the ego cannot get rid of the body: it can only negate
it, and by negating it, dialectically affirm it. Hence all symbolism, even in the highest flights of sublimation, remains body
symbolism. "The derisive remark was once made against psychoanalysis," says Ferenczi, "that the unconscious sees a penis
in every convex object and a vagina or anus in every concave
one. I find that this sentence well characterizes the facts." [49]
Infantile sexuality (in the infantile sexual organizations) negates
the world and attempts to make a world out of its own body.
Sublimation negates the body of childhood and seeks to construct the lost body of childhood in the external world. Infantile sexuality is an autoplastic compensation for the loss of the
Other; sublimation is an alloplastic compensation for the loss of
Self.

Hence the hidden aim of sublimation and the cultural process is the progressive discovery of the lost body of childhood.
As we saw in the last chapter, the repressed unconscious can
become conscious only by being transformed into an external
perception, by being projected. According to Freud, the mythological conception of the universe, which survives even in the
most modern religions, is only psychology projected onto the
outer world.[50] Not just mythology but the entirety of culture
is projection. In the words of Spender, "The world which we
create—the world of slums and telegrams and newspapers—is a
kind of language of our inner wishes and thoughts." [51]

The first breakthrough of the insight which flowers into
psychoanalysis occurs in German idealism, in Hegel's notion of
the world as the creation of spirit and, even more, in Novalis'
notion of the world as the creation of the magic power of fantasy. In fact, there is a certain loss of insight reflected in the
tendency of psychoanalysis to isolate the individual from culture. Once we recognize the limitations of talk from the couch,
or rather, once we recognize that talk from the couch is still
an activity in culture, it becomes plain that there is nothing
for psychoanalysis to psychoanalyze except these projections—
the world of slums and telegrams and newspapers—and thus
psychoanalysis fulfills itself only when it becomes historical

and cultural analysis. It also follows that consciousness of the repressed unconscious is itself a cultural and historical product, since the repressed unconscious can become conscious only by being transformed into an external perception in the form of a cultural projection.

Cultures therefore differ from each other not in the content of the repressed—which consists always in the archetypical fantasies generated by the universal nature of human infancy—but in the various kinds and levels of the return of the repressed in projections made possible by various kinds and levels of environment, technology, etc. Hence those psychoanalytically minded anthropologists who attempt to explain the varieties of culture from the variable actualities of infant-rearing practices are chasing a will-o'-the-wisp. The pathogenic material in culture, as in the individual, is not the real experience of childhood, but fantasy. Hence, on the other hand, psychoanalysis, as a new and higher mode of consciousness of the unconscious, was made possible by the industrial revolution and its new revelation, or projection, of human psychology. Psychoanalysis is part of the romantic reaction.

Sublimation is the search for lost life; it presupposes and perpetuates the loss of life and cannot be the mode in which life itself is lived. Sublimation is the mode of an organism which must discover life rather than live, must know rather than be. As a result of its origin in object-loss (first loss of the Other, then loss of Self) human consciousness (the ego) is burdened not only with a repressive function distinguishing men from other animals, but also with a cognitive function distinguishing men from animals. The human consciousness, in addition to the function of exploring the outside world, is burdened with the additional task of discovering the sequestered inner world. The result is an inevitable distortion of both the outer and the inner world. Projections, with their fetishistic displacement of inner fantasies, must distort the external world. In Freud's words, the boy saves his own penis at the cost of giving the lie to reality.[52] Projections bring the inner world to consciousness only under the general sign of negation or alienation; their relation to the inner world must be denied. Sublimation perpetuates the incapacity of the infantile ego to bear the full reality of living and dying, and continues the infantile mechanism (fantasy) for diluting (desexualizing) experience to the point where we can bear it. From the psychology of dreams Freud derived the basic law that the conscious system (the "secondary process") can cathect an idea only when it is able to inhibit any pain that may arise from that idea.[53] Sublimation inhibits pain by keeping experience at a distance and interposing a veil between consciousness and life. We project, says Freud, only those things about which we do not know and do not want to know,[54] so that we can know without knowing all. Again quoting Freud: [55]

> To be thus able not only to recognize, but at the same time to rid himself of, reality is of great value to the individual, and he would wish to be equipped with a similar weapon against the often merciless claims of his instincts. That is why he takes such pains to *project,* i.e., to transfer outwards, all that becomes troublesome to him from within. . . .
>
> A particular way is adopted of dealing with any internal excitations which produce too great an increase of unpleasure: there is a tendency to treat them as though they were acting, not from the inside, but from the outside, so that it may be possible to bring the shield against stimuli into operation as a means of defence against them. This is the origin of *projection,* which is destined to play such a large part in the causation of pathological processes.

The basic mechanism for producing this desexualization of life, this holding of life at a distance, is, as we have seen, negation; sublimation is life entering consciousness on condition that it is denied. The negative moment in sublimation is plain in the inseparable connection between symbolism (in language, science, religion, and art) and abstraction. Abstraction, as Whitehead has taught us, is a denial of the living organ of experience, the living body as a whole; [56] in Freud's words, "Subordinating sense-perception to an abstract idea was a triumph of spirituality [*Geistigkeit*] over the senses; more precisely an instinctual renunciation accompanied by its psychologically necessary consequences." [57] The dialectic of negation and alienation appears in the history of the sublimating consciousness as a law of ever increasing abstraction. Our deepest knowledge of ourselves is attained only on condition of the highest abstraction. Abstrac-

tion, as a mode of keeping life at a distance, is supported by
that negation of the "lower" infantile sexual organizations
which effects a general "displacement from below upwards" of
organ eroticism to the head, especially to the eyes: [58] *Os homini
sublime dedit caelumque videre jussit.* The audiovisual sphere
is preferred by sublimation because it preserves distance; the
incest taboo in effect says you may enjoy your mother only
by looking at her from a distance.[59] Whitehead too has criticized as a form of abstraction the restriction of cognition to
"a few definite avenues of communication with the external
world . . . preferably the eyes." [60] As life restricted to the seen,
and by hallucinatory projection seen at a distance, and veiled by
negation and distorted by symbolism, sublimation perpetuates
and elaborates the infantile solution, the dream.

If the mechanism of sublimation is the dream, the instinctual
economy which sustains it is a primacy of death over life in
the ego. The path which leads from infantile dreaming to sublimation originates in the ego's incapacity to accept the death
of separation, and its inauguration of those morbid forms of
dying—negation, repression, and narcissistic involution. The end
result is to substitute for the reality of living-and-dying the
desexualized or deadened life. This conclusion, so shattering to
the hope of finding in sublimation a "way out"—and therefore
omitted in the encyclopedias of psychoanalytical orthodoxy—
is squarely faced and stated by Freud in *The Ego and the Id:*
"By thus obtaining possession of the libido from the object-
cathexes, setting itself up as the love-object, and desexualizing
or sublimating the libido of the id, the ego is working in opposition to the purposes of Eros and placing itself at the service
of the opposing instinctual trends." [61]

And since the dialectic of sublimation in civilization is cumulative, cumulatively abstract and cumulatively deadening,
Freud's intuition that civilization moves towards the primacy of
intellect and the atrophy of sexuality is correct.[62] At the end
of the road is pure intelligence, and, in the aphoristic formula
of Ferenczi, "Pure intelligence is a product of dying, or at
least of becoming mentally insensitive." [63] But, as Freud also
stated in *The Ego and the Id*, this solution disrupts the harmony
between the two instincts, resulting in a "defusion of Eros into

aggressiveness": "After sublimation the erotic component no longer has the power to bind the whole of the destructive elements that were previously combined with it, and these are released in the form of inclinations to aggression and destruction." [64] Thus the path of cumulative sublimation is also the path of cumulative aggression and guilt, aggression being the revolt of the baffled instincts against the desexualized and inadequate world, and guilt being the revolt against the desexualized and inadequate self.

If there is a "way out" from the dialectic of cumulative repression, guilt, and aggression, it must lie not in sublimation but in an alternative to sublimation. To understand our present predicament we have to go back to its origins, to the beginning of Western civilization and to the Greeks, who taught and still teach us how to sublimate, and who worshiped the god of sublimation, Apollo. Apollo is the god of form—of plastic form in art, of rational form in thought, of civilized form in life. But the Apollonian form is form as the negation of instinct. "Nothing too much," says the Delphic wisdom; "Observe the limit, fear authority, bow before the divine." Hence Apollonian form is form negating matter, immortal form; that is to say, by the irony that overtakes all flight from death, deathly form. Thus Plato, as well as his shamanistic predecessors Abaris and Aristeas, is a son of Apollo. Apollo is masculine; but, as Bachofen saw, his masculinity is the symbolical (or negative) masculinity of spirituality. Hence he is also the god who sustains "displacement from below upward," who gave man a head sublime and told him to look at the stars. Hence his is the world of sunlight, not as nature symbol but as a sexual symbol of sublimation and of that sunlike eye which perceives but does not taste, which always keeps a distance, like Apollo himself, the Far-Darter. And, as Nietzsche divined, the stuff of which the Apollonian world is made is the dream. Apollo rules over the fair world of appearance as a projection of the inner world of fantasy; and the limit which he must observe, "that delicate boundary which the dream-picture must not overstep," [65] is the boundary of repression separating the dream from instinctual reality.

But the Greeks, who gave us Apollo, also gave us the alternative, Nietzsche's Dionysus. Dionysus is not dream but drunkenness; not life kept at a distance and seen through a veil but life complete and immediate. Hence, says Nietzsche, "The entire symbolism of the body is called into play, not the mere symbolism of the lips, face, and speech, but the whole pantomime of dancing, forcing every member into rhythmic movement" [66] (Rilke's "natural speech by means of the body" [67]). The Dionysian "is no longer an artist, he has become a work of art." [68] Hence Dionysus does not observe the limit, but overflows; for him the road of excess leads to the palace of wisdom; Nietzsche says that those who suffer from an overfullness of life want a Dionysian art.[69] Hence *he does not negate any more.* This, says Nietzsche, is the essence of the Dionysian faith.[70] Instead of negating, he affirms the dialectical unity of the great instinctual opposites: Dionysus reunifies male and female, Self and Other, life and death.[71] Dionysus is the image of the instinctual reality which psychoanalysis will find the other side of the veil. Freud saw that in the id there is no negation, only affirmation and eternity. In an earlier chapter we saw that the reality from which the neurotic animal flees in vain is the unity of life and death. In this chapter we have seen the dreams of infantile sexuality and of Apollonian sublimation are not, are negations of, the instinctual reality. The instinctual reality is Dionysian drunkenness; in Freud's words, "We can come nearer to the id with images, and call it a chaos, a cauldron of seething excitement." [72]

The human ego must face the Dionysian reality, and therefore a great work of self-transformation lies ahead of it. For Nietzsche was right in saying that the Apollonian preserves, the Dionysian destroys, self-consciousness. As long as the structure of the ego is Apollonian, Dionysian experience can only be bought at the price of ego-dissolution. Nor can the issue be resolved by a "synthesis" of the Apollonian and the Dionysian; the problem is the construction of a Dionysian ego. Hence the later Nietzsche preaches Dionysus, and to see in this Dionysus a synthesis of Apollo and Dionysus is to sacrifice insight for peace of mind. Not only does Dionysus without the Dionysian ego threaten us with dissolution of consciousness; he also threatens us with that "genuine witches' brew," "that horrible mixture of sensuality and cruelty" (Nietzsche again [73]), which is the revolt of the Dionysian against the Apollonian, and an ambivalent mixture, but no fusion, between the instinctual opposites.

Since we are dealing with bodily realities, not abstract intellectual principles, it is well to listen to one who knew not only the life of the mind, but also the life of the body and the art of the body as we do not—Isadora Duncan, who tells how she experienced the Dionysian ecstasy as "the defeat of the intelligence," "the final convulsion and sinking down into nothingness that often leads to the gravest disasters—for the intelligence and the spirit." [74] But her Dionysian ecstasy is the orgasm —that one moment, she says, worth more and more desirable than all else in the universe. The Dionysian ego would be freed from genital organization and of that necessity of "ridding the organism of sexual cravings and concentrating these in the genital" (Ferenczi [75]). While the Apollonian ego is the ego of genital organization, the Dionysian ego would be once more a body-ego and would not have to be dissolved in body-rapture.

The work of constructing a Dionysian ego is immense; but there are signs that it is already under way. If we can discern the Dionysian witches' brew in the upheavals of modern history—in the sexology of de Sade and the politics of Hitler— we can also discern in the romantic reaction the entry of Dionysus into consciousness. It was Blake who said that the road of excess leads to the palace of wisdom; Hegel was able to see the dialectic of reality as "the bacchanalian revel, in which no member is not drunk." [76] And the heirs of the romantics are Nietzsche and Freud. The only alternative to the witches' brew is psychoanalytical consciousness, which is not the Apollonian scholasticism of orthodox psychoanalysis, but consciousness embracing and affirming instinctual reality—Dionysian consciousness.

Part Five

STUDIES IN ANALITY

> But Love has pitched his mansion in
> The place of excrement.
>
> —YEATS *

We have tried to reshape psychoanalysis into a general theory of human nature, culture, and history. In this effort the concept of sublimation is crucial, and the last chapter attempted a technical revision both of the theory of sublimation and of the (interconnected) theory of the ego. It is time to confront these abstractions with the facts, to see what use they are for the interpretation of the actualities of human culture. And since the cutting edge of psychoanalysis is always paradox, we have chosen to investigate the most paradoxical of psychoanalytical specifications of sublimation, anality. "Perhaps the most astonishing of Freud's findings," says Ernest Jones, "and certainly the one that has evoked the liveliest incredulity, repugnance, and opposition, was his discovery that certain traits of character may become profoundly modified as the result of sexual excitations experienced by the infant in the region of the anal canal. I imagine that every one on first hearing this statement finds it almost inconceivably grotesque, a fact which well illustrates the remoteness of the unconscious from the conscious mind, for of the truth of the statement itself no one who has undertaken any serious psychoanalytical study can have any doubt." [1]

The Excremental Vision

A NY READER of Jonathan Swift knows that in his analysis of human nature there is an emphasis on, and attitude toward, the anal function that is unique in Western literature. In mere quantity of scatological imagery he may be equaled by Rabelais and Aristophanes; but whereas for Rabelais and Aristophanes the anal function is a part of the total human being which they make us love because it is part of life, for Swift it becomes the decisive weapon in his assault on the pretensions, the pride, even the self-respect of mankind. The most scandalous pieces of Swiftian scatology are three of his later poems—*The Lady's Dressing Room, Strephon and Chloe, Cassinus and Peter*—which are all variations on the theme:

Oh! *Caelia, Caelia, Caelia* ———.

Aldous Huxley explicates, saying, "The monosyllabic verb, which the modesties of 1929 will not allow me to reprint, rhymes with 'wits' and 'fits.' " [1] But even more disturbing, because more comprehensively metaphysical, is Swift's vision of man as Yahoo, and Yahoo as excrementally filthy beyond all other animals, in the fourth part of *Gulliver's Travels*. Nor is the anal theme a new feature in Swift's mature or later period; it is already adumbrated in *A Tale of a Tub*, that intoxicated overflow of youthful genius and fountainhead of the entire Swiftian apocalypse. The understanding of Swift therefore begins with the recognition that Swift's anatomy of human nature, in its entirety and at the most profound and profoundly disturbing level, can be called "The Excremental Vision."

"The Excremental Vision" is the title of a chapter in Middleton Murry's book (1954) on Jonathan Swift. [2] The credit for recognizing the central importance of the excremental theme in Swift belongs to Aldous Huxley. In an essay in *Do What You Will* (1929) he says, "Swift's greatness lies in the intensity, the almost insane violence of that 'hatred of the bowels' which is the essence of his misanthropy and which underlies the whole of his work." [3] Murry deserves credit for his arresting phrase, which redirects criticism to the central problem in Swift. Aldous Huxley's essay had no effect on Quintana's book *The Mind and Art of Jonathan Swift* (1936), which perfectly illustrates the poverty of criticism designed to domesticate and housebreak this tiger of English literature. Quintana buries what he calls the "noxious compositions" in a general discussion of Swift's last phase as a writer, saying, "From scatology one turns with relief to the capital verses entitled *Helter Skelter, or The Hue and Cry after the Attorneys going to ride the Circuit,* which exhibits Swift's complete mastery of vigorous rhythm." The excremental theme in the fourth part of *Gulliver's Travels* is dismissed as bad art (criticism here, as so often, functioning as a mask for moral prejudice): "The sensationalism into which Swift falls while developing the theme of bestiality. . . . Had part IV been toned down, *Gulliver's Travels* would have been a finer work of art." [4] It is reassuring to know that English literature is expounded at our leading universities by men who, like Bowdler, know how to improve the classics. The history of Swiftian criticism, like the history of psychoanalysis, shows that repression weighs more heavily on anality than on genitality. Psychoanalytical theorems on the genital function have become legitimate hypotheses in circles which will not listen to what Freud has to say about anality, or to what Swift had to say (and who yet write books on *The Mind and Art of Jonathan Swift*).

Even Huxley and Murry, though they face the problem, prove incapable of seeing what there is to see. After admitting into consciousness the unpleasant facts which previous criticism had repressed, they proceed to protect themselves and us against the disturbing impact of the excremental vision by systematic distortion, denunciation, and depreciation. It is a perfect example, in the field of literary criticism, of Freud's notion that the first way in which consciousness becomes conscious of a repressed idea is by emphatically denying it.[5] The basic device for repudiating the excremental vision is, of course, denunciation. Huxley adopts a stance of intellectual superiority—"the absurdity, the childish silliness, of this refusal to accept the universe as it is given." [6] Murry, echoing that paradoxically conservative philosopher of sexuality, D. H. Lawrence, adopts a stance of moral superiority—"so perverse, so unnatural, so mentally diseased, so humanly *wrong*." [7] The transparently emotional character of their reaction to Swift is then masked as a psychoanalytical diagnosis; the excremental vision is a product of insanity. Huxley speaks of the "obsessive preoccupation with the visceral and excrementitious subject," "to the verge of insanity," and suggests a connection between it and the "temperamental coldness" of Swift's relations to Stella and Vanessa, implying a disturbance in the genital function.[8]

Murry's attempt to transform Huxley's suggestions into a full-dress biography is a case study in perverted argumentation. The texts of the "noxious compositions" and the fourth part of *Gulliver* are crudely distorted, as we shall see later, so as to transform Swift's misanthropy into misogyny; then the entire excremental vision can be explained away as an attempt to justify his genital failure (with Varina, Vanessa, and Stella) by indicting the filthiness of the female sex. It is falsely insinuated that the excremental vision is restricted to Swift's latest phase. This insinuation not only has the advantage of suggesting that there is a Swiftian vision which is not excremental (on this point Huxley is more tough-minded than Murry); it has the further advantage of linking the excremental vision with Swift's final mental breakdown. The fact that the mental breakdown came ten years later (1742) will not stop anyone ignorant of psychopathology and determined to lobotomize Swift's scatology; the chronological gap is filled by an enthusiastic vision of Swift's mental breakdown as God's punishment for the scatology. The fact that the excremental theme is already prominent in the fourth part of *Gulliver* (1723) is explained away by a little psychoanalytical jargon buttressed by a little flight of historical imagination: "Evidently the whole complex was working in Swift's mind when he wrote the fourth part of *Gulliver*. . . . Its emergence at that moment may have been the outcome

of a deep emotional upheaval caused by the death of Vanessa."
The prominence of the same complex in the *Letter of Advice
to a Young Poet* (1721), two years before the death of Vanessa,
is ignored. Murry's amateur diagnosis finds the origin of the
entire complex in Swift's rejection by Varina (1696). It is
therefore essential to his thesis to regard *A Tale of a Tub*
(1696–1698) as uninfected by the complex. Murry sustains
this interpretation by averting his eyes from the prominence
of anality in the *Tale* and by interpreting the whole book
as wonderful tomfoolery which is not to be taken seriously—
that is, by a notion of comedy which denies meaning to wit.[9]

If the duty of criticism toward Jonathan Swift is to judge
him insane, criticism should be turned over to the psychoanalysts. They have risen to the occasion and have shown that
they can be counted on to issue a medical certificate of insanity
against genius. Their general verdict is substantially the same
as that of Huxley and Murry, with the addition of some hand-
some new terminology. Thus Ferenczi (1926): "From the psychoanalytical standpoint one would describe his neurotic behaviour as an inhibition of normal potency, with a lack of courage in relation to women of good character and perhaps with
a lasting aggressive tendency towards women of a lower type.
This insight into Swift's life surely justifies us who come after
him in treating the phantasies in *Gulliver's Travels* exactly as
we do the free associations of neurotic patients in analysis, especially when interpreting their dreams." [10] Karpman (1942):
"It is submitted on the basis of such a study of *Gulliver's
Travels* that Swift was a neurotic who exhibited psychosexual
infantilism, with a particular showing of coprophilia, associated
with misogyny, misanthropy, mysophilia and mysophobia." [11]
Greenacre (1955): "One gets the impression that the anal fixation was intense and binding, and the genital demands so impaired or limited at best that there was a total retreat from
genital sexuality in his early adult life, probably beginning with
the unhappy relationship with Jane Waring, the first of the
goddesses." [12]

In developing their diagnosis, the psychoanalysts, as might
be expected, trace the origin of Swift's neurosis to his earliest
childhood. If the psychoanalytical theory of the neuroses is

correct, we must abandon Murry's attempt to isolate the excremental vision as a late excrescence; we must also abandon Murry's thesis (interconnected with his attempt to salvage part of Swift for respectability) that until he was rejected by her, Swift's love for Varina (Jane Waring) was "the healthy natural love of a naturally passionate, and naturally generous nature." [13] We shall have to return to Huxley's more tough-minded literary judgment that Swift *is* the excremental vision, and to his more tough-minded psychological judgment that Swift's sexuality was structurally abnormal from the start. And the biographical evidence, most carefully analyzed by Greenacre, supplies more than enough confirmation. Swift lost his father before he was born; was kidnaped from his mother by his nurse at the age of one; was returned to his mother only three years later, only to be abandoned by his mother one month after his return to her at the psychoanalytically crucial Oedipal period.[14] By psychoanalytical standards such a succession of infantile traumata must establish more than a predisposition to lifelong neurosis.

The case, then, would appear to be closed. The psychoanalytical experts concur with the critics that Swift was mad and that his works should be read only as documents in a case history. Not just the fourth part of *Gulliver* and the "noxious compositions" but all of Swift. For if we cry "insane" to the objectionable parts of Swift, in all honesty we must hand the case over to the psychoanalysts. But after psychoanalytical scrutiny, there is nothing left of Swift that is not objectionable. We must not underestimate the ability of psychoanalysis to uncover the real meaning of symbols. For example, a psychoanalytical comment on Gulliver as a little man in a little boat on the island of Brobdingnag says that "the common symbolism of the man in the boat as the clitoris suggests the identification with the female phallus thought to be characteristic of the male transvestite." Similarly, psychoanalysis leaves the Dean's character without a shred of integrity. "Swift showed marked anal characteristics (his extreme personal immaculateness, secretiveness, intense ambition, pleasure in less obvious dirt [sc. satire], stubborn vengefulness in righteous causes) which indicate clearly that early control of the excretory function was achieved under great stress and perhaps too early." [15]

At this point common humanity revolts. If personal immaculateness, ambition, and the championship of righteous causes are neurotic traits, who shall 'scape whipping? And certainly no genius will escape if this kind of psychoanalysis is turned loose on literary texts. Common humanity makes us turn in revulsion against Huxley, Murry, and the psychoanalysts. By what right do they issue certificates of lunacy? By virtue of their own pre-eminent sanity? Judged for sanity and truthfulness, *Gulliver's Travels* will not suffer in comparison with the works of Murry and Huxley. Only Swift could do justice to the irony of Huxley condemning Swift for misanthropic distortion in a volume of essays devoted to destroying the integrity not only of Swift, but also of St. Francis and Pascal. Nor is the sanity of psychoanalysts—and their interpretations of what a man in a boat signifies—utterly beyond question. Only Swift could do justice to the irony of psychoanalysts, whose capacity for finding the anus in the most unlikely places is notorious, condemning Swift for obsessive preoccupation with anality. Fortunately Swift is not himself speechless in the face of these accusations of insanity:

> He gave the little Wealth he had
> To build a House for Fools and Mad.[16]

In Dr. Swift's mental hospital there is a room for Huxley and Murry; their religious eccentricities are prefigured under the name of Jack, the prototype of religious enthusiasm in *A Tale of a Tub*. For Huxley, as for Jack, it later came to pass that "it was for certain reported that he had run out of his Wits. In a short time after, he appeared abroad, and confirmed the Report by falling into the oddest Whimsies that ever a sick Brain conceived." [17] Swift has also prepared a room for the psychoanalysts with their anal complex; for are they not prophetically announced as those "certain Fortune-tellers in Northern America, who have a Way of reading a Man's Destiny, by peeping in his Breech"? [18]

The argument thus ends in a bedlamite babel filling the air with mutual accusations of madness. If we resist the temptation to stop our ears and run away, if we retain a psychiatric interest and a clinical detachment, we can only conclude that the accusations are all justified; they are all mad. And the crux of their madness is their proud insistence that everybody except themselves—Huxley, Murry, the psychoanalysts—are mad. We can only save ourselves from their madness by admitting that we are all mad. Psychoanalysis deserves the severest strictures, because it should have helped mankind to develop this kind of consciousness and this kind of humility. Freud saw psychoanalysis as the third great wound, comparable to the Newtonian and Darwinian revolutions, inflicted by science on human narcissism.[19] The Epigoni of Freud have set themselves up as a proud elect exempt from the general damnation. As we have argued elsewhere, the proper aim of psychoanalysis is the diagnosis of the universal neurosis of mankind, in which psychoanalysis is itself a symptom and a stage, like any other phase in the intellectual history of mankind.

If we reorient psychoanalysis in this direction, then a different method for the application of psychoanalysis to Swift (or any other literary figure) is in order. We no longer try to explain away Swift's literary achievements as mere epiphenomena on his individual neurosis. Rather we seek to appreciate his insight into the universal neurosis of mankind. Then psychoanalysis becomes a method not for explaining away but for explicating Swift. We are not disturbed by the fact that Swift had his individual version of the universal human neurosis; we are not even disturbed by the thought that his individual neurosis may have been abnormally acute, or by the thought that his abnormality may be inseparable from his art.

Intense suffering may be necessary, though not sufficient, for the production of genius; and psychoanalysis has never thought through its position towards the age-old tradition of an affinity between genius and madness. Perhaps there is that "necessity of doctors and nurses *who themselves are sick*" of which Nietzsche spoke.[20] Psychoanalysis is then not less necessary for the study of Swift, but more so, though in a different way. It is necessary in order to sustain the requisite posture of humility—about ourselves, about mankind, and toward genius. It is also necessary in order to take seriously the Swiftian exploration of the universal neurosis of mankind. The thesis of this chapter is that if we are willing to listen to Swift we will find startling anticipations of Freudian theorems about anality, about sublimation, and about the universal neurosis of mankind. To anticipate objections, let me say that Swiftian psychoanalysis differs from the Freudian in that the vehicle for the exploration of the unconscious is not psychoanalysis but wit. But Freud himself recognized, in *Wit and the Unconscious,* that wit has its own way of exploring the universal neurosis of mankind.

Psychoanalysis is apparently necessary in order to explicate the "noxious compositions"; at least the unpsychoanalyzed neurotic appears to be incapable of correctly stating what these poems are about. These are the poems which provoke Murry to ecstasies of revulsion—"nonsensical and intolerable," "so perverse, so unnatural, so mentally diseased, so humanly *wrong.*" What Murry is denouncing is the proposition that woman is abominable because she is guilty of physical evacuation. We need not consider whether the proposition deserves such denunciation, for the simple reason that it comes from Murry's imagination, not Swift's. Murry, like Strephon and the other unfortunate men in the poems, loses his wits when he discovers that Caelia -----, and thus unconsciously bears witness to the truth of Swift's psychological insight. Any mind that is at all open to the antiseptic wisdom of psychoanalysis will find nothing extraordinary about the poems, except perhaps the fact that they were written in the first half of the eighteenth century. For their real theme—quite obvious on a dispassionate reading— is the conflict between our animal body, appropriately epitomized in the anal function, and our pretentious sublimations, more specifically the pretensions of sublimated or romantic-Platonic love. In every case it is a "goddess," "so divine a Creature," "heavenly Chloe," who is exposed; or rather what is exposed is the illusion in the head of the adoring male, the illusion that the goddess is all head and wings, with no bottom to betray her sublunary infirmities.

The peculiar Swiftian twist to the theme that Caelia ----- is the notion that there is some absolute contradiction between the state of being in love and an awareness of the excremental function of the beloved. Before we dismiss this idea as the fantasy of a diseased mind, we had better remember that Freud said the same thing. In an essay written in 1912 surveying the disorder in the sexual life of man, he finally concludes that the deepest trouble is an unresolved ambivalence in the human attitude toward anality: [21]

> We know that at its beginning the sexual instinct is divided into a large number of components—or rather it develops from them—not all of which can be carried on into its final form; some have to be surpassed or turned to other uses before the final form results. Above all, the coprophilic elements in the instinct have proved incompatible with our aesthetic ideas, probably since the time when man developed an upright posture and so removed his organ of smell from the ground; further, a considerable proportion of the sadistic elements belonging to the erotic instinct have to be abandoned. All such developmental processes, however, relate only to the upper layers of the complicated structure. The fundamental processes which promote erotic excitation remain always the same. Excremental things are all too intimately and inseparably bound up with sexual things; the position of the genital organs—*inter urinas et faeces*—remains the decisive and unchangeable factor. The genitals themselves have not undergone the development of the rest of the human form in the direction of beauty; they have retained their animal cast; and so even today love, too, is in essence as animal as it ever was.

Again, in *Civilization and Its Discontents*, Freud pursues the thought that the deepest cause of sexual repression is an organic factor, a disbalance in the human organism between higher and lower functions: [22]

> The whole of sexuality and not merely anal erotism is threatened with falling a victim to the organic repression consequent upon man's adoption of the erect posture and the lowering in value of the sense of smell; so that since that time the sexual function has been associated with a resistance not susceptible of further explanation, which puts obstacles in the way of full satisfaction and forces it away from its sexual aim towards sublimations and displacements of libido. . . . All neurotics, and many others too, take exception to the fact that "*inter urinas*

et faeces nascimur." . . . Thus we should find, as the deepest
root of the sexual repression that marches with culture, the
organic defense of the new form of life that began with the erect
posture.

Those who, like Middleton Murry, anathematize Swift's
excremental vision as unchristian might ponder the quotation
from St. Augustine that Freud uses in both these passages.

That Swift's thought is running parallel with Freud's is
demonstrated by the fact that a fuller explication of the poems
would have to use the terms "repression" and "sublimation."
It is of course not ignorance but repression of the anal factor
that creates the romantic illusions of Strephon and Cassinus and
makes the breakthrough of the truth so traumatic. And Swift's
ultimate horror in these poems is at the thought that sublimation—that is to say, all civilized behavior—is a lie and cannot
survive confrontation with the truth. In the first of his treat-
ments of the theme (*The Lady's Dressing Room,* 1730) he
reasons with Strephon that sublimation is still possible:

> Should I the Queen of Love refuse,
> Because she rose from stinking Ooze?

Strephon should reconcile himself to—

> Such Order from Confusion sprung,
> Such gaudy Tulips rais'd from Dung.

But in *Strephon and Chloe* (1731) sublimation and awareness
of the excremental function are presented as mutually exclusive,
and the conclusion is drawn that sublimation must be cultivated
at all costs, even at the cost of repression:

> Authorities both old and recent
> Direct that Women must be decent:
> And, from the Spouse each Blemish hide
> More than from all the World beside . . .
> On Sense and Wit your Passion found,
> By Decency cemented round.

In *Cassinus and Peter,* the last of these poems, even this solution is exploded. The life of civilized sublimation, epitomized
in the word "wit," is shattered because the excremental vision
cannot be repressed. The poem tells of two undergraduates—

> Two College Sophs of *Cambridge* growth
> Both special Wits, and Lovers both—

and Cassinus explains the trauma which is killing him:

> Nor wonder how I lost my Wits;
> Oh! *Caelia, Caelia Caelia* sh—.

That blessed race of horses, the Houyhnhnms, are free from the illusions of romantic-Platonic love, or rather they are free from love. "Courtship, Love, Presents, Joyntures, Settlements, have no place in their thoughts; or Terms whereby to express them in their Language. The young Couple meet and are joined, merely because it is the Determination of their Parents and Friends: it is what they see done every Day; and they look upon it as one of the necessary Actions in a reasonable Being."[23] If the Houyhnhnms represent a critique of the genital function and genital institutions of mankind, the Yahoos represent a critique of the anal function.

The Yahoos represent the raw core of human bestiality; but the essence of Swift's vision and Gulliver's redemption is the recognition that the civilized man of Western Europe not only remains Yahoo but is worse than Yahoo—"a sort of Animals to whose Share, by what Accident he could not conjecture, some small Pittance of *Reason* had fallen, whereof we made no other use than by its Assistance to aggravate our *natural* Corruptions, and to acquire new ones which Nature had not given us." And the essence of the Yahoo is filthiness, a filthiness distinguishing them not from Western European man but from all other animals: "Another Thing he wondered at in the *Yahoos*, was their strange Disposition to Nastiness and Dirt; whereas there appears to be a natural Love of Cleanliness in all other Animals." The Yahoo is physically endowed with a very rank smell—"the Stink was somewhat between a *Weasel* and a *Fox*"—which, heightened at mating time, is a positive attraction to the male of the species. The recognition of the rank odor of humanity stays with Gulliver after his return to England: "During the first Year I could not endure my Wife or Children in my Presence, the very Smell of them was intolerable"; when he walked the street, he kept his nose "well stopt with Rue, Lavender, or Tobacco-leaves." The Yahoo eating habits are equally filthy: "There was nothing that rendered the *Yahoos* more odious, than their undistinguishing Appetite to devour everything that came in their Way, whether Herbs, Roots, Berries, corrupted Flesh of Animals, or all mingled together."

But above all the Yahoos are distinguished from other animals by their attitude towards their own excrement. Excrement to the Yahoos is no mere waste product but a magic instrument for self-expression and aggression. This attitude begins in infancy: "While I held the odious Vermin in my Hands, it voided its filthy Excrements of a yellow liquid Substance, all over my Cloaths." It continues in adulthood: "Several of this cursed Brood getting hold of the Branches behind, leaped up into the Tree, from whence they began to discharge their Excrements on my Head." It is part of the Yahoo ritual symbolizing the renewal of society: when the old leader of the herd is discarded, "his Successor, at the Head of all the *Yahoos* in that District, Young and Old, Male and Female, come in a Body, and discharge their Excrements upon him from Head to Foot." Consequently, in the Yahoo system of social infeudation, "this *Leader* had usually a Favourite as *like himself* as he could get, whose Employment was to *lick his Master's Feet and Posteriors, and drive the Female* Yahoos *to his Kennel.*" This recognition that the human animal is distinguished from others as the distinctively excremental animal stays with Gulliver after his return to England, so that he finds relief from the oppressive smell of mankind in the company of his groom: "For I feel my Spirits revived by the Smell he contracts in the Stable." Swift does not, as Huxley says he does, hate the bowels, but only the human use of the bowels.[24]

This demonic presentation of the excremental nature of humanity is the great stumbling block in *Gulliver's Travels*—an aesthetic lapse, crude sensationalism, says Quintana; a false libel on humanity, says Middleton Murry, "for even if we carry the process of stripping the human to the limit of imaginative possibility, we do not arrive at the Yahoo. We might arrive at his cruelty and malice; we should never arrive at his nastiness and filth. That is a gratuitous degradation of humanity; not a salutary, but a shocking one." [25] But if we measure

Swift's correctness not by the conventional and complacent prejudices in favor of human pride which are back of Quintana's and Murry's strictures, but by the ruthless wisdom of psychoanalysis, then it is quite obvious that the excremental vision of the Yahoo is substantially identical with the psychoanalytical doctrine of the extensive role of anal erotism in the formation of human culture.

According to Freudian theory the human infant passes through a stage—the anal stage—as a result of which the libido, the life energy of the body, gets concentrated in the anal zone. This infantile stage of anal erotism takes the essential form of attaching symbolic meaning to the anal product. As a result of these symbolic equations the anal product acquires for the child the significance of being his own child or creation, which he may use either to obtain narcissistic pleasure in play, or to obtain love from another (feces as gift), or to assert independence from another (feces as property), or to commit aggression against another (feces as weapon). Thus some of the most important categories of social behavior (play, gift, property, weapon) originate in the anal stage of infantile sexuality and—what is more important—never lose their connection with it. When infantile sexuality comes to its catastrophic end, non-bodily cultural objects inherit the symbolism originally attached to the anal product, but only as second-best substitutes for the original (sublimations). Sublimations are thus symbols of symbols. The category of property is not simply transferred from feces to money; on the contrary, money is feces, because the anal erotism continues in the unconscious. The anal erotism has not been renounced or abandoned but repressed.[26]

One of the central ambiguities in psychoanalytical theory is the question of whether the pregenital infantile organizations of the libido, including the anal organization, are biologically determined. We have elsewhere taken the position that they are not biologically determined but are constructed by the human ego, or rather that they represent that distortion of the human body which *is* the human ego. If so, then psychoanalysis concurs with Swift's thesis that anal erotism—in Swift's language, "a strange Disposition to Nastiness and Dirt"—is a specifically human privilege; on the other hand, psychoanalysis would differ from Swift's implication that the strange Disposition to Nastiness and Dirt is biologically given. It comes to the same thing to say that Swift errs in giving the Yahoos no "Pittance of Reason" and in assigning to Reason only the transformation of the Yahoo into the civilized man of Western Europe. If anal organization is constructed by the human ego, then the strange Disposition to Nastiness and Dirt is a primal or infantile manifestation of human Reason. Swift also anticipates Freud in emphasizing the connection between anal erotism and human aggression. The Yahoos' filthiness is manifested primarily in excremental aggression: psychoanalytical theory stresses the interconnection between anal organization and human aggression to the point of labeling this phase of infantile sexuality the anal-sadistic phase. Defiance, mastery, will to power are attributes of human reason first developed in the symbolic manipulation of excrement and perpetuated in the symbolic manipulation of symbolic substitutes for excrement.

The psychoanalytical theory of anal erotism depends on the psychoanalytical theory of sublimation. If money etc. are not feces, there is not much reason for hypothesizing a strange human fascination with excrement. By the same token it is hard to see how Swift could have come by his anticipation of the doctrine of anal erotism if he did not also anticipate the doctrine of sublimation. But Swift did anticipate the doctrine of sublimation. Full credit for perceiving this goes to William Empson. Referring to *A Tale of a Tub* and its appendix, *The Mechanical Operation of the Spirit,* Empson writes: [27]

> It is the same machinery, in the fearful case of Swift, that betrays not consciousness of the audience but a doubt of which he may himself have been unconscious. "Everything spiritual and valuable has a gross and revolting parody, very similar to it, with the same name. Only unremitting judgement can distinguish between them"; he set out to simplify the work of judgement by giving a complete set of obscene puns for it. The conscious aim was the defense of the Established Church against the reformers' Inner Light; only the psychoanalyst can wholly applaud the result. Mixed with his statement, part of what he satirized by pretending (too convincingly) to believe, the source of his horror, was "everything spiritual is really material;

Hobbes and the scientists have proved this; all religion is really a perversion of sexuality."

The source of Swift's horror, according to Empson, is the discovery of that relation between higher and lower, spiritual and physical, which psychoanalysis calls sublimation. Swift hit upon the doctrine of sublimation as a new method for the psychological analysis of religion, specifically religious enthusiasm. His new method sees religious enthusiasm as the effect of what he calls the "Mechanical Operation of the Spirit." At the outset he distinguishes his psychology of religion from traditional naturalistic psychology, which treats religious enthusiasm as "the Product of Natural Causes, the effect of strong Imagination, Spleen, violent Anger, Fear, Grief, Pain, and the like." If you want a distinctive label for Swift's new psychology of religion, it can only be called psychoanalysis. The first step is to define religious enthusiasm as "a lifting up of the Soul or its Faculties above Matter." Swift then proceeds to the fundamental proposition that "the Corruption of the Senses is the Generation of the Spirit." By corruption of the senses Swift means repression, as is quite clear from his explanation: [28]

> Because the Senses in Men are so many Avenues to the Fort of Reason, which in this Operation is wholly block'd up. All Endeavours must be therefore used, either to divert, bind up, stupify, fluster, and amuse the Senses, or else to justle them out of their Stations; and while they are either absent, or otherwise employ'd or engaged in a Civil War against each other, the Spirit enters and performs its Part.

The doctrine that repression is the cause of sublimation is vividly implied in the analogy which Swift sets up for the "Mechanical Operation of the Spirit": [29]

> Among our Ancestors, the Scythians, there was a Nation, call'd Longheads, which at first began by a Custom among Midwives and Nurses, of molding, and squeezing, and bracing up the Heads of Infants; by which means, Nature shut out at one Passage, was forc'd to seek another, and finding room above, shot upwards, in the Form of a Sugar-Loaf.

Swift affirms not only that the spirit is generated by repression of bodily sensuousness, but also, as is implied by the anal-

ogy of the Scythian Longheads, that the basic structure of sublimation is, to use the psychoanalytical formula, displacement
from below upward. Displacement from below upward, conferring on the upper region of the body a symbolic identity
with the lower region of the body, is Swift's explanation for
the Puritan cult of large ears: the ear is a symbolic penis. According to psychoanalysis, displacement of the genital function to another organ is the basic pattern in conversion hysteria. "Conversion hysteria genitalizes those parts of the body
at which the symptoms are manifested"; maidenly blushing,
for example, is a mild case of conversion hysteria—that is, a mild
erection of the entire head.[30] According to Swift's analysis of
the Puritans, "The Proportion of largeness, was not only lookt
upon as an Ornament of the Outward Man, but as a Type of
Grace in the Inward. Besides, it is held by Naturalists, that if
there be a Protuberancy of Parts in the *Superiour* Region of
the Body, as in the Ears and Nose, there must be a Parity also
in the *Inferior.*" Hence, says Swift, the devouter Sisters 'lookt
upon all such extraordinary Dilatations of that Member, as
Protrusions of Zeal, or spiritual Excrescencies" and also "in
hopes of conceiving a suitable Offspring by such a Prospect." [31]
By this road Swift arrives at Freud's theorem on the identity of
what is highest and lowest in human nature. In Freud's language: "Thus it is that what belongs to the lowest depths in
the minds of each one of us is changed, through this formation
of the ideal, into what we value highest in the human soul." [32]
In Swift's language: [33]

> Whereas the mind of Man, when he gives the Spur and
> Bridle to his Thoughts, doth never stop, but naturally sallies
> out into both extreams of High and Low, of Good and Evil;
> His first Flight of Fancy, commonly transports Him to Ideas
> of what is most Perfect, finished and exalted; till having soared
> out of his own Reach and Sight, not well perceiving how near
> the Frontiers of Height and Depth, border upon each other;
> With the same Course and Wing, he falls down plum into the
> lowest Bottom of Things; like one who travels the *East* into the
> *West;* or like a strait Line drawn by its own Length into a
> Circle.

Such is the demonic energy with which Swift pursues his vision that twice, once in *A Tale of a Tub* and once in *The Mechanical Operation of the Spirit,* he arrives at the notion of the unity of those opposites of all opposites, God and the Devil. Men, "pretending . . . to extend the Dominion of one Invisible Power, and contract that of the other, have discovered a gross Ignorance in the Natures of Good and Evil, and most horribly confounded the Frontiers of both. After Men have lifted up the Throne of their Divinity to the *Coelum Empyraeum; . . .* after they have sunk their *Principle* of *Evil* to the lowest Center . . . I laugh aloud, to see these Reasoners, at the same time, engaged in wise Dispute, about certain walks and Purlieus, whether they are in the Verge of God or the Devil, seriously debating, whether such and such Influences come into Men's Minds, from above or below, or whether certain Passions and Affections are guided by the Evil Spirit or the Good. . . . Thus do Men establish a Fellowship of Christ with Belial, and such is the Analogy they make between *cloven Tongues,* and *cloven Feet.*" [34] Empson has shown how and by what law of irony the partially disclaimed thought is Swift's own thought.

As we have argued elsewhere, psychoanalysis finds far-reaching resemblances between a sublimation and a neurotic symptom. Both presuppose repression; both involve a displacement resulting from the repression of libido from the primary erogenous zones. Thus the psychoanalytic theory of sublimation leads on to the theory of the universal neurosis of mankind. In the words of Freud: [35]

> The neuroses exhibit on the one hand striking and far-reaching points of agreement with . . . art, religion and philosophy. But on the other hand they seem like distortions of them. It might be maintained that a case of hysteria is a caricature of a work of art, that an obsessional neurosis is a caricature of religion and that a paranoic delusion is a caricature of a philosophical system.

Swift develops his doctrine of the universal neurosis of mankind in the "Digression concerning the Original, the Use and Improvement of Madness in a Commonwealth," in *A Tale of a Tub.* Here Swift attributes to Madness "the greatest Actions that have been performed in the World, under the Influence of

Single Men; which are, *the Establishment of New Empires by Conquest: the Advance and Progress of New Schemes in Philosophy; and the contriving, as well as the propagating of New Religions.*" Psychoanalysis must regret the omission of art, but applaud the addition of politics, to Freud's original list; Freud himself added politics in his later writings. And Swift deduces the universal neurosis of mankind from his notion of sublimation; in his words:

> For the *upper Region* of Man, is furnished like the *middle Region* of the Air; The Materials are formed from Causes of the widest Difference, yet produce at last the same Substance and Effect. Mists arise from the Earth, Steams from Dunghils, Exhalations from the Sea, and Smoak from Fire; yet all Clouds are the same in Composition, as well as Consequences: and the Fumes issuing from a Jakes, will furnish as comely and useful a Vapour, as Incense from an Altar. Thus far, I suppose, will easily be granted me; and then it will follow, that as the Face of Nature never produces Rain, but when it is overcast and disturbed, so Human Understanding, seated in the Brain, must be troubled and overspread by vapours, ascending from the lower Faculties, to water the Invention, and render it fruitful.

After a witty review of kings, philosophers, and religious fanatics Swift concludes: "If the *Moderns* mean by *Madness,* only a Disturbance or Transposition of the Brain, by force of certain *Vapours* issuing up from the lower Faculties; then has this *Madness* been the Parent of all these mighty Revolutions, that have happened in *Empire,* in *Philosophy,* and in *Religion.*" And Swift ends the Digression on Madness with a humility and consistency psychoanalysis has never known, by applying his own doctrine to himself: [36]

> Even I myself, the Author of these momentous Truths, am a Person, whose Imaginations are hard-mouthed, and exceedingly disposed to run away with his *Reason,* which I have observed from long Experience to be a very light Rider, and easily shook off; upon which account, my Friends will never trust me alone, without a solemn Promise, to vent my Speculations in this, or the like manner, for the universal Benefit of Human kind.

Swift, as we have seen, sees in sublimation, or at least certain kinds of sublimation, a displacement upward of the genital function. So much was implied in his attribution of genital signifi-cance to the Puritans' large ears. He makes a similar, only more elaborately obscene, derivation of the nasal twang of Puritan preachers. He also speaks of "certain Sanguine Brethren of the first Class," that "in the Height and *Orgasmus* of their Spirit-ual exercise it has been frequent with them *****; immediately after which they found the *Spirit* to relax and flag of a sudden with the Nerves, and they were forced to hasten to a Conclu-sion." Swift explains all these phenomena with his notion of sublimation: [37]

> The Seed or Principle, which has ever put Men upon *Visions* in Things *Invisible*, is of a corporeal Nature. . . . The Spinal Marrow, being nothing else but a Continuation of the Brain, must needs create a very free Communication between the Su-perior Faculties and those below: And thus the *Thorn in the Flesh* serves for a *Spur* to the *Spirit.*

Not only the genital function but also the anal function is displaced upward, according to Swift. The general theorem is already stated in the comparison of the upper Region of Man to the middle Region of the Air, in which "the Fumes issuing from a Jakes, will furnish as comely and useful a Vapour, as Incense from an Altar." [38] The idea is developed in the image of religious enthusiasts as Aeolists, or worshipers of wind. Swift is here punning on the word "spirit," and as Empson says, "The language plays into his hands here, because the spiritual words are all derived from physical metaphors." [39] Psychoanal-ysis, of course, must regard language as a repository of the psy-chic history of mankind, and the exploration of words, by wit or poetry or scientific etymology, as one of the avenues into the unconscious. [40] At any rate, Swift's wit, pursuing his "Physico-logical Scheme" for satirical anatomy, "dissecting the Carcass of Humane Nature," [41] asks where all this windy preaching comes from, and his answer gives all the emphasis of obscenity to the anal factor: [42]

> At other times were to be seen several Hundreds link'd to-gether in a circular Chain, with every Man a Pair of Bellows applied to his Neighbour's Breech, by which they blew up each other to the Shape and Size of a *Tun;* and for that Reason, with

great Propriety of Speech, did usually call their Bodies, their *Vessels.* When by these and the like Performances, they were grown sufficiently replete, they would immediately depart, and disembogue for the Public Good, a plentiful Share of their Acquirements into their Disciples Chaps.

Another method of inspiration involves a Barrel instead of a Bellows:

Into this *Barrel,* upon Solemn Days, the Priest enters; where, having before duly prepared himself by the methods already described, a secret Funnel is also convey'd from his Posteriors, to the Bottom of the Barrel, which admits of new Supplies Inspiration from a *Northern* Chink or Crany. Whereupon, you behold him swell immediately to the Shape and Size of his *Vessel.* In this posture he disembogues whole Tempests upon his Auditory, as the Spirit from beneath gives him Utterance; which issuing *ex adytis,* and *penetralibus,* is not performed without much Pain and Gripings.

Nor is Swift's vision of sublimated anality limited to religious preaching or *A Tale of a Tub.* In *Strephon and Chloe* the malicious gossip of women is so explained:

You'd think she utter'd from behind
Or at her Mouth were breaking Wind.

And more generally, as Greenacre observes, there is throughout Swift "a kind of linking of the written or printed word with the excretory functions." [43] When Swift writes in a letter to Arbuthnot, "Let my anger break out at the end of my pen," [44] the psychoanalytically uninitiated may doubt the psychoanalytical interpretation. But Swift makes references to literary polemics (his own literary form) as dirt-throwing (compare the Yahoos). More generally he meditates that "mortal man is a broomstick," which "raiseth a mighty Dust where there was none before; sharing deeply all the while in the very same Pollutions he pretends to sweep away." [45] In the *Letter of Advice to a Young Poet,* he advocates the concentration of writers in a Grub Street, so that the whole town be saved from becoming a sewer: "When writers of all sizes, like freemen of cities, are at liberty to throw out their filth and excrementitious

productions, in every street as they please, what can the consequence be, but that the town must be poisoned and become
such another jakes, as by report of great travellers, Edinburgh
is at night." [46] This train of thought is so characteristically
Swift's that in the *Memoirs of Martinus Scriblerus*, now thought
to have been written by Pope after talks with Arbuthnot and
Swift, the story of Scriblerus' birth must be an inspiration of
Swift's: "Nor was the birth of this great man unattended with
prodigies: he himself has often told me, that on the night before he was born, Mrs. Scriblerus dreamed she was brought to
bed of a huge ink-horn, out of which issued several large streams
of ink, as it had been a fountain. This dream was by her hus-
band thought to signify that the child should prove a very
voluminous writer." [47] Even the uninitiated will recognize the
fantasy, discovered by psychoanalysis, of anal birth.

It would be wearisome to rehearse the parallels to Swift in
psychoanalytical literature. The psychoanalysts, alas, think they
can dispense with wit in the exploration of the unconscious.
Fenichel in his encyclopedia of psychoanalytical orthodoxy refers to the "anal-erotic nature of speech" without intending to
be funny.[48] Perhaps it will suffice to quote from Ferenczi's essay on the proverb "Silence is golden" (for Ferenczi the proverb itself is one more piece of evidence on the anal character
of speech): [49]

> That there are certain connections between anal erotism and
> speech I had already learnt from Professor Freud, who told me
> of a stammerer all whose singularities of speech were to be
> traced to anal phantasies. Jones too has repeatedly indicated
> in his writings the displacement of libido from anal activities
> to phonation. Finally I too, in an earlier article ("On Obscene
> Words") was able to indicate the connection between musical
> voice-culture and anal erotism.

Altogether Ernest Jones' essay on "Anal-Erotic Character
Traits" [50] leaves us with the impression that there is no aspect
of higher culture uncontaminated by connections with anality.
And Swift leaves us with the same impression. Swift even anticipates the psychoanalytical theorem that an anal sublimation
can be decomposed into simple anality. He tells the story of a

furious conqueror who left off his conquering career when
"the *Vapour* or *Spirit*, which animated the Hero's Brain, being
in perpetual Circulation, seized upon that Region of the Human
Body, so renown'd for furnishing the *Zibeta Occidentalis*, and
gathering there into a Tumor, left the rest of the World for
that Time in Peace." [51]

The anal character of civilization is a topic which requires
sociological and historical as well as psychological treatment.
Swift turns to the sociology and history of anality in a poem
called *A Panegyrick on the Dean*. The poem is written as if
by Lady Acheson, the lady of the house at Market Hill where
Swift stayed in 1729–1730. In the form of ironic praise, it describes Swift's various roles at Market Hill, as Dean, as conver-
sationalist with the ladies, as Butler fetching a bottle from the
cellar, as Dairymaid churning Butter. But the Dean s greatest
achievement at Market Hill was the construction of "Two
Temples of magnifick Size," where—

> In sep'rate Cells the He's and She's
> Here pay their vows with *bended Knees*,

to the "gentle Goddess *Cloacine*." As he built the two out-
houses, Swift seems to have meditated on the question of why
we are ashamed of and repress the anal function:

> Thee bounteous Goddess *Cloacine*,
> To Temples why do we confine?

The answer he proposes is that shame and repression of anality
did not exist in the age of innocence (here again we see how far
wrong Huxley's notion of Swift's "hatred of the bowels" is):

> When *Saturn* ruled the Skies alone
> That *golden* Age, to *Gold* unknown;
> This earthly Globe to thee assign'd
> Receiv'd the Gifts of all Mankind.

After the fall—the usurpation of Jove—came "*Gluttony* with
greasy Paws," with her offspring "lolling *Sloth*," "Pale *Dropsy*,"
"lordly *Gout*," "wheezing *Asthma*," "voluptuous *Ease*, the
Child of *Wealth*"—

> This bloated Harpy sprung from Hell
> Confin'd Thee Goddess to a Cell.

The corruption of the human body corrupted the anal function and alienated the natural Cloacine:

> . . . unsav'ry Vapours rose,
> Offensive to thy nicer Nose.

The correlative doctrine in psychoanalysis is of course the equation of money and feces. Swift is carried by the logic of the myth (myth, like wit, reaches into the unconscious) to make the same equation: the age of innocence, "the *golden* Age, to *Gold* unknown," had another kind of gold. The golden age still survives among the Swains of Northern Ireland—

> Whose Off'rings plac't in golden Ranks,
> Adorn our Chrystal River's Banks.

But the perspectives now opening up are too vast for Swift, or for us:

> But, stop ambitious Muse, in time;
> Nor dwell on Subjects too sublime.

The Protestant Era

LUTHER describes the circumstances under which he received
the illumination which became the fundamental axiom
of the Protestant Reformation—the doctrine of justification by faith—in the following words: [1]

> These words "just" and "justice of God" were a thunderbolt
> in my conscience. They soon struck terror in me who heard
> them. He is just, therefore He punishes. But once when in
> this tower I was meditating on those words, "the just lives by
> faith," "justice of God," I soon had the thought whether we
> ought to live justified by faith, and God's justice ought to be
> the salvation of every believer, and soon my soul was revived.
> Therefore it is God's justice which justifies us and saves us.
> And these words became a sweeter message for me. This knowl-
> edge the Holy Spirit gave me on the privy in the tower.

Luther with his freedom from hypocrisy, his all-embracing
vitality, and his all-embracing faith, records the scene of his
crucial religious experience with untroubled candor. It was in
a tower of the Wittenberg monastery, where the privy was located. Grisar explains, "In olden times it was very usual to establish this adjunct on the city wall and its towers, the sewage
having egress outside the town boundaries." [2]

Luther's candor has been too much for the Lutherans. Recognizing the crucial importance of the "experience in the
tower," the *Thurmerlebnis*, as it is called in Lutheran hagi-
ography, Lutheran scholars have either monkeyed with the
texts in an attempt to separate the tower from the privy, or
else interpreted the tower not as a geographical location but as
an allegory of spiritual captivity. It was thus left to the Jesuit
Father Grisar (1911) to recover the facts, only to be received

by outcries, from Harnack and a pack of lesser Lutherans, that he was hitting below the belt, indulging in "vulgar Catholic polemics." [3]

When the smoke of controversy died away, the location of the *Thurmerlebnis* was established, but both the Jesuit and his Lutheran critics were agreed that the location was of no significance. Grisar agreed with Harnack that "the locality in which Luther first glimpsed this thought is of small importance"; he agreed with the Lutheran Scheel that Roman Catholics, like all Christians, believe that God is present everywhere. [4]

Psychoanalysis, alas! cannot agree that it is of no significance that the religious experience which inaugurated Protestant theology took place in the privy. The psychoanalytical theory of infantile sexuality and its sublimation insists that there is a hidden connection between higher spiritual activity and lower organs of the body. Ever since Freud's essay on "Character and Anal Erotism" (1908), psychoanalysis has accepted as a demonstrated theorem that a definite type of ethical character, exhibiting a combination of three traits—orderliness, parsimony, and obstinacy—is constructed by the sublimation of a special concentration of libido in the anal zone, and it is therefore labeled the anal character. [5] Erich Fromm, in one of his real contributions to psychoanalytical theory, showed the connection between Freud's anal character—with its orderliness, parsimony, and obstinacy—and the sociological type of the capitalist as delineated by Sombart and Max Weber. [6] And Weber, of course, followed by Troeltsch, Tawney, and others, postulated a far-reaching connection between the capitalist spirit and the ethic of Protestantism.

It is characteristic of the neo-Freudian school to which Fromm belongs to connect psychoanalytical categories with socio-historical categories; it is also characteristic of the neo-Freudian school to make such connections by sacrificing the primal psychoanalytical insight into the bodily base of all ideological superstructures. In Erich Fromm's *Escape from Freedom*, his study of the social psychology of Protestantism and capitalism, the concept of the "authoritarian character" is substituted for Freud's "anal character," and the "authori-

tarian character" is treated as an autonomous spiritual attitude with no basis in the body. With the loss of the Freudian
materialism of the body, psychology becomes in neo-Freudian
hands, as also in Jungian hands, once more what it was before
the Freudian revolution, a psychology of the autonomous soul.
This is the "advance" celebrated in neo-Freudian circles as
overcoming Freud's "biological orientation." Freud, says
Fromm, "mistook the causal relation between erogenous zones
and character traits for the reverse of what they really are."
What is primary is an "attitude," and if there is a reference to
the infantile erogenous zones, it is merely "the expression of
an attitude toward the world in the language of the body."
Hence Fromm explicitly repudiates the notion that there is anything anal about the anal character, except for residual and
peripheral use of anal imagery, to express "one form of related-
ness to others, rooted in the character-structure." Thus neo-
Freudianism returns to the wisdom that character is rooted in
character structure—that is to say, is autonomous from the
body.[7] It is therefore no surprise that Erich Fromm's study of
Luther in *Escape from Freedom* makes no reference to the
Thurmerlebnis or to anality.

It was therefore left to a psychoanalytically more orthodox
(though more amateur) writer, G. Rattray Taylor, in his recent book, *Sex in History,* to say that it was important that
Luther was sitting on the privy when he received his great moment of enlightenment.[8] But, as Rattray Taylor sees, to introduce the concept of the anal character into the discussion of
Protestantism is to raise a problem and not to solve it. For the
psychoanalytical theory of the anal character is involved in all
the ambiguities and contradictions of the general psychoanalytical theory of sublimation. Vulgar psychoanalytical dogmatists
—those for whom psychoanalysis is a closed system rather than
a problem—seem to believe that the adult anal character is to be
understood as a fixation to a trauma occurring in the process
of infantile toilet training—"the anal character traits formed in
the conflicts around this training," says Fenichel.[9]

But whatever merits this theory may have as a working
hypothesis in dealing with neurotically abnormal individuals,
when confronted with the anal character as a socio-historical

phenomenon it is useless. For, assuming that there is some connection between Protestantism and anality, the orthodox psychoanalytical dogma can yield no explanatory hypothesis except the notion that Protestantism is the result of a change in toilet-training patterns, presumably in the direction of greater strictness. Or, assuming that our capitalistic civilization exhibits anal neurotic traits on a mass scale and not just an individual scale, the orthodox psychoanalytical dogma can yield no program of social therapy except a change in toilet-training patterns, presumably in the direction of greater permissiveness.

But the attempts to validate this explanation of the anal character with historical or cross-cultural evidence have been not only unsuccessful but also halfhearted in the first place. And even if they were successful, the problem would not be solved, but only displaced by the problem of explaining the shift in parental attitudes toward the toilet training of children. Actually this whole approach makes parental attitude decisive and so betrays the classic Freudian axiom that the Child is Father to the Man. While apparently deriving the adult anal character from infantile anal erotism, it is really deriving infantile anal erotism from the adult anal character: the efficient cause is the cleanliness complex in the parents.[10]

Hence in the final result the orthodox psychoanalytical dogma ends in the same cul-de-sac as the neo-Freudian revisionists: adult anal character is derived from adult anal character. The only difference is that orthodox psychoanalysis views infantile sexuality as the mechanism for the transmission of the anal character from one generation to the next. And when called upon to explain a change in the character of a culture, orthodox psychoanalysis can have nothing to offer, because of the iron ring of psychological determinism it postulates, while the neo-Freudians at this point cease to be psychologists and invoke traditional non-psychological factors. For Erich Fromm, economic changes cause the changes in character structure; that is to say, capitalism generates the capitalistic spirit.[11]

This impasse illustrates concretely the difficulties in the theory of sublimation. Freud, with good evidence, postulated a far-reaching but mysterious connection between the human body and human character and ideology; but the rationale of the connection escaped him, and he was unable to provide the necessary links between his psychoanalytical postulate and the facts of human history. The neo-Freudians, on the other hand, open the door to historical considerations, but do so only at the cost of abandoning the theory of sublimation. They thus return to what are essentially pre-Freudian categories of man and history, decorated with unessential (and confusing) psychologistic patter.

At the abstract theoretical level, psychoanalytical paradox and historical common sense are so far apart that one can only despair of ever unifying them. It therefore seems inevitable that progress will be made, if at all, by concrete empirical investigation. And since in general psychoanalytical considerations grope so far beneath the surface that they can easily be dismissed as arbitrary constructions not based on facts, such concrete empirical investigations must take as their point of departure, not psychoanalytical imputations as to what may (or may not) be going on in the Unconscious, but historical fact.

Such a solid point of departure is provided by the historical fact that the Protestant illumination came to Luther while seated on the privy. Such historical facts are hard to come by (few of the world's great men had Luther's honesty), and historical science should make the most of them. The hypothesis to be investigated is that there is some mysterious intrinsic connection between the Protestant illumination and the privy. The issue is: What exactly does the privy mean to Luther? But since the theory of sublimation is at stake in such an investigation, we cannot use the theory of sublimation to impute to Luther's unconscious unconscious meanings for the privy. Rather we must rely on the historical evidence of his writings for documented fact as to what the privy meant to Luther (in psychoanalytical terms, his "associations" to the idea of the privy). Such an empirical investigation of Luther's writings reveals the existence of a middle term, unexplored by both the psychoanalysts and the historians, connecting the privy with Protestantism on the one hand and capitalism on the other. This middle term is the Devil.

Psychoanalytical studies of the Devil, following Freud himself, have emphasized the Oedipal aspect of the Devil, his status as a father-substitute, the ambivalent combination of emulation of and hostility against the father in the Devil, and the identity of God and the Devil (as father-substitutes) underlying their opposition.[12] The persistently anal character of the Devil has not been emphasized enough. The color pre-eminently associated with the Devil and the Black Mass is black—not because of his place of abode (a circular explanation) but because of the association of black and filth. "The painters paint the Devil black and filthy," says Luther. Equally persistent is the association of the Devil with a sulphurous or other evil smell, the origin of which is plainly revealed in the article "*De crepitu Diaboli*" in an eighteenth-century compendium of folklore. The climax of the ritual of the Witches' Sabbath was to kiss the Devil's posteriors or a facial mask attached to the Devil's posteriors. In the central ceremony of the Black Mass, as the Queen of the Sabbath lay prone, "The sacred host was prepared by kneading on her buttocks a mixture of the most repulsive material, faeces, menstrual blood, urine, and offal of various kinds." Hence Dante makes the still point of the turning world, round which he passes upward to Purgatory, Satan's anus; hence Bosch, in the panel depicting this world as Hell, enthrones Satan on a privy, from which the souls that have passed out of his anus drop into the black pit.[13]

Luther's idea of the Devil is a compound of current folklore, personal experience, and theological speculation; but of these ingredients the element of personal experience is decisive.[14] It is an error to think of Luther's diabolism, or the general diabolism of the period, as a reverberation of a medieval theme. The age which gave birth to Protestantism experienced the Devil with a peculiar immediacy, power, and pervasiveness, and Luther, who personally experienced the Devil with more immediacy, power, and pervasiveness than any other leader of the age, is in this respect only the most representative man of the age. Personal experience was the touchstone by which Luther tested current folklore of the Devil; and personal experience was, of course, the touchstone for his theological speculations.

In Luther's personal encounters with the Devil—remember

we are dealing with materialized apparitions—the anal character of the Devil is sensuously perceived and sensuously recorded by Luther (in his *Table-Talk*) with a gross concreteness that latter-day Protestantism cannot imagine and would not tolerate. An encounter with the Devil is for Luther an encounter with something black and "filthy." [15] Latter-day Lutheranism has encouraged the circulation of the stories of how the Devil threw ink at Luther, and Luther threw ink at the Devil; here the anality has a thin but sufficient disguise. [16] But there is no disguise in Melancthon's additional details: "Having been worsted by this saying the Demon departed indignant and murmuring to himself, after having emitted a crepitation of no small size, which left a train of foul odour in the chamber for several days afterwards." [17] Personal experience therefore authorized Luther to give credibility to the story of a Lutheran pastor to whom the Devil appeared in the confessional, blasphemed Christ, and "departed leaving a horrible stench." [18] The materialized anality which is the Devil consists not only of anal smells but also anal sights; twice at least Luther was assaulted by an apparition of the Devil "showing him his posterior." [19] And, as passages too numerous to cite show, Luther's most general word for the assaults of the Devil is the homely German verb *bescheissen.* [20]

As striking as the anality of the Devil's attacks is the anality of Luther's counterattacks. When Luther pours verbal abuse at the Devil or throws the ink at him, the anality of his weapons is perhaps disguised. But there is no disguise when Luther records that in one encounter, when Lutheran doctrines had not sufficed to rout the Devil, he had routed him *"mit einem Furz"* [21]—the same weapon the Devil used against Luther in Melancthon's story. Personal experience therefore authorized Luther to tell with approval the story of the lady who had routed the Devil with the same device. [22] Other anal weapons employed by Luther in his fight with the Devil—my language is here more refined than Luther's—are injunctions to "lick (or kiss) my posteriors" or to "defecate in his pants and hang them round his neck," and threats to "defecate in his face" or to "throw him into my anus, where he belongs." [23]

The last quotation exhibits the psychic logic and psycho-analytical understanding underlying Luther's warfare with the

Devil. The Devil is virtually recognized as a displaced material-ization of Luther's own anality, which is to be conquered by be-ing replaced where it came from. The same pattern of anal at-tack and counterattack is exhibited in Luther's notions of witch-craft. Luther says that "people who eat butter that has been bewitched, eat nothing but mud"; and as a counterattack on the witchcraft that is spoiling the butter-churning, he recom-mends "Dr. Pommer's plan" as the best—"Dr. Pommer came to the rescue, scoffed at the Devil, and emptied his bowels into the churn." [24]

Given the importance of the Devil in Lutheran theology—a subject to which we shall come in a moment—it is Luther's grossly concrete image of the anal character of the Devil that made the privy the appropriate scene for his critical religious experience. And the appropriate comment is not that milk-and-water piety, proposed by nineteenth-century Lutherans and assented to by the Jesuit Grisar, that "God is everywhere." We are reminded of Luther's acid test of a Christian teacher: "Does he know of death and the Devil? Or is all sweetness and light?" [25] Protestantism was born in the temple of the Devil, and it found God again in extremest alienation from God. The dark ambivalence of the situation is expressed in Luther's story of the proper answer to the Devil given by a monk sitting on the privy:

> Monachus super latrinam
> Non debet orare primam?
> Deo quod supra,
> Tibi quod cadit infra.[26]

The situation is apparently proverbial. Sir John Harrington wrote the same answer to the Devil on an emblem hung in the privy of his house: "To God my pray'r I ment, to thee the durt." [27] Whether or not there was a materialized apparition of the Devil in Luther's experience in the tower, the Devil was present in some sense of psychic reality. Again we must re-member the intimate and everyday familiarity of Luther's ex-perience with the Devil. The Wartburg castle was full of devils, who never left him at peace but "behave in such a way that he is never alone even when he seems to be so." In his old age Luther's steps were dogged by two particular devils, who walked with him whenever he went in the dormitory (*auf dem Schlafhause*). And the Wittenberg cloister, where the *Thurmerlebnis* took place, was no less full of devils.[28]

WE HAVE established the relation between the Devil and anality. We have now to establish the relation between the Devil and Protestantism. Everybody knows that Luther and Luther's Protestantism are haunted by a sense of the Devil; every time we sing *"Ein feste Burg"* and celebrate the victory over our "ancient foe" it stares us in the face. But rationalists nursed on eighteenth-century Enlightenment, and optimists nursed on nineteenth-century Liberalism, who themselves cannot take the Devil seriously, could not take Luther's Devil seriously. We are reminded of Baudelaire's epigram—"The neatest trick of the Devil is to persuade you he does not exist." [29] Luther's diabolism was regarded as either an individual psychological aberration or as a hang-over from medieval superstition. In this spirit Troeltsch, Weber, Tawney and their countless followers (including Fromm) have defined Protestantism simply as a new relation to God. Thus Troeltsch: "The whole change of view in Protestantism is summed up and expressed in its Idea of God"; the essence of Protestantism is "the reduction of the whole of religion . . . to that idea of God." [30]

But Protestantism and its social and psychological implications must be understood as a new relation to the Devil, a relation which explains the new relation to God. If we want to understand Luther, we may, if we like, take neither his God nor his Devil seriously, and substitute psychological explanations for both. What we may not do is to take one seriously and explain away the other. For Luther, as for John Wesley, "No Devil, no God." [31] In thus taking Luther's Devil as seriously as we take Luther's God, we draw on the twentieth-century reaction in theology against Enlightenment rationalism and Liberal optimism. The twentieth-century trend in Protestant theology is to restore to the Devil his due; the best-known example is Tillich's concept of the demonic.[32] The neo-orthodox trend has given Protestant scholarship a truer appreciation of the role of the Devil in Luther's thought. A typical achievement of the school is Obendiek's book *Der Teufel bei Martin Luther*, which demonstrates that Luther's anthropology is not merely incomplete, but rather falsified, if the idea of the Devil is omitted or slurred.[33]

"Far from decreasing the power of the Devil in the world, the Reformation brought him strong reinforcements"; so speaks the Devil's most authoritative historian.[34] The psychological premise of Protestantism is conviction of sin. Protestantism, as a new relation to God, is a response to a new experience of evil. The novelty consists first in the scope and intensity of the evil experienced, and second in the sense of absolute powerlessness in the face of it. This new experience of evil reaches back into the waning period of the Middle Ages; Protestantism and Protestant diabolism are the offspring of a long gestation. Huizinga writes of the fifteenth century: [35]

> Is it surprising that the people could see their fate and that of the world only as an endless succession of evils? Bad governments, exactions, the cupidity and violence of the great, wars and brigandage, scarcity, misery and pestilence—to this is contemporary history nearly reduced in the eyes of the people. The feeling of general insecurity which was caused by the chronic form wars were apt to take, by the constant menace of the dangerous classes, by the mistrust of justice, was further aggravated by the obsession of the coming end of the world, and by the fear of hell, of sorcerers and of devils. The background of all life in the world seems black. Satan covers a gloomy earth with his sombre wings.

In Luther this experience of omnipresent and uncontrollable evil generates the theological novelty that this world, in all its outward manifestations, is ruled not by God but by the Devil. "It is an article of faith," says Luther, "that the Devil is *Princeps mundi, Deus huius seculi.*" It is an article of faith, based on experience: "The Devil is the lord of the world. Let him who does not know this, try it. I have had some experience of it: but no one will believe me until he experiences it too." "The world and all that belongs to it must have the Devil as its master." "We are servants in a hostelry, where Satan is the householder, the world his wife, and our affections his children." "The whole world is possessed by Satan." "The whole world is enslaved to his machinations." "The world is the Devil and the Devil is the world." "Everything is full of devils, in the courts of princes, in houses, in fields, in streets, in water, in wood, in fire." [36]

Luther finds the autonomous demonic power of evil not only in the macrocosm of society but also in the microcosm of the individual. It is his experience of the dominion of Satan over the individual that generates another theological innovation, the denial of free will; Melancthon (in 1559) and other critics correctly apprehend the trend of Luther's thought when they call his predestinarianism Manichaean. Luther's predestinarianism is partly based on a sense of the power of temptation— "No man could face the devil with his free will" [37]—but at a deeper level it is based on the sense that temptation and sin are the work of an autonomous force outside of the individual. The result is to eliminate the traditional notion of vices, faults for which the individual is responsible, and substitute the Devil. "The German reformer and his disciples thus filled Germany with devils by diabolizing all vices." [38] A Lutheran compilation, the *Theatrum Diabolorum* (1569), lists the new discoveries, the devil of blasphemy, the dance-devil, the laziness-devil, the pride-devil, etc.

Not content with diabolizing the vices, Luther diabolizes the virtues also. Man is justified not by works but by faith alone; and faith is not a virtue in our power but a gift of God. The whole domain of traditional virtue, pejoratively re-evaluated as mere "works," is handed over to the Devil. "For seeing that, outside of Christ, death and sin are our masters and the devil our God and sovereign, there can be no power or might, no wit or understanding whereby we could make ourselves fit for, or could even strive after, righteousness and life, but on the contrary we must remain blind and captive, slaves of sin and the devil." Therefore, "in the man who does not believe in Christ not only are all sins mortal, but even his good works are sins." Hence piety in the Romish style is the devil's work: "The Devil lets his own do many good works, pray, fast, build churches, establish Masses and holy days, and behave as if he were quite holy and pious." "Men of holy works (*die Werk-heiligen*) are Satan's captive servants, no matter how much they appear outwardly to surpass others in good works and in strictness and holiness of life." Thus the Devil as "lord of the world," so that "men must think, speak and do what the Devil wills," is the guiding spirit behind the traditional religious virtue of pious works.[39]

And by the same token the Devil is seen to be the guiding spirit behind natural reason, the anchor sheet of natural virtue in the Aristotelian and Thomistic tradition. Reason is the Devil's "bride and whore." Not only is reason a positive enemy to scriptural faith, but it is also linked to the Aristotelian principle that good works make a man good. Reason is the source of all achievement in this world; but good works and achievements in this world are the domain of the Devil; therefore the teaching of reason can only be the Devil's teaching, and the voice of reason the voice of the Devil.[40] Even that citadel of later Protestant morality, conscience, does not escape Luther's devaluation of human virtue; he discovers its counterfeit character and transfers it to the Devil's account. "Conscience is a beast and bad devil. Hence the poets invented the Erinnyes and Furies, that is to say hellish devils which avenged all wrongdoing." "Conscience stands in the cruel service of the devil; a man must learn to find consolation even against his own conscience," which is the most cruel instrument of death.[41]

Luther's experience of the autonomous demonic could not but lead to new metaphysical formulations, formulations which attribute to the Devil an autonomy not granted him in medieval Catholic theology. How close Luther comes to Manichaeism— or for that matter how close Luther's favorite doctor Augustine is to Manichaeism—is an abstract question which produces only partisan answers and endless theological hairsplitting. Suffice it to say that Luther is compelled to reformulate the essential nature of the cosmic drama of Redemption. In the medieval synthesis—for Anselm, for Thomas, for Abelard—Redemption sets right the relation between man and God; the divine man atones mankind and God, either by paying the debt to God incurred by human sin, or by exhausting the wrath of God against mankind, or by melting the rebellion which estranged man from God. But for Luther the antagonists in the cosmic drama are not man and God, but God and the Devil, and the relation

between them is essentially combative; the incarnate God conquers the Devil. And man is passive in the cosmic drama of
Redemption. Man is no third power; he belongs either to Christ
or to the Devil. And man has no free will to determine his allegiance. As Obendiek puts it, we must think of the situation
as a battle between God and the Devil for control of the human will.[42]

True, Luther cannot permit his experience of dualism to
submerge Christianity's traditional faith in the monarchy of
God; to reconcile the two he has such formulations as that
God *permits* the Devil to rage or that God *withdraws* to leave
space for the Devil. But the net effect is still to recognize the
Devil's power as a positive antidivine structure in its own right.
Hence when Luther is arguing for man's lack of free will, he
does not simply argue from the omnipotence of God, but also
from the power and rights of the Devil and from original sin,
which established and perpetuates Satan's domination over mankind.[43] "In the Protestant Church, the Devil must have his pay,
and the Devil's pay is the soul of the sinner. Thus ever since the
days of the Reformation, Satan's power in this world has con-
siderably increased." [44] According to the more merciful Catholic
tradition, even those who had made pacts with the Devil might,
even in the eleventh hour, be saved by some outward act of
penitence (the "works" that Luther despised) or by the inter-
cession of the saints (another concept that fell victim to Protestant fundamentalism). The new Lutheran notion of inescapable
damnation takes over the Faust legend and makes it a profound
symbol of modern man.[45]

Nor does Christian faith withdraw the Christian from the
domination of Satan. Here the central doctrine is the impossibility of overcoming sin, a Lutheran innovation which, as
Troeltsch says, is all the more remarkable for being a diver-
gence from Pauline Christianity.[46] The doctrine of the impossibility of overcoming sin can be deduced from the doctrine of
the vanity of good works, and it results in the Lutheran dualism between the inner world of grace and the outer world of
works, the world of the spirit and the world of the flesh. Following Troeltsch's explication of the Lutheran position, we may
say that an active fulfillment of the Christian ideal is impossible

upon earth and realizable only in the future life. Hence the Lutheran conception of grace and of the impossibility of overcoming sin leaves no outwardly visible distinction between Christian and non-Christian. Christianity consists in the inner possession of grace, not in any outward achievement. Although to some extent faith should issue in good works, such good works affect neither the quality of Christian piety nor the fact of personal salvation.[47] This is tantamount to saying—and Luther says it—that the Christian remains under the dominion of the Devil, and nevertheless is lord over the Devil and the Devil has no power over him. This paradox means that the Christian is split into two dimensions, spirit that belongs to Christ and flesh that belongs to the Devil. Again we see the tremendous extension of the Devil's empire in Protestantism. The whole realm of visible reality, the world and the flesh, belong to the Devil; God has retired into invisibility—*Deus absconditus*.[48]

Not only does the Christian as flesh continue to be under the Devil, but as spirit he obtains the victory over the Devil by voluntary submission of himself as flesh to the Devil. The English reformer John Wycliffe had taken the dark view that here on earth God must obey the Devil;[49] in Luther's new *theologia crucis* the Christian, like Christ himself, must voluntarily submit to crucifixion by the Devil. "To take up the cross is voluntarily to take upon oneself and bear the hate of the Devil, of the world, of the flesh, of sin, of death." And as Christ harrowed hell by offering Himself for hell whole and entire (a point denied in Roman Catholic theology), so "God leads down to hell those whom He predestines to heaven, and makes alive by slaying." Hence it is one of the signs of predestination to heaven not merely "to be resigned in very deed to hell" but even to "desire to be lost and damned."[50]

It would be hard to find a clearer illustration of the actuality and effective power of that death instinct which Freud postulated and which the non-Freudian world has ridiculed. For hell, Luther said, is not a place, but is the experience of death, and Luther's devil is ultimately personified death.[51] Luther's new *theologia crucis* rejects the traditional Aristotelian-Thomistic goal of actualizing the potentialities of life as *amor concupis-*

centiae, and calls us to experience hell on earth, to experience life on earth as ruled by the death instinct, and to die to such a death-in-life, in the hope of a more joyful resurrection.

> Whoever is not destroyed and brought back by the cross and suffering to the state of nothingness, attributes to himself works and wisdom, but not to his God. . . . But whoever is annihilated by suffering (*exinanitus*) ceases to do anything, knowing that God is working in him and doing all. . . . For himself, this he knows, it is enough that he should suffer and be destroyed by the cross, so that he may advance more and more toward annihilation. This is what Christ teaches us in John iii.3: "Ye must be born again." If we are to be born again, we must first die and be raised with the Son of God [on the cross]; I say die, i.e., taste death as though it were present.[52]

It is the hope of a more joyful resurrection that alone saves Luther from the dominion of death. Satan is the lord of this life, but there is another life where Christ is King, and to have faith in the existence of that other life is to conquer this death-in-life while in it. To make psychological sense of Luther's central paradox we had to invoke Freud's two immortal antagonists, the life instinct and the death instinct. Under Luther's symbols, we perceive that Luther sees this life as being under the domination of the death instinct. Those who take Freud's *Civilization and Its Discontents* seriously can only agree, and must recognize Luther's insight as a decisive advance in the task, as old as human history, of reclaiming id territory for the human ego. This recognition of life as death-in-life reflects and crystallizes an immense withdrawal of libido from life.[53] In other words, whereas in previous ages life had been a mixture of Eros and Thanatos, in the Protestant era life becomes a pure culture of the death instinct. Luther's faith and grace—the hope of a more joyful resurrection—form an enclave in the dominion of death which will not bow the knee and call death life, but on the other hand they form no real exception to the fact that death has dominion over life. Luther cannot affirm life, but can only die to this death-in-life. Therefore for him, too, holy living is holy dying. "God . . . makes alive by slaying." [54]

Thus the insight of Protestantism is its insight into the dominion of death in life, and its service to life and to love is its

hope in another life which would be true life. The positive
features in Luther are his diabolism and his eschatology. Actually the diabolism and the eschatology are two sides of the
same coin. It would be psychically impossible for Luther to
recognize the Devil's dominion over this world (Luther is not
yet de Sade) without the faith that the Devil's dominion is
doomed, and that the history of man on earth will end in the
kingdom of God, when grace will be made visible. Hence it is
an integral part of Luther's position to believe, as the earliest
Christians had, that he is living in the last age of time. In fact,
in Luther's eyes the new power of the Devil points to the end
of time: our devils are far worse than those known in previous
ages; compared to ours, medieval devils are child's play; the
whole age is Satanic; the world cannot last much longer, and
"from so Satanic a world" Luther would fain be "quickly
snatched." [55]

Hence the decadence of Protestantism may be measured by
the decline of diabolism and eschatology. Theologies (including later Lutheranism) which lack a real sense of the Devil
lack Luther's capacity for critical detachment from the world,
lack Luther's disposition to fight the Devil, and end by calling
the Devil's work God's work. The elimination of diabolism
and eschatology are the theological premises for the degeneration of the social doctrine of Lutheranism into a "religious
sanction of the existing situation," to use Troeltsch's description.[56] Later Protestantism substituted for Luther's vision that
we are bondsmen in the Devil's hostelry the notion that our
calling is divinely appointed. "It is harder for the men of this
century to believe in the Devil than to love him," says Baudelaire,[57] and one of the ways of loving him is to call him God.
Already Luther had discerned that the worst of the new assaults of the Devil were those in which "one does not know
whether God is the devil or the devil God." [58] Decadent Protestantism does not have this problem.

Similarly, when Protestantism ceases to be able to affirm the
hope of a more joyful resurrection, it ceases to perform any service for the life instinct. Christianity cannot be separated from the
hope that some day, in spite of all the rational evidence, the kingdom of grace will be made visible. Neo-orthodox Protestant the-

ology, with its triumphant vindication of the demonic and its failure to produce an eschatology, is not hope, and it is in danger of becoming, like so much in the modern world, merely the love of death. Luther's ethic, like the ethic of primitive Christianity, is an interim ethic looking forward to the speedy abolition of its own premises. If neo-orthodox Christianity cannot foresee the kingdom of Christ on earth, it consigns this earth to the eternal dominion of Satan.

IF THE central axiom in Luther's attitude toward the world is the proposition that the Devil is lord of this world, then Luther's relation toward capitalism—and the general relation of Protestantism to capitalism—will have to be reformulated. Ever since Max Weber's celebrated essay, the socio-psychological literature on the question has been dominated by the notion that Protestantism's essential contribution to capitalism was the sanctification of secular vocations as appointed by God. The implication of this contention is, of course, that Protestantism is essentially friendly to capitalism. Since Luther is notoriously critical of capitalism, the basic contention involves the odd corollary that the founder of Protestantism was not really a Protestant, or at least not a Protestant in his social doctrine. Luther's explicit views on economic problems are therefore regarded as "traditionalist," "reactionary," medieval, and basically Catholic.[59]

But if the essence of Protestantism is that this world is ruled by the Devil, then in the first place the notion that our visible vocation in this world is appointed by God, while not formally inconsistent (since the Devil rules by God's permission), grossly misrepresents the psychological ambivalence of the Protestant attitude toward this world. And in the second place it is immediately obvious that the new Protestant attitude toward the world contains in itself the basis for a new critique of capitalism as precisely the work of the Devil—a new critique which is much more devastating in that it is capitalism itself, and not the "abuses" discerned by Catholic casuistry, that is indicted.[60]

Experience taught Luther that the Devil is lord of this world —the experience of his age, the waning Middle Ages, and the rise of capitalism. All around him Luther felt the irresistible attraction and power of capitalism, and interpreted it as the Devil's final seizure of power in this world, therefore foreshadowing Christ's Second Coming and the Devil's final overthrow.[61] "Accursed avarice and usury have utterly destroyed Germany." "Germany is sheerly swallowed up by the merchants and companies, by means of usury." "Usury lives all secure in Germany, and rages as if he were God and lord in all lands; no one may oppose him." "Leipzig is sunk in avarice: in short *mundus est diaboli, Genitivi casus, et diaboli, Nominativi casus*." (The world is the Devil's, and the people in it have become pure devils.) Denouncing the greed for gain, "Devour everything in the Devil's name," he cries; "Hell will glut you. Come, Lord Jesus, come, hearken to the sighing of Thy Church, hasten Thy coming; wickedness is reaching its utmost limit; soon it must come to a head, Amen." "God must intervene and make an end, as He did with Sodom, with the world at the Deluge, with Babylon, with Rome and such like cities, that were utterly destroyed. This is what we Germans are asking for." [62]

Our generation, which has happily thrown away the accumulated wisdom of the race as to the nature of the Devil, is liable to dismiss Luther's vision of the demonic in capitalism as mere rhetoric, as a way of expressing irrational and hysterical dislike. Thus Tawney on Luther: [63]

> Confronted with the complexities of foreign trade and financial organization, or with the subtleties of economic analysis, he is like a savage introduced to a dynamo or a steam-engine. He is too frightened and angry even to feel curiosity. Attempts to explain the mechanism merely enrage him: he can only repeat that there is a devil in it.

Tawney never sees that the proposition that "there is a devil in it" is Luther's most profound attempt to explain. We are beginning to realize that the mythical archetypes of the race, of which the Devil is one, say things which it is still not possible to say in any other way (unless psychoanalysis has found a way). Through the archetype of the Devil mankind has said something about the psychological forces, inside man himself, sustaining the economic activity which ultimately flowered into capitalism. The Devil is the lineal descendant of the Trickster and Culture-hero type in the primitive mythologies. The Trickster is a projection of the psychological forces sustaining the economic activity of primitive peoples; and the evolution of the Trickster, through such intermediary figures as the classical Hermes, into the Christian Devil, parallels the changing forms of human economic (especially commercial) activity.[64] Hence when Baudelaire and Blake declare the essentially Satanic character of commerce, they exploit a great mythological tradition to say something which has not yet been said in any other way.[65]

Luther's identification of the spirit of capitalism with the Devil draws on this tradition of the Devil as Trickster. For Luther the Devil is the father of lies, of deceit, of trickery (*List, Tücke, Schalkheit*), a robber and thief. And usury is, in Luther's eyes, self-evidently trickery, robbery, and theft also. But Luther, as always, brings the tradition up to date; his experience of the new capitalistic spirit and his conception of the Devil reciprocally influence each other. Thus Luther stresses the busy restlessness of the Devil (*emsig, unruhig*), and his mastery of all techniques (*Tausendkünstler*). Conversely, Luther's concept of the Devil as the personified death instinct sustains his vision of the usurer as a murderer, and usury as a plague killing Germany.[66]

The crucial point, however, is to see the essential connection between Luther's notion of the demonic character of capitalism and his new theology of the demonic. Luther says that the traffic in interest, "undoubtedly the greatest misfortune of the German nation," was invented by the Devil. Usurers, "the big world-eaters," are denounced as the servants of Mammon and the Devil, or as devils. The general trend toward acquisitiveness is seen as bondage to the Devil: "It is the world's way to think of nothing but money, as though it hung as soul and body. God and our neighbour are despised and the people serve Mammon. Horrible times will come, worse even than befell Sodom and Gomorrha." [67] With the general diabolization of the vices intrinsic in the new Protestant theology, usury becomes a devil rather than a sin; and Luther sees a characteristic feature of the modern age in the fact that the Devil has aggravated the form of his attacks, and instead of operating as in the Middle Ages through the petty nuisances of a noisy poltergeist, has made usury and heresy his main instruments.[68]

The autonomous demonic of capitalism, like the autonomous demonic altogether, is a consequence of original sin, and exhibits the structure of original sin. Original sin consists in the turning from God to other gods, more specifically in the attempt to make a god out of oneself. But the demonic of capitalism, at the deepest level, consists in its drive to become God and king of this world. "Usury lives securely and rages, as if he were God and lord in all lands." "There is therefore no worse enemy of mankind on earth, next to the Devil himself, than the covetous man and the usurer, for he wishes to become God over all men." The fundamental aim of Satan himself is the same as the fundamental aim of capitalism—to make himself *princeps mundi* and *deus huius seculi*. And Luther sees the final coming to power in this world of Satan in the coming to power of capitalism. The structure of the entire kingdom of Satan is essentially capitalistic: we are the Devil's property.[69] Hence Luther's deepest sentence on capitalism is the statement that "money is the word of the Devil, through which he creates all things, the way God created through the true word." [70] Money is, in the words of Ben Jonson's Volpone, "the world's soul." [71] In Luther's theology capitalism, as demonic, exhibits the essential structure of the demonic as ape of God, *simia dei*.[72]

Consequently the psychological commitment of Protestantism to capitalism is mediated by the notion of the Devil, not God, and can be understood only in the light of Luther's new *theologia crucis*. First of all, it is a consequence of Luther's notion of the objective autonomy of the demonic that bondage to capitalism, like bondage to tyrants, can no more be avoided than bondage to original sin: the Devil is lord of this world. "The world cannot go on without usury, without avarice, without pride, without whoring, without adultery, without murder, without stealing, without blaspheming of God and all manner of sins; otherwise the world would cease to be the world, and the world would be without the world and the Devil without the Devil. Usury must be, but woe to the usurers." To those who argued that his position on usury was unrealistic, in view of its prevalence, Luther replied, "It is nothing new or strange that the world should be hopeless, accursed, damned; this it had always been and would ever remain." Hence capitalism is the inevitable bondage to Satan consequent on original sin: "In truth the traffic in interest is a sign and a token that the world is sold into the Devil's slavery by grievous sins." [73]

What then shall the Christian do? On this point it is not possible to claim that Luther was consistent. Sometimes, in what Troeltsch would call a sectarian mood, he seems to contradict his own theology and prescribe complete avoidance of usury, as if the Christian could avoid bondage to Satan in this world. Sometimes, in a mood of more practical accommodation to this world, he lapses into essentially Catholic-scholastic casuistry about permissible and impermissible usury. But if we look to the essence of his new *theologia crucis,* then Luther's essential directive is to be in this world but not of it. The world is the Devil's hostelry, and we his captive bondsmen. But while our flesh is surrendered to the Devil, our spirit is not; hence "whosoever would walk peacefully in this world, must be money's guest, and money a guest with him," and maintain this detached attitude, unlike the attitude of the godless money-makers. By thus keeping the spirit free while surrendering the flesh to the Devil, the Christian, while in inevitable bondage to Mammon, is also lord over Mammon. [74]

Max Weber was not wrong in stressing the importance, for the spirit of capitalism, of Luther's critique of monasticism and the acceptance of this world and its secular vocations as the area where salvation is to be won. [75] The mistake was to leave out the crucifixion from Luther's theology of salvation. The Protestant surrenders himself to his calling as Christ surrendered himself to the cross. "To take up one's cross was understood under Popery to mean to scourge oneself as the monks do." But "to take up the cross means freely to take upon oneself and bear the hate of the Devil, of the world, of the flesh, of sins and of death." Therefore "it is not necessary for you, like monks and hermits, to take up a special cross: remain with people and in your calling *(Beruf)*; there the Devil and the World will lay cross enough upon you." [76] The Protestant surrender to calling and to capitalism is a mode of surrender to the Devil and to death.

The subsequent history of Protestantism's attitude toward capitalism confirms the centrality of the idea of the Devil. Luther's Protestantism rested on two fundamental psychological premises: a realistic recognition that this life is under the domination of the Devil and the death instinct, and a religious faith and hope in Christ's Second Coming to put an end to the dominion of death in life and make grace visible. It was only the mystical hope that made the realism psychologically bearable. Later Protestantism loses Luther's historical eschatology, his faith in the end of the world, and his hope that it would come soon. And then the realistic recognition of the dominion of the Devil and death in this world is no longer psychologically possible.

But with the enfeeblement of the sense of the Devil, as Troeltsch recognizes, "existing conditions, which are permanent because they are founded on reason or appointed by God, become more and more the normal condition, and the Christian ethic becomes, as modern Lutherans say increasingly, 'the truth of the natural order'; the work of Redemption consists more and more in the 'glorification of the natural order created by God.'" [77] Elsewhere Troeltsch recognizes that it is Luther's belief in the Devil and in the end of the world that saves him from the socially conservative interpretation placed upon him by later Lutherans.[78] With the elimination of the Devil, secular callings can be celebrated as simply appointed from God. Although Weber's and Troeltsch's interpretations of Luther are vitiated by attributing this position to him, Troeltsch does also recognize that it is a deviation from Luther when modern Lutherans exalt Luther's doctrine of the "calling" and interpret it as "a certain religious consecration and sanction of modern civilization." The happy consequences of the elimination of the Devil are celebrated by the Protestant Uhlhorn as quoted by Troeltsch: "With that the dualism of the present and the future life, of the natural and the supernatural, of Christian and worldly, of the perfect Christian and the average Christian, has been overcome. Science, trade, and commerce gain once more their free movement." [79]

From the standpoint of the original Protestant theology, the deification of capitalism and of the calling is the deification of the Devil, or at least an utter confusion between God and the Devil. From the psychoanalytical point of view, if the Devil is Death, and if capitalism is the Devil, then modern Protestantism's alliance with capitalism means its complete surrender to the death instinct.

It is therefore no accident that Tillich, the theologian who has done most to recover the sense of the demonic, is also the theologian who has done most to disentangle Protestantism from its alliance with capitalism. Tillich speaks like Luther when he speaks of "a demonic possession in the grip of which modern society lives," and of capitalism as "the demonry of autonomous economics," which, together with the demonry of nationalism, surpasses all others in significance for our times.[80] But again we wonder what the outcome of neo-orthodox theology is, as long as it fails to recover Luther's historical eschatology. Tillich's exponent James Luther Adams may say that "the way out of the present era can be found only if men can be released from the 'possession' of the demonic powers that now carry through or protect the bourgeois principle." [81] But as long as (to quote Tillich) "the Protestant principle cannot admit any identification of grace with a visible reality," [82] and cannot repeat with conviction the traditional Christian faith that the time will come when grace will be made visible, and that this goal is the meaning of history, it looks as if neo-orthodox theology will remain incapable of casting out demons, and therefore will be of limited service to the life instinct in its war against the death instinct. It diagnoses, but it does not cure.

WE BEGAN with the location of Luther's moment of illumination. We showed that the location could be connected with Luther's theology through the anal character of Luther's Devil. We then showed the centrality of the Devil in Luther's theology. Finally we showed that in Luther's theology capitalism is a manifestation of the Devil. We must now return to the problem of anality; the question is whether the demonic in Luther's higher theology and in his notion of capitalism retains its anal character, or whether the grossly anal character of the Devil in Luther's hallucinatory experiences remains quite distinct from his higher theology. We must return to the problem of sublimation.

Now whether we agree or disagree with the Freudian paradox of the scope of sublimated anality in the structure of civilization, there can, I think, be no doubt that Luther takes essentially the same point of view as Freud, and arrives at it from his knowledge of the Devil. Luther detects the Devil at work wherever he sees disguised (sublimated) anality, and conceives it to be the function of the Gospel to expose the disguise and reveal the anality behind the sublimation. "The Devil does not come in his filthy black colours, but slinks around like a snake, and dresses himself up as pretty as may be." "No thing is as hateful to the Devil as the Gospel, for that shows him up, so that he cannot conceal himself, and everyone sees how black he is." [83] Hence Luther's grossly anal abuse of the Devil is not hysterical rhetoric but a correct exposure of his exact nature.

Hence also, when Luther uses grossly anal imagery to denounce his opponents, the imagery is not to be criticized as vulgar abuse or explained away as part of Luther's "peasant background": the anal imagery strips the disguise off the Devil's instruments (to speak in theological terms), or (to speak in psychoanalytical terms) reveals the anality behind the sublimation. Thus—to give only a few examples—"The Devil has indeed smeared us well over with fools"; "The Devil fouls and poisons with his venom the pure and true knowledge of Christ"; "The members of the body must not wait till filth says and decrees whether the body is healthy or not. We are determined to learn this from the members themselves and not from the urine, excrement and filth. In the same way we shall not wait for the Pope and bishops in Council to say: This is right. For they are no part of the body, or clean and healthy members but merely the filth of squiredom, merd spattered on the sleeve and veritable ordure, for they persecute the true Evangel, well knowing it to be the Word of God. Therefore we can see they are but filth, stench and limbs of Satan." [84]

And since the Devil is lord of this world, we may say, in psychoanalytical terms, that Luther sees civilization as having an essentially anal-sadistic structure, as essentially constructed by the sublimation of anality. Luther uses the verb *bescheissen* to describe the general nature of the Devil's attacks, and the function of grace is to make us clean. Thus Luther can describe the cosmic drama of Redemption in the following words: [85]

> Thanks be to the good God, who can so make use of the Devil and his wickedness, that it must all serve for our good; otherwise (were it up to his wicked will) he would quickly slaughter us with his knife, and stink us and stab us with his dung. But now God takes him into His hand and says: "Devil, you are indeed a murderer and a wicked spirit, but I will use you for my purposes; you shall be only my pruning-knife, and the world, and all that depends on you, shall be my manure-dung for my beloved vineyard."

To see the Devil as lord of this world is to see the world as a manure heap, to see universal filth: *"Scatet totus orbis,"* Luther says. The avarice in Leipzig is the Devil's work and by the same token "filth." [86] And since in Luther's historical eschatology the world was going to get worse before it got better, he sees the approaching end of the world as taking the form of a "rain of filth." The Second Coming will reduce sublimations to the anality out of which they are constructed. The Devil turns cow dung into a crown, but "Christ, Who will shortly come in His glory, will quiet them, not indeed with gold, but with brimstone." [87] And in this world, in line with Luther's new *theologia crucis,* though grace may keep the inward spirit clean, the Christian must surrender his flesh to the extremest assaults of anality. Here Luther picks up Bosch's vision of this world as a hell in which we pass through the Devil's digestive system: "We live in the Devil's worm-bag (*Madensack*)"; "We are nothing but a worm in ordure and filth, with no good or hope left in us, a loathsome abomination and object of scorn because of the loathsome stench and scorn for the sake of the cross." [88] Hence Luther expresses his readiness to depart this world in the formula, "I am the ripe shard and the world is the gaping anus." [89] The world's anus is the Devil's anus.

Here we see, to speak in psychoanalytical terms, the final identity of the Devil as death instinct and the Devil as anality. We can see also that Luther is under no illusion that faith liberates the Christian from the universal filth; such a position would contradict his basic notion of original sin. Luther's insight into the anal character does not mean that he does not share the anal character himself. Anal character belongs to the realm of the flesh, which remains in bondage to the Devil: "The Devil is moored to me with mighty cords." In such a way, presumably, Luther would interpret the anality of his own condemnation of anality. Luther's language in attacking the Papacy is, as we shall see in a moment, grossly anal; but he himself said, "I am the Pope's devil." [90]

Luther applies his general vision of civilization as anality in his appraisal of concrete specific social institutions, especially the social institution he knew best, the Papacy. Here again the degeneration of modern Protestantism makes it difficult for us to recognize, let alone take seriously, Luther's point of view. In this age of entente cordiale between Protestantism and Catholicism, it is rare to find Protestant intellectuals—simple Protestant fundamentalists tend to retain the wisdom of folly— who retain that vision with which Protestantism began, the vision of the Pope as devil incarnate (*leibhaftiger Teufel*) and as Antichrist.[91] And since neither Luther's view of the Papacy nor his view of the Devil is taken seriously, the substance of Luther's view of the Papacy is lost.

The superficial (liberal Protestant) view, with its implicit philosophy of progress, identifies Protestantism with the modern age (as it identifies Protestantism with capitalism) and Catholicism with medievalism. Then Luther's quarrel with the Papacy becomes a fight against the dead hand of the past which is obstructing Progress. But, as we have seen, Luther had no such idea of Progress; on the contrary, his philosophy of history is based on the axiom that things are getting worse and are approaching the end of the world. And consequently the Papacy is not for Luther the dead hand of the past, but representative of the demonic forces which are coming to power in the modern age: the Pope is Antichrist, who comes at the end of time. Luther's schism was intended to separate Protestantism not from the medieval, but from the modern world; again we see the profound change in Protestantism's social orientation.

correlative with the disintegration of Protestantism's original diabolism and eschatology.

"The Pope is the devil incarnate." "The Devil is the false god (*Abgott*) of the Pope." "The Devil founded the Papacy." "The Papacy is the Devil's church." "The Devil rules throughout the entire Papacy." "The Papacy is Satan's highest head and greatest power." "The Pope is *Satanissimus*." [92] These expressions are not rhetorical flourishes, but reflect the sober conviction which made the Protestant schism possible and necessary. Ultimately Luther's conviction that the Papacy is a demonry rests on his rejection of outwardly good works—that is to say, his conviction that visible reality is under the domination of the Devil. In Luther's eyes the ultimate sin of the Papacy is its accommodation to this world, its attempt to spiritualize this world: in psychoanalytical terms, its allegiance to the Platonic-Aristotelian ideal of sublimation. Given Luther's sense of the irredeemable (until the Second Coming) evil of this world, the effort to spiritualize this world only confuses the two realms which according to Lutheran theology must be kept separate, the flesh and the spirit. "The Papacy has so confused worldly and spiritual rule, that neither has stayed in its own power and right." "Under the Papacy the great and special secret has been forgotten, that Christ's kingdom is not a temporal, perishable, earthly kingdom, but a spiritual one." [93]

But this confusion of good works with grace, of the earthly and the heavenly, is, as we have seen, the finest trick of the Devil, the Father of Lies, in order to secure man's allegiance to the world and the flesh and the Devil. Hence the Papacy exhibits all the characteristic symptoms of demonic possession. First of all the Papacy exhibits a drive for power: "That which Christ denied and avoided, namely worldly rule, power and glory, that the Papacy pursues with raging madness." The structure of this power drive is essentially demonic; like the Devil himself, and like capitalism, the Pope seeks to be prince of this world and God on earth.[94] But money is the ultimate powerful word of the Devil; hence the Papacy reveals its allegiance to the Devil in its capitalistic spirit. "The God of the Papists is Mammon." [95] In Luther's denunciation of papal avarice, the affinity between the Papacy and the spirit of capitalism is seen particularly in the commercialization of ceremonies, such as the sale of indulgences. The dispute over the sale of indulgences dramatizes the anticapitalistic character of the Reformation. In Luther's eyes, "The Papists have made out of God a merchant, who would give the Kingdom of Heaven not freely, out of grace, but for money and human achievement." "Under the Papacy the Devil has established a market in souls." "The Papacy has made an annual market out of the Mass and out of the forgiveness of sins." [96] Hence the Papacy exhibits also that other structural feature shared also by the Devil and by capitalism (and, according to psychoanalysis, intrinsic to all sublimation): deception, lies, and tricks. The Papacy, as the Devil's church, is full of lies, theft, and robbery.[97]

But the structure of the demonic is essentially anal-sadistic; and so, says Luther, is the structure of the Papacy. That he says so is known to any reader of any except the most drastically expurgated editions of the *Table-Talk;* how he says so in serious theological writings may be sampled in the more than one hundred pages of his manifesto entitled "Wider das Pabstthum zu Rom, vom Teufel gestiftet." [98] All we suggest is that the facts be not suppressed or repressed, and the text, as the literary critics say, be allowed to speak for itself. To indicate in general, without the gross detail of the original, what may be found in the text, let me only say that the Papacy is the Devil's ordure, or the Devil is the Pope's ordure; Papal *gloria* is *stercus diaboli;* Papal decretals are the Pope's (or the Devil's) excretals; monastic life is "a latrine and the devil's own sweet Empire." Great play is made with the word *Furz,* especially in connection with the symbol of the Pope-Ass (*Pabstesel, Farzesel,* etc.) to reveal the anal-sadistic character of the Pope's words. The Pope's words are lies (*Lüge*), that is to say, farts, which get coined into money. The whole picture is based on Bosch's vision of the world as hell with the center of hell being the Devil's anus. "Because of God's wrath the Devil has bedunged us with big and gross asses at Rome." [99]

If there is anything to psychoanalysis, we must again regret the loss in modern Protestantism of Luther's insight into the problem of anality; thus the problem was surrendered by default to psychoanalysis. The degeneration set in early. Already in the seventeenth century, a true follower of Luther, arguing against no less an authority than Martin Bucer, who was disposed to admit the lawfulness of taking twelve per cent interest, wrote: "What has become of the book Dr. Luther of blessed memory addressed to the ministers on the subject of usury? Where do we see in any of our countries which claim to be Evangelical anyone refused the Sacrament of the altar or Holy Baptism on account of usury? Where do we see one of them buried on the dungheap?" [100]

THOSE WHO reject psychoanalysis may well be able to offer another explanation of the facts here considered; only when they attempt to do so will it be possible to evaluate the psychoanalytical interpretation by confronting it with an alternative. Our effort has been in another direction—to determine how psychoanalysis itself is to be interpreted if it is applied to history and culture. We therefore conclude by summarizing the implications of our inquiry for some of the questions to which this book is addressed:

(1) The Devil is a middle term connecting Protestantism and anality. As against the neo-Freudians, anality means real bodily anality, and not just "an attitude in interpersonal relationships." As against the orthodox Freudians, the pathogenic factor in anality is not real bodily toilet training, but peculiar fantasies (the Devil) connected with the anal zone. Furthermore, these fantasies are not private or individual products, but exist as social projections into the world of culture. [101] It follows that the precipitating factor in a psychological upheaval such as the Protestant Reformation is not any change in toilet-training patterns, but an irruption of fresh material from deeper strata of the unconscious made possible by a large-scale transformation in the structure of the projective system (the culture). The dynamic of history is the slow return of the repressed.

(2) The inquiry confirms the theoretical postulate of a close connection between anal fantasies on the one hand and the death instinct on the other. While orthodox psychoanalysis is accustomed to the notion that the anal organization is also the sadistic organization, its notion that the anal organization is

essentially a sexual organization, and the implication that in it Eros somehow takes sadistic forms, underestimates the role of the death instinct in the anal organization and in the formation of the sexual organizations altogether. To put it another way, the whole theory of the sexual organizations, formulated by Freud in terms of his earliest theory of the instincts, should be revised in terms of the death instinct. We are reminded once more of Ferenczi's argument that the sexual organizations are constructed by the "thalassal regressive trend," i.e., the death instinct.[102]

(3) The relation between psychoanalysis and religion is not the simple polarity of science and wishful thinking, as suggested by Freud's title, *The Future of an Illusion*. Lutheranism can be explicated not only as theology but also as psychoanalysis. Luther, like a psychoanalyst, penetrates beneath the surface of life and finds a hidden reality; religion, like psychoanalysis, must say that things are not what they seem to be. And psychoanalysis must admit that the hidden reality revealed in religion is the same as the hidden reality revealed by psychoanalysis, namely, the unconscious: both psychoanalysis and religion represent phases in the return of the repressed to human consciousness. Psychoanalysis may claim that it represents a full return of the repressed, and religion only a partial and distorted return. Religion perceives the repressed only in the form of projections, such as Luther's devil; the unconscious self is perceived but in an alienated form, as the not-self. Psychoanalysis, coming at the end of a long process of the withdrawal of projections (Jung's phrase) or *"Entzauberung der Welt"* (Max Weber's phrase), may claim that with its awareness of the body and the bodily base of all symbolism, alienation is about to be overcome and the return of the repressed about to be completed. But this superior wisdom does not authorize psychoanalysis to dismiss religion as neurotic. As Freud pointed out, there is "not only method in madness, but also a fragment of historical truth." [103] If we take seriously the position that human history is the history of a neurosis, then psychoanalysis (unless Freud was sent to us by God) is inside the neurosis, and the neurosis itself must always have contained those "attempts at explanation and cure" which Freud at the end of his life

came to regard as the only basis for therapeutic hope.[104] But then Luther must be understood as a stage in a process which leads to Freud. Protestantism then represents a new stage in human history, a fuller return of the repressed. It is true that as long as basic repression is maintained, a return of the repressed can take place only under the general condition of denial and negation; therefore a fuller return of the repressed is accompanied by greater distortion of consciousness and a general aggravation of the neurosis. But, as we have argued elsewhere, psychoanalysis itself is no exception to this law of the evolution of consciousness under general conditions of repression. The neurotic process and the historical process are dialectical.

(4) The deepest psychoanalytical insight of Lutheran Protestantism is its unmasking and repudiation of the traditional path to salvation for Western man, sublimation. This is the psychoanalytical meaning of the emphasis on original sin: no matter how anality is sublimated, human nature remains essentially filthy. There is an affinity here between Luther's position and Freud's critique of sublimation. But psychoanalysis must recognize that Luther's repudiation of all efforts to rise above the body is if anything more consistent than Freud's.

(5) Protestantism's critique of sublimation is either the cause or the effect, or both cause and effect, of a massive withdrawal of Eros from sublimations and therefore from life in this world. But since life in this world is the life we actually live, the effect is to surrender this life to the driving power of Eros' antagonist, the death instinct. Protestantism would therefore seem to mark an important stage in the psychic history of civilization: the death instinct becomes the master of the house. This psychic fact is registered in Luther's consciousness, and expressed in the doctrines that the Devil is lord of this world and that holy living is holy dying.

(6) Luther's vision of the dominion of death in life is correlative to his eschatological hope in the transformation of life on earth, and the transformation of the human body—the resurrection of the body, in a form, as Luther says, free from death and filth.[105] Luther's eschatology challenges psychoanalysis to formulate the conditions under which the dominion of death

and anality could be abolished. In thus challenging psycho-analysis, Christianity would perform the function, proper to all religion, of voicing the substance of things hoped for, the evidence of things unseen. And, in answering the challenge, psychoanalysis would be fulfilling its claim of turning the full light of consciousness on what has hitherto been seen only through a glass darkly. Current psychoanalysis has no utopia; current neo-orthodox Protestantism has no eschatology. This defect cripples both of them as allies of the life instinct in that war against the death instinct which is human history; both are crippled in their capacity to cast out demons. Competition between the two to produce an eschatology for the twentieth century is the way to serve the life instinct and bring hope to distracted humanity.

Filthy Lucre

Aurum in stercore quaero.
—VIRGIL [1]

1. *Rationality and Irrationality*

ONE OF THE great stumbling blocks in the way of a psychoanalytical approach to money is the close connection between money and rationality. We may concede to psychoanalysis legitimate concern with the irrational; but what is more rational than *Homo economicus?* Of course we know that man is never *Homo economicus,* and therefore we might permit psychoanalysis to investigate human deviations from that ideal norm. But the psychoanalytical theorems about money question the rationality of the norm itself, of which money is the center. The connection between money thinking and rational thinking is so deeply ingrained in our practical lives that it seems impossible to question it; our practical experience is articulated in one whole school of economic theorists who define economics as the "science which studies human behavior as a relationship between ends and scarce means which have alternative uses." The disposal of scarce means among competing ends—what could be more rational than that? At a more philosophic level, sociology (on this point most elaborately articulated by Simmel) correctly says that money reflects and promotes a style of thinking which is abstract, impersonal, objective, and quantitative, that is to say, the style of thinking of modern science—and what can be more rational than that? [2]

That the instinct of psychoanalysis—for it too has instincts which it represses—makes it want to attack the rationality of prudential calculation and quantitative science is an indubitable but not widely advertised fact. It is concealed by the use of a quite naïve and traditional (therefore unpsychoanalytical) notion of the "reality-principle" and "reality-thinking." Behind this naïve notion of "reality-thinking" is Freud's unquestioning (he could not question everything) attitude to science, that Comtian attitude which saw man passing through the stages of magic and religion till it finally arrives at the scientific stage, where he is at last mature—i.e., where he has abandoned the pleasure-principle, has adapted himself to reality, and has learned to direct his libido toward real objects in the outer world.[3] Behind this scientist pose of the psychoanalyst lies the repressed problem of the psychoanalysis of psychoanalysis itself.

There is a connection between money and what may be called quantifying rationality, and the psychoanalytical theorems on money make no sense if not brought into relation with the psychoanalytical critique of quantifying rationality. This critique is an integral, though awkward, theme throughout Freud's writings; it can be stated in terms of the early libido theory or in terms of the later ego theory. Freudian theory derives character from repressed perverse sexual trends; the prudential calculating character (the ideal type of *Homo economicus*) is an anal character.[4] There are equivocations in the psychoanalytical literature; but taken strictly, the Freudian theory of the anal character—like classical economic theory—has no room for the concept of an *excessively* prudential calculating disposition. Prudential calculation as such is an anal trait; the theory of the anal character is a theory of what Max Weber called the capitalist spirit, and not just of deviant exaggerations such as the miser.

Hence psychoanalysis cannot honestly limit itself simply to offering an explanation of some curious excrescences on the money economy (such as currency-hoarding, or even such a major fetish as the gold standard). If it is both honest and courageous, psychoanalysis must frankly offer a psychology of the capitalist spirit as a whole. And its psychology of the capitalist spirit contains Simmel's notion of the affinity between the capitalist spirit and scientistic rationality. Freud derives "the desire for knowledge" from anal sources, saying that "it is at bottom an offshoot, sublimated and raised to the intellectual sphere, of the possessive instinct." [5] And Ferenczi, the *enfant terrible* of psychoanalysis (and therefore at times the most profound), in his discussion of mathematics, says, "Thinking is after all only a means of preventing a squandering through action," so that thinking is only a "special expression of the tendency to economize," and as such has "its origin in anal-eroticism." [6] Freud's later theory of the ego consolidates the doctrine that there is a significant irrational factor in areas of human behavior which we normally regard as in the domain of reason and consciousness. The core of the later theory of the ego is the notion that a large part of the ego is unconscious and is governed by unconscious connections with the id.[7]

There is an attack on the great god Science in psychoanalysis; but the nature of the attack needs careful explanation. What is being probed, and found to be in some sense morbid, is not knowledge as such, but the unconscious schemata governing the pursuit of knowledge in modern civilization—specifically the aim of possession or mastery over objects (Freud), and the principle of economizing in the means (Ferenczi). And the morbidity imputed to these schemata, if interpreted in the context of the whole libido theory, amounts to this: possessive mastery over nature and rigorously economical thinking are partial impulses in the human being (the human body) which in modern civilization have become tyrant organizers of the whole of human life; abstraction from the reality of the whole body and substitution of the abstracted impulse for the whole reality are inherent in *Homo economicus.* In contrast, what would a nonmorbid science look like? It would presumably be erotic rather than (anal) sadistic in aim. Its aim would not be mastery over but union with nature. And its means would not be economizing but erotic exuberance. And finally, it would be based on the whole body and not just a part; that is to say, it would be based on the polymorphous perverse body.[8]

So stated, the psychoanalytical critique of modern rationality is softened by slurring over the grossly concrete psychoanalytical emphasis on the anus; and to the anus we shall return later. But in this complexity, one thing at a time. This softened statement is necessary to obtain an initial comprehension of what real problems in the great world psychoanalysis is talking about. For this softened statement does not indeed reconcile the psychoanalytical critique of modern rationality with common sense, but at least it relates it to serious currents of nonpsychoanalytical thought.

In the area of science, it is related to Whitehead's philosophy of organism. Whitehead's critique of abstraction is a critique of the abstract, impersonal, quantifying rationality; and his objection to abstraction is precisely that through it a partial impulse becomes equated with the whole. Whitehead's philosophy of organism protests against quantifying rationality on behalf of the living body as a whole: "But the living organ of experience is the living body as a whole." And he protests "on behalf of value"; he insists that the real structure of the human body, of human cognition, and of the events cognized is erotic, creative "self-enjoyment." [9]

Christian mysticism and poetical mysticism have also protested against the economizing principle as a violation of Eros, of the life instinct. "Exuberance is beauty," says Blake. And Rilke, advocating art as a way of life, says:

> Consequently not any self-control or self-limitation for the sake of specific ends, but rather a carefree letting go of oneself. . . . Not caution but rather a wise blindness. . . . Not working to acquire silent, slowly increasing possessions, but rather a continuous squandering of all shifting values. . . . This way of being has something naïve and instinctive about it and resembles that period of the unconscious best characterized by a joyous confidence: namely the period of childhood.[10]

And thirdly, the psychoanalytical critique of quantifying rationality has an affinity with Marx; not the Marx of *Das Kapital*, which recognizes the irrationality of modern civilization but locates the irrationality in the "system," but the early Marx of the "economic-philosophic manuscripts," [11] with his conception of the radical viciousness of the civilized mind, labeled "the alienated consciousness." The alienated consciousness is correlative with a money economy. Its root is the compulsion to work. This compulsion to work subordinates man to things, producing at the same time confusion in the valuation of things (*Verwertung*) and devaluation of the human body (*Entwertung*). It reduces the drives of the human being to greed and competition (aggression and possessiveness, as in the anal character). The desire for money takes the place of all genuinely human needs. Thus the apparent accumulation of wealth is really the impoverishment of human nature, and its appropriate morality is the renunciation of human nature and desires—asceticism. The effect is to substitute an abstraction, *Homo economicus,* for the concrete totality of human nature, and thus to dehumanize human nature. In this dehumanized human nature man loses contact with his own body, more specifically with his senses, with sensuality and with the pleasure-principle. And this dehumanized human nature produces an inhuman consciousness, whose only currency is abstractions divorced from real life—the industrious, coolly rational, economic, prosaic mind. Capitalism has made us so stupid and one-sided that objects exist for us only if we can possess them or if they have utility.[12]

Marx thus finds economic man and his consciousness defective by comparison with the ideal of a truly human man. Compare the modern economist F. H. Knight: "Economic relations are *impersonal.* . . . It is the market, the exchange opportunity, which is functionally real, not the other human beings; these are not even means to action. The relation is neither one of cooperation nor one of mutual exploitation, but is completely non-moral, non-human." [13]

The great economist von Mises tried to refute socialism by demonstrating that, in abolishing exchange, socialism made economic calculation, and hence economic rationality, impossible. "Just because no production good will ever become the object of exchange, it will be impossible to determine its monetary value. . . . Money could never fill in a socialist state the role it fills in a competitive society in determining the value of production goods. Calculation in terms of money will here be impossible. . . . There would be no means of determining what was rational, and hence it is obvious that production could never be directed by economic considerations." But if von Mises is right, then what he discovered is not a refutation but a psy-

choanalytical justification of socialism, as a system which by
its very nature transcends the psychology of *Homo economicus.*

It is one of the sad ironies of contemporary intellectual life
that the reply of socialist economists to von Mises' arguments
was to attempt to show that socialism was not incompatible
with "rational economic calculation"—that is to say, that it
could retain the inhuman principle of economizing. More recently, Maurice Dobb's reappraisal of the whole controversy
shows signs of recognizing that socialist economics must submerge economizing calculation in "welfare" considerations. But
Dobb does not face up to the magnitude of the problem of
establishing those truly human needs which comprise welfare,
and of constructing a new model of rationality which can dismiss *Homo economicus* as simply irrational. In the last resort
Dobb tries to find a middle ground, and thus he contaminates
his socialism with the sordid rationality of the past.[14] The problems of the "welfare economists" have psychoanalytical dimensions, whether they know it or not.

2. Sacred and Secular

A SECOND stumbling block in the way of a psychoanalytical
approach to money can be expressed simply, but abstractly,
as the absence of a middle term. What has neurosis to do with
money? Even if we are prepared to recognize the existence in
the domain of the public, the social, the historical, of something
that might be called the universal neurosis of mankind, we do
not recognize money as part of it. If there is a universal neurosis, it is reasonable to suppose that its core is religion. We
might therefore tolerate psychoanalytical investigation of religion and still see no point to a psychoanalytical investigation
of money. Is not money essentially secular—not only outside
the domain of religion, but even its opposite?

Our common-sense feelings have been articulated by the
sociologists, who in various ways contrast the sacred and the
secular as polar opposites, always with money and rationality
as syndromes in the Gestalt of the secular. In fact the notion
of money as essentially secular is interconnected with our notion of its essential rationality. Hence, although sociology has

used the antithesis of sacred and secular to probe irrational elements in society, and (e.g., Pareto, Durkheim) has even taken the position that society must always be a secular superstructure on a sacred base—i.e., that society can never get rid of irrational residues—yet sociology has not connected money with the irrational and the sacred. Money remains anchored in the domain of the secular. And since the essence of modern rationalism as a whole is simply autonomy from religion, money as secular is also rational.

But this static contrast of the sacred and the secular as mutually exclusive opposites is misleading, because it is undialectical. The secular is the negation of the sacred, and both Freud's and Hegel's negation affirms its own opposite. The psychological realities here are best grasped in terms of theology, and were already grasped by Luther. Modern secularism, and its companion Protestantism, do not usher in an era in which human consciousness is liberated from inhuman powers, or the natural world is liberated from supernatural manifestations; the essence of the Protestant (or capitalist) era is that the power over this world has passed from God to God's negation, God's ape, the Devil. And already Luther had seen in money the essence of the secular, and therefore of the demonic. The money complex is the demonic, and the demonic is God's ape; the money complex is therefore the heir to and substitute for the religious complex, an attempt to find God in things.

In psychoanalytical terms, modern secularism is no release from the Oedipus complex, from which Freud said religion was derived; it is only the transfer of the projections originating in the Oedipus complex from the world of spirits to the world of things. "The last figure in the series beginning with the parents is that dark supremacy of Fate," says Freud, indicating the residues of the parental complex in secular thought.[15] It still remains true that religion is the middle term connecting psychoanalysis and society. If there is to be a psychoanalysis of money it must start from the hypothesis that the money complex has the essential structure of religion—or, if you will, the negation of religion, the demonic. The psychoanalytical theory of money must start by establishing the proposition that money is, in Shakespeare's words, the "visible god"; in Luther's words, "the God of this world." [16]

The first paradox in the psychoanalytical theory of money is the imputation of irrationality; the second paradox is the imputation of sacredness to the money complex. This paradox also needs careful explanation. Already Marx (again in the "economic-philosophic manuscripts") had compared the money complex with the religious complex, as two forms of human self-alienation. Marx even entertained the hypothesis that the money complex is derived from the religious complex, only to reject it decisively in words well worth considering:

> If my own activity does not belong to me, if it is an alien compulsive activity, to whom does it belong? To a being other than myself. Who is this being? The gods? Certainly it appears that at the earliest times the main production, as for example temple-building in Egypt, India, Mexico, belonged to the service of the gods, as the product belonged to them also. But the gods alone were never masters of labor. Just as little was nature. And what a contradiction indeed would there be if, the more man subjects nature to himself through labor, and the more the miracles of the gods become superfluous because of the miracles of industry, man should renounce in favor of these powers the joy of production and the enjoyment of the product. The alien being, to whom labor and the product of labor belongs, in whose service and for whose enjoyment labor and the product of labor stand, can only be man himself. If the product of work does not belong to the worker, but confronts him as an alien power, this is possible only if it belongs to another man outside of the worker.[17]

Marx comes close to recognizing alienated (compulsive) work as an inner psychological necessity. He seems to recognize that if it is an inner psychological necessity, it amounts to the same thing to say that it is a necessity due to the gods; he is aware that the earliest forms of money-capital fit in with the hypothesis of the religious nature of alienated (compulsive) work. But the psychological implications of this line of thought are too bewildering (cf. "and what a contradiction," etc.); and Marx withdraws to the position that the primary datum is the domination of man over man. In doing so he contradicts his own formulations on the alienated (compulsive) character of all labor as such, as well as his formulation that private property is to be derived from alienated (compulsive) labor and not vice versa.[18] And, of course, the domination of man over man, which itself has to be explained, particularly by one who seeks to abolish it, is left as an ultimate. The ultimate category is presumably force, the force which appropriates another man's labor.

We are here at one of the ultimate crossroads in social theory. We have seen elsewhere how Freud himself (with his Primal Father), as well as Hegel (with his Master) and Nietzsche (with his Master Race) are, like Marx in this passage, compelled in the last resort to postulate external domination and its assertion by force in order to explain repression. And we have argued that to take this line is to renounce psychological explanation ("force" being substituted for psychology) and to miss the whole point of the riddle: How can there be an animal which represses itself? [19] And to miss the nature of the human disease is also to miss the nature of the cure. If the cause of the trouble were force, to "expropriate the expropriators" would be enough. But if force did not establish the domination of the master, then perhaps the slave is somehow in love with his own chains. If there is such a deeper psychological malady, then a deeper psychological regeneration is needed.

To take the path of psychological explanation means that the money complex is to be derived from the religious complex. The question then is how such a proposition is to be established. The answer, I think, is that the proposition can be validated only historically; the word "derived" has no verifiable meaning unless it means historically derived. To understand the secular is to understand its relation to the sacred; to understand the civilized is to understand its relation to the primitive, or archaic, as we prefer to call it; to understand modern economics (and money) is to understand its relation to archaic economics (and money). But such a historical, and because historical also philosophical, approach to money is precisely what is lacking in the entire range of modern economic theory.

Classical economic theorists, assuming the basic rationality of economic activity, assumed likewise that archaic economic activity was a core of secular rationalism in an otherwise rude and superstitious milieu. They assumed that economic activity was always and everywhere essentially the same in the fundamental motivation; economic activities were governed by economic motives—that is, by economizing calculation. Assuming the psychology of economizing calculation, they correctly postulated its sociological correlate, the institution of ownership (property). Again from the psychology of economizing calculation, they deduced the division of labor and its institutional correlate, exchange in a market. Thus Adam Smith: [20]

> In a tribe of hunters or shepherds a particular person makes bows and arrows, for example, with more readiness and dexterity than any other. He frequently exchanges them for cattle or for venison with his companions; and he finds at last that he can in this manner, get more cattle and venison than if he himself went to the field to catch them. From a regard to his own interest, therefore, the making of bows and arrows grows to be his chief business.

And then finally the institution of money was derived from the institution of the market, as medium of exchange or standard of value.

In spite of the cultural relativists' busy warfare against all attempts to generalize (i.e., reach any important conclusion), it is a safe generalization to say that the postulates of classical economic theory have no relation whatever to the anthropological facts. Archaic economics is not governed by the psychology of economizing calculation. We can safely follow Karl Polanyi, the only economist who faces the facts and the problems they pose, when he says, "It is on this one negative point that modern ethnographers agree: the absence of the motive of gain; the absence of the principle of laboring for remuneration; the absence of the principle of least effort; and especially the absence of any separate and distinct institution based on economic motives." [21] (Even the cultural relativist Herskovits cannot avoid generalizations tending in the same direction; he provides much data to support Polanyi's statement and none to contradict it.[22])

And, on the other hand, archaic economics includes often very elaborate systems of ownership, division of labor, and exchange.

Is there money in the ideal type of archaic economy? The radical disjunction between archaic and modern psychology, and therefore terminology, creates difficulties which are only too apparent in the literature on the subject. In a sense Malinowski is right in saying that if we define money as it is defined in modern economic theory, as an object which fulfills the three functions of being a medium of exchange, a standard of value, and a store of wealth, then archaic economics has no money.[23] The classical definition takes the medium-of-exchange function as primary; the reason why there is nothing in the archaic economy that really corresponds to money is not so much that the exchanges are limited in scope, but rather that the psychology of the (often quite elaborate) archaic exchange is not the psychology of self-interest and economizing calculation which the modern definition assumes. But a philosophy of economics cannot leave archaic money flatly distinct from money, just as a philosophy of rationality cannot be satisfied with a flat disjunction between the sacred and the secular. More dialectical thinking is needed. And the fact—recognized by Malinowski himself and the generality of writers on the subject—is that archaic economy does set aside a special class of objects which serve one of the three functions ascribed to modern money, that of being an instrument for condensing and storing wealth.[24] If the study of archaic economics shows that, at least in the historical sense, the prime function of money is to condense and store wealth, it invites modern economic theory to reconsider its traditional emphasis on the medium-of-exchange function. Modern economic theory, with its unsolved problems in the theory of money and the rate of interest, might well profit by accepting the invitation.

This wealth that can be condensed and stored—what is it? It is a well-known fact that the objects characteristically chosen in archaic economies to serve as stores of wealth, and therefore referred to as "primitive money," are, to the modern mind, bizarre in the extreme—shells, dogs' teeth, feather bands, the famous stone money of the island of Yap.[25] That is to say, the condensed wealth of archaic economies is practically useless, and in that sense irrational. We have to stay with common sense here, and avoid the ethical relativism of modern utilitarian economics with its assumption of the "randomness of ends," [26] as well as the cultural relativism of the anthropologists with its assumption that the law of reason is to do when in Rome what the Romans do. But even official cultural relativists have common sense: Herskovits writes, "There are but few objects employed as money by non-literate peoples that have use value other than to bring prestige to those who display them." [27]

What irrational considerations confer value on shells, dogs' teeth, and feather bands? Herskovits' concept of prestige is certainly not wrong, and it has the advantage of linking up with Veblen's conceptual framework, which the still-to-be-written psychology of economics cannot afford to ignore. But I think we can go further and say that the value conferred on the useless object, and the prestige conferred on the owner, is magical, mystical, religious, and comes from the domain of the sacred. Just as an example, in the Trobriand Islands the "tokens of wealth" are "big ceremonial axe-blades," made of a material "rare and difficult to obtain" and fashioned with "much time and labor," but which "are hardly ever put to any real use." [28] Herskovits himself shows the intimate connection between social prestige and supernatural power in nonliterate cultures.[29] The only alternative explanation is to regard these archaic moneys as ornaments and to derive their value from their ornamental purposes; [30] but Laum, in his treatise on the sacral origins of Greek money, correctly argues that ornamentation can hardly be accepted as an ultimate psychological category, and that ornaments in fact are basically magic amulets or tokens.[31] The decisive reason, however, for insisting on the sacred character of archaic money is not so much the object itself as the context of its circulation. All the authorities insist that archaic economic activity is submerged in "noneconomic" relations; and they all emphasize the ceremonial (ritual) character of these noneconomic relations.[32] Hence, when Firth says that primitive money sometimes comprises articles of practical use, his statement cannot be accepted at face value.[33] It is certain that some archaic moneys, which have been taken to be practically useful articles elevated into a standard of value by the process of exchanging utilities as postulated by modern economic theory, became money in no such way. Utility is ambiguous; many useful articles in archaic cultures have also a useless, sacred value. This applies especially to food, which besides serving the useful purpose of satisfying hunger can also be the magic substance of communion or the means for paying religious debts (in the sacrifice). Laum has demonstrated that the famous cattle money in Homer must be derived not from any role of cattle as utilitarian commodities but from the sacred significance of cattle in the sacrifice and in the ceremonial (communion) meal.[34] Compare Herskovits on cattle wealth among the East African Nuer: [35]

> It is striking how non-economic factors enter into every aspect of their ownership. . . . The cattle play an important part in determining affinal relationships. . . . Such facts as these, and the manner in which they enter into the religious life together with their essential place in various rituals, all differentiate them from other kinds of property among this people.

It has been long known that the first markets were sacred markets, the first banks were temples, the first to issue money were priests or priest-kings. But these economic institutions have been interpreted as in themselves secular-rational, though originally sponsored by sacred auspices. The crucial point in Laum's argument is that the institutions are in themselves sacred. Laum derives the very idea of equivalence (equal value) from ritual tariffs of atonement, the very idea of a symbol of value from rituals of symbolic substitution, and the very idea of price from ritual distribution of the sacred food. In other words, the money complex, archaic or modern, is inseparable from symbolism; and symbolism is not, as Simmel thought, the mark of rationality but the mark of the sacred.

If we recognize the essentially sacred character of archaic money, we shall be in a position to recognize the essentially sacred character of certain specific features of modern money—certainly the gold standard, and almost certainly also the rate of interest. As far as gold and silver are concerned it is obvious to the eye of common sense that their salient characteristic is their absolute uselessness for all practical purposes. John Locke put his finger on the essential point with his formula of "mankind having consented to put an *imaginary* value upon gold and silver." [36]

Measured by rational utility and real human needs, there is absolutely no difference between the gold and silver of modern economy and the shells or dogs' teeth of archaic economy. There is no difference between those great stone cartwheels on the island of Yap which, "even though under the sea, continue to symbolize value," and the gold under the ground at Fort Knox.[37] And that the imaginary value placed on gold and silver in the modern economy is derived from the domain of the sacred is a point already fully recognized by Keynes in the *Treatise on Money*. In the chapter entitled *"Auri sacra fames,"* Keynes (correctly, I believe) sees the history of civilized money as continuous from the urban revolution with which civilization began: "The magical properties, with which the Egyptian priestcraft anciently imbued the yellow metal, it has never altogether lost." [38]

Keynes also recognizes that the special attraction of gold and silver is due not to any of the rationalistic considerations generally offered in explanation but to their symbolic identification with Sun and Moon, and to the sacred significance of Sun and Moon in the new astrological theology invented by the earliest civilizations. Heichelheim, the authority on ancient economics, concurs on the essentially magical-religious nature of the value placed on gold and silver in the ancient Near East.[39] Laum states that the value ratio of gold to silver remained stable throughout classical antiquity and into the Middle Ages and even modern times at $1:13\frac{1}{2}$. It is obvious that such a stability in the ratio cannot be explained in terms of rational supply and demand. The explanation, says Laum, lies in the astrological ratio of the cycles of their divine counterparts, the Sun and Moon.[40]

The history of money from this point of view has yet to be written. Greek money, which contributed to modern money the institution of coinage, was recognized by Simmel to be essentially sacred and to have originated not in the market but in the temple.[41] Laum has amplified and established the thesis. But

Simmel and Laum are confused by the illusion that modern money is secular, and hence they confuse the past by describing as "secularization" a process which is rather only a metamorphosis of the sacred. Even Keynes perhaps shares this illusion, although he sees the real secularization of money as still lying in the future. The historian must doubt the possibility of having capitalism without gold fetishism in some form or other. At any rate, the historian must conclude that the ideal type of the modern economy retains, at its very heart, the structure of the archaic sacred. And once again the undialectical disjunction of sacred and secular is seen to be inadequate.

The rate of interest is a "highly psychological phenomenon," says Keynes. It presents problems which, I believe, are still unsolved in economics: "A queer beast," says Professor Robertson.[42] Although the notion that the rate of interest is the price of money would be disputed, it would not be disputed, I think, that there is some close connection between the rate of interest and money. Here I wish to comment on only one of the aspects which puzzle economists, the curious long-range stability of rate of interest. It has been common for economists to go outside of economics for possible explanations; there are theories connecting it with the average rate of growth of animals and plants or with the length of human life. F. H. Knight says the problem can be discussed only as philosophy or theory of history.[43] Keynes postulates the operation of certain "constant psychological characters." [44]

It is possible that the rate of interest is a second sacred residue in the secular world of modern economy. Stability of prices is a general characteristic of the archaic economy, because, as Malinowski says, prices are rigidly prescribed by custom and not by supply and demand.[45] Is there not an essential element of determination by custom, not by supply and demand, in the rate of interest? But if this is granted, the question must be pushed further to inquire what determines the custom. Custom is, in sociological theory, essentially sacred, and why should the custom determinant in the rate of interest be any exception? We remember Laum's solution to the analogous riddle of the stability of the ratio between gold and silver. The institution of interest, like the institution of money based on

gold and silver, is coeval with urban civilization. In fact, Heichelheim proposes to take the institution of interest-bearing capital investment as the strategic key factor in the economic development called the urban revolution. Then Heichelheim looks
for the source of the new economic institution; he answers only
that the source must be sought in the transvaluation of religious
values which accompanied the urban revolution.[46]

At a deeper level, the hidden middle term connecting money
and the whole domain of the sacred is power (social power).
Classical economic theory, with its model of perfect competition, ignores the factor of power. Ruskin was not deceived—
Ruskin whom Mumford rightly raised from the dead as the
"fundamental economist of the biotechnic order": [47] "Mercan-
tile economy . . . signifies the accumulation, in the hands of
individuals, of legal and moral claim upon, or power over, the
labour of others"; "What is really desired, under the name of
riches, is, essentially, power over men." [48] Karl Marx' ambiguity
on this subject reveals some of the fundamental dilemmas in
Marxism. In the first volume of *Capital* he sets out to establish
a model of capitalism as a self-contained system governed by
the principle of economizing calculation; it was therefore logical for him to incorporate in this system the (to my mind erroneous) notion of classical economic theory that money is
basically a medium of exchange originating in a market where
economizing calculators meet each other. Even in this first system, however, psychological realities which do not fit in with
his basic psychological postulates do not escape his acute eye.

Marx notes the operation of a "desire after hoarding"
which clings to the money form, and is therefore a "greed for
gold"—and which is an intrinsic factor in capitalism inherited
from the precapitalist stage: "With the very earliest development of the circulation of commodities, there is also developed
the necessity, and the passionate desire, to hold fast to the product of the first metamorphosis . . . its gold-chrysalis."

Marx also notes the fact, inexplicable by the medium-of-
exchange theory of money, that it is intrinsic to the nature of
money to get condensed in useless objects, and that this is also
an intrinsic feature of capitalism inherited from the precapitalist
stage: "In the early stages of the circulation of commodities it

is the surplus use-values alone that are converted into money. Gold and silver thus become of themselves social expressions for superfluity of wealth." [49] Here Marx comes close to the notion of money as prestige, and to the connection between prestige and the practically useless, the "surplus use-value." This strange term, "surplus use-value," is so far as I know nowhere elaborated by Marx. It implies that a psychology of money has to be a psychology which can discriminate between useless (irrational) demands and truly human needs; but, as we have seen in another connection, where such a psychology of real human needs should be, there is in Marxism a great gap. The ultimate direction of this other line of thought in the first volume of *Capital* is to make prestige the essential value of money; that is to say, the essence of money is not its function in exchange, but power. And Marx says this: Under capitalism "social power becomes the private power of private persons." [50]

This other line of thought in Marx is elaborated in the third volume of *Capital*, which, as a whole, clearly shows that Marx was aware that there were problems not solved in the first volume, especially in the topics of hoarding (and precapitalist accumulation), money, and the rate of interest. There the essence of money and interest emerges more clearly as power: "They represent in this form a command over the labor of others"; "Interest is, therefore, merely the expression of the fact that value in general . . . faces living labor-power as an independent power." [51]

But correlative with this emphasis on power is an explicit recognition that the labor theory of money, which is the automatic consequence of the labor theory of value plus the medium-of-exchange theory of money adopted in his first volume, is wrong. There is the recognition that the price of money in borrowing and lending does not obey the basic law for all commodities laid down there, namely that the price is determined not by use-value but by exchange-value (i.e., amount of labor incorporated into the object, according to the labor theory of value). Hence there is the recognition that there is something irrational about interest: "If interest is to be called the price of money-capital, it will be an irrational form of price, which is quite at variance with the conception of the price of commodities." Interest—again at variance with the labor theory of value —is seen to arise "outside of the process of production," "the fruit of mere ownership." [52] Hence the real essence of money is not disclosed by the labor theory of value but by a theory of ownership—i.e., power. "But how are gold and silver distinguished from other forms of wealth? Not by the magnitude of their value, for this is determined by the quantity of labor materialized in them; but by the fact that they represent independent incarnations, expressions of the social character of wealth." [53] The value of money does not lie in the value with which the labor theory of value is concerned. And conversely—this is the crucial point—the labor theory of value does not contain the answer to the problem of power.

The ultimate category of economics is power; but power is not an economic category. Marx fills up the emergent gap in his theory with the concept of force (violence)—i.e., by conceiving power as a material reality. We have argued elsewhere that this is a crucial mistake; power is in essence a psychological category. And to pursue the tracks of power, we will have to enter the domain of the sacred, and map it: all power is essentially sacred power. Here again the crucial problem is to understand archaic man and the archaic economy. Marxian anthropology, with its assumption of the economic derivation of power and its correlative assumption that the psychology of economics is universally the psychology of appropriation, is committed to deny or belittle the existence of power in the archaic society; "primitive communism" is conceived as in principle egalitarian. But the fact is, to quote Herskovits: [54]

> In the great political groupings of Africa and Indonesia, as well as in the less complex societies in these and other areas, the same mechanisms found to be operative in the cultures of Oceania and the Americas are also active. With but rare exceptions we find that, to the extent to which the economic system, the technological level of achievement, and the natural setting permit, some men enjoy more favored positions than others.

The line of development is continuous from the simplest societies to the great theocratic structures of the first civilizations. If the emergence of social privilege marks the Fall of Man, the

Fall took place not in the transition from "primitive communism" to "private property" but in the transition from ape to man. And secondly, the anthropological data—again we can follow Herskovits—show the inherent connection, in the archaic society, between this expanding sector of privilege and the expanding sector of the sacred.[55] Privilege is prestige, and prestige, in its fundamental nature as in the etymology of the word, means deception and enchantment. Again the line of development is continuous from the magician-leader of the simpler societies to the priest-king or god-king of the first civilizations, as indeed Frazer showed fifty years ago.[56]

Power was originally sacred, and it remains so in the modern world. Again we must not be misled by the flat antinomy of the sacred and the secular, and interpret as "secularization" what is only a metamorphosis of the sacred. If there is a class which has nothing to lose but its chains, the chains that bind it are self-imposed, sacred obligations which appear as objective realities with all the force of a neurotic delusion. The perception that class war is sustained by myths underlies Sorel's classic *On Violence.*[57] And on the other side, the perception that the essence of capitalism is the magnetic leadership of the entrepreneur was systematically elaborated into an economic theory by Schumpeter. Already Ruskin wrote in the margin of his copy of Mill the aphorism "Industry dependent on Will, not Capital." [58] Along these lines, I believe, a deeper anatomy, a psychological anatomy, of modern civilization can be pursued. And the underlying phenomenon of leadership was assimilated into the domain of psychoanalysis when Freud published his book on mass psychology. Psychoanalysis takes the final step of showing the origin of the myths which sustain social power and power struggles in the repression of the human body.

3. *Utility and Uselessness*

WE SAID that it was essential to the nature of money for the objects into which wealth or value is condensed to be practically useless, and that this theorem was equally true for modern money (gold) and for archaic money (dogs' teeth). But to support the proposition we simply invoked common sense. We

had to invoke common sense because there is no currently accepted body of theory which can accommodate this common-
sense observation. It is a normative statement, and as such it
offends the prudent rule of ethical neutrality with which economists and anthropologists have amputated the disturbing possibility that their sciences might have critical implications.
Common sense on this point reflects our profounder human
feelings, and, on the uselessness of money, is supported by the
entire tradition of religious and poetic thought. The social scientists, even more than the physical scientists, need to follow
Whitehead's advice and correct their science with the more
concrete deliverances of poetry.

Still there is need for a science, and not just a poetry of common sense; and from our present vantage point we can deduce
the formal nature of a science of economics which could accommodate the proposition that money is in the first place useless.
In Marxian terminology, to grasp money as a surplus use-value,
we need a science of use-values, not a science of exchange-
values. Or, more accurately, the science of exchange-values
would have to be comprehended in the larger framework of a
science of use-values. Then the science of economics would
have the structure of that science of economy which Aristotle
distinguished as the art of using from money-making (*chrema-
tistike*) or the art of acquisition.[59] And, like Aristotle's science
of economy, the science of use-values would have to be based
on a science of human nature, able to distinguish real human
needs from (neurotic) consumer demands. It was his notion of
human nature that permitted Aristotle to make the normative
statement that money-making is an unnatural perversion. And
finally in a science of use-values the ultimate guiding problem
would not be production but consumption, not economizing
but satisfaction: the dismal science would become the science
of enjoyment. "The real science of political economy," says
Ruskin, "which has yet to be distinguished from the bastard
science, as medicine from witchcraft, and astronomy from as-
trology, is that which teaches nations to desire and labor for
the things that lead to life."[60]

We begin to discern the true connection between psychoanalysis and economics. Like Aristotle, psychoanalysis seeks to

relate economics to a fundamental notion of human nature; unlike Aristotle, its fundamental notion of human nature begins to assume the structure of a science. And its scientific theory of human nature is striving to grasp money-making as what Aristotle felt it to be, an unnatural perversion (a neurosis). Furthermore, psychoanalysis diagnoses the perversion of money because it is the science of enjoyment (the pleasure-principle). "Happiness," says Freud, "is the deferred fulfillment of a prehistoric wish. That is why wealth brings so little happiness; money is not an infantile wish." [61] And finally, in its famous paradox, the equation of money and excrement, psychoanalysis becomes the first science to state what common sense and the poets have long known—that the essence of money is its absolute worthlessness.

We thus arrive at a third paradox in the psychoanalytical theory of money; and this paradox also needs careful explanation. And again, to explain the psychoanalytical doctrine we shall try to connect it with the relevant parallel stream of modern thought. In this case the crucial figure is Veblen. There is, as John Gambs, Veblen's most perceptive modern explicator, says, no Veblen system; it is germane to our problem that a theory of money is, as Gambs notes, a crying need in Veblenian institutionalism. Veblen had extraordinary psychological insights, but his psychological theory was an improvisation. Gambs himself points out that Veblen's psychology in its most penetrating insights surprisingly resembles Freudian theory; we are following Gambs' own suggestion if we try to incorporate Veblen into psychoanalysis. [62] When the core of the economic problem becomes not production but consumption, when the core of the sociological problem is the jungle pattern of irrational human demands, Veblen is the pioneer. And fortunately Veblen's ideas have already been applied by Herskovits to the anthropological data on the archaic economy.

Veblen's masterpiece is focused on what I hope will be the main problem facing the next generation, the problem of consumption. Statesmen who think that there are no psychological problems, that social control over productive forces and increased production will automatically bring happiness, should read it. One of the advances toward reality-thinking in Dobb's article on "Economic Calculation in a Socialist Economy" is his (still somewhat oblique) recognition that Veblenesque patterns of irrational consumption are not restricted to capitalist economies.[63]

To effect a juncture between economic theory and Veblen's insights into the psychological realities of economic behavior, a missing link needs to be established—the concept of an economic surplus. The economic correlate of Veblen's sociological concept of the leisure class is the existence of an economic surplus over and above the minimum necessary for subsistence. We are back once more at Marx' statement, which Marx cannot clarify, that it is "the surplus use-values alone that are converted into money." As a result of the invention of money, says Locke, "The desire of having more than men needed altered the intrinsic value of things, which depends only on their usefulness to the life of man." We have to pick up Plato's distinction between the most elementary ("most necessary") city and the luxurious city; we have to pick up Thoreau's desperate insistence on the distinction between the necessary and the superfluous. Thoreau, Plato, and Veblen all agree that (to use psychoanalytical terminology) the human neurosis is interrelated with the economic surplus. Thoreau says luxury results in impoverishment: "That seemingly wealthy, but most terribly impoverished class of all, who have accumulated dross, but know not how to use it, or get rid of it, and thus have forged their own golden or silver fetters."[64] Plato's second city, the luxurious city, automatically becomes the swollen city, the sick city that has to be purged by the regimen of philosopher-kings. And for Veblen the logic of leisure is the logic of "reputable wastefulness and futility."[65] The time has come to ask liberal humanists—who, to their honor, entertain "freedom from want" as a goal—how they will deal with Plato's point that poverty consists not so much in small property as in large desires.[66]

The existence of an economic surplus, or luxury, certainly antedates the urban revolution, and it is a regular feature in the ideal type of the archaic economy. There is on this point, except in Herskovits, considerable confusion in the anthropological literature. Veblen himself confuses the issue by equating luxury with the leisure class on the one hand and with the "predatory habit of life" on the other. Since the "predatory habit of life" and the leisure class did not seem to him to be aboriginal, he postulated an "archaic structure" without these and without luxury. And in the literature of economic determinism, followers of Marx, who, like Marx, have no psychology of use-values and therefore no concept of surplus use-values, confuse in the concept of "economic necessities" all discrimination between what is economically necessary for survival and other, in some sense superfluous, economic demands. And, confusing economic surplus with surplus-value in the standard Marxian sense (surplus exchange-value), they too, like Veblen, equate luxury and leisure class and therefore (with the Marxian view of classes) ignore the existence of an economic surplus in the archaic economy, which they call primitive communism.

But the fact is that the human animal is distinctively characterized, as a species and from the start, by the drive to produce a surplus; it is not true that this drive appears only when coercively imposed by a ruling class. There is some of this error in Veblen's notion of the leisure class. Actually there never has been a leisure class in history. Veblen himself brilliantly showed how his leisure class is involved in a pattern not of enjoyment but of ceremonial work, "the exhibition of difficult and costly achievements in etiquette," [67] etc. There is something in the human psyche which commits man to nonenjoyment, to work (*negotium,* nonleisure). Thus the issue here is the same question of alienated (compulsive) labor. To postulate an inner, not externally imposed, compulsion to work is to postulate an inner need to produce a surplus. Actually no other assumption can explain the phenomenon of technological progress which Marxists must ascribe to their stage of primitive communism. That "unceasing bent for discovery," which Engels ascribes to the very structure of that labor which according to him is the essence of the species,[68] is the drive to produce a surplus.

There is something in the structure of the human animal which compels him to produce superfluously, but obviously the compulsion will apply only so long as the human animal draws no distinction between the necessary and the superfluous. It is an integral part of the money complex and the compulsion to work to confuse the superfluous with the necessary;

the confusion still reigns in all the vague talk about "economic necessity." But the core of the necessary is the need for food. We may therefore say that it is inherent in the money complex to attribute to what is not food the virtue that belongs to food. In Freud's succinct formula, excrement becomes aliment; [69] but it remains excrement, as Midas, with his *auri sacra fames*, discovered when he became hungry. "All *essential* production is for the Mouth; and is finally measured by the mouth," says Ruskin; "the want of any clear insight of this fact is the capital error, issuing in rich interest and revenue of error among the political economists. Their minds are continually set on money-gain, not on mouth-gain." And Ruskin perceives money-gain as the pursuit of the dream of sublimated anality; it is to "take dust for deity, spectre for possession, fettered dream for life." [70] The Inca even possessed gardens in which the trees and plants were imitated "all in gold and silver, with their leaves, flowers and fruit; some just beginning to sprout, others half-grown, others having reached maturity. They made fields of maize with their leaves, heads, canes, roots and flowers, all exactly imitated. The beard of the maize-head was of gold, and all the rest was of silver, the parts being soldered together." [71]

The superfluity complex thus invades and corrupts the domain of human consumption; in technical psychoanalytical terms, the anal complex is displaced to, and fused with, the oral complex. "Wherefore do you spend money for that which is not bread? and your labor for that which satisfieth not?" (Isaiah); "Fools! They know not how much the half is more than the whole, nor how great enjoyment there is in mallow and asphodel" (Hesiod). [72] The resultant confusion is exhibited not only in the bottomless consumer demand for inedible goods which satisfy not, but also in the demand that food itself assume luxurious—i.e., superfluous—forms. This neurotic perversion of needs is not a child of civilization or class domination, but begins in archaic man. Archaic food production, distribution, and consumption patterns, as Malinowski and Herskovits show, [73] exhibit the logic of what Veblen called conspicuous consumption—that is, the logic of the irrational superfluous. Modern economic theory, which accepts as given and unquestionable the demands that appear on the market (the "randomness of ends"), is accepting as given and unquestionable the irrationality of human demand and consumption patterns. Once again we see the spurious character of modern "rationality." What the elegant laws of supply and demand really describe is the antics of an animal which has confused excrement with aliment and does not know it, and which, like infantile sexuality, pursues no "real aim." [74] Having no real aim, acquisitiveness, as Aristotle correctly said, has no limit. Hence the psychological premise of a market economy is not, as in classical theory of exchange, that the agents know what they want, but that they do not know what they want. In advanced capitalist countries advertising exists to create irrational demands and keep the consumer confused; without the consumer confusion perpetuated by advertising, the economy would collapse. Thus, as Ruskin again saw, the science of political economy must perpetuate darkness and nescience: [75]

> So far, therefore, as the science of exchange relates to the advantage of one of the exchanging persons only, it is founded on the ignorance or incapacity of the opposite person. . . . It is therefore a science founded on nescience. . . . *This* science, alone of sciences, must, by all available means, promulgate and prolong its opposite nescience. . . . It is therefore peculiarly and alone the science of darkness.

With the transformation of the worthless into the priceless and the inedible into food, man acquires a soul; he becomes the animal which does not live by bread alone, the animal which sublimates. Hence gold is the quintessential symbol of the human endeavor to sublimate—"the world's soul" (Jonson). The sublimation of base matter into gold is the folly of alchemy and the folly of alchemy's pseudosecular heir, modern capitalism. The profoundest things in *Capital* are Marx' shadowy poetic presentiments of the alchemical mystery of money and of the "mystical," "fetishistic" character of commodities. "This social existence [represented in gold and silver] assumes the aspect of a world beyond, of a thing, matter, commodity, by the side of and outside of the real elements of social wealth." "In the case of interest-bearing capital the self-reproducing character of capital, the self-expansion of value, the surplus-value, surrounds itself with the qualities of the occult." Commodities are "thrown into the alchemistical retort of circulation" to "come out again in the shape of money." "Circulation is the great social retort into which everything is thrown, to come out again as a gold-crystal." "Circulation sweats money from every pore." [76] Freud's critique of sublimation foreshadows the end of this flight of human fancy, the end of the alchemical delusion, the discovery of what things really are worth, and the return of the priceless to the worthless. In a letter to Fliess Freud writes, "I can hardly tell you how many things I (a new Midas) turn into—excrement." [77]

The drive to sublimate is the same as the drive to produce an economic surplus. What then underlies the drive to produce a surplus? Marx, to explain man's historicity (i.e., for him, technological progress), attributes to man a psychological-physiological structure such that the act of satisfying a need, and making an instrument to satisfy a need, provokes a new need. Such an assumption makes man eternally Faustian and restless and therefore precludes happiness; it also precludes the possibility of an "economy of abundance." [78] This dark shadow hangs over the third volume of *Capital*. Marx writes: [79]

> The realm of freedom does not commence until the point is passed when labor under the compulsion of necessity and of external utility is required. . . . Just as the savage must wrestle with nature, in order to satisfy his wants, in order to maintain his life and to reproduce it, so the civilized man has to do it in all forms of society and under all possible modes of production. With his development the realm of natural necessity expands, because his wants increase; but at the same time the forces of production increase, by which these wants are satisfied.

In the second volume of *Capital* Marx says that "capitalism is destroyed in its very foundation, if we assume that its compelling motive is enjoyment instead of the accumulation of wealth." [80] But Marx' psychology is unable to emancipate socialism or any economy whatsoever from the motive of accumulation, and therefore it is unable to guide mankind to enjoyment. From this nightmare of infinitely expanding technological progress and human needs, only a science of enjoyment can deliver us. But how?

Our problem is also the problem of the division of labor. No one has denounced the dehumanizing consequences of the civilized division of labor more emphatically than Marx.[81] It is fatal to freedom; it produces the development in a man of one single faculty at the expense of all other faculties, and to subdivide a man's faculties is to kill him; it produces a crippled monstrosity, industrial pathology; intelligence is alienated into the process as a whole while the individual specialist becomes stupid and ignorant. More dispassionately, Durkheim has demonstrated that the division of labor is not a consequence of the individual's search for happiness and does not promote the happiness of the individual; progress, the work of the division of labor, has nothing to do with human happiness.[82] Durkheim's argument stresses the antinomy between the determinate nature of human happiness and needs and the indeterminate goal of progress, between the harmony principle in happiness and the disharmonious effects of the division of labor, and, underlying all, the antinomy between happiness and work. But Marx had to recognize that the division of labor is "common to economic formations of society the most diverse," is "spontaneous" and natural. Hence the gloomy conclusion that "some crippling of body and mind is inseparable even from the division of labor as a whole." Hence Marx can hope only to reduce the excesses of contemporary industrial pathology, and Durkheim only to regulate them.[83]

The division of labor does not grow out of the realm of economic necessities in the strict sense, but out of the realm of economic surplus. It is only at a very advanced level of organization that households dare to depend on something other than their own production for economic necessities. Marx in his description of the ancient Indian communities says, "The chief part of the product is destined for direct use by the community itself. . . . It is the surplus alone that becomes a commodity." [84] Hence the superfluous character of the objects round which primitive trade centered—paleolithic amber, ancient oriental gold; hence the superfluous character of the first specialist, the magician. Here we are once more back at sacred money.

Durkheim failed to connect the division of labor with economic surplus, and so was led to conceive of it as an abstract principle of social solidarity; and having satisfied himself that it had no connection with individual happiness, he hypostatized the abstract principle of social solidarity as a real power over against the individual, not grounded in the psychology of the individual. Another line of thought is taken by Herskovits, following Veblen.[85] He connects the division of labor with economic surplus, and connects economic surplus with prestige and privilege, and, as we have seen, connects prestige and privilege with the domain of the sacred. And it is easy to show a continuous development of the division of labor as an integral part of the expanding sector of the sacred-superfluous, climaxing in the elaborate organization of the divine household by the priest-kings of the earliest civilizations.[86]

"Man does not live by bread alone." This was already true of archaic man. Instinctively committed to create an economic surplus, archaic man was by the same token instinctively committed to nonenjoyment, self-repression, and compulsive work. The psychological complex which made the economic surplus possible by the same token directed the economic surplus toward irrational—i.e., sacred—ends. This sacred complex is the parent of the division of labor. Our acceptance of the division of labor as rational is part of our general illusion that the secular is the rational: it is really a demonolatry. We no longer give the surplus to God; the process of producing an ever expanding surplus is in itself now our God. And since God is more human than civilization, the emancipation of the economic process from control by God completes the dehumanization of man. To quote Schumpeter: "Capitalist rationality does not do away with sub- or super-rational impulses. It merely makes them get out of hand by removing the restraint of sacred or semi-sacred tradition." [87] A genuine release from the division of labor and from compulsive work—and the inauguration of an economy of enjoyment—therefore depends on release from the commitment to the sacred-superfluous. But how? We must probe more deeply into the nature of this commitment.

4. *Owe and Ought*

IN OUR ideal type of archaic economy we have postulated a psychological principle of nonenjoyment—in Freudian terminology, repression; in Marxian terminology, alienated (compulsive) work. We have derived from the psychological principle of nonenjoyment the economic institution of the surplus or superfluous. We have seen that those two plagues of the modern economy, power and the division of labor, are already inherent in the archaic economy because they are endemic in the sector of the superfluous. Finally we have seen that the sector of the superfluous is essentially the sector of the sacred.

But it is not enough to postulate a psychological principle of nonenjoyment; our aim is to understand it. Is it immutable? Biologically given? Or is it possible that mankind may one day live to enjoy itself? There is a seeming clue in the connection between the principle of nonenjoyment and the devotion to the sacred. Further reflection—as well as psychoanalytical theory—suggest the two are the same; there is one problem—the superfluous-sacred. And the problem of the superfluous-sacred exists already in the archaic economy.

Following Polanyi, we have already seen that archaic economics is not governed by the psychology of economizing calculation. What principle does it obey, then? Polanyi says the essential point is that: [88]

> Man's economy, as a rule, is submerged in his social relationships. He does not act so as to safeguard his individual interest in the possession of material goods; he acts so as to safeguard his social standing, his social claims, his social assets. He values material goods only in so far as they serve this end. . . . The economic system will be run on non-economic motives.

And again Herskovits supports the generalization. But Polanyi's formulation, though it accurately reflects the general line of thought among anthropologists, does not answer the question of the psychology of archaic economics. The sociological concept of "social relationships," "social assets," is too vague, and it implies, if anything, simply a functional view of economics as interconnected with all the other aspects of a culture. But the sophisticated articulation of the ideal type of *Homo economicus* in modern economic theory, together with the admitted fact of its total inapplicability to the whole area of archaic economics, compel us to look for an ideal type for archaic *Homo economicus*, in full awareness that ideal types are ideal and that in concrete actuality there is only individual complexity. Polanyi realizes the need, and he tries to fill it by pointing to strategic principles of social organization, which he lists as reciprocity (symmetry), redistribution (centricity), and householding (autarky). But this is still sociology, not psychology, and for our purposes it is not adequate.

Anthropology, so far as I know, has produced only one concept which attempts in a philosophic manner to define the psychological essence of primitive economics, and that is the gift. It was the philosophic eye of Malinowski which first saw how in the Trobriand Islands the incentive to work and the division of labor are based on an elaborate system of obligations to give and to return gifts.[89] It was the philosophic mind of Marcel Mauss which generalized the concept and advanced it as the fundamental category of primitive economics as a whole.[90] The category of the gift in fact states more concretely and more fundamentally what Polanyi referred to more vaguely as reciprocity and redistribution. We can get an image of how an economy based on the gift works and feels if we study our own Christmas. As Lévi-Strauss, who attempts to explain archaic kinship systems in terms of the gift, points out, Christmas giving is nowhere so elaborate as in capitalist America, as if the year-round psychology of taking was canceled and atoned by an annual ritual which returns to the archaic psychology of giving.[91]

Thus the myth of a primitive communism, like all myths, turns out to have a core of psychological truth. The archaic economy is governed by the rule of giving and sharing. But this rule is a psychological principle, and its character is quite distorted if it is interpreted as based on an economic principle of common ownership. Such a concept imports into the archaic world our modern psychology of property and possession. It treats the collective as one big owner. Man remains the self-interested *Homo economicus*, who shares not because he has an intrinsic disposition to give but because he is only a part-owner in a collective enterprise. Hence the stalemate and confusion in the whole debate as to whether the archaic economy was collectivistic (in the sense of common ownership).[92] The real point is that the modern psychology of possession is superimposed over a deeper psychology of giving, and is constructed, by the process of denial, out of its archaic opposite.

The archaic institution of the gift is the clue to the psychology of the whole sector of the sacred-superfluous. In the archaic economy gift and countergift organize the division of labor; prestige and power are conferred by ability to give; gifts are sacred and the gods exist to receive gifts (*do ut des*).[93] Hence the principle of nonenjoyment, the compulsion to work and to produce an economic surplus, is contained in the need to give. An economic surplus is created in order to have something to give; archaic man does not enjoy because he needs to give.

We must get rid of the prejudice of *Homo economicus* that economic activity is based on the psychology of "rational" utilitarian egoism. The psychological postulate on which Marx based labor and technological progress—that in man need-satisfaction always begets new needs—postulates utilitarian egoism. Durkheim's whole sociology of the division of labor turns on the axiom, "The desire to become happier is the only individual source which can take account of progress." [94] Durkheim assumes that the domain of individual psychology is comprehended in the search for happiness—i.e., is egoistic. Then, having shown (correctly) that the division of labor cannot be derived from the search for happiness, he is sure that it cannot be derived from the psychology of the individual, and therefore he is free to hypostatize as a real force society and a supraindividual principle of solidarity. Even Mauss, in the essay to which we are so indebted, seems to mistake the problem, because he is not free from the egoist fallacy. According to Mauss, the fundamental problem is to determine what obligates the recipient of a gift to make a return gift.[95] He assumes that the original giver needs such an assurance before he will give, an assurance that he will not lose in the transaction; here we see the assumption of a psychology of egoism. But the psychology of egoism is incapable of explaining the institution of gift exchange. For gift exchange in the archaic economy is broadly governed by the principle of reciprocity, so that although the giver may not lose, he does not gain. The psychology of egoism cannot explain activities resulting in no gain, merely no loss. The question is not what obligates the recipient of a gift to return a gift, but why give in the first place? In the end Mauss has to take the same position on the gift as Durkheim took on the division of labor: gift exchange is a primal act of social solidarity.[96]

It is a great step forward to indicate that the concrete institution of the gift creates social solidarity, and therefore that the basic psychology of human social organization may be contained in the psychology of giving. But we are not going to understand either the gift or social organization if we simply derive the gift from a not-further-analyzable principle of social solidarity.

What then is the psychology of the need to give? We have already postulated a connection between the need to give and the principle of nonenjoyment: that is to say, the psychology of giving takes us beyond egoism, beyond the desire for individual happiness—in Freud's phrase, beyond the pleasure-principle. Archaic gift-giving (the famous potlatch is only an extreme example) is one vast refutation of the notion that the psychological motive of economic life is utilitarian egoism. Archaic man gives because he wants to lose; the psychology is not egoist but self-sacrificial. Hence the intrinsic connection with the sacred. The gods exist to receive gifts, that is to say sacrifices; the gods exist in order to structure the human need for self-sacrifice.[97]

In *Beyond the Pleasure Principle* Freud declared the existence of a function of the mental apparatus independent from the pleasure-principle, more primitive than the pleasure-principle, which seems to impose on the human organism "another task, which must be accomplished before the dominance of the pleasure-principle can even begin." [98] *Beyond the Pleasure Principle* inaugurated the last phase in Freud's thought; the rest of his life was devoted to exploring the nature of this other principle. His exploration disclosed many aspects—anxiety, the repetition compulsion, sadism and masochism, guilt, the death instinct. In Freud's mind these aspects were all interrelated, and all ultimately were to be grasped as manifestations of the death instinct. We suggest that it is in this area, the sector of the death instinct, that the psychology of economics lies.

But to avoid being confronted all at once with all the complications of death-instinct theory, we begin with the more limited hypothesis that the psychology of economics is the psychology of guilt. Giving is self-sacrificial; self-sacrifice is self-punishment—"Work is still for most men a punishment and a scourge," says Durkheim [99]—the derivation of work from Adam's sin expresses the psychological truth. In the archaic institution of the gift, what the giver wants to lose is guilt. We thus arrive at a further level of meaning in the psychoanalytical paradox of the anal character of money. Money is condensed wealth; condensed wealth is condensed guilt. But guilt is essentially unclean. "Monks eat the world's excrement, that is to say sins," says Rabelais. "In one of my patients," says Abraham, "the idea of eating excrement was connected with the idea of being punished for a great sin." [100] Money is human guilt with the dross refined away till it is a pure crystal of self-punishment; but it remains filthy because it remains guilt.

Freud says of Dostoevsky that his "burden of guilt had taken tangible shape as a burden of debt." [101] We proceed to generalize the implications of Freud's observation. The classic psychoanalytical essays on money and the anal character (Freud, Abraham, Ferenczi, Jones) do not pay enough attention to the factor of guilt. Róheim alone, with his familiarity with anthropological data, does justice to it, although in his usual unfortunately obscure manner.[102] Actually the essential points in the psychoanalytical theory of money as guilt are made by Nietzsche in his essay on guilt in the *Genealogy of Morals.* Nietzsche is not systematic nor even consistent; and still he is the best point of departure.

Nietzsche begins by defining man as the "animal that can promise," and takes it to be the very problem of man to understand how such an animal came into existence. The ability to promise involves the loss of the natural animal forgetfulness of the past, which is the precondition for healthy living in the present. Man's ability to promise involves an unhealthy (neurotic) constipation with the past (the anal character!); he can "get rid of" nothing. Thus, through the ability to promise, the future is bound to the past. It is therefore what gives man the power to calculate and to be calculable, to owe and to pay. It is what makes man responsible; it is his conscience.

Nietzsche then expands the interconnection between morality and economy thus postulated by showing the structural identity of debt and guilt ("ought" and "owe"), contract and duty, price and retaliation. (I discard, and am going to reverse, his proposition that conscience derives from trade; I also discard his distinction between "conscience" and "bad conscience.") He notes that both the economy sector (the creditor-debtor relation) and the morality sector (the categorical imperative) reek of cruelty (sadism). In the morality sector he postulates as underlying cause an instinctual repression which turns aggression inward and produces self-denial and self-sacrifice (masochism). He connects the whole complex with a religion of sadism and masochism. In the religious sector the basic notion is that present culture is a debt owed to ancestors. Nietzsche postulates that with the accumulation of culture (civilization) the sense of indebtedness to ancestors (guilt) increases, climaxing in Christianity as a theology of unpayable debt. And, returning to his original point of departure (the unhealthiness of the animal that can promise), Nietzsche ends by connecting the religion of self-sacrifice with instinctual repression and disease (neurosis).[103]

The importance of this whole set of ideas for economic theory can be measured by contrasting Nietzsche with a great economic psychologist who lacks them. Veblen's predatory instinct (sadism) attempts to explain economic institutions without Nietzsche's notion of convertibility of sadism and masochism, without guilt, without repression. Hence the limitations of Veblen's notion of leisure.

To introduce psychoanalytical system into Nietzsche's insights we must start with his last idea, the sense of indebtedness to ancestors. Psychoanalysis can accept the idea that the sense of indebtedness to ancestors is the governing idea of the religion of self-sacrifice. Psychoanalysis can accept the idea that the religion of self-sacrifice is the cause of the life (and economy) of instinctual repression and renunciation (nonenjoyment), and that the religion of self-sacrifice is cumulative in its effects. Freud explains the process in *Civilization and Its Discontents* better than Nietzsche, by invoking Nietzsche's other ideas, the convertibility of sadism and masochism, and the derivation of the whole complex from the repression of full enjoyment of life in the present. The repression of full enjoyment in the present inevitably releases aggression against those ancestors out of love of whom the repression was instituted. Aggression against those simultaneously loved is guilt. And the more fully the debt to the past is paid, the more complete are its inroads on the enjoyment of life in the present; but then fresh quantities of aggression are released, bringing fresh quantities of guilt.

Whatever the ultimate explanation of guilt may be, we put forward the hypothesis that the whole money complex is rooted in the psychology of guilt. "All money, properly so called, is an acknowledgement of debt," says Ruskin. He also observes that the goddess of guilt and revenge, Tisiphone, is "a person versed in the highest branches of arithmetic, and punctual in her habits" [104] (i.e., in Freudian terminology, an anal character). Certainly the Indo-European languages confirm Nietzsche's observation that the semantics of debt and payment (owe) are the semantics of guilt (ought). Since, for reasons already given, we must abandon Nietzsche's notion (the old Adam Smith notion) that trade is an aboriginal human institution, we must reverse his explanation of the semantic facts and derive trade from guilt. Actually the derivation of trade from guilt follows automatically if you grant the basic premise of the sacred character of the money complex, and also allow the equation of the domain of the sacred with the domain of guilt.

Durkheim was right that the division of labor and all that results from it are not derived from the pleasure-principle ("the desire for individual happiness"); he was wrong in thinking that the psychology of the individual is summed up in the pleasure-principle. Archaic man gives to get rid of the burden of guilt. But *ex hypothesi*, the recipient has his burden of guilt too; and in our ideal archaic economy the net result of the exchange of gifts is a structure of reciprocity, symmetry, and balance.

How then does reciprocal giving help to get rid of the burden of guilt? Of course it does not get rid of guilt, as the whole history of archaic and modern man shows. But it does represent man's first attempt at a solution. Guilt is mitigated by being shared; man entered social organization in order to share guilt. Social organization (including the division of labor) is a structure of shared guilt. Social organization brings the repressed unconscious guilt to consciousness (in a distorted form, of course); we remember Freud's proposition that unconscious ideas can become conscious only if they are transformed into external perceptions, i.e., projected out on to the real world.[105] Social organization is a symbolic mutual confession of guilt.

We thus arrive at Freud's notion that social organization is formed by complicity in a primal crime (the totemic brotherhood).[106] The logic of gift-giving is the same as the logic of the totemic communion-meal, on which Freud commented that only through the solidarity of all the participants could the sense of guilt be assuaged.[107] All the ceremonies of food distribution participate in the nature of the communion-meal. It is not sufficient to accept, as Mauss does, the explanation of archaic man, that the objects shared and exchanged have a magic quality which prescribes their socialization.[108] Their magical quality, like that of the totemic food, is derived from their symbolic relation to the unconscious sense of guilt, and the first demand of the unconscious sense of guilt is to be shared. Similarly archaic kinship systems, which are so intimately connected with the institution of gift-giving, are not explained by the abstract need for social organization but by the psychology of guilt. It is not sufficient to say, as Lévi-Strauss does,[109] that the incest taboo is the foundation of the familial organization; we must return to Freud and say that incest guilt created the familial organization.

But we must immediately differentiate ourselves from Freud. For Freud the primal crime was a historical fact. And since it is a historical fact whose consequences are reproduced, according to Freud, in every generation, it is also a biological fact. Freud's position is inseparable both from his position that the "archaic heritage" consists of "memory-traces of the experiences of former generations" [110] and from his position that the infantile sexual organizations (which are the bodily carriers of the basic human trauma) are biologically given.[111] It then follows that the problem of guilt is insoluble. Freud, who abandoned many illusions, did not abandon the illusion that Adam really fell, and thus his allegiance to sublimation and civilization—the consequences of original sin—holds fast on the essential point. Given Freud's perception that civilization is constructed out of guilt and his knowledge of the logic of guilt, the result can only be complete pessimism.

We on the other hand cling to the position that Adam never really fell; that the children do not really inherit the sins of their fathers; that the primal crime is an infantile fantasy, created out of nothing by the infantile ego in order to sequester by repression its own unmanageable vitality (id); that the sexual organizations are constructed by the infantile ego to repress its bodily vitality; and that adult life remains fixated to this world of infantile fantasy until the adult ego is strong enough to undo the basic repression and enter the kingdom of enjoyment. "Atheism and a kind of second innocence complement and supplement each other," says Nietzsche.[112] Only second innocence could recognize the whole debt and guilt complex as fantasy, as nightmare; only second innocence could be atheistical. Again we see the limitations of pseudosecular "rationalism." The ultimate problem is not guilt but the incapacity to live. The illusion of guilt is necessary for an animal that cannot enjoy life, in order to organize a life of nonenjoyment.

If the money complex is constructed out of an unconscious sense of guilt, it is a neurosis. Hence the symbolism inseparable from the money complex. Laum argued that the symbolism of the money complex must be derived from the home of symbolism, the domain of the sacred. But the symbolism of the sacred is itself a mystery. The ultimate rationale of symbolism lies in the unconscious. Condensation, displacement, and symbolic substitution are, as Freud showed, the necessary schemata through which the unconscious passes as it seeks to enter consciousness. Money as "condensed value," as "symbol of value," as "universal representative equivalent," has passed through these schemata and comes from the unconscious. And the ultimate reason why the money complex cannot dispense with symbolism is that it originates in denial of reality (fantasy) and has, as Freud said of the fantasies of infantile sexuality, no real aim. Money is symbolical because it is derived from unconscious guilt and because there is nothing in reality that corresponds to it. We may therefore say of money what Freud said of the symptoms (symbols) produced by unconscious fantasies: [113]

> One must, however, never allow oneself to be misled into applying to the repressed creations of the mind the standard of reality; this might result in underestimating the importance of phantasies in symptom-formation on the ground that they are not actualities; or in deriving a neurotic sense of guilt from another source because there is no proof of actual committal of a crime. One is bound to employ the currency that prevails in the country one is exploring; in our case it is the neurotic currency.

All currency is neurotic currency in this sense.

But all currency is not equally neurotic, or at least not neurotic in the same sense. The dialectic of neurosis contains its own "attempts at explanation and cure," [114] energized by the ceaseless upward pressure of the repressed unconscious and producing the return of the repressed to consciousness, though in an increasingly distorted form, as long as basic repression (denial) is maintained and the neurosis endures. The modern economy is characterized by an aggravation of the neurosis, which is at the same time a fuller delineation of the nature of the neurosis, a fuller return of the repressed. In the archaic consciousness the sense of indebtedness exists together with the illusion that the debt is payable; the gods exist to make the debt payable. Hence the archaic economy is embedded in religion, limited by the religious framework, and mitigated by the consolations of religion—above all, removal of indebtedness and guilt. The modern consciousness represents an increased sense of guilt, more specifically a breakthrough from the unconscious of the truth that the burden of guilt is unpayable. This, as we saw in the last chapter, is the moment of history represented by Luther. At this point the gods retreat into invisibility (*Deus absconditus*); man is bankrupt.

Thus the increased sense of guilt brings about the emancipation of the economic process from divine controls and divine ends. The secularization of the economy means the abandonment of the comfortable illusion that work achieves redemption; as Luther said, man is not justified by works. At the same time the compulsion to work is retained and intensified. The result is an economy driven by the pure sense of guilt, unmitigated by any sense of redemption; as Luther said, the Devil (guilt) is lord of this world. Nor is classical political economy (again in a distorted way) unaware of the situation; the labor theory of value corresponds to an economy driven simply by the compulsion to work, unmitigated by any enjoyment. But work without enjoyment is pure self-punishment, and therefore it is a pure culture of guilt. The illusion that Christ redeemed is abandoned, but not the illusion that Adam fell, and therefore man must punish himself with work. The economy unconsciously obeys the logic of guilt.

The abandonment of the illusion that work redeems signifies a disillusionment with the dreams of infantile narcissism, a strengthened capacity to endure harsh truth, and, on both counts, a general strengthening of the ego. But the neurosis goes on, and the harsh truth is actualized only on condition of denying it (negation). Luther's notion of capitalism as the work of the Devil still admits the problem of guilt into consciousness, even if in a distorted way. Secular "rationalism" and liberal Protestantism deny the existence of the Devil (guilt). Their denial makes no difference to the economy, which remains driven by the sense of guilt; or rather it makes this difference, that the economy is more uncontrollably driven by the sense of guilt because the problem of guilt is repressed by denial into the unconscious.

5. *Time Is Money*

THE PROVERB says that "time is money." In the labor theory of value, value consists of units of labor-time. The result, according to Marx, is that "time is everything, man is nothing; he is no more than the carcase of time." Fromm explains, "Capital, the dead past, employs labor, the living vitality and power of the present." [115] From that point of view, interest is a trib-

ute levied on present activity by past achievement. From another point of view, the dynamics of capitalism is postponement of enjoyment to the constantly postponed future—in
Keynes' words, "a case of jam tomorrow and never jam today";
in Ruskin's words, "bulb issuing in bulb, never in tulip." [116] The
rate of interest has been called "impatience crystallized into a
market-rate"; Schumpeter says that in the phenomenon of interest "time itself becomes in a certain sense an element of
cost." [117] The problem is therefore summarized in Professor
Hicks' formula, "The rate of interest is the price of time." [118]

The economists are not going to track "that queer beast,
the rate of interest" to its lair unless they stop repressing from
their consciousness what has been happening to the concept of
time. It is becoming increasingly clear to philosophically
minded physicists, biologists, and anthropologists both that
Kant was right in saying that time was not a thing in itself out
there but a schema of the human mind, and that Kant was
wrong in assuming that the human mind was immutably endowed with this schema. A recent review of the discussion
draws the correct (as far as it goes) conclusion that the choice
of a time-schema depends on biological and cultural needs.[119]
Kant's assumption of the universality of the time-schema is
correlative with his assumption of man's universal rationality;
and the epistemological assumption of the universality of *Homo
rationalis* can now be seen to be really the psychological assumption of the universality of *Homo economicus*. The collapse
of the rationalist notion of time leaves the current theory of
time irrationally culturally relativistic; and the irrational relativism of time is connected with the irrational relativism of
human needs. Therefore progress toward a higher rationality
in our understanding of time depends on a psychology which
explores the irrational in general and specifically the irrational
in human needs. Such a psychology is psychoanalysis.

The intermediate term between psychoanalysis and time, as
between psychoanalysis and money, is religion. Economists and
scientists must face up to the fact that in dealing with time at
all they are dealing with a religion. It did not escape the acute
eye of Whorf, who opened the eyes of American anthropologists to the cultural relativity of the time sense, that for exam-

ple the Hopi sense of time is rooted in religious valuations.[120] But the essential point is to see that the classical Western sense of time, Newtonian time, was a religion, which, like all religions, was taken by its adherents (both the physicists and the economists) to be absolute objective truth. Once again we see that "secular rationalism" is really a religion; the new relativist notion of time is really the disintegration of a religion.

The religious nature of time was already adumbrated in Spengler's antithesis of Apollonian and Faustian time;[121] but for our purposes the best point of departure is Mircea Eliade's brilliant (though, as we shall see, psychologically confused) exposition of the antithesis between archaic and modern time.[122] Archaic time is cyclical, periodic, unhistoric: modern time is progressive (historical), continuous, irreversible. Eliade shows that the periodicity of archaic time is based on a religion of periodic redemption, and modern progressive time is based on a religion of ultimate redemption at the end of time, Hebrew in origin and given classic formulation in Christianity. Once again it appears that "secular rationalism," in this case the classical rationalist theory of time, is really the prolongation of the basic premises of Christianity, but minus (the crucial point) the idea of Redemption.

If time is a religious notion, it is a proper object for psychoanalytical investigation. "As a result of certain psychoanalytic discoveries, we are today in a position to embark on a discussion of the Kantian theorem that time and space are 'necessary forms of thought,'" wrote Freud in 1920.[123] Actually the fundamental psychoanalytical discovery about time was made in the initial discovery of the unconscious: in the unconscious there is no time. "Unconscious mental processes are in themselves timeless"; "In the id there is nothing corresponding to the idea of time."[124] From this theorem we have already in an earlier chapter drawn the conclusion that a healthy human being, in whom ego and id were unified, would not live in time. To put it another way, time, both archaic and modern, is, like money, neurotic and correlative with instinctual repression.[125]

Under conditions of general repression, consciousness cannot discard the veil of time, and only the mystical consciousness has been able to divine what lies beyond it. Psychoanalysis claims to be a new and scientific way of making conscious the unconscious; but the difficulties it faces can be seen in Freud's own failure with the problem of time. At the end of his life he wrote: "It is constantly being borne in on me that we have made far too little use for our theory of the indubitable fact that the repressed remains unaltered by the passage of time. This seems to offer us the possibility of an approach to some very profound truths. But I myself have made no further progress here." [126] In 1920 Freud made the mistake of concluding that since time is not in the unconscious, it must be derived from the conscious system: "Our abstract idea of time seems to be wholly derived from the method of working of the system Perception-Consciousness"; and he proposed to derive it from a certain rhythmic periodicity inherent in the operation of the perceptual system.[127] And then Freud reached a dead end. But in the psychoanalytical map of man there are more domains than just the unconscious and the conscious. Time belongs to the ego indeed, but to the unconscious sector of the ego—that is to say, to those basic structures of reality distortion necessary to sustain and endure repression. What Kant took to be the necessary schemata of rationality are really the necessary schemata of repression. What the cultural relativity of time concepts really signifies—and it is a hopeful sign—is that the structure of basic repression is not immutable. What Eliade really discovered is a significant difference in the structure of repression between archaic and modern man.

If time belongs to the unconscious sector of the ego, it belongs with the components in this sector discovered by psychoanalysis—the super-ego (conscience, guilt), the defense mechanisms, and character structure. Actually the relation between time and this unconscious sector of the ego was noted by Freud, though not connected into a theory. As early as 1914 Freud suggested a connection between the watching institution of conscience and the time sense.[128] In his fully developed theory, the super-ego is a shadow of the lost past incorporated (by identification) into the personality. It "represents more than anything the cultural past"; "it unites in itself the influences of the present and of the past"; it is "an example of the way in which the present is turned into the past." [129] In Nietzsche's terms, that indebtedness to ancestors which is the guilty conscience, and which makes man constipated with the past and capable of promising, is formed in childhood by the incorporation of the parents and the wish to be father of oneself.

Freud also discerned the time factor—a "dichronous" structure—in the defense mechanism he called "undoing," which is defined by Fenichel as follows: "Something positive is done which, actually or magically, is the opposite of something which, again actually or in the imagination, was done before." [130] Fenichel correctly adds that "the idea of expiation is nothing but an expression of belief in the possibility of a magical undoing." Therefore time has to be constructed by an animal that has guilt and seeks to expiate.

And time is also a factor in the defense mechanism known as isolation. Isolation is a technique for protecting the ego from being overwhelmed by its own instinctual urges, and consists in fragmenting experience into separate parts; time intervals are interpolated, and the result is a safe obsession with routine as a protection against the demands of the instincts. [131] As Lucile Dooley pointed out, [132] this method of preserving the ego against the instincts is peculiarly developed in modern Western man; in Whiteheadian terminology, the reification and idolatry of time sustain the abstract character of modern Western life and protect it against instinctual concreteness. But the fragmentation, by isolation, of time parcels it into units that can be "counted," are "valuable," can be "saved," just like property and money; the point of the division of labor, says Adam Smith, is to save time. Therefore the defense mechanism of isolation prepares the way for those particular id gratifications which are dear to the anal character.

Actually the connection between time and money is closer than resemblance. Lucile Dooley showed that objects have to be seen as crystallized time in order to be possessed as property; on this point the labor-time theory of value comes closest to psychoanalysis. And, from another point of view, Spengler showed the connection between Apollonian time and Apollonian money, between Faustian time and Faustian money. [133] Hence, although Freud did not, Abraham and Jones did introduce into standard psychoanalytical dogma the paradox that not only money but also time is excrement, and they have case-histories to prove it.[134]

Finally, to complete this survey of the psychoanalytical investigation of time, there must be a connection between time and the death instinct. If the death instinct deserves its name, it must have something to do with time. Freud specifically postulated some special connection between the death instinct and the repetition compulsion;[135] repetition compulsion, like the defense mechanism of undoing, like Freud's postulated rhythmic periodicity in perception, is a temporal structure. Separation—the decisive act in the defense mechanism of isolation—is also a manifestation of the death instinct.[136] The connection between time and the death instinct has suffered the general neglect of the death instinct in psychoanalytical literature.[137] In an earlier chapter we attempted to develop the connection between the death instinct and negation, and between negation and the sense of time.

The psychoanalytical theory of time does not cohere; nothing in psychoanalysis coheres except what the master put together, and on this problem he was derelict. But separate insights have been developed to the point where they can be used. We are in a position to exploit the theorem of the connection between time and "undoing": time is a schema necessary for the expiation of guilt. Western philosophy begins with Anaximander's sentence: "To that out of which their birth is, their destruction returns, according to debt [or "fate," or "necessity"; the Greek word is significantly ambiguous]; for they give justice and payment to each other for their injustice according to the order of time." The sentence is pregnant with economics, but its parent is the religion of guilt, in which the schema of time originates. The problem is mistaken in Eliade's existentialist formulations. The problem is not the meaninglessness of profane existence, or its absurdity, or the sinfulness of historical existence, or the terror of history. The real problem is the sense of guilt in the human species, which causes the nightmare of history and the compensatory rituals of cyclical regeneration and messianic redemption.

Archaic man must not be idealized by attributing to him the power to abolish time and "live in a continual present";[138] no religion of expiation, but only the abolition of guilt, can abolish time. Archaic man experiences guilt, and therefore time; that is why he makes such elaborate efforts, once a year, to deny it. "The subject-matter of a repressed image or thought can make its way into consciousness on condition that it is denied." [139] Actually the defense mechanism of undoing is a special case of the defense mechanism of denial. And as Freud showed, denial is always accompanied by affirmation of the denied, and therefore results in a split in the ego.[140] In archaic man (and archaic time) the split in the ego is institutionalized in the all-pervasive dialectic, exhibited by Durkheim, between the sacred and the profane.[141] Eliade's distinction between archaic and modern time still stands, but it is to be understood as representing different structures of guilt. In modern man guilt has increased to the point where it is no longer possible to expiate it in annual ceremonies of regeneration. Guilt is therefore cumulative, and therefore time is cumulative. The annual expiation of guilt, as Eliade shows, ensured that archaic society had no history. Cumulative guilt imposes on modern societies a historical destiny; the sins of the fathers are visited upon the children even unto the third and fourth generations. And the schema of cumulative guilt and cumulative time makes possible the economics of compound interest. Faustian time and Faustian money, to use Spengler's metaphor, are the time and money of the irredeemably damned.

6. *Giving and Taking*

CUMULATIVE GUILT disrupts the archaic economy of gift-giving. The principle of reciprocity is inseparable from cyclical time, while in cumulative time accounts are always unbalanced. The first solution to the problem of guilt, to share it (the totemic brotherhood), is no longer adequate. But cumulative time, which disrupts the old solution to the problem of guilt, organizes a new solution, which is to accumulate the tokens of atonement, the economic surplus. Prestige and power, always attached to virtuosity in the arts of expiation, are now conferred not by giving but by taking, by possessing. The need to share the guilt is to some extent transcended; in accumulating possessions the individual shoulders his own burden of guilt and thus negates the first solution. The modern psychology of taking is constructed, by a process of denial, out of its archaic opposite, giving. Thus the individual (and the economic surplus) is emancipated to some extent from the archaic submergence in the social group. The new equally guilt-ridden schema of possession inaugurates the predatory pattern which Veblen described, and transforms archaic masochism into modern sadism.

At the same time the new schema imposes on the human being a second degree of dehumanization. The archaic man, to assuage his guilt, used his freedom, his surplus, to construct society, and hid himself in the group. The possessive individual emancipates himself to some extent from the group, but he is still in flight from himself; his essence now passes into things, his property. (Consider the etymology of "property.") The compulsion to work remains; life remains an exercise in overcoming guilt. Property accumulations are outward and visible signs of an inward and spiritual grace; they are also the man's life. And being the man's life, things become alive and do what the man would like to do. Things become the god (the father of himself) that he would like to be: money *breeds*. The institution of interest presupposes not only cumulative time but also the displacement of the parental complex from the totemic group to the totemic possession, money. Thus money in the civilized economy comes to have a psychic value it never had in the archaic economy.

We thus arrive at a further level of meaning in the equation of money and excrement. Money is inorganic dead matter which has been made alive by inheriting the magic power which infantile narcissism attributes to the excremental product. Freud pointed out that it was an integral part of the anal symbolic complex to equate the feces with the penis.[142] The infantile fantasy of becoming father of oneself first moves out to make magic use of objects instead of its own body when it gets attached to that object which both is and is not part of its own body, the feces. Money inherits the infantile magic of excrement and then is able to breed and have children: interest is an increment (cf. Greek *tokos*, Latin *faenus*, etc.).[143]

This emergent individualism has other complicated and obscure psychological dimensions.[144] In psychoanalytical terms it appears to involve a restructuring of the core of the guilt complex (the Oedipus complex and castration complex).[145] The psychology of giving is intimately feminine; the psychology of possession and taking is masculine.[146] And factually, the new guilt complex appears to be historically connected with the rise of patriarchal religion (for the Western development the Hebrews are decisive).[147] In psychoanalytical terms, the gift complex resolves guilt by identification with the mother, while the possession complex resolves guilt by identification with the father. And it would seem that identification with the father involves a transformation of guilt into aggression. In the gift complex dependence on the mother is acknowledged, and then overcome by mothering others. Identification with the father is a way of denying dependence on the mother. (And, like all sustained denials, simultaneously affirms it; the classic Oedipus complex is a superstructure based on relations to the "pre-Oedipal" mother.) "Taking" is a denial of dependence, and thus transforms the guilt of indebtedness into aggression; and the masculinity complex, the obsessive denial of feminity, is inherently aggressive. We therefore in principle agree with Bettelheim: "Only with phallic psychology did aggressive manipulation of nature by technological inventions become possible." [148] In another terminology, we can identify the new individualism with Apollonian masculinity and Apollonian sublimation. But as long as the psychoanalytical theory of the pre-Oedipal mother remains backward, and as long as psychoanalysis leaves it to the Jungians to exploit Bachofen's discovery of the religion of the Great Mother,[149] this turning point in history remains psychologically obscure.

Whatever the mechanisms involved, the history of the neurosis (the neurosis of history) produces over the long term a definite strengthening of the human ego, as measured by its capacity to face the problem of guilt.[150] The man who gives seeks to get rid of his guilt by sharing it. The man who takes is strong enough to shoulder his own burden of guilt. Christian man is strong enough to recognize that the debt is so great that only God can redeem it. Modern secular Faustian man is strong enough to live with irredeemable damnation.

7. The City Sublime

THIS TRANSFER of the arena for the drama of the parental complex from the totemic group to the magic object opens the path for sublimation. Whereas for archaic man the crucial defense mechanism is undoing (expiation), for civilized man the crucial defense mechanism is sublimation. The basic characteristic of sublimation is the desexualization of sexual energy by its redirection toward new objects. But as we have seen, desexualization means disembodiment. New objects must substitute for the human body, and there is no sublimation without the projection of the human body into things; the dehumanization of man is his alienation of his own body. He thus acquires a soul (the higher spirituality of sublimation), but the soul is located in things. Money is "the world's soul." And gold is the proper symbol of sublimation, both as the death of the body and as the quest for a "higher" life which is not that of the body. Spengler says: [151]

> Gold is not a colour; colours . . . are natural. But the metallic gleam, which is practically never found in natural conditions, is unearthly. . . . The gleaming gold takes away from the scene, the life and the body their substantial being. . . . And thus the gold background possesses, in the iconography of the Western Church, an explicit dogmatic significance. It is an express assertion of the existence and activity of the divine spirit.

Money is the heart of the new accumulation complex; the capacity of money to bear interest is its energy; its body is that fundamental institution of civilized man, the city. The archeologists note the complete rupture with the previous style of life which marks the foundations of the first cities. Heichelheim showed that the institution of interest-bearing capital is the key to this abrupt reorganization, and looked for the origin of the new economic institution in a transvaluation of religious values.[152] When we reach the urban stratum of a Mesopotamian archeological site, "One is no longer standing in a village green but on the square of a cathedral city," says Gordon Childe.[153]

What then is a city? A city reflects the new masculine aggressive psychology of revolt against the female principles of dependence and nature. Frankfort on the first cities says: "The modest life of the prehistoric villager had fitted well enough into the natural surroundings, but the city was a questionable institution, at variance, rather than in keeping, with the natural order." [154] Ortega y Gasset says of the classical polis, "The Graeco-Roman decides to separate himself from the fields, from Nature," and builds walls to mark off his "new kind of space." [155] The late city, says Spengler, "contradicts Nature in the lines of its silhouette, *denies* all Nature," while "the gigantic megalopolis, the *city-as-world,* . . . suffers nothing beside itself and sets about *annihilating* the country picture." [156]

In the new space of the city, which is always a sacred space, man succeeds for the first time in constructing a new life which is wholly superfluous, and wholly sacred. A city is by definition divorced from primary food production, and therefore by definition superfluous; its whole economy is based on the economic surplus. "What is a city in the economic sense?" asks Sombart. "A city is a settlement of men who for their sustenance depend on the production of agricultural labor which is not their own." [157] Sombart goes on to quote with approval Adam Smith: "It is the surplus produce of the country only . . . that constitutes the subsistence of the town, which can therefore increase only with the increase of this surplus produce." But the sector of the surplus is always the sector of the sacred. Hence the first city is a "cathedral city" and its whole economy devoted to sacred ends, "a divine household." [158] Behind the façade of modern secularization we can still see the truth of Tunnard's statement: "From earliest time, the city has had such an attraction and fascination for man that he has given it symbolic meaning, has made it a god." [159]

The devotion of the economic surplus to sacred ends is nothing new. What is new is the primacy of sublimation in the domain of the sacred. "Come let us build us a city, and a tower, whose top may reach unto heaven." [160] Hence the Apollonian character of the urban consciousness: "Intellect, *Geist, esprit,* is the specific urban form of the understanding," says Spengler; "these stone visages that have incorporated in their light-world the humanness of the citizen himself and, like him, are all eye and intellect—how distinct the language of form they talk, how different from the rustic drawl of the landscape!"[161]

But the essence of sublimation is the reification of the superfluous-sacred in monumental, enduring form. Hence it is in the city that money finally settles upon the most durable precious metals. The city, in Gordon Childe's theory, presupposes metallurgy; but the metallurgy it presupposes is not metallurgy in the service of "rational" "mastery over nature," or even in the service of war, but metallurgy in the service of conspicuous (and sacred) waste. As Stuart Piggott pointed out, "In Central and South America, stone-using communities had achieved a notable degree of urban development without any accompanying metallurgy save the use of gold ornaments."[162] The city is a deposit of accumulated sublimation, and by the same token a deposit of accumulated guilt. The temple buildings which dominate the first cities are monuments of accumulated guilt and expiation. The process of expiation, no longer a totemic communion of persons, has been reified and passes into piles of stone and gold and many other things beside. Hence a city is itself, like money, crystallized guilt. "To look at the plan of a great City," said Frank Lloyd Wright, "is to look at something like the cross-section of a fibrous tumor."[163] But guilt is time: "In the city, time becomes visible," says Mumford.[164] In monumental form, as money or as the city itself, each generation inherits the ascetic achievements of its ancestors; not, as Joan Robinson says of the gold fund,[165] as a "free gift from history," but as a debt to be paid by further accumulation of monuments. Through the city the sins of the fathers are visited upon the children; every city has a history and a rate of interest.

8. *Immortality*

EVERY CITY is an eternal city: civilized money lasts forever. Eliade, citing the annual re-enactment of the Creation myth in ancient Babylon, seems to believe that the first cities still moved in archaic time, although he recognizes them as the first to build "history," a notion which on his own definitions is incompatible with archaic time.[166] But to endure through time, the same yesterday, today, and forever, is not the same as to abolish time periodically and periodically return to the primeval plenitude. Although the ancient Near Eastern city does not yet say, as the Hebrew-Christian city says, that its last days shall be greater than its first, yet it has already made the decisive step. It endures; time and the city accumulate. But to endure is to conquer death. Civilization is an attempt to overcome death; and thus we come to the lowest circle in Freud's inferno, the death instinct.

The death instinct is the core of the human neurosis. It begins with the human infant's incapacity to accept separation from the mother, that separation which confers individual life on all living organisms and which in all living organisms at the same time leads to death. It is in the nature of finite things, says Hegel, that the hour of their birth is the hour of their death.[167] Hence the incapacity of the human species to die, and therefore to live, begins at birth, in what psychoanalysis calls the birth trauma. Thus the Platonic argument for immortality really amounts to a denial that we were ever born.[168] Humanity is that species of animal that cannot die. This decisive posture in the human animal is grounded in human biology; it is grounded in the fetalization which physical anthropologists say is the distinctive feature of the human body;[169] it is grounded in the biology of prolonged infancy; it is grounded in the social correlate of prolonged infancy, the human family.

This incapacity to die, ironically but inevitably, throws mankind out of the actuality of living, which for all normal animals is at the same time dying; the result is denial of life (repression). The incapacity to accept death turns the death instinct into its distinctively human and distinctively morbid form. The distraction of human life to the war against death, by the same inevitable irony, results in death's dominion over life. The war against death takes the form of a preoccupation with the past and the future, and the present tense, the tense of life, is lost—that present which Whitehead says "holds within itself the complete sum of existence, backwards and forwards, that whole amplitude of time, which is eternity."[170] And mankind's diversion from the actuality of living-and-dying, which is always in the present, is attained by reactivation in fantasy of the past and regressive attachment to fantasy of the past, ultimately the womb from which life came. Thus again the incapacity to accept death only results in the morbidity of an active death wish. Hence at the deepest level the morbid human death instinct is at the back of the human sense of time.

This human posture of life at war with death is epitomized in the fantasy—originating in infancy but energizing all human history—the wish to become the father of oneself.[171] To this ambition life and the enjoyment of life is sacrificed. It is the moving force behind the archaic economy of gift-giving and behind the civilized economy of accumulation. Economies, archaic and civilized, are ultimately driven by that flight from death which turns life into death-in-life. In fact, as Ruskin saw, there is no way of defining work, as distinct from enjoyable effort, except as effort spent in fighting death: [172]

> I have already defined Labour to be the Contest of the life of man with an opposite. . . . It is usually confused with effort itself, or the application of power (*opera*); but there is much effort which is merely a mode of recreation, or of pleasure. The most beautiful actions of the human body, and the highest results of the human intelligence, are conditions, or achievements, of quite unlaborious—nay, of recreative—effort. But labour is the *suffering* in effort. It is the negative quantity. . . . In brief, it is "that quantity of our toil which we die in."

Archaic man conquers death by living the life of his dead ancestors. As Eliade brilliantly describes,[173] profane (actual) living is submerged by assimilation with ancestral archetypes: what we do now is only a repetition of what they did then. This is the pattern of eternal return. Hence archaic society has no real history; and within archaic society there is no individuality. There is no history because there is no individuality; individuality is asserted by breaking with the ancestral archetypes and thus making history. Immortality—the wish to be father of oneself—is attained by assimilation into the fund of ancestral souls, out of which comes each generation and into which they return. Again the pattern of eternal return. Among the Murngins, "the most unifying concept in the whole of the clan ideology is that of the sacred waterhole in which reposes the spiritual unity of clan life. It is the fundamental symbol of clan solidarity. From it comes all the eternal qualities, and to it those qualities return when they have been lived or used by members of the clan." [174]

Civilized man asserts his individuality, and makes history. But the individuality he asserts is not life-affirming or life-enjoying, but the life-negating (ascetic) individuality of (Faustian) discontent and guilt. Civilized individuality, in Nietzsche's image, does not want itself, but wants children, wants heirs, wants an estate. [175] Life remains a war against death—civilized man, no more than archaic man, is not strong enough to die—and death is overcome by accumulating time-defying monuments. These accumulations of stone and gold make possible the discovery of the immortal soul. "Perhaps it is not an accident," says Keynes in his most profound appraisal of economic behavior, "that the race which did most to bring the promise of immortality into the heart and essence of our religions has also done most for the principle of compound interest." [176]

The ambition of civilized man is revealed in the pyramid—the achievement of the first modern individualists. [177] In the pyramid repose both the hope of immortality and the fruit of compound interest. As Heichelheim showed, the Iron Age, at the end of which we live, democratized the achievements of the Bronze Age (cities, metals, money, writing) and opened up the pursuit of kings (money and immortality) to the average citizen. [178] But the inevitable irony redresses the balance in favor of death. Death is overcome on condition that the real actuality of life pass into these immortal and dead things; money is the man; the immortality of an estate or a corporation resides in the dead things which alone endure. By the law of the slow return of the repressed, the last stage of history is, as Luther said, the dominion of death in life; the last stage of the polis is, as Mumford said, Nekropolis. Spengler saw in the late city "a metaphysical turn towards death." Mumford says: [179]

> The metropolis is rank with forms of *negative vitality*. Nature and human nature, violated in this environment, come back in destructive forms. . . . In this mangled state, the impulse to live departs from apparently healthy personalities. The impulse to die supplants it. . . . Is it any wonder that Dr. Sigmund Freud found a death wish at the seat of human activity?

Civilized economic activity has this death-defying and dead-ening structure because economic activity is sustained by psy-chic energy taking the form of sublimation. All civilized sub-limation, and not only the pursuit of money, has this structure. Thus in the first of his odes Horace sees poetry as a career, like all careers (trader, soldier, athlete, etc.), basically characterized by self-sacrifice and instinctual renunciation; it is nevertheless worth while if success will enable him "to strike the stars with head sublime." And at the end of the third book he celebrates his success: "I have wrought a monument more enduring than bronze, and loftier than the royal accumulation of the pyramids. Neither corrosive rain nor raging wind can destroy it, nor the innumerable sequence of years nor the flight of time. I shall not altogether die." [180] I shall not altogether die—the hope of the man who has not lived, whose life has been spent conquer-ing death, whose life has passed into those immortal pages.

9. *The Human Body*

WE ARE now in a position to focus attention on the nerve center of the psychoanalytical theory of money—the relation between the money complex and the human body.

Ferenczi, in a famous essay "On the Ontogenesis of the In-terest in Money," derived money from the infantile impulse to play with feces, sublimated by the impingement, on this play impulse, of a repudiation of feces which he connects with the development of upright posture. Money is the end result, which, says Ferenczi, "after what has been said is seen to be nothing other than odourless dehydrated filth that has been made to shine. *Pecunia non olet.*" [181] With the cause of the turn away from the human body, which we discussed in a previous chap-ter, we are not at the moment concerned. We are concerned with the central proposition that money is derived from anal erotism. The proposition has behind it the authority of Freud's essay on "Character and Anal Erotism" (1908); [182] actually Ferenczi is only filling out the central idea in Freud's essay. And for the most part orthodox psychoanalysis has stayed with this interpretation of the anal complex.

Yet this interpretation must be rejected as inadequate and

misleading. To derive money from anal erotism is to derive it from (part of) the play instinct. The implication is that the money complex contains an element of play; that (as Ferenczi puts it), besides serving the reality-principle, it also serves the pleasure-principle. Now in a previous chapter on the concept of play we recognized that the money complex, archaic and civilized, has an element in it of what Veblen called the "game of ownership," that element which the recent *Theory of Games and Economic Behavior* tries to grasp in mathematical form.[183] But our whole inquiry shows that the money complex is a great deal more than sublimated play.

In the first place, the money complex involves more regions of the body than just the anal. Since excrement becomes aliment, the oral region is involved; since money breeds, the genital region is involved. In other words anal erotism cannot be isolated, and the money complex involves the whole problem of all the sexual organizations and their interrelations—that is, the whole problem of the human body. The proper point of departure, in the literature of psychoanalysis, is not Freud's essay of 1908, but his essay of 1916, "On the Transformation of Instincts with Special Reference to Anal Erotism." [184] There Freud diagrammed the complicated set of symbolic equations, sustained, he says, by fantasies in the unconscious, which energize the disposal of anal erotism. Freud discriminates, and relates, feces as "thing" (*Lumpf*), as "gift," as "child," as "penis." Our whole essay goes to show that the money complex is not derived from feces but from these fantasies about feces. Our previous argument that the pathogenic material in the human psyche consists of fantasies is sustained. And by the same token the vulgar psychoanalytical derivation of anal character from the experience of toilet training is refuted.

The fantasies about feces that Freud lays bare consist essentially in the attribution to feces of the value of some other bodily function. Ferenczi in his later, and greatest, contribution to psychoanalysis showed that the sexual organization in the human body was constructed by substitutive displacement of the function and value of one organ onto another, a process which he termed "amphimixis of erotisms." [185] "Amphimixis of erotisms" is what in the human body corresponds to the symbolic equations in fantasy diagrammed by Freud. This "amphimixis of erotisms" *is* the sexual organizations. The anal sexual organization of the body in itself refers to other parts of the body, being the effect of a displacement onto the anal region of the function and value of other parts of the body. Sublimation, we said in an earlier chapter, is a search in the outside world for the lost body of childhood; but the body that was lost was already a befuddled body, befuddled by the confusion caused by the fantasy of becoming father of oneself (and therefore, for example, attributing to feces the value of "penis" or "child"). Thus if the money complex is derived from an anal complex, the anal complex is, to use Whiteheadian terminology, a prehensive unification, at a particular region, of the totality of the disorder in the human body—a prehensive unification whose relations to other regions (the oral, the genital) are internal.

And secondly, the anal complex cannot be formulated, as the Ferenczi essay on money formulates it, without reference to the Oedipus complex and the castration complex—to speak less technically, without reference to the whole problem of guilt. In our essay on money the concept of guilt has been central; and in Freud's second essay on the anal complex the equation of feces with "child" and with "penis," as well as his references to the castration complex, introduce what can only be called Oedipal dimensions into the anal complex. The anal complex (and its social derivatives) is really a peculiar anal-and-Oedipal complex.[186] In the psychoanalytical literature the proper weight is given to the Oedipal factor only in Róheim's essay on primitive money and in Harnik's essay on time.[187] Róheim and Harnik take the proper starting point, Freud's second essay, and make advances; their work, however, can only be called obscure groping in the right direction.

The difficulty here, on the psychoanalytical side, is the backwardness and confusion, which we have previously discussed, in the theory of the "pre-Oedipal" mother. The psychoanalytical anal stage is a pre-Oedipal stage, but it must not be interpreted as an erotic phenomenon untroubled by the dark clouds associated in the classical theory with the epiphany of the threatening father. The problem of guilt is misconstrued if it is construed as a reaction to the threatening father and not from the inherently ambivalent relation to the mother; likewise the castration complex, and the burden of symbolic meaning which the human race attaches to the genital and to masculinity, develop, as we have argued in an earlier chapter, in the child's relation with the "pre-Oedipal" mother.[188]

Thirdly—and this is the most important error in the orthodox psychoanalytical interpretation—the infantile anal complex, and its social derivative the money complex, is primarily not a manifestation of Eros, not anal erotism, but a manifestation of the death instinct. (Here again Róheim and Harnik are exceptions, who nevertheless confuse more than they clarify by their admission of more of the real complexities of the problem). There is of course always Eros in the human body; and, as Freud repeatedly said, the death instinct can manifest itself only in subtle fusion with Eros. There is an element of play in infantile anality, and in the money complex; but our whole argument goes to show that the main architects of the complex are guilt, the aggressive fantasy of becoming father of oneself, and death anxiety or separation anxiety.

Guilt, aggression, anxiety pertain to the ego, the mental side of human nature. What corresponds to them on the bodily side of human nature—the bodily legacy of infantile anxiety—is the sexual organizations of the human body, all the sexual organizations of the human body (oral, anal, and genital). They too must be recognized as creations of the death instinct. On this point the decisive theoretical advance was made by Ferenczi in his masterpiece, *Thalassa*, which proposed not only that the sexual organizations were constructed by that functional distortion which Ferenczi called "amphimixis of erotisms," but also that the power which constructed them was what he called the "thalassal [i.e., oceanic] regressive trend" [189]—the desire to get back to the womb, the incapacity to accept the individuality of life, the morbid death instinct.

From this it follows that as long as the human body retains the sexual organizations, both the pregenital and the genital, it is in bondage (fixated) to the infantile traumata which disorganized it and to the morbid death instinct. And as long as the human body remains fixated to its infantile structure, so long on the psychic side the human mind remains fixated to the fantasies of infancy, stored in the unconscious sector of the ego, in the form of character structures, and projected outward onto the world in the form of sublimations. We resolutely follow Ferenczi: "Character-traits are, so to speak, secret psychoses." [190] But again we must emphasize the unity of mind and body. What we call "character" is really a disorganization or malfunctioning of the body. Character formation, according to Ferenczi, is "the psychic superstructure and psychic transcript" of the amphimixis of erotisms, the functional distortion of organs, which establishes the sexual organizations. [191] Wilhelm Reich (we are in no position to reject a wise word from any source) has proposed the term "character-armour" to describe the muscular rigidities whereby the human body protects itself from the natural disposition to that erotic exuberance, that overflowing life which non-neurotic species of life display. [192] Compare Ferenczi: "Character is from the point of view of the psychoanalyst a sort of abnormality, a kind of mechanization of a particular way of reaction." [193] And sublimation, viewed as an activity of the human body, is, as Freud implied, structurally a hysteria, a displacement upward onto other organs (above all hand and eye) of the pathogenic libido concentrated, by an original displacement downward as postulated by Ferenczi, in the anal, and genital zones. [194]

If we can imagine an unrepressed man—a man strong enough to live and therefore strong enough to die, and therefore what no man has ever been, an individual—such a man, having overcome guilt and anxiety, could have no money complex. But at the same time such a man would have a body freed from all the sexual organizations—a body freed from unconscious oral, anal, and genital fantasies of return to the maternal womb. Such a man would be rid of the nightmares which Freud showed to be haunting civilization; but freedom from those fantasies would also mean freedom from that disorder in the human body which Freud pitilessly exposed. In such a man would be fulfilled on earth the mystic hope of Christianity, the resurrection of the body, in a form, as Luther said, free from death and filth. Freedom from filth would be freedom from the infantile fantasies which concentrate libido on the excremental function and make man a Yahoo. Freedom from death would be freedom from that dominion of death-in-life which Luther grasped as the dominion of Satan; but the freedom from death would be the strength to live-and-die. "What has become perfect, all that is ripe—wants to die." [195]

With such a transfigured body the human soul can be reconciled, and the human ego become once more what it was designed to be in the first place, a body-ego and the surface of a body, sensing that communication between body and body which is life. But the path to that ultimate reunification of ego and body is not a dissolution but a strengthening of the human ego. The human ego would have to become strong enough to die; and strong enough to set aside guilt. Archaic consciousness was strong enough to recognize a debt of guilt; Christian consciousness is strong enough to recognize that the debt is so great only God can redeem it; modern secular Faustian man is strong enough to live with irredeemable damnation; full psychoanalytical consciousness would be strong enough to cancel the debt by deriving it from infantile fantasy.

10. *Excrement*

THE WHOLE problem of the human body, as well as the whole problem of living and dying, is involved in sublimation; and yet psychoanalysis inexorably insists that there is a special connection between sublimation and anality. The psychoanalytical doctrine is a painful assault on human pride—what have we to be proud of except our sublimity?—and would not be tolerable or profitable if psychoanalysis cannot simultaneously offer a hope of better things. We have argued that there is a better way; that hope alone makes it possible to explore the bitter dregs of psychoanalytical theory.

What the psychoanalytical paradox is asserting is that "things" which are possessed and accumulated, the property and the universal condensed precipitate of property, money, are in their essential nature excremental. Psychoanalysis must take a position not only as to the origin of the money complex but also as to its ultimate validity. Vulgar psychoanalytical exegesis limits itself to the argument that the category of property originates in infantile manipulation of the excremental product. But the real point is that property remains excremental, and is known to be excremental in our secret heart, the unconscious. Jokes and folklore and poetic metaphor, the wisdom of folly, tell the secret truth. The wisdom of folly is the wisdom of childhood. What the child knows consciously, and the adult unconsciously, is that we are nothing but body. However much the repressed and sublimating adult may consciously deny it, the fact remains that life is of the body and only life creates values; all values are bodily values. Hence the assimilation of money with excrement does not render money valueless; on the contrary, it is the path whereby extraneous things acquire significance for the human body, and hence value. If money were not excrement, it would be valueless.

But why particularly excrement? Possession, according to psychoanalysis, gratifies bodily Eros concentrated in the anal zone. But the concentration of libido in the anal zone reflects the attachment to the anal zone of the infantile narcissistic project of becoming father of oneself.[196] The project of becoming father of oneself, and thus triumphing over death, can be worked out with things, and at the same time retain bodily meaning, only if the things produced by the body at the same time nourish it. Possessions are worthless to the body unless animated by the fantasy that they are excrement which is also aliment. Wealth brings so little happiness, said Freud, because money is not an infantile wish;[197] the infantile wish which sustains the money complex is for a narcissistically self-contained and self-replenishing immortal body. Therefore only if excrement were aliment could the infantile wish sustaining the money complex be gratified.

But, as we have seen, the narcissistic project of becoming father of oneself is at the deepest level the result of that incapacity to accept death which is also the incapacity to live. All sublimation as such presupposes repudiation (negation) of the body. The repudiation of the body does not and cannot alter the fact that life in the body is all we have, and the unconscious holds fast to the truth and never makes the repudiation; in the id, says Freud, there is nothing corresponding to the act of negation.[198] Hence the net effect of the ego's repudiation of bodily life can only be the diversion of bodily Eros from its natural task of sustaining the life of the body to the unnatural task of constructing death-in-life for the body.

Thus the morbid attempt to get away from the body can only result in a morbid fascination (erotic cathexis) in the death of the body. In the simple and true, because bodily, language of the unconscious, Eros can be deflected from the life of the body only by being deflected onto the excremental function. In the true life of the body (which is also the life of the id) value can be detached from the body only by attaching value to the nonbodily excreta of the body, which are at the same time the dead matter produced by the body, and which incorporate the body's daily dying. In more technical terms, sublimated anality presupposes the castration complex, the decisive death of the body which according to Freud desexualizes and paralyzes the penis.[199] With the death of the penis the center of erotic attention is transferred to the dead body par excellence, the feces: [200]

> When the child has unwillingly imbibed the knowledge that there are human beings who do not possess a penis, that organ seems to him something which can be detached from the body, and an unmistakable analogy is drawn between it and the excrement which was the first piece of bodily substance that had to be given up.

Better than the psychoanalysts, Coleridge saw the true nature of the anal complex: [201]

> Remark the seeming identity of body and mind in infants, and thence the loveliness of the former; the commencing separation in boyhood, and the struggle of equilibrium in youth: thence onward the body is first simply indifferent; then demanding the translucency of the mind not to be worse than indifferent; and finally all that presents the body as body becoming almost of an excremental nature.

What makes man, in Swift's language, a Yahoo, with a "strange Disposition to Nastiness and Dirt, whereas there appears to be a natural Love of Cleanliness in all other Animals," [202] is, ironically, his disposition to negate the body and rise above it. Swift, with his vision of how the soaring spirit of sublimation ends by falling down "plum in the lowest Bottom of Things, like a straight line drawn by its own Length into a Circle," [203] understood the irony better than Freud. Freud, with his commitment to sublimation, in the last analysis saw an ultimate conflict between the disposition to sublimate, which he connects with upright posture, and anal erotism. In his view, sublimation is a defense of a higher form of life against residual animality.[204] But the irony is that sublimation activates the morbid animality (anality), and the higher form of life, civilization, reveals that lower form of life, the Yahoo. To rise above the body is to equate the body with excrement.

In the last analysis, the peculiar human fascination with excrement is the peculiar human fascination with death. Freud saw that the regression of libido from the genital to the sadistic-anal level represents what he calls a defusion of instincts, a disbalancing of the relation between life instinct and death instinct such that the death instinct gets into the saddle.[205] And because all human sublimation represents a dying to the body, all human sublimation whatsoever must pass through the anal complex; by the dialectic of negation and the return of the repressed, the negation of infantile anality confers an anal quality upon the entire life in culture. Hence the extravagant psychoanalytical claims of finding anality behind all art, science, etc., are legitimate, though unless formulated in terms of the death instinct they make no sense. Excrement is the dead life of the body, and as long as humanity prefers a dead life to living, so long is humanity committed to treating as excrement not only its own body but the surrounding world of objects, reducing all to dead matter and inorganic magnitudes. Our much prized "objectivity" toward our own bodies, other persons, and the universe, all our calculating "rationality," is, from the psychoanalytical point of view, an ambivalent mixture of love and hate, an attitude appropriate only toward excrement, and appropriate to excrement only in an animal that has lost his own body and life.

How far the Yahoo man has poisoned his whole view of nature may be measured by the fact that the philosophic and scientific concept of "matter" is, from the psychoanalytical point of view, radically infected by the excremental imagination. J. O. Wisdom has taken Berkeley's *Siris: A Chain of Philo-*

sophical Reflexions and Inquiries Concerning the Virtues of Tar-Water out of the closet where philosophers had buried it—tarwater is, according to Berkeley, as a medicine "a powerful and safe deobstruent," and metaphysically akin to that "light that cannot be defiled by filth of any kind," which represents a divine infusion into this baser world.[206] Wisdom has demonstrated the excremental character of "matter" in Berkeley's philosophic imagination; but unfortunately—since it gives the philosophers an excuse for ignoring his demonstration—he belittles his own achievement by disclaiming any intent to impugn the validity of Berkeley's philosophy and by limiting the role of psychoanalysis to the investigation of origins.[207]

Our interpretation of psychoanalysis cannot accept such a divorce of origins from validity; Wisdom is making the same mistake as the psychoanalytical critics of Swift. What he has before him is not the anal character of the individual Berkeley, but the anal character of the Western philosophic tradition, or rather, the anal character of man. The vision of the human body as excremental; the command for man to sublimate; the vision of a component of "base matter" in all this sublunary world, making the universe one vast alembic of cosmic sublimation—all this goes back to Plato: and is not all Western philosophy, as Whitehead said, but a series of footnotes to Plato?[208]

Consequently the psychoanalytical point of view cannot take the traditional debate between materialism and idealism at face value. If there is a real question in this dispute it seems to be whether the idea of God is necessary in order to sublimate; for neither materialists nor idealists question the principle of sublimation. Nor can psychoanalysis abstain from wondering whether the contradictions in the scientific concept of "matter," so searchingly probed by Emile Meyerson,[209] do not reflect the unconscious projection—palpable in Plato or in Berkeley's tarwater philosophy—of man's anal disturbance into his picture of the world.

The commitment to mathematize the world, intrinsic to modern science, is a commitment to sublimation. Mathematics is coeval with city life, because in the city culture is organized by the principle of sublimation. Plato was right: God geometrizes, and mathematics is the crucial discipline in converting human love to a suprasensual life. Bertrand Russell is right: Mathematics has "a beauty cold and austere," "without any appeal to our weaker nature," and gives "the sense of being more than man." [210] The psychoanalytical paradox of the anal character of mathematical thinking merely specifies what part of the life of the body is affirmed by negation—by denial, as Russell says, of "our weaker nature"—in order to construct the nonbodily life.

The connection between sublimation, the death instinct, and excrement is not static, but subject to the dynamics of the neurosis which is human history. Culture originates in the denial of life and the body, and the impossibility of denying life in the body is what makes all cultures unstable defusions of life instinct and death instinct. It follows that the recovery of life in the body is the hidden aim of history, in the sense that the recovery of life in the body would put an end to the dynamic disequilibrium. The historical series of cultural patterns—the stages in the history of the neurosis—exhibit a dialectic of two seemingly contradictory trends: on the one hand, ever increasing denial of the body, and, on the other hand, the slow return of the repressed in an alienated form.

Actually these seemingly contradictory trends are two sides of the same coin. The ever increasing denial of the body is, in the form of a negation, an ever increasing affirmation of the denied body. Sublimations are these negations of the body which simultaneously affirm it; and sublimations achieve this dialectical tour de force by the simple but basic mechanism of projecting the repressed body into things. The more the life of the body passes into things, the less life there is in the body, and at the same time the increasing accumulation of things represents an ever fuller articulation of the lost life of the body. Hence increasing sublimation is a general law of history. Technological progress makes increased sublimation possible; and, as we argued in an earlier chapter, the hidden aim of technological progress is the discovery and recovery of the human body.[211]

It follows that what we call historical progress, or higher civilization, means an increase in the domain of the death instinct at the expense of the life instinct. Sublimation is a mortification of the body and a sequestration of the life of the body into dead things. There is a death of the body in every sublimation; but we must be clear as to the specific nature of the bodily Eros so denied. Sublimation attacks the Eros attached to the infantile sexual organizations, more specifically anal erotism. But, as we have seen, anal erotism is sustained by the infantile fantasy of a magic body which would fulfill the narcissistic wish for self-contained and self-replenishing immortality. Sublimation, in denying the body, is denying body-magic and renouncing fantasies and bodily instinctual aims that never could be gratified in reality. As such, sublimation represents a gain for the reality-principle. On the other hand, in so far as sublimation unconsciously continues to seek gratification for the same infantile aims, in so far as things, like money, are as a result of sublimation animated by the magic powers and wishes that originally were attached to the body, sublimation perpetuates the unreal aims of infantile narcissism. It comes to the same thing to say that the sublimating ego is still the ego in flight from death. But at the same time, by a fortunate irony, as a result of the attempt to cure which is part of the neurosis, the sublimating ego in its flight from death acquires an ever increasing capacity to die by increasingly mortifying the body. The transformation of life into death-in-life, which is the achievement of higher civilization, prepares mankind to accept death.

These theoretical considerations put us in a position to consider the historical evolution of the anal complex. Sublimation, we said earlier, is the defense mechanism characteristic of civilized man, undoing (expiation) the defense mechanism characteristic of archaic man. It cannot be denied that archaic man does sublimate, and does sublimate anality. There is archaic money, and native folklore shows its excremental associations; shell money, for example, is the excrement of the sea.[212] But the development of money, and sublimation, remains backward, because relations to things rather than to persons have not yet become charged with the main weight of the desire to overcome guilt and death. Archaic man devotes the economic surplus to establishing and maintaining the social group as a device for sharing guilt.

In more technical terms, archaic man is preoccupied with

the castration complex, the incest taboo, and the desexualization of the penis—that is to say, the transformation of genital impulses into that aim-inhibited libido which sustains the kinship systems in which archaic life is embedded. The low degree of sublimation, corresponding to the low level of technology, means, by our previous definitions, a weaker ego, an ego which has not yet come to terms (by negation) with the pregenital impulses in its own body. But the pregenital impulses are there. The result is that the pregenital impulses, all the fantastic wishes of infantile narcissism, express themselves in unsublimated form, so that archaic man retains the magic body of infancy.

Hence archaic man characteristically has a massive structure of excremental magic, which indicates the degree to which his anality remains unsublimated, and at the same time indicates the bodily fantasies from which the disembodied fantasies of sublimation are derived. Actually the archaic tradition of magic dirt dies hard and survives in high civilizations: the newspapers report that the new monarch of Nepal in the coronation ceremony "was anointed with Himalayan mud for wisdom, horse stable mud for speed, and elephant pen mud for muscle." [213] The Himalayas are, I suppose, the seat of the gods.

Nor are these residues of excremental magic confined to the mysterious East. The *materia medica* of eighteenth-century Europe included, under such sublimated names as *"eau de Mille-fleurs,"* distillations of animal and human excrement.[214] Or we may illustrate the repressed and sublimated fantasies of capitalism by the unrepressed and semisublimated fantasies of its more archaic prototype, alchemy. The salt the alchemists manipulate is an "excrement of nature"; their aim is to distill from the excremental salt the "seminal" salt or "spirits"; the procedure of "cohobation" consisted in "returning the spirits to their feces." [215] The monetary system itself of the European Middle Ages still retained archaistic memories of the true worth of money; at the bridge of Montluçon in France the toll required of prostitutes was *"quatuor denarios," "aut unum bumbum."* [216] Incurable quantifiers who seek to grasp the psychoanalytical paradox in mathematical terms may base on this Rosetta Stone their tables of equivalence. Actually this intellectual tour de force was already anticipated by Chaucer in *The Summoner's Tale:*

> In ars-metryke shal ther no man finde
> Biforn this day, of swich a questioun.
> Who sholde make a demonstracioun,
> That every man sholde have y-liche his part
> As of the soun or savour of a fart?

In really primitive thought, however, that power over persons which civilization attributes to money is conferred by possession of their "dirt"—excrement, hair, nail parings, etc.; [217] the "dirt" is the person in the same sense in which the ancient Greek proverb said that money is the man. The category of "possession," and power based on possession, is apparently indigenous to the magic-dirt complex. Even in societies where the economic surplus is in the main governed by the principle of reciprocal giving, the magic-dirt complex can be exploited by that first individualist, the potent sorcerer, to levy an economic tribute. And in the magic-dirt complex we can discern the fear of death and the fantastic wish for an immortal self-replenishing body. Hence rituals of scatophagy, and that close homologue of scatophagy, necrophagy, and the more generally constant association of dirt with funereal ceremonies. Priam, on the death of Hector, rolled in the dung heap; primitive tribes smear themselves as a sign of mourning, and we wear black; the Tonga Islanders raised a pious mound of ordure on the grave; our Indo-European ancestors raised a mound of stones.[218] One example is necessary, and should suffice, to show the fantasies by which the human body is haunted. The matriarchal Seri Indians, taken by Briffault as the prototype of humanity at its rudest level, have a ritual of scatophagy in which their anthropologist observer found "the germ of industrial economy and a feeble thrift-sense emerging." To quote his words: [219]

> It is impossible to portray justly the food habits of the Seri without some reference to a systematic scatophagy, which seems to possess fiducial as well as economic features. In its simplest aspect this custom is connected with the tuna harvests; the fruits are eaten in enormous quantity, and are imperfectly di-

gested, the hard-coated seeds especially passing through the system unchanged; the feces containing these seeds are preserved
with some care, and after the harvest is passed the hoard (desic-
cated, of course, in the dry climate) is ground . . . and win-
nowed. The product is then eaten. . . . In superficial view this
food factor is the precise homologue of the "second harvest"
of the California Indians as described by Clavigero, Baegert,
and others; but it gains importance, among the Seri at least, as
the sole method of storing or preserving food supplies, and
hence as the germ of industrial economy out of which a feeble
thrift-sense may be regarded as emerging. And the rise of thrift
in Seriland, like esthetic and industrial beginnings generally, is
shaped by faith and attendant ceremony; for the doubly con-
sumed food is credited with intensified powers and virtues.

In Seri magic, excrement is literally aliment; but before we
read them out of the roll of humanity, let us remember what
happened to Midas. The unsublimated body magic of the Seri
Indian reveals the only bodily meaning that can be attached to
the dreams of avarice. And since the only life meanings are
body meanings, the dreams of avarice are not less, but more,
unreal than the body magic of the Seris.

Until the advent of psychoanalysis and its doctrine of the
anal character of money, the profoundest insights into the nature of the money complex had to be expressed through the
medium of myth—in modern times, the myth of the Devil. The
Devil, we said in our chapter on Luther, is the lineal descendant of the Trickster in primitive mythologies; the evolution
of the Trickster, through such intermediary figures as the
classical Hermes, into the Christian Devil reflects the history of
anality. The Trickster of primitive mythologies is surrounded
by unsublimated and undisguised anality. For example, of the
Winnebago Trickster Paul Radin writes: [220]

He comes upon a bulb which tells him that whoever chews it
will defecate. . . . So he takes the bulb and chews it to find
that he does not defecate but only breaks wind. This expulsion
of gas increases in intensity progressively. He sits on a log, but
is propelled into the air with the log on top of him; he pulls
up trees to which he clings, by their roots. In his helplessness
he has the inhabitants of a village pile all their possessions upon

him, their lodges, their dogs, and then they themselves climb
upon him. . . . And so the whole world of man is now on
Wakdjunkaga's back. With a terrific expulsion of gas he scatters
the people and all their possessions to the four quarters of the
earth. . . . He now begins to defecate. The earth is covered
with excrement. To escape it he takes refuge in a tree, but to
no avail, and he falls into mountains of his own excrement. . . .

At the same time, as all students of comparative mythology
know, this Trickster, with his "filthy" tricks, is a great Culture-
hero, the source of man's material culture. Indeed the Trickster can create the world by a filthy trick, out of excrement
or that thinly disguised substitute for excrement, mud or clay,
reflecting, in Abraham's words, the idea of the omnipotence of
the products of the bowel.[221] In classical antiquity, the period
of the most perfect sublimation, the figure of Hermes is produced by sublimation-negation of anality. Though vestiges of
unsublimated anality remain, simple excrement is replaced first
by the symbolic heap of stones and then by the symbolic bag
of money (compare the bag in which, according to Margaret
Mead, the Arapesh carefully collect their magic dirt).[222] Luther's Devil is a negation of the classical sublimation; sublimation is repudiated because the body is perceived as fallen and
filthy; the Devil regains, by a return of the repressed, his excremental character, but his anality is not cathected with libido
or magic life, as in the magic-dirt complex, but is seen as death.
The whole evolution from Trickster to Devil and on into the
pseudosecular demonic of capitalism shows the progressive triumph of the death instinct.

The sublimations of civilized man desiccate the magic out
of the human body and thus represent a victory for the reality-
principle. But to desiccate the magic out of the human body is
to desexualize it; on the path of sublimation a victory for the
reality-principle is also a victory for the death instinct. The
process must end where Luther said it ended, in the dominion
of death over the body and the entire realm of visible reality.
A new stage in the history of the money complex begins in
modern times, with the Reformation and the rise of capitalism.
On the one hand definitive sublimation is attained at last by a

final repression of the awareness of the anal-erotic sources of the complex: up till then the pursuit of money appears to have been inhibited by the knowledge that lucre is filthy. And on the other hand there is a turn against the sublimation, a withdrawal of libido from sublimation, a desexualization of the sublimation itself. The psychology of precapitalist hoarding ("primitive accumulation") differs from that of capitalist enterprise ("creative destruction," Schumpeter called it) precisely in the fact that the accumulation, the gold or the real estate, yielded bodily satisfaction to the owner. "Let me kiss thee," says Volpone to his gold, "thou being best of things, and far transcending all style of joy; such are thy beauties and our loves!" [223] True capitalism, on the other hand, as Marx said, is destroyed in its very foundation if we assume that its compelling motive is enjoyment instead of the accumulation of wealth.[224]

This withdrawal of Eros hands over culture to the death instinct; and the inhuman, abstract, impersonal world which the death instinct creates progressively eliminates all possibility of the life of sublimated Eros, which we nostalgically so admire in the ancient Greeks. Thus the path of sublimation ends in its own self-refutation and sets the stage for its own abolition. At the same time this transformation of life into death-in-life is a victory for the reality-principle. The withdrawal of Eros from sublimation is the great disillusionment.[225] As modern civilization ruthlessly eliminates Eros from culture, modern science ruthlessly demythologizes our view of the world and of ourselves. In getting rid of our old loves, modern science serves both the reality-principle and the death instinct. Thus science and civilization combine to articulate the core of the human neurosis, man's incapacity to live in the body, which is also his incapacity to die. The human body had to be handed over to death before culture could produce psychoanalysis—the last assault on man's old loves and the first turn to face the body.

Thus the general consciousness of mankind needs to appropriate psychoanalysis, the science of neurosis, in order to vindicate, and then pass beyond, the intuitive judgment of John Maynard Keynes: [226]

When the accumulation of wealth is no longer of high social importance, there will be great changes in the code of morals. We shall be able to rid ourselves of many of the pseudo-moral principles which have hag-ridden us for two hundred years, by which we have exalted some of the most distasteful of human qualities into the position of the highest virtues. We shall be able to afford to dare to assess the money-motive at its true value. The love of money as a possession—as distinguished from the love of money as a means to the enjoyments and realities of life—will be recognized for what it is, a somewhat disgusting morbidity, one of those semi-criminal, semi-pathological propensities which one hands over with a shudder to the specialists in mental disease.

Part Six

THE WAY OUT

"The cultural era is past. The new civilization, which may take centuries or a few thousand years to usher in, will not be another civilization—it will be the open stretch of realization which all the past civilizations have pointed to. The city, which was the birth-place of civilization, such as we know it to be, will exist no more. There will be nuclei of course, but they will be mobile and fluid. The peoples of the earth will no longer be shut off from one another within states but will flow freely over the surface of the earth and intermingle. There will be no fixed constellations of human aggregates. Governments will give way to management, using the word in a broad sense. The politician will become as superannuated as the dodo bird. The machine will never be dominated, as some imagine; it will be scrapped, eventually, but not before men have understood the nature of the mystery which binds them to their creation. The worship, investigation and subjugation of the machine will give way to the lure of all that is truly occult. This problem is bound up with the larger one of power—and of possession. Man will be forced to realize that power must be kept open, fluid and free. His aim will be not to possess power but to radiate it." *

Utopian speculations, such as these of Henry Miller, must come back into fashion. They are a way of affirming faith in the possibility of solving problems that seem at the moment insoluble. Today even the survival of humanity is a utopian hope.

* From Henry Miller, *Sunday After the War* (New York: New Directions), pp. 154-155. Copyright, 1944, by Henry Miller. Reprinted by permission.

The Resurrection of the Body

THE PATH of sublimation, which mankind has religiously followed at least since the foundation of the first cities, is no way out of the human neurosis, but, on the contrary, leads to its aggravation. Psychoanalytical theory and the bitter facts of contemporary history suggest that mankind is reaching the end of this road. Psychoanalytical theory declares that the end of the road is the dominion of death-in-life. History has brought mankind to that pinnacle on which the total obliteration of mankind is at last a practical possibility. At this moment of history the friends of the life instinct must warn that the victory of death is by no means impossible; the malignant death instinct can unleash those hydrogen bombs. For if we discard our fond illusion that the human race has a privileged or providential status in the life of the universe, it seems plain that the malignant death instinct is a built-in guarantee that the human experiment, if it fails to attain its possible perfection, will cancel itself out, as the dinosaur experiment canceled itself out. But jeremiads are useless unless we can point to a better way. Therefore the question confronting mankind is the abolition of repression—in traditional Christian language, the resurrection of the body.

We have already done what we could to extract from psychoanalytical theory a model of what the resurrected body would be like. The life instinct, or sexual instinct, demands activity of a kind that, in contrast to our current mode of activity, can only be called play. The life instinct also demands a union with others and with the world around us based not on anxiety and aggression but on narcissism and erotic exuberance.

But the death instinct also demands satisfaction; as Hegel

says in the *Phenomenology,* "The life and knowledge of God may doubtless be described as love playing with itself; but this idea sinks into triviality, if the seriousness, the pain, the patience and the labor of the Negative are omitted." [1] The death instinct is reconciled with the life instinct only in a life which is not repressed, which leaves no "unlived lines" in the human body, the death instinct then being affirmed in a body which is willing to die. And, because the body is satisfied, the death instinct no longer drives it to change itself and make history, and therefore, as Christian theology divined, its activity is in eternity.

At the same time—and here again Christian theology and psychoanalysis agree—the resurrected body is the transfigured body. The abolition of repression would abolish the unnatural concentrations of libido in certain particular bodily organs—concentrations engineered by the negativity of the morbid death instinct, and constituting the bodily base of the neurotic character disorders in the human ego. In the words of Thoreau: "We need pray for no higher heaven than the pure senses can furnish, a purely sensuous life. Our present senses are but rudiments of what they are destined to become." [2] The human body would become polymorphously perverse, delighting in that full life of all the body which it now fears. The consciousness strong enough to endure full life would be no longer Apollonian but Dionysian—consciousness which does not observe the limit, but overflows; consciousness which *does not negate any more.*

If the question facing mankind is the abolition of repression, psychoanalysis is not the only point of view from which the question can and should be raised. We have already indicated that the question is intrinsic to Christian theology. The time has come to ask Christian theologians, especially the neo-orthodox, what they mean by the resurrection of the body and by eternal life. Is this a promise of immortality after death? In other words, is the psychological premise of Christianity the impossibility of reconciling life and death either in "this" world or the "next," so that flight from death—with all its morbid consequences—is our eternal fate in "this world" and in "the next"? For we have seen that the perfect body, promised by Christian theology, enjoying that perfect felicity promised by Christian theology, is a body reconciled with death.

In the last analysis Christian theology must either accept death as part of life or abandon the body. For two thousand years Christianity has kept alive the mystical hope of an ultimate victory of Life over Death, during a phase of human history when Life was at war with Death and hope could only be mystical. But if we are approaching the last days, Christian theology might ask itself whether it is only the religion of fallen humanity, or whether it might be asleep when the bridegroom comes. Certain it is that if Christianity wishes to help mankind toward that erasure of the traces of original sin which Baudelaire said was the true definition of progress,[3] there are priceless insights in its tradition—insights which have to be transformed into a system of practical therapy, something like psychoanalysis, before they are useful or even meaningful.

The specialty of Christian eschatology lies precisely in its rejection of the Platonic hostility to the human body and to "matter," its refusal to identify the Platonic path of sublimation with ultimate salvation, and its affirmation that eternal life can only be life in a body. Christian asceticism can carry punishment of the fallen body to heights inconceivable to Plato; but Christian hope is for the redemption of that fallen body. Hence the affirmation of Tertullian: *Resurget igitur caro, et quidem omnis, et quidem ipsa, et quidem integra*—The body will rise again, all of the body, the identical body, the entire body.[4] The medieval Catholic synthesis between Christianity and Greek philosophy, with its notion of an immortal soul, compromised and confused the issue; only Protestantism carries the full burden of the peculiar Christian faith. Luther's break with the doctrine of sublimation (good works) is decisive; but the theologian of the resurrected body is the cobbler of Görlitz, Jacob Boehme. When Tillich and Barth finally get round to the substance of things hoped for, their eschatology, they will have to reckon with Boehme. Meanwhile, as neo-orthodox theology plunges deeper into the nature of sin and death, Boehme's *theologia ex idea vitae deducta* is neglected except by the lonely mystic and revolutionary Berdyaev.[5]

Whatever the Christian churches do with him, Boehme's

position in the Western tradition of mystic hope of better things is central and assured. Backward he is linked, through Paracelsus and alchemy, to the tradition of Christian gnosticism and Jewish cabalism; forward he is linked, through his influence on the romantics Blake, Novalis, and Hegel, with Freud. We have argued that psychoanalysis has not psychoanalyzed itself until it places itself inside the history of Western thought—inside the general neurosis of mankind. So seen, psychoanalysis is the heir to a mystical tradition which it must affirm.

Mysticism, in the mind of the general public, is identified with that flight from the material world and from life preached by such popularizers as Evelyn Underhill and Aldous Huxley [6] —which, from the psychoanalytical point of view, may be termed Apollonian or sublimation mysticism. But there is in the Western tradition another kind of mysticism, which can be called Dionysian or body mysticism, which stays with life, which is the body, and seeks to transform and perfect it. Western body mysticism—a tradition which urgently needs re-examination—contains three main strands: the Christian (Pauline) notion of the "spiritual" body, the Jewish (cabalistic) notion of Adam's perfect body before the Fall, and the alchemical notion of the subtle body.[7] All of these strands unite in Boehme, and even a little knowledge of the real Boehme—for example Ernst Benz' first-rate book, not available in English [8]— makes it plain that Boehme and Freud have too much in common to be able to dispense with each other.

Boehme, like Freud, understands death not as a mere nothing but as a positive force either in dialectical conflict with life (in fallen man), or dialectically unified with life (in God's perfection). Thus, says Benz, "Our life remains a struggle between life and death, and as long as this conflict lasts, anxiety lasts also." [9] In Boehme's concept of life, the concept of play, or love-play, is as central as it is in Freud's; and his concept of the spiritual or paradisical body of Adam before the Fall recognizes the potent demand in our unconscious both for an androgynous mode of being and for a narcissistic mode of self-expression, as well as the corruption in our current use of the oral, anal, and genital functions. It is true that Boehme does not yet accept the brutal death of the individual physical body, and therefore makes his paradisical body ambiguously immaterial, without oral, anal, and genital organs; and yet he clings obstinately to the body and to bodily pleasure, and therefore says that Adam was "magically" able to eat and enjoy the "essence" of things, and "magically" able to reproduce and to have sexual pleasure in the act of reproduction. Boehme is caught in these dilemmas because of his insight into the corruption of the human body, his insight that all life is life in the body, and, on the other hand, his inability to accept a body which dies. No Protestant theologian has gone further; or rather, later Protestantism has preferred to repress the problem and to repress Boehme.

Oriental mysticism also, to judge from Needham's survey of Taoism or Eliade's study of Yoga,[10] has reached the same point. Needham (quoting Maspéro) is right in stressing that the Taoist quest for a more perfect body transcends the Platonic dualism of soul and matter. But Needham's enthusiasm for Taoism as a human and organismic response to life in the world must be qualified by recognizing that the Taoist perfect body is immortal: Taoism does not accept death as part of life. (In an earlier chapter we argued that there is the same defect in Needham's other enthusiasm, Whitehead's philosophy of nature.)

Psychoanalysis accepts the death of the body; but psychoanalysis has something to learn from body mysticism, occidental and oriental, over and above the wealth of psychoanalytical insights contained in it. For these mystics take seriously, and traditional psychoanalysis does not, the possibility of human perfectibility and the hope of finding a way out of the human neurosis into that simple health that animals enjoy, but not man.

As Protestantism degenerated from Luther and Boehme, it abandoned its religious function of criticizing the existing order and keeping alive the mystical hope of better things; in psychoanalytical terminology, it lost contact with the unconscious and with the immortal repressed desires of the unconscious. The torch passed to the poets and philosophers of the romantic movement. The heirs of Boehme are Blake, Novalis, Hegel, and, as Professor Gray has recently shown, Goethe.[11] These are the poets whom Freud credited with being the real discoverers of the unconscious.[12]

Not only toward the mystics but also toward the poets psychoanalysis must quit its pretension of supramundane superiority. Instead of exposing the neuroses of the poets, the psychoanalysts might learn from them, and abandon the naïve idea that there is an immense gap, in mental health and intellectual objectivity, between themselves and the rest of the world. In the world's opinion, in the eyes of common sense, Novalis is crazy, and Ferenczi also: the world will find it easier to believe that we are all mad than to believe that the psychoanalysts are not. And further, it does not seem to be the case that the psychoanalytical mode of reaching the unconscious has superannuated the poetic, or artistic, mode of attaining the same objective. Anyone conversant both with modern literature and with psychoanalysis knows that modern literature is full of psychoanalytical insights not yet grasped, or not so clearly grasped, by "scientific" psychoanalysis. And anyone who loves art knows that psychoanalysis has no monopoly on the power to heal. What the times call for is an end to the war between psychoanalysis and art—a war kept alive by the sterile "debunking" approach of psychoanalysis to art—and the beginning of cooperation between the two in the work of therapy and in the task of making the unconscious conscious. A little more Eros and less strife.

Modern poetry, like psychoanalysis and Protestant theology, faces the problem of the resurrection of the body. Art and poetry have always been altering our ways of sensing and feeling—that is to say, altering the human body. And Whitehead rightly discerns as the essence of the "Romantic Reaction" a revulsion against abstraction (in psychoanalytical terms, sublimation) in favor of the concrete sensual organism, the human body.[13] "Energy is the only life, and is from the Body. . . . Energy is Eternal Delight," says Blake.

A young critic, whose first book represents a new mode of criticism—a criticism for which poetry is an experience both mystical and bodily—has traced the persistent quest in modern poetry for the resurrection of the body and the perfection of the body.[14] Wordsworth, in contrast with the sublime (and sublimating) tendency of Milton, "considers that his revelation can be expressed in the forms and symbols of daily life" and "sees Paradise possible in any sweet though bare nook of the earth." Hopkins "is engaged on a theodicy, and has taken for his province the stubborn senses and the neglected physical world"; "no one has gone further than Hopkins in presenting Christ as the direct and omnipresent object of perception, so deeply ingrained in the eyes, the flesh, and the bone (and the personal sense of having eyes, flesh, and bone), that the sense of self and the sense of being in Christ can no longer be distinguished." Rilke's plaint throughout his career is that "we do not know the body any more than we know nature": Rilke believes (in his own words) that "the qualities are to be taken away from God, the no longer utterable, and returned to creation, to love and death"; so that the outcome of his poetry is that "for Rilke, the body becomes a spiritual fact." Valéry's poetry "may be considered as the Odyssey of Consciousness in search of its true body"; and "the intellectual pursuit of Valéry is to this end, that the body may be seen as what it virtually is, a magnificent revelation and instrument of the soul. Could it be viewed as such, the eyes would not be symbol, but reality." [15]

The "magical" body which the poet seeks is the "subtle" or "spiritual" or "translucent" body of occidental mysticism, and the "diamond" body of oriental mysticism, and, in psychoanalysis, the polymorphously perverse body of childhood. Thus, for example, psychoanalysis declares the fundamentally bisexual character of human nature; Boehme insists on the androgynous character of human perfection; Taoist mysticism invokes feminine passivity to counteract masculine aggressivity; and Rilke's poetic quest is a quest for a hermaphroditic body.[16] There is an urgent need for elucidation of the interrelations between these disparate modes of articulating the desires of the unconscious. Jung is aware of these interrelations, and orthodox psychoanalysts have not been aware of them. But no elucidation results from incorporation of the data into the Jungian system, not so much because of the intellectual disorder in the system, but rather because of the fundamental orientation of Jung, which is flight from the problem of the body, flight from the concept of repression, and a return to the path of sublimation. Freudianism must face the issue, and Freud himself said: "Certain practices of the mystics may succeed in upsetting the normal relations between the different regions of the mind, so that, for example, the perceptual system becomes able to grasp relations in the deeper layers of the ego and in the the id which would otherwise be inaccessible to it." [17]

Joseph Needham's interest in what we have called body mysticism, an interest which underlies his epoch-making work *Science and Civilization in China,* reminds us that the resurrection of the body has been placed on the agenda not only by psychoanalysis, mysticism, and poetry, but also by the philosophical criticism of modern science. Whitehead's criticism of scientific abstraction is, in psychoanalytical terms, a criticism of sublimation. His protest against "The Fallacy of Misplaced Concreteness" is a protest on behalf of the living body as a whole: "But the living organ of experience is the living body as a whole"; and his protest "on behalf of value" insists that the real structure of the human body, of human cognition, and of the events cognized is both sensuous and erotic, "self-enjoyment." [18] Whitehead himself recognized the affinity between himself and the romantic poets; and Needham of course recognizes the affinity between the philosophy of organism and mysticism. Actually Needham may be exaggerating the uniqueness of Taoism. The whole Western alchemical tradition, which urgently needs re-examination, is surely "Whiteheadian" in spirit, and Goethe, the last of the alchemists, in his "Essay on the Metamorphosis of Plants" produced the last, or the first, Whiteheadian scientific treatise. Goethe, says a modern biologist, "reached out to the reconciliation of the antithesis between the senses and the intellect, an antithesis with which traditional science does not attempt to cope." [19]

Needham has recognized the crucial role of psychology in the philosophy of science. The refutation of Descartes, he has said, will come from psychology, not biology. [20] And yet he seems to be unaware of the profound affinities between the Tao, which he so much admires, and psychoanalysis. He seems to be unaware of Ferenczi's brilliant essay attempting to reorganize the whole theory of biological evolution in the light of psychoanalysis. [21] But the function of psychoanalysis in relation to Whitehead and Needham's critique of science is not that of supplementing their ideology with sympathetic support; rather it is indispensable if their critique of science is to amount to more than mere ideology. For what they are calling in question is the subjective attitude of the scientist, and if their critique is to amount to more than mere dislike, it must be supplemented by a psychoanalysis of the subject. In fact a psychoanalysis of the subject (the "observer") seems necessary if science is to remain "objective." The essential point has been seen by Ferenczi, who coined the term "utraquism" to indicate the required combination of analysis of the subject and analysis of the object: "If science is really to remain objective, it must work alternately as pure psychology and pure natural science, and must verify both our inner and outer experience by analogies taken from both points of view. . . . I called this the 'utraquism' of all true scientific work." [22]

Ferenczi's formulations date from 1923–1926: today we would presumably think of "integration" rather than alternation. Ferenczi saw psychoanalysis as marking a significant step forward in general scientific methodology, a step which he defined as "a return to a certain extent to the methods of ancient animistic science" and "the re-establishment of an animism no longer anthropomorphic." [23] But the re-establishment of an animism is precisely the outcome of Whitehead and Needham's line of thought. And Ferenczi argues that psychoanalysis is necessary in order to differentiate the new "purified" animism from the old naïve animism: [24]

> Insofar as Freud attempts to solve problems of biology as well as of sexual activity by means of psychoanalytic experience, he returns to a certain extent to the methods of ancient animistic science. There is a safeguard, however, against the psychoanalyst falling into the error of such naïve animism. Naïve animism transferred human psychic life *en bloc* without analysis onto natural objects. Psychoanalysis, however, dissected human psychic activity, pursued it to the limit where psychic and physical came into contact, down to the instincts, and thus freed psychology from anthropocentrism, and only then did it trust itself to evaluate this purified animism in terms of biology. To have been the first in the history of science to make this attempt is the achievement of Freud.

We therefore conclude with a plea for "utraquistic" integration between psychoanalysis and the philosophy of science.

Ferenczi, in his important analysis of Ernst Mach entitled "The Psychogenesis of Mechanism," put it this way: "When will the physicist, who finds the soul in the mechanism, and the psychoanalyst, who perceives mechanisms in the soul, join hands and work with united forces at a *Weltanschauung* free from one-sidedness and 'idealizations'?" [25]

Perhaps there are even deeper issues raised by the confrontation between psychoanalysis and the philosophy of organism. Whitehead and Needham are protesting against the inhuman attitude of modern science; in psychoanalytical terms, they are calling for a science based on an erotic sense of reality, rather than an aggressive dominating attitude toward reality. From this point of view alchemy (and Goethe's essay on plants) might be said to be the last effort of Western man to produce a science based on an erotic sense of reality. And conversely, modern science, as criticized by Whitehead, is one aspect of a total cultural situation which may be described as the dominion of death-in-life. The mentality which was able to reduce nature to "a dull affair, soundless, scentless, colourless; merely the hurrying of material endlessly, meaninglessly"—Whitehead's description [26]—is lethal. It is an awe-inspiring attack on the life of the universe; in more technical psychoanalytical terms, its anal-sadistic intent is plain. And further, the only historian of science who uses psychoanalysis, Gaston Bachelard, concludes that it is of the essence of the scientific spirit to be mercilessly ascetic, to eliminate human enjoyment from our relation to nature, to eliminate the human senses, and finally to eliminate the human brain: [27]

> It does indeed seem that with the twentieth century there begins a kind of scientific thought in opposition to the senses, and that it is necessary to construct a theory of objectivity *in opposition to* the object. . . . It follows that the entire use of the brain is being called into question. From now on the brain is strictly no longer adequate as an instrument for scientific thought; that is to say, the brain is the *obstacle* to scientific thought. It is an obstacle in the sense that it is the coordinating center for human movements and appetites. It is necessary to think *in opposition to* the brain.

Thus modern science confirms Ferenczi's aphorism: "*Pure intelligence* is thus a product of dying, or at least of becoming mentally insensitive, and is therefore *in principle madness*." [28]

What Whitehead and Needham are combating is not an error but a disease in consciousness. In more technical psychoanalytical terms, the issue is not the conscious structure of science, but the unconscious premises of science; the trouble is in the unconscious strata of the scientific ego, in the scientific character-structure. Whitehead called the modern scientific point of view, in spite of its world-conquering successes, "quite unbelievable." [29] Psychoanalysis adds the crucial point: it is insane. Hence there is unlikely to be any smooth transition from the "mechanistic" point of view to the "organismic" point of view. It is unlikely that problems generated in the mechanistic system will lead to organismic solutions. The two points of view represent different instinctual orientations, different fusions of life and death. It is even doubtful that the adoption of an organismic point of view under present conditions would be a gain; it might be a relapse into naïve animism. Thus the kind of thinking which Needham hails as Taoist wisdom (alchemy, etc.), is attacked by Bachelard as unconscious projection, dreaming, and naïve mythologizing; he sees science (and psychoanalysis) as sternly committed to the task of demythologizing our view of nature. It would seem, therefore, in line with Ferenczi's argument, that Taoist ideology without psychoanalytical consciousness could be a relapse into naïve animism. And psychoanalytical consciousness means psychoanalytical therapy also. Psychoanalytical therapy involves a solution to the problem of repression; what is needed is not an organismic ideology, but to change the human body so that it can become for the first time an organism—the resurrection of the body. An organism whose own sexual life is as disordered as man's is in no position to construct objective theories about the Yin and the Yang and the sex life of the universe.

The resurrection of the body is a social project facing mankind as a whole, and it will become a practical political problem when the statesmen of the world are called upon to deliver happiness instead of power, when political economy becomes a science of use-values instead of exchange-values—a science of enjoyment instead of a science of accumulation. In the face of this tremendous human problem, contemporary social theory, both capitalist and socialist, has nothing to say. Contemporary social theory (again we must honor Veblen as an exception) has been completely taken in by the inhuman abstractions of the path of sublimation, and has no contact with concrete human beings, with their concrete bodies, their concrete though repressed desires, and their concrete neuroses.

To find social theorists who are thinking about the real problem of our age, we have to go back to the Marx of 1844, or even to the philosophers influencing Marx in 1844, Fourier and Feuerbach. From Fourier's psychological analysis of the antithesis of work and pleasure Marx obtained the concept of play, and used it, in a halfhearted way to be sure, in some of his early utopian speculations. From Feuerbach Marx learned the necessity of moving from Hegelian abstractions to the concrete senses and the concrete human body. Marx' "philosophic-economic manuscripts" of 1844 contain remarkable formulations calling for the resurrection of human nature, the appropriation of the human body, the transformation of the human senses, and the realization of a state of self-enjoyment. Thus, for example, "Man appropriates himself as an all-sided being in an all-sided way, hence as total man. [This appropriation lies in] every one of his human relationships to the world—seeing, hearing, smell, taste, feeling, thought, perception, experience, wishing, activity, loving, in short, all organs of his individuality." [30] The human physical senses must be emancipated from the sense of possession, and then the humanity of the senses and the human enjoyment of the senses will be achieved for the first time. Here is the point of contact between Marx and Freud: I do not see how the profundities and obscurities of the "philosophic-economic manuscripts" can be elucidated except with the aid of psychoanalysis.

Psychoanalysis, mysticism, poetry, the philosophy of organism, Feuerbach, and Marx—this is a miscellaneous assemblage; but, as Heraclitus said, the unseen harmony is stronger than the seen. Common to all of them is a mode of consciousness that can be called—although the term causes fresh difficulties—the dialectical imagination. By "dialectical" I mean an activity of consciousness struggling to circumvent the limitations imposed by the formal-logical law of contradiction. Marxism, of course, has no monopoly of "dialectics." Needham has shown the dialectical character of Whitehead's philosophy, and he constantly draws attention to dialectical patterns in mystical thought.[31] The goal of Indian body mysticism, according to Eliade, is the "conjunction of contrarieties" (*coincidentia oppositorum*). Scholem, in his survey of Jewish mysticism, says, "Mysticism, intent on formulating the paradoxes of religious experience, uses the instrument of dialectics to express its meaning. The Kabbalists are by no means the only witnesses to this affinity between mystical and dialectical thinking." [32]

As for poetry, are not those basic poetic devices emphasized by recent criticism—paradox, ambiguity, irony, tension—devices whereby the poetic imagination subverts the "reasonableness" of language, the chains it imposes? (Compare Valéry's theory of poetry; see chapter VI.) And from the psychoanalytical point of view, if we, with Trilling (see above, chapter V), accept the substantial identity between poetic logic (with its symbolism, condensation of meaning, and displacement of accent) and dream logic, then the connection between poetry and dialectics, as defined, is more substantially grounded. Dreams are certainly an activity of the mind struggling to circumvent the formal-logical law of contradiction.[33]

Psychoanalytical thinking has a double relation to the dialectical imagination. It is, on the one hand (actually or potentially), a mode of dialectical consciousness; on the other hand, it contains, or ought to contain, a theory about the nature of the dialectical imagination. I say "actually or potentially" because psychoanalysis, either as a body of doctrine or an experience of the analysand, is no total revelation of the unconscious repressed. The struggle of consciousness to circumvent the limitations of formal logic, of language, and of "common sense" is under conditions of general repression never ending (see Freud's essay, "Analysis Terminable and Interminable").[34] "Dialectical" are those psychoanalysts who continue this struggle; for the rest, psychoanalytical terminology can be a prison house of Byzantine scholasticism in which "word-consciousness" is substituting for consciousness of the unconscious (see above, chapter XI).

And even if we take Freud as the model of psychoanalytical consciousness, we have argued that at such crucial points as the relation between the two instincts and the relation between humanity and animality, Freud is trapped because he is not sufficiently "dialectical." Nevertheless, the basic structure of Freud's thought is committed to dialectics, because it is committed to the vision of mental life as basically an arena of conflict; and his finest insights (for example, that when the patient denies something, he affirms it [35]) are incurably "dialectical." Hence the attempt to make psychoanalysis out to be "scientific" (in the positivist sense) is not only vain but destructive.[36] Empirical verification, the positivist test of science, can apply only to that which is fully in consciousness; but psychoanalysis is a mode of contacting the unconscious under conditions of general repression, when the unconscious remains in some sense repressed. To put the matter another way, the "poetry" in Freud's thought cannot be purged away, or rather such an expurgation is exactly what is accomplished in "scientific" textbooks of psychology; but Freud's writings remain unexpurgatable. The same "poetical" imagination marks the work of Róheim and Ferenczi as superior, and explains why they are neglected by "scientific" anthropologists and psychoanalysts. The whole nature of the "dialectical" or "poetical" imagination is another problem urgently needing examination; and there is a particular need for psychoanalysis, as part of the psychoanalysis of psychoanalysis, to become conscious of the dialectical, poetical, mystical stream that runs in its blood.

The key to the nature of dialectical thinking may lie in psychoanalysis, more specifically in Freud's psychoanalysis of negation. There is first the theorem that "there is nothing in the id which can be compared to negation," and that the law of contradiction does not hold in the id. Similarly, the dream does not seem to recognize the word "no." [37] Instead of the law of contradiction we find a unity of opposites: "Dreams show a special tendency to reduce two opposites to a unity"; "Anything in a dream may mean its opposite." [38] We must therefore entertain the hypothesis that there is an important connection between being "dialectical" and dreaming, just as there is between dreaming and poetry or mysticism. Furthermore, in his essay "The Antithetical Sense of Primal Words" [39] Freud compares the linguistic phenomenon of a hidden (in the etymological root) identity between words with antithetical meanings; he reveals the significant fact that it was the linguistic phenomenon that gave him the clue to the dream phenomenon, and not vice versa. It is plain that both psychoanalysis and the study of language (philosophical and philological) need a marriage or at least a meeting.

And, on the other hand, Freud's essay "On Negation" [40] may throw light on the nature of the "dialectical" dissatisfaction with formal logic. Negation is the primal act of repression; but it at the same time liberates the mind to think about the repressed under the general condition that it is denied and thus remains essentially repressed. With Spinoza's formula *omnis determinatio est negatio* in mind, examine the following formulations of Freud: "A negative judgment is the intellectual substitute for repression; the 'No' in which it is expressed is the hall-mark of repression. . . . By the help of the symbol of negation, the thinking process frees itself from the limitations of repression and enriches itself with the subject-matter without which it could not work efficiently." But: "Negation only assists in undoing one of the consequences of repression—the fact that the subject-matter of the image in question is unable to enter consciousness. The result is a kind of intellectual acceptance of what is repressed, though in all essentials the repression persists." [41]

We may therefore entertain the hypothesis that formal logic and the law of contradiction are the rules whereby the mind submits to operate under general conditions of repression. As with the concept of time, Kant's categories of rationality would then turn out to be the categories of repression. And conversely, "dialectical" would be the struggle of the mind to circumvent repression and make the unconscious conscious. But by the same token, it would be the struggle of the mind to overcome the split and conflict within itself. It could then be identified with that "synthesizing" tendency in the ego of which Freud spoke, [42] and with that attempt to cure, inside the neurosis itself, on which Freud came finally to place his hope for therapy.[43] As an attempt to unify and to cure, the "dialectical" consciousness would be a manifestation of Eros. And, as consciousness trying to throw off the fetters of negation, the "dialectical" consciousness would be a step toward that Dionysian ego which does not negate any more.[44]

What the great world needs, of course, is a little more Eros and less strife; but the intellectual world needs it just as much. A little more Eros would make conscious the unconscious harmony between "dialectical" dreamers of all kinds—psychoanalysts, political idealists, mystics, poets, philosophers—and abate the sterile and ignorant polemics. Since the ignorance seems to be mostly a matter of self-ignorance, a little more psychoanalytical consciousness on all sides (including the psychoanalysts) might help—a little more self-knowledge, humility, humanity, and Eros. We may therefore conclude with the concluding words of Freud's *Civilization and Its Discontents:* [45]

> Men have brought their powers of subduing the forces of nature to such a pitch that by using them they could now very easily exterminate one another to the last man. They know this —hence arises a great part of their current unrest, their dejection, their mood of apprehension. And now it may be expected that the other of the two "heavenly forces," eternal Eros, will put forth his strength so as to maintain himself alongside of his equally immortal adversary.

And perhaps our children will live to live a full life, and so see what Freud could not see—in the old adversary, a friend.

Reference Notes

THE FOLLOWING abbreviations are used for reference to Freud's works most often cited in the text:

BPP   *Beyond the Pleasure Principle*, tr. J. Strachey. (International Psycho-Analytical Library, ed. E. Jones, no. 4.) London: Hogarth Press, 1950.

BW   *The Basic Writings of Sigmund Freud*, tr. & ed. A. A. Brill. New York: The Modern Library, 1938. Contains six major works, herein distinguished as follows:

Life	*The Psychopathology of Everyday Life*
Dreams	*The Interpretation of Dreams*
Sex	*Three Contributions to the Theory of Sex*
Wit	*Wit and Its Relation to the Unconscious*
T & T	*Totem and Taboo*
History	*The History of the Psychoanalytic Movement*

Civ.   *Civilization and Its Discontents*, tr. J. Riviere. (International Psycho-Analytical Library, ed. E. Jones, no. 17.) London: Hogarth, 1930.

CP I–V   *Collected Papers*, ed. J. Riviere & J. Strachey. 5 vols. (International Psycho-Analytical Library, no. 7–10, 37.) New York, London: The International Psycho-Analytical Press, 1924–50.

DD   *Delusion and Dream and Other Essays*, ed. P. Rieff. Boston: Beacon Press, 1956.

EI   *The Ego and the Id*, tr. J. Riviere. (International Psycho-Analytical Library, no. 12.) London: Hogarth Press and The Institute of Psycho-Analysis, 1927.

FI   *The Future of an Illusion*, tr. W. D. Robson-Scott. (International Psycho-Analytical Library, no. 15.) London: Hogarth Press and The Institute of Psycho-Analysis, 1928.

GI   *A General Introduction to Psycho-Analysis*, tr. J. Riviere. New York: Perma Giants, 1953. Copyright 1935 by Edward L. Bernays. (Quotations from this source by permission of Liveright Publishers, New York, and G. Allen & Unwin Ltd., London.)

GP   *Group Psychology and the Analysis of the Ego*, tr. J. Strachey. (International Psycho-Analytical Library, no. 6.) London, Vienna: The International Psycho-Analytical Press, 1922.

ISA   *Inhibitions, Symptoms and Anxiety*, tr. A. Strachey. (International Psycho-Analytical Library, no. 28.) London: Hogarth Press and The Institute of Psycho-Analysis, 1936.

L   *Leonardo da Vinci: A Study in Psychosexuality*, tr. A. A. Brill. New York: Random House, 1947.

MM   *Moses and Monotheism*, tr. K. Jones. (International Psycho-Analytical Library, no. 33.) London: Hogarth Press and The Institute of Psycho-Analysis, 1939; (New York, Knopf, 1939).

NIL   *New Introductory Lectures on Psychoanalysis*, tr. W. J. H. Sprott. (International Psycho-Analytical Library, no. 24.) London: Hogarth Press and The Institute of Psycho-Analysis, 1933.

Out. *An Outline of Psychoanalysis*, tr. J. Strachey. (International Psycho-Analytical Library, no. 35.) London: Hogarth Press, 1949.

Works *The Standard Edition of the Complete Psychological Works of Sigmund Freud*, ed. James Strachey, Anna Freud, Alix Strachey, & Alan Tyson. [24] vols. London: Hogarth Press and The Institute of Psycho-Analysis, 1954- .

PART ONE

Chapter I: The Disease Called Man

1. BW (History) 939.
2. BW (Dreams) 527.
3. BW (Dreams) 542.
4. GI 397.

5. NIL 92. Cf. EI 12.
6. CP IV, 86. Cf. GI 304, 358–59; EI 11; NIL 25–26.
7. EI 12.
8. EI 12. Cf. DD 70.
9. BW (Dreams) 473, 510–11, 540–41; GI 146–47. Cf. BW (Dreams) 519; GI 70, 136, 311, 369.
10. GI 87, 236, 307, 368, 464; NIL 15, 26.
11. GI 367–68, 464–65; NIL 80; CP II, 120; CP V, 337; DD 65.
12. BW (Dreams) 539.
13. DD 70.
14. BW (Dreams) 510.
15. GI 365. Cf. CP V, 339.
16. *Civ.* 27.
17. *Civ.* 27, 39.
18. GI 27, 310, 353–54, 363; *Civ.* 33, 51, 68, 74; FI 16–17; MM 182–87.
19. *Civ.* 37; BW (Dreams) 500, 518, 536, 549; EI 30; NIL 98; BPP 56.
20. CP IV, 13–21; EI 19–33; NIL 100–101; GI 359, 365, 436.
21. CP II, 114–15, 277–82; CP IV, 13; ISA 136.
22. GI 308, 375, 453; ISA 20.
23. ISA 20–28, 34; BPP 7.
24. GI 27, 199, 321, 363; FI 16; *Civ.* 74.
25. GI 421; BW (Sex) 622; ISA 134; MM 121.
26. Nietzsche, *The Philosophy of Nietzsche*, p. 702.

Chapter II: Neurosis and History

1. *Civ.* 141.
2. BW (T & T) 831. Cf. BW (T & T) 875; CP III, 454; CP IV, 93; ISA 61, 71; MM 122–29, 201.
3. MM 94.
4. MM 129.
5. These passages, and their importance, were first drawn to my attention by Rieff, "The Meaning of History and Religion in Freud's Thought," p. 115.
6. CP V, 343; MM 159. Cf. MM 204–205.
7. MM 208.
8. Freud, *Questions of Lay Analysis*, p. 167, quoted by Rieff, "The Authority of the Past," p. 430.
9. Marx, *Der historische Materialismus*, p. 264.
10. BW (T & T) 876–77.
11. *Civ.* 142.
12. Cf. Lukács, *Goethe und seine Zeit*, p. 131.

13. Joyce, *Ulysses*, p. 35.
14. Nietzsche, *The Philosophy of Nietzsche*, p. 712.
15. *Civ.* 121–22.
16. CP IV, 350–55.
17. NIL 228.
18. GI 321.
19. Cf. Popitz, *Der entfremdete Mensch*, pp. 151–52.
20. Marx, *Capital*, III, 954.
21. BPP 56.

Part Two

Chapter III: Sexuality and Childhood

1. GI 211–22, 349–73, 416; ISA 125–29.
2. GI 308, 312–47.
3. EI 46; CP IV, 78n.
4. GI 421.
5. CP IV, 14–18; ISA 140.
6. ISA 105–108, 117, 140; NIL 114–16.
7. BW (Sex) 588 and note; CP IV, 41.
8. GI 332.
9. GI 337.
10. CP II, 129.
11. Fenichel, *The Psychoanalytic Theory of Neurosis*, p. 496. Cf. Abraham, *Selected Papers*, pp. 407–15; Reich, *The Function of the Orgasm*.
12. NIL 106.
13. Cf. Huxley, *Tomorrow and Tomorrow*, pp. 289–301; Eliade, *Le Yoga*, pp. 250, 267, 270, 396.
14. Needham, *Science and Civilization in China*, II, 149.
15. BW (Sex) 599–602.
16. Blake, *The Marriage of Heaven and Hell*.
17. CP IV, 51.
18. Cf. BW (Dreams) 294.
19. BW (T & T) 872; CP IV, 17, 174–76.
20. Guardini quoted by Huizinga, *Homo Ludens*, p. 19; cf. Huizinga, *op. cit.*, pp. 1–27.
21. Sartre, *Being and Nothingness*, pp. 580–81; Schiller, *Essays Aesthetical and Philosophical*, p. 71.
22. Brinton, *The Mystic Will*, pp. 217–18.
23. Brinton, *op. cit.*, p. 252.
24. Keynes, *Essays in Persuasion*, pp. 366–67.
25. Veblen, *Theory of the Leisure Class*, p. 28.

26. Von Neumann and Morgenstern, *Theory of Games and Economic Behavior*.
27. Ferenczi, *Sex in Psychoanalysis*, pp. 319–31.

Chapter IV: The Self and the Other: Narcissus

1. GP 60–62; NIL 86.
2. CP IV, 44–45; BW (Sex) 614 and note; GI 433–34.
3. CP IV, 47; EI 40–44.
4. CP V, 281.
5. GP 60–61; NIL 86.
6. CP IV, 78–81.
7. EI 35.
8. CP IV, 57. Cf. EI 36 and note; GP 73–76.
9. ISA 105–10, 117, 122, 140; NIL 115–16.
10. CP IV, 55; NIL 170.
11. FI 41.
12. CP IV, 152–70; NIL 86.
13. EI 36; ISA 27–28; Ferenczi, *Further Contributions*, pp. 97, 164.
14. CP IV, 57. Cf. BW (T & T) 876.
15. BPP 57, 68; *Out.* 6; CP V, 185, 350; *Civ.* 97.
16. CP IV, 78–79; *Civ.* 12.
17. *Civ.* 13.
18. CP IV, 79.
19. CP IV, 81.
20. CP IV, 57.
21. *Civ.* 21.
22. CP V, 185.
23. Spinoza, *Ethics*, Part III, "Definitions of the Emotions," II and VI. Cf. Hampshire, *Spinoza*, pp. 142–43, 168–71.
24. Hampshire, *op. cit.*, pp. 141–44.
25. Spinoza, *Ethics*, Part III, Prop. LIX, note.
26. Spinoza, *Ethics*, Part III, Prop. XI.
27. Spinoza, *Ethics*, Part IV, Prop. XXXVIII.
28. Spinoza, *Ethics*, Part V, Prop. XXXIX, note.
29. Spinoza, *Ethics*, Part V, Prop. XXXIX, demonstration.
30. GP 38–39.
31. Nygren, *Agape and Eros*, p. 711 and note.
32. D'Arcy, *The Mind and Heart of Love*, p. 87.
33. Nygren, *op. cit.*, pp. 729–30; Plato, *Symposium*, 206E.
34. Blake, *The Marriage of Heaven and Hell*.
35. EI 63; *Out.* 8; CP IV, 350; GI 423.
36. CP IV, 42. Cf. GI 428.

37. CP V, 81.
38. Freud, *Gesammelte Werke*, XIV, 443, note; cf. *Civ.* 41.
39. Cf. Benz, *Der vollkommene Mensch nach Jacob Boehme*, pp. 9–11, 25–26, 31, 35.
40. Kaufmann, *The Portable Nietzsche*, pp. 128, 302.
41. BW (Sex) 614.
42. CP IV, 58.
43. GI 323.
44. Goethe, *Faust*, Part II, vs. 8479.
45. CP IV, 57.
46. CP IV, 44. Cf. BW (Sex) 587; GI 322–23, 434; GP 60–62.
47. BW (T & T) 854; GP 61; EI 61; NIL 159; CP V, 263.
48. NIL 129.
49. NIL 129.
50. Abraham, *Selected Papers*, p. 481.
51. CP II, 253, 395; ISA 33, 36, 61, 71; MM 125; CP V, 326, 337.
52. Abraham, *loc. cit.*; Ferenczi, *Further Contributions*, p. 372.

Chapter V: Art and Eros

1. Trilling, *The Liberal Imagination*, p. 61.
2. Trilling, *op. cit.*, pp. 57, 60.
3. Contrast GI 384–85 with L 120, CP V, 222 and Freud, *Gesammelte Werke*, XIII, 265, note 1
4. CP IV, 14; GI 365.
5. Keats, *Endymion*, Book I, vss. 1–13.
6. Nietzsche, *The Philosophy of Nietzsche*, p. 1088.
7. Rilke, "Ueber Kunst," pp. 41–49.
8. BW (History) 938.
9. Reich, *The Function of the Orgasm*, pp. 63–64.
10. BW (Wit) 692, 782, 791.
11. CP V, 215–21.
12. BW (Wit) 692.
13. BW (Wit) 803.
14. BW (Wit) 721, 794.
15. Poe, "The Poetic Principle," pp. 273–74.
16. Scheler, *The Nature of Sympathy*, pp. 197–99.
17. BW (Wit) 754; cf. BW (Wit) 717, 721, 761.
18. Freud, *Gesammelte Werke*, VI (*Der Witz . . .*), 204. (Author's trans.)
19. Trilling, *op. cit.*, p. 53.
20. BW (Wit) 730–31, 736–37, 740–42.
21. DD 117.
22. Trilling, *op. cit.*, p. 44.
23. BW (Wit) 722; cf. BW (Wit) 702.
24. Trilling, *op. cit.*, p. 61.

25. Freud, *Gesammelte Werke*, VI (*Der Witz . . .*), 196–197.
    (Author's trans.)
26. BW (Wit) 697, 721.
27. BW (Wit) 712, 719.
28. BW (Wit) 730–31, 736–37, 766.
29. Freud, *Gesammelte Werke*, VI (*Der Witz . . .*), 154. (Author's
    trans.)
30. BW (Wit) 801–802.
31. BW (Wit) 761.
32. *Civ.* 37.
33. BW (Wit) 761.
34. Rilke, "Ueber Kunst," pp. 41–49.
35. Freud, *The Origins of Psychoanalysis*, p. 244.
36. *Civ.* 122.

Chapter VI: Language and Eros

1. LaBarre, *The Human Animal*, pp. 163–207.
2. GI 175.
3. CP V, 181–85.
4. Engels, *The Part Played by Labor in the Transition from
   Ape to Man*, p. 8.
5. CP IV, 111, 126; CP V, 185.
6. Jespersen, *Language*, p. 436.
7. Langer, *Philosophy in a New Key*, p. 96.
8. Cassirer, *An Essay on Man*, p. 109; cf. J. Huizinga, *Homo
   Ludens*, p. 4.
9. Jespersen, *op. cit.*, p. 433.
10. Cassirer, *op. cit.*, p. 110.
11. Wittgenstein, *Philosophical Investigations*, p. 47.
12. Wittgenstein, *op. cit.*, p. 133; Wittgenstein, *Tractatus Logico-
    Philosophicus*, p. 189.
13. BW (T & T) 865–83.
14. BW (T & T) 872.
15. Boehme, *Mysterium Magnum*, chap. 35, secs. 59–60.
16. Hytier, *La poétique de Valéry*, p. 29.
17. Hytier, *op. cit.*, p. 74.
18. Hytier, *op. cit.*, pp. 57, 289.
19. Hartman, *The Unmediated Vision*, pp. 73–76.

PART THREE

Chapter VII: Dualism and Dialectics

1. NIL 124.
2. CP IV, 34.

3. CP IV, 60.
4. BPP 72; BW (History) 972–77.
5. CP IV, 64.
6. Cf. *Civ.* 94–98; NIL 124–39; BPP 83–84n.
7. CP V, 345, 347.
8. CP V, 355.
9. *Civ.* 120–21, 136, 144.
10. NIL 140–41; CP V, 345.
11. CP V, 348–50.
12. Nietzsche, *The Philosophy of Nietzsche*, pp. 706, 745.
13. NIL 101; ISA 33, 61, 71; CP II, 253, 395; CP V, 326, 337.
14. NIL 101.
15. Cf. Popitz, *Der entfremdete Mensch.*

Chapter VIII: Death, Time, and Eternity

1. BPP, *passim;* CP II, 255–68; NIL 134–42.
2. Contrast BPP 76, 85–88 with CP II, 256.
3. BPP 57, 68; *Civ.* 97n.
4. *Civ.* 37.
5. CP II, 257.
6. CP II, 256.
7. CP IV, 136; CP V, 370–71; MM 125.
8. Augustine, *De Civitate Dei*, Book XXII, chap. XXX.
9. Cf. Popitz, *Der entfremdete Mensch*, pp. 151–52.
10. BPP 46–48.
11. BPP 55–56.
12. BPP 45.
13. Cf. above chap. II, note 2.
14. BPP 33; NIL 99.
15. BPP 33.
16. Schopenhauer, *The World as Will and Idea*, III, 283.
17. BPP 33; NIL 99.
18. Bonaparte, *Chronos, Eros, Thanatos*, pp. 11–12.
19. See below, chap. XV, sec. 5.
20. NIL 99.
21. Cf. von Bertalanffy, "An Essay on the Relativity of Categories," 243–63.
22. Schiller, *Humanism*, pp. 204–27; Schiller, *Riddles of the Sphinx*, pp. 255–58, 423–24.
23. Aristotle, *Ethica Nicomachea*, Book X, chap. IV.
24. Aristotle, *Ethica Nicomachea*, Book VII, chap. XIV.
25. Schiller, *Humanism*, pp. 217, 226–27.
26. Augustine, *De Civitate Dei*, Book XIV, chap. XXVIII.

27. BPP 50.
28. BPP 74–75; CP II, 261.
29. CP IV, 304–17; ISA 93.
30. Unamuno, *Tragic Sense of Life*, pp. 20, 41.
31. BPP 73; EI 56–57; CP II, 260.
32. Kojève, *Introduction à la lecture de Hegel*, pp. 11–34, 364–80, 490–513, 527–73; Marcuse, *Reason and Revolution*, pp. 224, 240; Kroner, "Bemerkungen zur Dialektik der Zeit," pp. 153–61.
33. CP V, 185.
34. Hegel, *Science of Logic*, I, 142.
35. Cf. Kojève, *op. cit.*, pp. 517, 549.
36. ISA 91–95.
37. Róheim, *The Origin and Function of Culture*, pp. 77, 79, 98.
38. ISA 93–95, 104–12.
39. Schopenhauer, *The World as Will and Idea*, III, 286, 298, 308.
40. Kaufmann, *The Portable Nietzsche*, p. 434.
41. Keynes, *Essays in Persuasion*, p. 370.
42. Kojève, *op. cit.*, p. 546.
43. Cf. Rehm, *Orpheus: Der Dichter und die Toten*, p. 583.
44. EI 87. Cf. ISA 105–18; NIL 114–16.
45. EI 85.
46. Kierkegaard, *Works of Love*, p. 253.

Chapter IX: Death and Childhood

1. Cf. Horney, *New Ways in Psychoanalysis*, pp. 47–78.
2. NIL 129, 153–59.
3. ISA 53. Cf. NIL 113.
4. NIL 159. Cf. *Civ.* 120–22.
5. BW (History) 939.
6. NIL 112.
7. ISA 103–16, 131–42, 151–53.
8. EI 87. Cf. ISA 105–18.
9. ISA 109–10.
10. EI 85. Cf. ISA 160; NIL 122.
11. NIL 123; MM 200.
12. CP II, 249. Cf. BW (Sex) 618; CP IV, 45; ISA 110.
13. Ferenczi, *Thalassa*, pp. 18, 26.
14. Ferenczi, *op. cit.*, pp. 20–24.
15. CP IV, 77–79.
16. CP IV, 14, 78, 82; CP V, 183.
17. CP IV, 119; CP V, 182, 185.
18. BW (Sex) 597–98; BPP 15; CP V, 119, 264–66; NIL 165.
19. CP II, 260; CP V, 266; BPP 74.

20. CP II, 248.
21. CP IV, 201. Cf. CP V, 265–66; NIL 154.
22. Contrast BW (Sex) 614–16 with CP V, 259–65, NIL 154–59, and MM 125–29.
23. CP II, 272; CP V, 188, 196, 199, 257.
24. CP IV, 48–49.
25. CP II, 272. Cf. CP II, 53, 190; CP V, 188–90, 267; NIL 154, 165.
26. Civ. 121; Civ. 117n. Cf. CP V, 262–63; NIL 156–59.
27. Out. 54.
28. NIL 159. Cf. Civ. 120–21.
29. Abraham, Selected Papers, p. 497.
30. CP V, 254.
31. CP V, 264–69; NIL 154.
32. CP V, 186–97, 262; NIL 162–63; CP II, 274.
33. CP V, 263.
34. GI 326; CP II, 246–47, 270–71; CP V, 105, 199, 256, 261; NIL 160; Out. 58.
35. CP V, 105–106, 191; NIL 37; CP II, 247, note 2. Cf. Pollack, Les idées des enfants sur la différence des sexes, p. 77.
36. EI 40–44.
37. NIL 114.
38. Kojève, Introduction à la lecture de Hegel, pp. 14–34, 494; Nietzsche, The Philosophy of Nietzsche, pp. 701–705. Cf. CP V, 275.
39. CP II, 273; NIL 166; CP V, 196.
40. Out. 59.
41. CP II, 273.
42. EI 19–31; Ferenczi, op. cit., p. 16. Cf. Ferenczi, Further Contributions, p. 86.
43. CP II, 272; CP V, 188, 196, 199, 257.
44. EI 36–49; MM 184.
45. Róheim, War, Crime and the Covenant, p. 37. Cf. Civ. 105, 115, 120.
46. Cf. Brinton, The Mystic Will, pp. 214–15.
47. Fromm, "Sex and Character," pp. 21, 25; Horney, op. cit., p. 38.
48. BW (Sex) 558, 612–13; CP II, 56–58, 246; CP V, 230, 251; NIL 146–49, 151.
49. EI 42–43. Cf. CP II, 198–201, 272; CP V, 230–32.
50. CP V, 354.
51. CP V, 356–57. Cf. Out. 63.
52. Cf. Lévi-Strauss, Les structures élémentaires de la parenté, p. 567.
53. CP V, 231; NIL 148. Cf. CP II, 248–49, 258.

54. CP V, 269. Cf. BW (Sex) 612; NIL 169.
55. BPP 79–80.
56. Baumann, *Das doppelte Geschlecht*, pp. 127–28, 171–72.
57. Cf. Benz, *Der vollkommene Mensch nach Jacob Boehme*, pp. 23, 38–43, 111, 121.
58. Berdyaev, *The Destiny of Man*, p. 64.
59. Needham, *Science and Civilization in China*, II, 58.
60. Rilke, *Letters to a Young Poet*, p. 38; Rilke, *Sämtliche Werke*, I, 349. Cf. Simenauer, "Pregnancy Envy in Rainer Maria Rilke," pp. 240–42.

PART FOUR

Chapter X: The Ambiguities of Sublimation

1. GI 175, 321; *Civ.* 63; GP 57, 118–20; CP II, 50, 82–83; BW (Sex) 584, 625.
2. Kroeber, "The Superorganic," pp. 163–213. Cf. Valabrega, "L'anthropologie psychanalytique," pp. 221–45.
3. CP II, 48; *Civ.* 33, 63; MM 182–87.
4. CP V, 132–33. Cf. GI 354.
5. GI 27.
6. *Civ.* 76–77.
7. CP IV, 52. Cf. BW (Sex) 625; L 49.
8. *Civ.* 33.
9. FI 12. Cf. FI 16; GI 321.
10. GI 175; *Civ.* 34n.
11. L 49–50.
12. Reich, *The Function of the Orgasm*, pp. 77, 111, 141.
13. *Civ.* 77n.
14. CP V, 171. Cf. GI 441.
15. Marcuse, *Eros and Civilization*, pp. 35, 37.
16. Reich, *op. cit.*, pp. 52–53, 92; Reich, *The Mass Psychology of Fascism*, pp. 183, 244, 337–38.
17. GI 463.
18. GI 355; CP II, 83.
19. *Civ.* 33–34; GI 355.
20. GP 118–19.
21. EI 65, 80. Cf. below, chap. XII.
22. CP V, 126, 128, 329, 331; *Out.* 44; FI 68.
23. *Works* (T & T), XIII, 73. Cf. CP II, 25–35; CP V, 92–97.
24. CP V, 94.
25. BW (T & T) 864.

26. Róheim, *The Origin and Function of Culture*, p. 74.
27. See above, chap. I, note 11.
28. GP 41–51.
29. *Civ.* 141.
30. Róheim, *op. cit.*, p. 24.
31. FI 77. Cf. GP 124–25; *Civ.* 42.

Chapter XI: Couch and Culture

1. GI 442; NIL 106.
2. GI 462. Cf. DD 115.
3. GI 453.
4. Cf. CP V, 334: the new conflicts artificially produced in the transference "lack the character of reality."
5. GI 452.
6. CP II, 319, 402.
7. Glover, "The Klein System of Child Psychology," p. 117, note 21.
8. Cf. CP II, 400.
9. CP V, 334. Cf. CP V, 370; *Out.* 41.
10. CP II, 322.
11. *Out.* 48.
12. EI 19–26.
13. EI 21.
14. FI 95.
15. EI 12.
16. CP IV, 111.
17. NIL 154.
18. CP II, 369.
19. CP IV, 133–34.
20. CP IV, 136.
21. LaBarre, *The Human Animal*, p. 207.
22. Cf. Ferenczi, *Further Contributions*, p. 374.
23. CP V, 300–301 and note.
24. See above, chap. X.
25. CP V, 329. Cf. *Out.* 44; contrast GI 463.
26. CP V, 331; *Civ.* 114–22.
27. CP V, 286.
28. *Civ.* 121–22.
29. *Out.* 36.
30. BW (T & T) 877; EI 30.
31. CP IV, 14, 16; *Out.* 2–3.
32. CP II, 279–80. Cf. CP II, 250–54, 277–82.

33. CP II, 322.
34. *Works* (T & T), XIII, 73; MM 137.

Chapter XII: Apollo and Dionysus

 1. *Prose Works of Jonathan Swift* (Oxford, 1939), I, 174.
 2. Cf. Ghiselin, *The Creative Process*, p. 114.
 3. B. Russell, *Philosophical Essays*, p. 73.
 4. Frazer, *The Golden Bough*, pp. 667–701.
 5. Cornford, *Principium Sapientiae*, pp. 88–127.
 6. Ferenczi, *Final Contributions*, p. 246.
 7. Cf. Fenichel, *The Psychoanalytic Theory of Neurosis*, p. 141.
 8. EI 30; NIL 102.
 9. EI 31 and note.
10. EI 30.
11. Fenichel, *op. cit.*, p. 35.
12. CP V, 182. Cf. CP IV, 119.
13. Cf. Ferenczi, *Further Contributions*, pp. 367–69.
14. CP III, 458.
15. EI 36.
16. EI 37.
17. EI 61–64. Cf. Róheim, *The Origin and Function of Culture*,
    pp. 73–78.
18. EI 37–38.
19. EI 36.
20. *Out.* 79–80.
21. CP V, 184.
22. CP V, 184.
23. BW (Dreams) 535. Cf. BW (Dreams) 533.
24. BW (Sex) 614.
25. CP IV, 14, 136.
26. BW (Dreams) 533.
27. BW (Dreams) 533.
28. Isaacs, "The Nature and Function of Phantasy," p. 94; Glover,
    "The Klein System of Child Psychology," pp. 75–118.
29. Isaacs, *op. cit.*, p. 90.
30. Cf. Feldmann, "The Illusions of Work," p. 266.
31. CP III, 584n.
32. CP IV, 20. Cf. BW (T & T) 874.
33. *Civ.* 121; NIL 114.
34. CP V, 259; CP II, 269; BPP 22.
35. Bartlett, "The Concept of Repression," pp. 326–39.
36. NIL 154.
37. CP III, 577.

38. MM 159. Cf. CP V, 343–44.
39. MM 160.
40. Ferenczi, *Further Contributions*, p. 407; CP IV, 136. Cf. Wilbur, "Freud's Life-Death Instinct Theory," pp. 144, 211.
41. *Out.* 59.
42. Cf. above, chap. V, note 19.
43. LaBarre, *The Human Animal*, p. 173.
44. *Out.* 74. Cf. CP V, 198–204, 372–75.
45. *Out.* 73–74; CP V, 372–75.
46. Ferenczi, *Final Contributions*, p. 164.
47. CP IV, 51.
48. Ferenczi, *Final Contributions*, p. 246; Schilder, *The Image and Appearance of the Human Body*, p. 136.
49. Ferenczi, *Sex in Psychoanalysis*, p. 227.
50. BW (Life) 164.
51. Cf. Ghiselin, *The Creative Process*, p. 119.
52. CP V, 374.
53. BW (Dreams) 535.
54. BW (T & T) 856.
55. CP IV, 148; BPP 35. Cf. ISA 86–87.
56. Whitehead, *Adventures of Ideas*, p. 289; Whitehead, *Science and the Modern World*, pp. 64–73.
57. MM 178–79.
58. Ferenczi, *Sex in Psychoanalysis*, p. 275; Ferenczi, *Further Contributions*, pp. 85, 99–102, 171–72.
59. Cf. Wilbur, "Freud's Life-Death Instinct Theory," pp. 246–53.
60. Whitehead, *Adventures of Ideas*, p. 289.
61. EI 65. Cf. Wilbur, "Freud's Life-Death Instinct Theory," pp. 241–44.
62. *Civ.* 74–78; CP V, 286. Cf. Róheim, *The Origin and Function of Culture*, pp. 99–100.
63. Ferenczi, *Final Contributions*, p. 246.
64. EI 80.
65. Nietzsche, *The Philosophy of Nietzsche*, p. 954.
66. Nietzsche, *The Philosophy of Nietzsche*, pp. 955, 960.
67. See above, chap. VI, note 19.
68. Nietzsche, *The Philosophy of Nietzsche*, p. 956.
69. Kaufmann, *Nietzsche*, p. 328.
70. Kaufmann, *Nietzsche*, p. 247.
71. Cf. Otto, *Dionysos, Mythos und Kultus*, pp. 74, 84–85, 95, 124, 159.
72. NIL 98.
73. Nietzsche, *The Philosophy of Nietzsche*, p. 958.
74. Duncan, *My Life*, p. 105.
75. Ferenczi, *Thalassa*, p. 16.

76. Blake, *The Marriage of Heaven and Hell;* Hegel, *The Phenom-
    enology of Mind,* p. 105.

PART FIVE

Introduction

1. Jones, *Papers on Psycho-Analysis,* p. 664.

Chapter XIII: The Excremental Vision

1. Huxley, *Do What You Will,* p. 94.
2. Murry, *Jonathan Swift,* pp. 432–48.
3. Huxley, *op. cit.,* p. 99.
4. Quintana, *The Mind and Art of Jonathan Swift,* pp. 327, 360.
5. CP V, 182.
6. Huxley, *op. cit.,* p. 101.
7. Murry, *op. cit.,* p. 440; Lawrence, *Sex, Literature and Censor-
    ship,* p. 60.
8. Huxley, *op. cit.,* pp. 94, 104.
9. Murry, *op. cit.,* pp. 78–82, 86, 346–55, 432–48.
10. Ferenczi, *Final Contributions,* p. 59.
11. Karpman, "Neurotic Traits of Jonathan Swift," p. 132.
12. Greenacre, "The Mutual Adventures of Jonathan Swift and
    Lemuel Gulliver," p. 60.
13. Murry, *op. cit.,* p. 60.
14. Greenacre, *op. cit.,* pp. 21–22.
15. Greenacre, *op. cit.,* pp. 41, 56.
16. Swift, *Verses on the Death of Dr. Swift,* vss. 479–80.
17. Swift, *A Tale of a Tub,* in *Prose Works of Jonathan Swift*
    (Oxford, 1939), I, 88.
18. Swift, *A Discourse Concerning the Mechanical Operation of
    the Spirit, Etc.,* in *Prose Works of Jonathan Swift* (Oxford,
    1939), I, 186.
19. CP IV, 351–55.
20. Nietzsche, *The Philosophy of Nietzsche,* p. 752.
21. CP IV, 215.
22. *Civ.* 78n.
23. Swift, *Gulliver's Travels,* in *Prose Works of Jonathan Swift*
    (Oxford, 1941), XI, 253.
24. *Gulliver's Travels,* pp. 243, 245–47, 250, 272–74.
25. Murry, *op. cit.,* p. 352; Quintana, *op. cit.,* p. 327.

26. Cf. CP II, 45–50, 164–71; Jones, *Papers on Psycho-Analysis*, pp. 664–88; Abraham, *Selected Papers on Psychoanalysis*, pp. 370–92.

27. Empson, *Some Versions of Pastoral*, p. 60.

28. Swift, *Mechanical Operation of the Spirit*, pp. 174–76.

29. Swift, *Mechanical Operation of the Spirit*, p. 175.

30. Ferenczi, *Further Contributions*, p. 90; Ferenczi, *Thalassa*, p. 14.

31. Swift, *A Tale of a Tub*, p. 129.

32. EI 48.

33. Swift, *A Tale of a Tub*, p. 99.

34. Swift, *Mechanical Operation of the Spirit*, pp. 179–80. Cf. Swift, *A Tale of a Tub*, pp. 99–100.

35. *Works* (T & T), XIII, 73.

36. Swift, *A Tale of a Tub*, pp. 102–103, 107–108, 114.

37. Swift, *Mechanical Operation of the Spirit*, pp. 184–85, 188–89.

38. Swift, *A Tale of a Tub*, p. 102.

39. Empson, *op. cit.*, p. 60.

40. GI 166, 174–75; CP IV, 184–91.

41. Swift, *A Tale of a Tub*, pp. 37, 77.

42. Swift, *A Tale of a Tub*, pp. 96, 98.

43. Greenacre, *op. cit.*, p. 56.

44. Cf. Greenacre, *op. cit.*, p. 56.

45. Swift, *A Tale of a Tub*, pp. 5, 63, 116; Swift, *A Meditation upon a Broomstick*, in *Prose Works of Jonathan Swift* (Oxford, 1939), I, 239–40.

46. Swift, *Letter of Advice to a Young Poet*, in *Prose Works of Jonathan Swift* (London, 1907), XI, 108.

47. Pope, *Works*, X, 281.

48. Fenichel, *The Psychoanalytic Theory of Neurosis*, p. 312.

49. Ferenczi, *Further Contributions*, p. 251.

50. See above, note 26.

51. Swift, *A Tale of a Tub*, p. 104.

Chapter XIV: The Protestant Era

1. Cf. Grisar, *Luther*, VI, 506.

2. Grisar, *Luther*, I, 396.

3. Grisar, *Luther*, I, 396–97, VI, 504–10. Cf. the treatment of the text on the J. G. Walch edition of Luther's *Table-Talk*: Luther, *Sämmtliche Schriften*, XXII, 463.

4. Grisar, *Luther*, VI, 504, 510. Cf. F. Funck-Brentano, *Luther*, pp. 84–87; Fife, *The Revolt of Martin Luther*, pp. 198–99, note 91.

5. CP II, 45–50.
6. Fromm, "Die psychoanalytische Charakterologie und ihre Bedeutung für die Sozialpsychologie," pp. 253–77.
7. Fromm, *Escape from Freedom*, pp. 291–94. Cf. Horney, *New Ways in Psychoanalysis*, pp. 168–82.
8. Taylor, *Sex in History*, pp. 166–68.
9. Fenichel, *The Psychoanalytic Theory of Neurosis*, p. 278.
10. Cf. above, chap. IX.
11. Cf. Fromm, *Escape from Freedom*, p. 73.
12. CP IV, 436–72; Jones, *On the Nightmare*, pp. 154–89; Reik, *Der eigene und der fremde Gott*.
13. Cf. Rudwin, *The Devil in Legend and Literature*, pp. 45, 207, 250; Rudwin, *Die Teufelszenen im geistlichen Drama des deutschen Mittelalters*, p. 76; Murray, *Witch Cult in Western Europe*, pp. 126–30; Bourke, *Scatalogic Rites of All Nations*, p. 163; Castelli, *Il Demoniaco nell' arte*, p. 89; Jones, *On the Nightmare*, pp. 122, 203; Ben Jonson, *Ballad of the Devil's Arse: The Gypsies Metamorphosed*, vss. 1061–1137; Luther, *Sämmtliche Schriften*, IX, 845; Dante, *Inferno*, XXXIV, vss. 76–93.
14. Cf. Obendiek, *Der Teufel bei Martin Luther*; Klingner, "Luther und der deutsche Volksaberglaube," pp. 18–91; Grisar, *Luther*, V, 275–305; VI, 122–40; Luther, *Sämmtliche Schriften*, XXIII, Index, s.v. "Teufel."
15. Luther, *Sämmtliche Schriften*, I, 174; VII, 43; IX, 825, 1288; XII, 1338.
16. Rudwin, *The Devil*, pp. 51, 110.
17. Bourke, *Scatalogic Rites*, p. 163.
18. Grisar, *Luther*, V, 315.
19. Grisar, *Luther*, VI, 132–33.
20. Luther, *Sämmtliche Schriften*, XXIII, Index, s.v. "Teufel."
21. Luther, *Sämmtliche Schriften*, XXII, 706.
22. Luther, *Sämmtliche Schriften*, XXII, 731, 1710.
23. Luther, *Sämmtliche Schriften*, XXII, 715, 729, 734, 762, 766, 770, 798; Grisar, *Luther*, V, 238, 355; VI, 364.
24. Grisar, *Luther*, V, 293, 304; Luther, *Sämmtliche Schriften*, XXII, 783.
25. Obendiek, *Der Teufel bei Martin Luther*, p. 51.
26. Luther, *Sämmtliche Schriften*, XXII, 515.
27. Harrington, *The Metamorphosis of Ajax*, p. 35.
28. Luther, *Sämmtliche Schriften*, XXII, 728–29, 767, 777; Grisar, *Luther*, V, 337; VI, 119, 122, 133.
29. Cf. Rudwin, *The Devil*, pp. 105–106.
30. E. Troeltsch, *The Social Teaching of the Christian Churches*, II, 469, 476.

31. Cf. Rudwin, *The Devil*, p. 106.
32. Tillich, *The Protestant Era*, pp. xx–xxi; Tillich, *The Interpretation of History*, pp. 77–122.
33. Obendiek, *Der Teufel bei Martin Luther*, p. 180.
34. Rudwin, *The Devil*, p. 23. Cf. Grisar, *Luther*, V, 277–78, 289.
35. Huizinga, *The Waning of the Middle Ages*, p. 21.
36. Obendiek, *op. cit.*, 53–57; Grisar, *Luther*, V, 5; Luther, *Sämmtliche Schriften*, XIII, 1259; XXII, 1917.
37. Grisar, *Luther*, VI, 153.
38. Rudwin, *The Devil*, p. 24; Grisar, *Luther*, V, 297.
39. Grisar, *Luther*, V, 48; Obendiek, *op. cit.*, p. 187; Luther, *Sämmtliche Schriften*, V, 1118; IX, 103, 839.
40. Grisar, *Luther*, VI, 365; Obendiek, *op. cit.*, p. 174; Rudwin, *The Devil*, p. 246; Luther, *Sämmtliche Schriften*, I, 757; III, 883; VI, 1762; IX, 842; XII, 207, 246; XIX, 1462–63; XXII, 1956.
41. Grisar, *Luther*, V, 330, 355, 356; Luther, *Sämmtliche Schriften*, II, 1514; V, 104.
42. Obendiek, *op. cit.*, pp. 169, 179, 183–84.
43. Obendiek, *op. cit.*, pp. 42–43, 178–80, 204.
44. Rudwin, *The Devil*, p. 136.
45. Butler, *The Fortunes of Faust*, p. 11. Contrast the Catholic Calderón, *El Magico Prodigioso*.
46. Troeltsch, *op. cit.*, II, 840, note 221.
47. Troeltsch, *op. cit.*, II, 498.
48. Obendiek, *op. cit.*, pp. 190–92; Grisar, *Luther*, II, 268–69, 284. Cf. Tillich, *The Protestant Era*, p. xx.
49. Rudwin, *The Devil*, p. 134.
50. Grisar, *Luther*, I, 192, 236–40, 376; VI, 113, 220; Luther, *Sämmtliche Schriften*, VII, 304; XII, 544.
51. Luther, *Sämmtliche Schriften*, III, 256; IV, 990, 1800; IX, 1497; XIV, 956.
52. Grisar, *Luther*, I, 191, 234–36.
53. Cf. Troeltsch, *op. cit.*, II, 475, 825.
54. Grisar, *Luther*, VI, 113.
55. Grisar, *Luther*, V, 230, 247, 298, 305, 352–53; VI, 117; Luther, *Sämmtliche Schriften*, XIII, 2777; XXII, 718–19, 810–11, 813. Cf. Troeltsch, *op. cit.*, II, 479–80, 490, 497, 510–11, 547, 560, 841.
56. Troeltsch, *op. cit.*, II, 570.
57. Cf. Rudwin, *Les écrivains diaboliques de France*, p. 85.
58. Grisar, *Luther*, V, 352.
59. Cf. Weber, *Gesammelte Aufsätze zur Religionssociologie*, I, 74–75, 77; Tawney, *Religion and the Rise of Capitalism*, pp. 82, 85, 91, 95; Troeltsch, *op. cit.*, II, 554, 557, 560, 873; Grisar, *Luther*, VI, 89, 96.

60. Cf. Troeltsch, *op. cit.*, II, 558; Grisar, *Luther*, VI, 82, 85, 89, 96.
61. Cf. Gener, *La mort et le diable*, pp. 582–90.
62. Barge, *Luther und der Frühkapitalismus*, pp. 37–39; Grisar, *Luther*, V, 227–28; VI, 95–96; Luther, *Sämmtliche Schriften*, X, 860, 874, 875; XX, 2197; XXII, 232.
63. Tawney, *op. cit.*, p. 89. Cf. Troeltsch, *op. cit.*, II, 479, 480, 490, 497, 510–11, 547, 560.
64. Cf. Brown, *Hermes the Thief*.
65. Blake, *The Laocoon Group: The Portable Blake*, pp. 497–98; Rudwin, *The Devil*, p. 246, note.
66. Luther, *Sämmtliche Schriften*, III, 74; IV, 2077; IX, 835–37, 1131, 1497; X, 850–51, 877, 906–907, 910–11, 916, 928, 935; XXII, 851.
67. Barge, *op. cit.*, pp. 33–40; Grisar, *Luther*, V, 228; VI, 93; Luther, *Sämmtliche Schriften*, X, 897, 906; XXII, 776. Cf. Luther, *Sämmtliche Schriften*, XXIII, Index, s.v. "Wucher," "Wucherer."
68. Grisar, *Luther*, V, 284; Luther, *Sämmtliche Schriften*, XXII, 777.
69. Barge, *op. cit.*, p. 37; Obendiek, *op. cit.*, p. 172; Luther, *Sämmtliche Schriften*, I, 183; X, 895–97; XX, 2197.
70. Barge, *op. cit.*, pp. 32, 50.
71. Jonson, *Volpone*, I, 1, 3.
72. Cf. Obendiek, *op. cit.*, p. 209; Rudwin, *The Devil*, pp. 120–29; Luther, *Sämmtliche Schriften*, III, 499.
73. Grisar, *Luther*, V, 244; VI, 88, 94; Luther, *Sämmtliche Schriften*, X, 873.
74. Obendiek, *op. cit.*, pp. 55, 192; Barge, *op. cit.*, p. 32; Troeltsch, *op. cit.*, II, 473–74; Luther, *Sämmtliche Schriften*, XXII, 1917.
75. Weber, *op. cit.*, pp. 69–71.
76. Luther, *Sämmtliche Schriften*, VII, 304; XIII, 1110.
77. Troeltsch, *op. cit.*, II, 509.
78. Troeltsch, *op. cit.*, II, 547, 560.
79. Troeltsch, *op. cit.*, II, 509n., 570.
80. Tillich, *The Protestant Era*, p. 168; *The Interpretation of History*, p. 119.
81. Tillich, *The Protestant Era*, p. 312.
82. Tillich, *The Protestant Era*, p. xx.
83. Luther, *Sämmtliche Schriften*, IX, 825, 1288; XII, 1338.
84. Grisar, *Luther*, IV, 318–22; V, 238, 239, 303, 324.
85. Obendiek, *op. cit.*, p. 49. Cf. Luther, *Sämmtliche Schriften*, XXII, 804.
86. Grisar, *Luther*, V, 226; VI, 215; Luther, *Sämmtliche Schriften*, XXII, 232.

87. Grisar, *Luther*, V, 233, 245, 247, 284.
88. Thiel, *Luther*, p. 336; Obendiek, *op. cit.*, p. 193; Luther, *Sämmtliche Schriften*, IV, 1252.
89. Grisar, *Luther*, V, 229, 249, 315.
90. Grisar, *Luther*, IV, 296; V, 337.
91. See the whole section of the *Table-Talk* on the topic "Von dem Anti-Christ, oder Pabst," *Sämmtliche Schriften*, XXII, 844–935. Cf. *Sämmtliche Schriften*, XXIII, Index, s.v. "Pabstthum," "Papisten." Cf. also Grisar, *Luther*, III, 141–53; IV, 295–301; VI, 154–61.
92. Luther, *Sämmtliche Schriften*, I, 1623; IV, 1303; IX, 857; XVII, 1120; XX, 64; XXII, 806, 845, 870.
93. Luther, *Sämmtliche Schriften*, V, 1144; X, 756.
94. Luther, *Sämmtliche Schriften*, VII, 301; XXII, 845, 875, 896.
95. Luther, *Sämmtliche Schriften*, IV, 1503.
96. Luther, *Sämmtliche Schriften*, II, 107; V, 1017; VII, 1059; XIV, 307.
97. Luther, *Sämmtliche Schriften*, I, 1623; XII, 1284; XVI, 1650–51; XXII, 856, 866, 885, 902, 910, 920, 922, 931.
98. Luther, *Sämmtliche Schriften*, XVII, 1019–1132.
99. Luther, *Sämmtliche Schriften*, XVII, 1019–1132; cf. XIV, 289; XXII, 848, 880–81, 897, 905. See also Grisar, *Luther*, III, 151; IV, 295–305, 319–22; V, 276, 342; VI, 158–59, 195, 201, 364.
100. Grisar, *Luther*, VI, 98.
101. Cf. above, chaps. XI, XII.
102. Cf. above, chap. IX.
103. CP V, 370.
104. CP V, 371.
105. Luther, *Sämmtliche Schriften*, XII, 961, 963, 1238.

Chapter XV: Filthy Lucre

1. Cf. Cassiodorus, *Institutiones*, Book I, chap. I, section 8.
2. Frazer, *Economic Thought and Language*, pp. 29–30; Simmel, *Philosophie des Geldes*, pp. 480–501. Cf. Spengler, *The Decline of the West*, II, 482, 489–90; Schumpeter, *Capitalism, Socialism and Democracy*, pp. 122–23.
3. BW (T & T) 876–77.
4. CP II, 45–50.
5. CP II, 130–31.
6. Ferenczi, *Final Contributions*, p. 188.
7. BPP 20; NIL 94.
8. Cf. above, chaps. III, IV.
9. Whitehead, *Adventures of Ideas*, pp. 249–50, 281, 289, 332.

10. See above, chap. V, note 34.
11. Marx, Engels, *Kleine ökonomische Schriften*, pp. 42–166.
12. Marx, Engels, *op. cit.*, pp. 97–99, 102, 104, 130–36, 151.
13. Knight, *The Ethics of Competition*, p. 282.
14. Cf. Dobb, *On Economic Theory and Socialism*, pp. 55–92; he quotes von Mises on p. 56.
15. CP II, 265. Cf. CP V, 306.
16. Shakespeare, *Timon of Athens*, IV, iii, 387; cf. above, chap. XIV.
17. Marx, Engels, *op. cit.*, pp. 102, 106–08.
18. Marx, Engels, *op. cit.*, pp. 98, 108, 110–11.
19. Cf. above, chap. IX.
20. Smith, *Wealth of Nations*, Book I, chap. II, p. 22.
21. Polanyi, *The Great Transformation*, p. 47.
22. Herskovits, *Economic Anthropology*.
23. Malinowski, "The Primitive Economics of the Trobriand Islanders," p. 13.
24. Malinowski, *loc. cit.*
25. Herskovits, *Economic Anthropology*, pp. 238–68; Firth, "Currency, Primitive."
26. Parsons, *The Structure of Social Action*, pp. 59–60.
27. Herskovits, *Economic Anthropology*, p. 214.
28. Malinowski, *op. cit.*, p. 9.
29. Herskovits, *Economic Anthropology*, pp. 439–60.
30. Firth, *op. cit.*; Simmel, *op. cit.*, pp. 116, 162.
31. Laum, *Heiliges Geld*, p. 128.
32. Herskovits, *Economic Anthropology*, pp. 11, 155–79.
33. Firth, *op. cit.*
34. Laum, *Heiliges Geld*, pp. 8–80. Cf. Einzig, *Primitive Money*, pp. 379–86; Van der Leeuw, *Religion in Essence and Manifestation*, p. 353.
35. Herskovits, *Economic Anthropology*, p. 389.
36. Locke, *Some Considerations of the Consequences of the Lowering of Interest and Raising the Value of Money*, in *Works*, V, 22.
37. Herskovits, *Economic Anthropology*, p. 264.
38. Keynes, *Treatise on Money*, II, 289–92.
39. Heichelheim, *Wirtschaftsgeschichte des Altertums*, I, 114–15.
40. Laum, *Heiliges Geld*, pp. 128–29.
41. Simmel, *Philosophie des Geldes*, p. 176.
42. Keynes, *General Theory*, p. 202; Robertson, *Utility and All That*, p. 96.
43. Knight, *Ethics of Competition*, p. 264.
44. Keynes, *General Theory*, p. 356.
45. Malinowski, "Primitive Economics," p. 14.

46. Heichelheim, *Wirtschaftsgeschichte*, I, 114–15.
47. Mumford, *The Culture of Cities*, p. 542.
48. Ruskin, *Unto This Last*, in *Works*, XVII, 44–45, 46.
49. Marx, *Capital*, I, 146–49.
50. Marx, *Capital*, I, 149.
51. Marx, *Capital*, III, 419, 445.
52. Marx, *Capital*, III, 415–16, 439–40, 443, 716.
53. Marx, *Capital*, III, 672–73.
54. Herskovits, *Economic Anthropology*, pp. 481–82.
55. Herskovits, *Economic Anthropology*, pp. 439–60.
56. Frazer, *The Golden Bough*, pp. 83–106.
57. Sorel, *Réflexions sur la violence*, pp. 32, 132.
58. Ruskin, *Works*, XVII, 176n; Schumpeter, *Theory of Economic Development;* Schumpeter, *Capitalism, Socialism and Democracy.* Cf. Spengler, *Decline of the West*, II, 492–93.
59. Aristotle, *Politics*, I, viii–x.
60. Ruskin, *Unto This Last*, in *Works*, XVII, 85.
61. Freud, *The Origins of Psychoanalysis*, p. 244.
62. Gambs, *Beyond Supply and Demand*, pp. 33, 47, 78, 90.
63. Dobb, *On Economic Theory and Socialism*, pp. 71–72, 84.
64. Locke, *Of Civil Government*, Book II, secs. 36–37; Thoreau, *Walden*, chap. I; Plato, *Republic*, II, 369–73.
65. Veblen, *Theory of the Leisure Class*, p. 177.
66. Plato, *Laws*, V, 736E.
67. Veblen, *Theory of the Leisure Class*, p. 76.
68. Engels, *Origin of the Family, Private Property and the State*, p. 23. Cf. above, chap. II, note 18.
69. CP II, 48n.
70. Ruskin, *Unto This Last*, in *Works*, XVII, 101–102; *Munera Pulveris*, in *Works*, XVII, 282–83.
71. Herskovits, *Economic Anthropology*, p. 481.
72. Isaiah 55:2; Hesiod, *Works and Days*, vss. 40–41.
73. Malinowski, "Primitive Economics," pp. 8–9; Herskovits, *Economic Anthropology*, pp. 461–83.
74. See above, chap. XII, note 34.
75. Ruskin, *Unto This Last*, p. 92.
76. Marx, *Capital*, III, 673, 715; I, 81–87, 127, 148.
77. Freud, *The Origins of Psychoanalysis*, p. 240 and note.
78. Cf. above, chap. II, note 18.
79. Marx, *Capital*, III, 954.
80. Marx, *Capital*, II, 136.
81. Marx, *Capital*, I, 389, 396–99.
82. Durkheim, *The Division of Labor in Society*, pp. 233–55.
83. Marx, *Capital*, I, 393, 394, 399; Durkheim, *Division of Labor*, pp. 364–73.

84. Marx, *Capital*, I, 392.
85. Herskovits, *Economic Anthropology*, pp. 142, 398, 461-83.
86. Heichelheim, *Wirtschaftsgeschichte*, I, 106-98.
87. Schumpeter, *Capitalism, Socialism and Democracy*, p. 144.
88. Polanyi, *The Great Transformation*, p. 46.
89. Malinowski, "Primitive Economics," pp. 1-16.
90. Mauss, *Sociologie et anthropologie*, pp. 145-279 ("Essai sur le don").
91. Lévi-Strauss, *Les structures élémentaires de la parenté*, pp. 71-72.
92. Cf. Herskovits, *Economic Anthropology*, pp. 496-501.
93. Malinowski, *op. cit.;* Mauss, *op. cit.;* Herskovits, *Economic Anthropology*, pp. 155-79, 439-83.
94. Durkheim, *Division of Labor*, p. 251.
95. Mauss, *op. cit.*, p. 148.
96. Mauss, *op. cit.*, pp. 277-79.
97. Cf. Van der Leeuw, *Religion in Essence and Manifestation*, pp. 350-60.
98. BPP 39.
99. Durkheim, *Division of Labor*, p. 242.
100. Abraham, *Selected Papers on Psychoanalysis*, p. 444.
101. CP V, 238.
102. Róheim, "Heiliges Geld in Melanesien," pp. 384-401.
103. Nietzsche, *The Philosophy of Nietzsche*, pp. 668-712.
104. Ruskin, *Unto This Last*, pp. 50n, 95n.
105. EI 21. Cf. above, chaps. XI, XII.
106. BW (T & T) 915-19.
107. BW (T & T) 919. Cf. G. Róheim, *The Origin and Function of Culture*, p. 79.
108. Mauss, *op. cit.*, p. 159.
109. Lévi-Strauss, *op. cit.*, pp. 9-53.
110. MM 159. Cf. above, chap. XII.
111. Cf. above, chap. IX.
112. Nietzsche, *The Philosophy of Nietzsche*, p. 709.
113. CP IV, 20. Cf. BW (T & T) 874.
114. CP V, 371.
115. Marx, *The Poverty of Philosophy*, p. 57; Fromm, *The Sane Society*, pp. 94-95, 149.
116. Keynes, *Essays in Persuasion*, p. 370; Ruskin, *Unto This Last*, p. 98.
117. Schumpeter, *Theory of Economic Development*, p. 202.
118. Robertson, *Utility and All That*, p. 90.
119. Von Bertalanffy, "An Essay on the Relativity of Categories," pp. 243-63.
120. Whorf, *Collected Papers on Metalinguistics*, p. 68.

121. Spengler, *Decline of the West*, I, 117–60.
122. Eliade, *The Myth of the Eternal Return*.
123. BPP 33.
124. BPP 33; NIL 99.
125. Contrast Eliade, *op. cit.*, pp. 141–62.
126. NIL 99.
127. BPP 34; CP V, 175–80.
128. CP IV, 54n. Cf. CP IV, 152–70.
129. *Out.* 79–80. Cf. EI 46; CP V, 308–12.
130. ISA 74–75; Fenichel, *The Psychoanalytic Theory of Neurosis*, p. 153.
131. ISA 76–77; Fenichel, *op. cit.*, pp. 155–56, 284.
132. Dooley, "The Concept of Time in Defence of Ego Integrity," pp. 13–23.
133. Spengler, *Decline of the West*, II, 486–93.
134. Abraham, *Selected Papers*, pp. 384–85; Jones, *Papers on Psychoanalysis*, pp. 671–72. Cf. Fenichel, *op. cit.*, p. 282.
135. BPP 45–52.
136. See above, chap. IX.
137. Some good intuitions, and much confusion, in the baroque poetry of Harnik, "Die triebhaft-affektiven Momente im Zeitgefühl," pp. 32–57.
138. Eliade, *Myth of the Eternal Return*, pp. 53–54, 79, 86, 157.
139. CP V, 182.
140. CP V, 200, 372–75; *Out.* 73–76.
141. Durkheim, *The Elementary Forms of the Religious Life*, pp. 38–42.
142. CP II, 164–71. Cf. Abraham, *Selected Papers*, pp. 379–81.
143. Cf. Heichelheim, *Wirtschaftsgeschichte*, I, 114.
144. Cf. Durkheim, *Division of Labor*, pp. 147–99.
145. Cf. Freud's tentative formulations on the hero, GP 112–15.
146. Cf. Veblen, *Theory of the Leisure Class*, pp. 3–8; *Instinct of Workmanship*, pp. 38–102.
147. Cf. Eliade, *op. cit.*, pp. 102–12.
148. Bettelheim, *Symbolic Wounds*, pp. 108, 136.
149. Cf. above, chap. IX.
150. Cf. Róheim, "The Evolution of Culture," pp. 387–418.
151. Spengler, *Decline of the West*, I, 248. Cf. Eliade, *Le Yoga*, pp. 281, 286.
152. Cf. above, note 46.
153. Childe, *What Happened in History*, p. 84.
154. Frankfort, *The Birth of Civilization in the Near East*, p. 51.
155. Ortega y Gasset, *The Revolt of the Masses*, p. 111.
156. Spengler, *Decline of the West*, II, 94.
157. Sombart, *Der moderne Kapitalismus*, II, 191–93. Cf. Nuss-

baum, *A History of the Economic Institutions of Modern Europe*, p. 36; Turner, *The Ancient Cities*, pp. 270–305.

158. Childe, *What Happened in History*, pp. 84, 88.
159. Tunnard, *The City of Man*, pp. 28–29.
160. Genesis 11:4.
161. Spengler, *Decline of the West*, II, 92–93. Cf. Simmel in Wolff, *The Sociology of Georg Simmel*, pp. 410–14.
162. Piggott, "The Role of the City in Ancient Civilizations," in Fisher (ed.), *The Metropolis in Modern Life*, p. 7.
163. Cf. Tunnard, *City of Man*, p. 43.
164. Mumford, *Culture of Cities*, p. 4.
165. Robinson, *The Rate of Interest*, p. 146.
166. Eliade, *Myth of the Eternal Return*, pp. 55–58, 74.
167. See above, chap. VIII, note 34.
168. Plato, *Phaedrus*, 245 C–E.
169. LaBarre, *The Human Animal*, pp. 149–58.
170. Whitehead, *The Aims of Education*, p. 26.
171. Cf. above, chap. IX. Cf. Róheim, *Origin and Function of Culture*, p. 97.
172. Ruskin, *Munera Pulveris*, pp. 182–83.
173. Eliade, *Myth of the Eternal Return*, pp. 6–48.
174. Róheim, *The Eternal Ones of the Dream*, p. 247; cf. pp. 149–50, 249–50.
175. Kaufmann (ed.), *The Portable Nietzsche*, p. 434.
176. Keynes, *Essays in Persuasion*, p. 371.
177. Cf. Durkheim, *Division of Labor*, pp. 174–99.
178. Heichelheim, *Wirtschaftsgeschichte*, I, 199–225. Cf. Childe, *What Happened in History*, pp. 177–223.
179. Spengler, *Decline of the West*, II, 103; Mumford, *Culture of Cities*, pp. 271, 291–92.
180. Horace, *Odes*, I, i; III, xxx. Classical scholars have disputed whether the word *situs*, here translated "accumulation," means "structure" or "dirt"; they can learn from psychoanalysis the unity of these opposites.
181. Ferenczi, *Sex in Psychoanalysis*, p. 327.
182. CP II, 45–50.
183. See above, chap. III, notes 19–20.
184. CP II, 164–71.
185. Ferenczi, *Thalassa*, pp. 5–14, 97.
186. Cf. the case of the boy who worked out his Oedipus complex with coins: Abraham, *Selected Papers*, pp. 387–88.
187. Róheim, "Heiliges Geld in Melanesien"; Harnik, "Die triebhaft-affektiven Momente im Zeitgefühl."
188. See above, chap. IX.
189. Ferenczi, *Thalassa*, pp. 5–36, 52.

190. Ferenczi, *Further Contributions*, p. 291.
191. Ferenczi, *Thalassa*, p. 12.
192. Reich, *The Function of the Orgasm*, pp. 99–112.
193. Ferenczi, *Final Contributions*, p. 66.
194. BW 863; Ferenczi, *Thalassa*, pp. 12, 16; Ferenczi, *Further Contributions*, pp. 78–89, 95–104, 170–74, 191–93.
195. Kaufmann, *The Portable Nietzsche*, p. 434.
196. CP II, 45, 170, 260; CP III, 559. Compare Hegel's derivation of the *Kunsttrieb* and *Bildungstrieb* from the anal function: *Naturphilosophie*, in *Werke*, XVII, Part I, pp. 635–36; cf. Bachelard, *La terre et les rêveries de la volonté*, pp. 106–107.
197. See above, note 61.
198. NIL 99.
199. CP II, 273.
200. NIL 131.
201. Coleridge, *On Poesy or Art*, in Shawcross, *Coleridge's Biographia Literaria*, II, 263.
202. See above, chap. XIII, note 24.
203. See above, chap XIII, note 33.
204. *Civ.* 66n, 76–78n.
205. EI 57, 80.
206. Wisdom, *The Unconscious Origin of Berkeley's Philosophy*, pp. 64, 73–74.
207. Wisdom, *op. cit.*, pp. 137, 230.
208. Further palpable evidence of the anal problem in Platonism can be found in the case of Henry More: see Powicke, *The Cambridge Platonists*, pp. 152–53. Cf. Bachelard, *La terre et les rêveries de la volonté*, p. 107n.
209. Meyerson, *Identity and Reality; De l'explication dans les sciences*.
210. See above, chap. XII, note 3.
211. See above, chap. XII.
212. Cf. Róheim, "Heiliges Geld in Melanesien," p. 399; Róheim, "The Evolution of Culture," pp. 401–402; Bourke, *Scatalogic Rites of All Nations*, pp. 266–67; Posinsky, "Yurok Shell Money and Pains," pp. 598–632.
213. *Life*, June 4, 1956.
214. Bachelard, *La formation de l'esprit scientifique*, pp. 134–37, 179–80.
215. Bachelard, *La formation de l'esprit scientifique*, pp. 120–22, 125. Cf. Eliade, *Le Yoga*, p. 280.
216. Bourke, *Scatalogic Rites*, p. 168; cf. pp. 166–67.
217. Frazer, *Taboo and the Perils of the Soul*, pp. 283–90; Mead, *Sex and Temperament*, pp. 20–21, 48–50; Bourke, *Scatalogic Rites*.

218. Róheim, "Heiliges Geld in Melanesien," pp. 389–91; Bourke, *Scatalogic Rites*, pp. 264–65. Cf. Abraham, *Selected Papers*, p. 444.
219. McGee, "The Seri Indians," pp. 209–12.
220. Radin, *The Trickster*, p. 140.
221. Bourke, *Scatalogic Rites*, pp. 266–67; Abraham, *Selected Papers*, pp. 320–21.
222. This paragraph is a psychoanalytical addendum to the author's *Hermes the Thief*. For vestiges of unsublimated anality, see *Homeric Hymn to Hermes*, vss. 295–96; Babrius, *Fabulae*, LXVIII. For the anal character of the stone heap, cf. Babrius, *loc. cit.*, and Frazer, *The Scapegoat*, pp. 3–30. On the Arapesh, see Mead, *Sex and Temperament*, pp. 21, 49.
223. Jonson, *Volpone*, I, i, 11–21.
224. Marx, *Capital*, II, 136.
225. Cf. R. F. Allendy, *Capitalisme et sexualité*, p. 14.
226. Keynes, *Essays in Persuasion*, p. 369.

PART SIX

Chapter XVI: The Resurrection of the Body

1. Hegel, *Phenomenology of Mind*, p. 81.
2. Thoreau, *A Week on the Concord and Merrimack Rivers;* cf. Read, *Icon and Idea*, p. 139.
3. Baudelaire, *Mon coeur mis à nu*. Cf. Marcuse, *Eros and Civilization*, p. 153.
4. Tertullian, *De Carnis Resurrectione*, p. 63. Cf. Mead, *The Doctrine of the Subtle Body in Western Tradition*, p. 111.
5. See above, chap. IX, note 58.
6. Underhill, *Mysticism;* Huxley, *The Perennial Philosophy*.
7. Mead, *The Doctrine of the Subtle Body in Western Tradition;* Scholem, *Major Trends in Jewish Mysticism;* Gray, *Goethe the Alchemist*. Cf. Savage, "Jung, Alchemy and Self," pp. 14–37.
8. Benz, *Der vollkommene Mensch nach Jacob Boehme*.
9. Benz, *op. cit.*, p. 138.
10. Needham, *Science and Civilization in China*, II, 139–54. Needham seems to underestimate Occidental body mysticism; cf. *op. cit.*, p. 464, the only reference to Boehme. See also Watts, "Asian Psychology and Modern Psychiatry," pp. 25–30.
11. Gray, *Goethe the Alchemist*.
12. See above, chap. V, note 22.

13. Whitehead, *Science and the Modern World*, pp. 93–118.
14. Hartman, *The Unmediated Vision*.
15. Hartman, *op. cit.*, pp. 27–28, 57, 64, 94, 96, 107, 109.
16. See above, chap. IX, notes 56–60.
17. NIL 106.
18. See above, chap. XV, note 9.
19. Cf. Gray, *Goethe the Alchemist*, pp. 98–99.
20. Needham, "Mechanistic Biology," in *Science, Religion and Reality*, p. 257.
21. Ferenczi, *Thalassa*.
22. Ferenczi, *Further Contributions*, p. 373.
23. Ferenczi, *Further Contributions*, p. 256; *Thalassa*, p. 2.
24. Ferenczi, *Further Contributions*, p. 256.
25. Ferenczi, *Further Contributions*, p. 393.
26. Whitehead, *Science and the Modern World*, p. 69.
27. Bachelard, *La formation de l'esprit scientifique*, pp. 250–51.
28. Ferenczi, *Final Contributions*, p. 246.
29. Whitehead, *Science and the Modern World*, p. 69.
30. Marx, Engels, *Kleine ökonomische Schriften*, p. 131; cf. pp. 127–37.
31. Needham, "A Biologist's View of Whitehead's Philosophy," in Schilpp (ed.), *The Philosophy of Alfred North Whitehead*, pp. 241–72; Needham, *Science and Civilization in China*, II, 75–77, 291, 454, 467.
32. Eliade, *Le Yoga*, pp. 110, 258, 269; Scholem, *Major Trends in Jewish Mysticism*, p. 218.
33. Cf. the role of paradox in philosophy: Wisdom, *Philosophy and Psycho-Analysis*, pp. 169–81, 248–82.
34. CP V, 316–57.
35. CP V, 181–82.
36. For the positivist approach to psychoanalysis, see Kris, "The Nature of Psychoanalytical Propositions and Their Validation," pp. 239–59; Frenkel-Brunswik, "Psychoanalysis and the Unity of Science," pp. 273–347; Pumpian-Mindlin (ed.), *Psychoanalysis and Science*.
37. BW (Dreams) 345–46; NIL 99; CP III, 559n; CP IV, 119, 184; CP V, 185.
38. CP IV, 184; BW (Dreams) 346.
39. CP IV, 184–91. Cf. BW (Dreams) 346n.
40. CP V, 181–85.
41. CP V, 182. Cf. CP III, 559n; CP IV, 119.
42. See above, chap. VII, note 13.
43. CP V, 369–71.
44. See above, chap. XII, note 70.
45. *Civ.* 144.

Bibliography

Abraham, K. *Selected Papers on Psycho-analysis*, tr. D. Bryan and A. Strachey. New York: Basic Books, 1953.

Allendy, R. F. *Capitalisme et sexualité*. Paris: Denoël et Steele [1932].

Bachelard, G. *La formation de l'esprit scientifique*. Paris: J. Vrin, 1947.

——. *La terre et les rêveries de la volonté*. Paris: J. Corti, 1948.

Barge, H. *Luther und der Frühkapitalismus*. Gütersloh: Bertelsmann, 1951.

Bartlett, F. "The Concept of Repression," *Science and Society*, XVIII (1954), pp. 326–39.

Baumann, H. *Das doppelte Geschlecht: ethnologische Studien zur Bisexualität in Ritus und Mythos*. Berlin: D. Reimer, 1955.

Benz, E. *Der volkommene Mensch nach Jacob Boehme*. Stuttgart: W. Kohlhammer, 1937.

Berdyaev, N. *The Destiny of Man*. London: G. Bles. 3rd ed., 1948.

Bertalanffy, L. von "An Essay on the Relativity of Categories," *Philosophy of Science*, XXII (1955), pp. 243–63.

Bettelheim, B. *Symbolic Wounds*. Glencoe: Free Press, 1954.

Blake, W. *The Portable Blake*, ed. A. Kazin. New York: Viking Press, 1953.

Bonaparte, M. *Chronos, Eros, Thanatos*. Paris: Presses Universitaires de France, 1952.

Bourke, J. G. *Scatalogic Rites of All Nations*. Washington: W. H. Lowdermilk & Co., 1891.

Brinton, H. H. *The Mystic Will*. New York: Macmillan, 1930.

Brown, N. O. *Hermes the Thief*. Madison: University of Wisconsin Press, 1947.

Butler, E. M. *The Fortunes of Faust*. Cambridge: Cambridge University Press, 1952.

Cassirer, E. *An Essay on Man*. New Haven: Yale University Press, 1944.

Castelli, E. *Il Demoniaco nell' arte*. Milan: Electa Milano, 1952.

Childe, V. G. *What Happened in History*. New York: Penguin Books, 1946.

Coleridge, S. T. *Biographia Literaria*, ed. J. Shawcross, 2 vols. Oxford: The Clarendon Press, 1907.

Cornford, F. M. *Principium Sapientiae, The Origins of Greek Philosophical Thought*. Cambridge: Cambridge University Press, 1952.

D'Arcy, M. C. *The Mind and Heart of Love, Lion & Unicorn; a study in Eros and Agape*. New York: Henry Holt, 1947.

Dobb, M. *On Economic Theory and Socialism*. London: Routledge & Kegan Paul, 1955.

Dooley, L. "The Concept of Time in Defence of Ego Integrity," *Psychiatry*, IV (1941), pp. 13–23.

Duncan, I. *My Life*. New York: Boni & Liveright, 1927.

Durkheim, E. *The Division of Labor in Society*, tr. G. Simpson. Glencoe: Free Press, 1947.

——. *The Elementary Forms of the Religious Life*, tr. J. W. Swain. London: G. Allen & Unwin, n.d.

Einzig, P. *Primitive Money*. London: Eyre & Spottiswoode, 1949.

Eliade, M. *The Myth of the Eternal Return*. New York: Pantheon Books, 1954.

——. *Le Yoga*. Paris: Payot, 1954.

Empson, W. *Some Versions of Pastoral*. London: Chatto & Windus, 1935.

Engels, F. *The Origin of the Family, Private Property and the State*. Chicago: C. H. Kerr, 1902.

——. *The Part Played by Labor in the Transition from Ape to Man*. Moscow: Foreign Languages Publishing House, 1949.

Feldmann, H. "The Illusions of Work," *Psychoanalytical Review*, XLII (1955), pp. 262–70.

Fenichel, O. *The Psychoanalytic Theory of Neurosis*. New York: W. W. Norton, 1945.

Ferenczi, S. *Final Contributions to the Problems and Methods of Psycho-analysis*, ed. M. Balint, tr. E. Mosbacher and others. London: Hogarth Press and the Institute of Psycho-analysis, 1955.

——. *Further Contributions to the Theory and Technique of Psycho-analysis*. (London: Hogarth); New York: Basic Books, 1952.

——. *Sex in Psycho-analysis*, tr. E. Jones. New York: Basic Books [1950]; (London: Hogarth).

——. *Thalassa: A Theory of Genitality*. New York: The Psychoanalytic Quarterly, 1938.

Fife, R. H. *The Revolt of Martin Luther*. New York: Columbia University Press, 1957.

Firth, R. "Currency, Primitive," in the *Encyclopaedia Britannica*, 14th ed. London: Encyclopaedia Britannica, Ltd., 1923.

Frankfort, H. *The Birth of Civilization in the Near East*. Bloomington: Indiana University Press, 1951.

Fraser, L. M. *Economic Thought and Language*. London: A. & C. Black, 1937.

Frazer, J. G. *The Golden Bough*, 3rd ed., 12 vols. New York: Macmillan, 1935.

———. *The Golden Bough*, abridged ed. New York: Macmillan, 1947.

Frenkel-Brunswik, E. "Psychoanalysis and the Unity of Science," *Proceedings of the American Academy of Arts and Sciences*, LXXX, No. 4 (Mar. 1954), pp. 271–350.

Freud, S. *The Basic Writings of Sigmund Freud*, tr. & ed. A. A. Brill. New York: The Modern Library, 1938.

———. *Beyond the Pleasure Principle*, tr. J. Strachey. (International Psycho-Analytical Library, ed. E. Jones, no. 4.) London: Hogarth Press, 1950.

———. *Civilization and Its Discontents*, tr. J. Riviere. (International Psycho-Analytical Library, ed. E. Jones, no. 17.) London: Hogarth Press, 1930.

———. *Collected Papers*, ed. J. Riviere & J. Strachey, 5 vols. (International Psycho-Analytical Library, no. 7–10, 37.) New York, London: The International Psycho-Analytical Press, 1924–50.

———. *Delusion and Dream and Other Essays*, ed. P. Rieff. Boston: Beacon Press, 1956.

———. *The Ego and the Id*, tr. J. Riviere. (International Psycho-Analytical Library, no. 12.) London: Hogarth Press and The Institute of Psycho-Analysis, 1927.

———. *The Future of an Illusion*, tr. W. D. Robson-Scott. (International Psycho-Analytical Library, no. 15.) London: Hogarth Press and The Institute of Psycho-Analysis, 1928.

———. *A General Introduction to Psycho-Analysis*, tr. J. Riviere. New York: Perma Giants, 1953; (London: G. Allen & Unwin Ltd.).

———. *Gesammelte Werke*. London: Imago Publishing Co., 1948.

———. *Group Psychology and the Analysis of the Ego*, tr. J. Strachey. (International Psycho-Analytical Library, no. 6.) London, Vienna: The International Psycho-Analytical Press, 1922.

———. *Inhibitions, Symptoms and Anxiety*, tr. A. Strachey. (International Psycho-Analytical Library, no. 28.) London: Hogarth Press and The Institute of Psycho-Analysis, 1936.

———. *Leonardo da Vinci: A Study in Psychosexuality*, tr. A. A. Brill. New York: Random House, 1947.

———. *Moses and Monotheism*, tr. K. Jones. (International Psycho-Analytical Library, no. 33.) London: Hogarth Press and The Institute of Psycho-Analysis, 1939; (New York: Knopf, 1939).

Freud, S. *New Introductory Lectures on Psycho-Analysis*, tr. W. J. H. Sprott. (International Psycho-Analytical Library, no. 24.) London: Hogarth Press and The Institute of Psycho-Analysis, 1933.

——. *The Origins of Psycho-analysis: Letters to Wilhelm Fliess, Drafts and Notes: 1877–1902*, ed. M. Bonaparte, A. Freud and E. Kris. New York: Basic Books, 1954.

——. *An Outline of Psycho-Analysis*, tr. J. Strachey. (International Psycho-Analytical Library, no. 35.) London: Hogarth Press, 1949.

——. *The Question of Lay Analysis*. London: Imago Publishing Co., 1948.

——. *The Standard Edition of the Complete Psychological Works of Sigmund Freud*, ed. James Strachey, Anna Freud, Alix Strachey, & Alan Tyson. [24] vols. London: Hogarth Press and The Institute of Psycho-Analysis, 1954– .

Fromm, E. *Escape from Freedom*. New York: Rinehart, 1941.

——. "Die psychoanalytische Charakterologie und ihre Bedeutung für die Sozialpsychologie," *Zeitschrift für Sozialforschung*, I (1932), pp. 253–77.

——. *The Sane Society*. New York: Rinehart, 1955.

——. "Sex and Character," *Psychiatry*, VI (1943), pp. 21–31.

Funck-Brentano, F. *Luther*, tr. E. F. Buckley. London: J. Cape, 1936.

Gambs, J. S. *Beyond Supply and Demand*. New York: Columbia University Press, 1946.

Gener, P. *La mort et le diable*. Paris: C. Reinwald, 1880.

Ghiselin, B., ed. *The Creative Process*. New York: New American Library, 1955.

Glover, E. "Examination of the Klein System of Child Psychology," in *The Psychoanalytic Study of the Child*, I (1945), pp. 75–118. New York: International Universities Press, 1945.

Gray, R. D. *Goethe the Alchemist*. Cambridge: Cambridge University Press, 1952.

Greenacre, P. "The Mutual Adventures of Jonathan Swift and Lemuel Gulliver," *Psychoanalytic Quarterly*, XXIV (1955), pp. 20–62.

Grisar, H. *Luther*, tr. E. M. Lamond, ed. L. Cappadelta. 6 vols. London: Kegan Paul, Trench, Trübner, 1913–17.

Hampshire, S. *Spinoza*. Harmondsworth, Middlesex [Eng.]: Penguin Books, 1951.

Harington, J. *The Metamorphosis of Ajax*. Chiswick: Press of C. Whittingham, 1814.

Harnik, J. "Die triebhaft-affektiven Momente im Zeitgefühl," *Imago*, XI (1925), pp. 32–57.

Hartman, G. H. *The Unmediated Vision*. New Haven: Yale University Press, 1954.

Hegel, G. W. F. *Phenomenology of Mind*, tr. J. B. Baillie, 2d ed. London: G. Allen & Unwin, 1931.

Hegel, G. W. F. *Science of Logic*, tr. W. H. Johnson and L. G. Struthers. London: G. Allen & Unwin, 1929.

——. *Werke*, 19 vols. in 21. Berlin: Duncker & Humblot, 1832–87.

Heichelheim, F. M. *Wirtschaftsgeschichte des Altertums*. Leiden: A. W. Sijthoff, 1938.

Herskovits, M. J. *Economic Anthropology*. New York: Knopf, 1952.

Horney, K. *New Ways in Psychoanalysis*. New York: W. W. Norton, 1939.

Huizinga, J. *Homo Ludens, A Study of the Play-Element in Culture*. New York: Roy, 1950.

——. *The Waning of the Middle Ages*. London: E. Arnold, 1927.

Huxley, A. *Do What You Will*. London: Chatto and Windus, 1931.

——. *The Perennial Philosophy*. New York: Harper, 1945.

——. *Tomorrow and Tomorrow and Tomorrow, and Other Essays*. New York: Harper, 1956.

Hytier, J. *La poétique de Valéry*. Paris: Colin, 1953.

Isaacs, S. "The Nature and Function of Phantasy," *International Journal of Psycho-Analysis*, XXIX (1948), pp. 73–97.

Jespersen, O. *Language: Its Nature, Development and Origin*. London: G. Allen & Unwin, 1922.

Jones, E. *On the Nightmare*, new ed. New York: Liveright, 1951.

——. *Papers on Psycho-Analysis*. London: Baillière, Tindall & Cox, 1918.

Jonson, B. [*Works of*] *Ben Jonson*, ed. C. H. Herford, P. and E. Simpson. Oxford: Clarendon Press, 1925–52.

Joyce, J. *Ulysses*. New York: Modern Library, 1934.

Karpman, B. "Neurotic Traits of Jonathan Swift," *Psychoanalytic Review*, XXIX (1942), pp. 165–84.

Kaufmann, W. *Nietzsche: Philosopher, Psychologist, Antichrist*. Princeton: Princeton University Press, 1950.

——. *The Portable Nietzsche*. New York: Viking Press, 1954.

Keynes, J. M. *Essays in Persuasion*. New York: Harcourt, Brace, 1932; (London: Macmillan & Co., Ltd.).

——. *The General Theory of Employment, Interest and Money*. New York: Harcourt, Brace, 1936.

——. *Treatise on Money*. New York: Harcourt, Brace, 1930.

Kierkegaard, S. *Works of Love*, tr. D. F. and L. M. Swenson. Princeton: Princeton University Press, 1946.

Klingner, E. "Luther und der deutsche Volksaberglaube," *Palaestra*, LVI (1912).

Knight, F. H. *The Ethics of Competition*. New York: Harper, 1935.

Kojève, A. *Introduction à la lecture de Hegel*. Paris: Gallimard, 1947.

Kris, E. "The Nature of Psychoanalytical Propositions and Their

Validation," in Hook and Konvitz (eds.), *Freedom and Experience*. Ithaca: Cornell University Press, 1947.

Kroeber, A. L. "The Superorganic," *American Anthropologist*, XIX (1917), pp. 163–213.

Kroner, R. "Bemerkungen zur Dialektik der Zeit," *Verhandlungen des dritten Hegelkongresses* (Rome, 1934), pp. 153–61.

LaBarre, W. *The Human Animal*. Chicago: University of Chicago Press, 1954.

Langer, S. *Philosophy in a New Key*. New York: Penguin Books, 1948.

Lawrence, D. H. *Sex, Literature and Censorship*. New York: Twayne, 1953.

Laum, B. *Heiliges Geld*. Tübingen: Mohr, 1924.

Leeuw, G. van der. *Religion in Essence and Manifestation*. London: G. Allen & Unwin, 1938.

Lévi-Strauss, C. *Les structures élémentaires de la parenté*. Paris: Presses Universitaires de France, 1949.

Locke, J. *The Works of John Locke*, 10 vols. London: T. Tegg, 1823.

Lukács, G. *Goethe und seine Zeit*. Bern: A. Francke, 1947.

Luther, M. *Sämmtliche Schriften*, ed. J. G. Walch. St. Louis: Concordia Publishing House, 1881–1910.

McGee, W. J. "The Seri Indians," in *Annual Report of the Bureau of American Ethnology*, XVII (1898), Washington: U. S. Government Printing Office, pp. 9–344.

Malinowski, B. "The Primitive Economics of the Trobriand Islanders," *Economic Journal*, XXXI (1921), pp. 1–16.

Marcuse, H. *Eros and Civilization*. Boston: Beacon Press, 1955.

———. *Reason and Revolution: Hegel and the Rise of Social Theory*. New York: Oxford University Press, 1941.

Marx, K. *Capital*, tr. E. Untermann, 3 vols. Chicago: C. H. Kerr, 1906–1909.

———. *Capital*. New York: Modern Library [c.1932].

———. *Der historische Materialismus, die Frühschriften*, ed. S. Landshut and J. P. Mayer. Leipzig: A. Kröner, 1932.

———. *The Poverty of Philosophy*. Chicago: C. H. Kerr, 1913.

——— and Engels, F. *Kleine ökonomische Schriften*. Berlin: Dietz, 1955.

Mauss, M. *Sociologie et anthropologie*. Paris: Presses Universitaires de France, 1950.

Mead, G. R. S. *The Doctrine of the Subtle Body in Western Tradition*. London: J. M. Watkins, 1919.

Mead, M. *Sex and Temperament in Three Primitive Societies*. New York: New American Library, 1950.

Meyerson, E. *De l'explication dans les sciences*. Paris: Payot, 1921.

Meyerson, E. *Identity and Reality*. London: G. Allen & Unwin, 1930.

Miller, H. *Sunday After the War*. Norfolk, Conn.: New Directions, 1944.

Mumford, L. *The Culture of Cities*. New York: Harcourt, Brace, 1938.

Murray, M. *Witch Cult in Western Europe*. Oxford: Clarendon Press, 1921.

Murry, J. M. *Jonathan Swift: A Critical Biography*. London: Jonathan Cape, 1954.

Needham, J. "A Biologist's View of Whitehead's Philosophy," in *The Philosophy of Alfred North Whitehead*, ed. P. A. Schilpp. Evanston & Chicago: Northwestern University, 1951, pp. 241–71.

———. "Mechanistic Biology and the Religious Consciousness," in *Science, Religion and Reality*, ed. J. Needham. New York: Macmillan, 1925, pp. 219–57.

———. *Science and Civilization in China*. Vol. II: *History of Scientific Thought*. Cambridge: Cambridge University Press, 1956.

Nietzsche, F. W. *The Philosophy of Nietzsche*. New York: Modern Library, 1927.

Nussbaum, F. L. *A History of the Economic Institutions of Modern Europe*. New York: F. S. Crofts, 1933.

Nygren, A. *Agape and Eros*. Philadelphia: Westminster Press, 1953.

Obendiek, H. *Der Teufel bei Martin Luther*. Berlin: Furche-verlag, 1931.

Ortega y Gasset. *The Revolt of the Masses*. New York: New American Library, 1950.

Otto, W. F. *Dionysos, Mythos und Kultus*. Frankfurt am Main: Klosterman [1933].

Parsons, T. *The Structure of Social Action*. Glencoe: Free Press, 1949.

Piggott, S. "The Rule of the City in Ancient Civilizations," in *The Metropolis in Modern Life*, ed. R. M. Fisher. Garden City: Doubleday, 1955.

Poe, E. A. "The Poetic Principle," *Complete Poetical Works*, ed. J. A. Harrison and R. A. Stewart. New York: Crowell, 1922.

Polanyi, K. *The Great Transformation*. New York: Rinehart, 1944.

Pollack, D. *Les idées des enfants sur la différence des sexes*. Thesis. Paris: Impr. Beresniak, 1936.

Popitz, H. *Der entfremdete Mensch: Zeitkritik und Geschichtsphilosophie des jungen Marx*. Basel: Verlag für Recht und Gesellschaft, 1953.

Posinsky, S. H. "Yurok Shell Money and Pains: a Freudian Interpretation," *Psychiatric Quarterly*, XXX (1956), pp. 598–632.

Powicke, F. J. *The Cambridge Platonists*. Cambridge: Harvard University Press, 1926.

Pumpian-Mindlin, E., ed. *Psychoanalysis as Science*. Stanford: Stanford University Press [1952].

Quintana, R. *The Mind and Art of Jonathan Swift*. New York: Oxford University Press, 1936.

Radin, P. *The Trickster: A Study in American Indian Mythology*. London: Routledge & Kegan Paul, 1956.

Read, H. *Icon and Idea*. Cambridge: Harvard University Press, 1955.

Rehm, W. *Orpheus: Der Dichter und die Toten*. Düsseldorf: L. Schwann, 1950.

Reich, W. *The Discovery of the Orgone*, Vol. I, *The Function of the Orgasm*. New York: Orgone Institute Press, 1948.

———. *The Mass Psychology of Fascism*, 3d rev. & enl. ed., tr. T. P. Wolfe. New York: Orgone Institute Press, 1946.

Reik, T. *Der eigene und der fremde Gott*. Vienna: Internationaler Psychoanalytischer Verlag, 1923.

Rieff, P. "The Authority of the Past," *Social Research*, XXI (1954), pp. 428–50.

———. "The Meaning of History and Religion in Freud's Thought," *Journal of Religion*, XXXI (1951), pp. 114–31.

Rilke, R. M. *Letters to a Young Poet*, tr. M. D. Herter. New York: W. W. Norton, 1934.

———. "Ueber Kunst," *Verse und Prosa aus dem Nachlass*. Leipzig: Gesellschaft der Freunde der Deutschen Bücherei, 1929.

Robertson, D. H. *Utility and All That, and Other Essays*. New York: Macmillan, 1952.

Robinson, J. *The Rate of Interest*. London: Macmillan, 1952.

Róheim, G. *The Eternal Ones of the Dream*. New York: International Universities Press, 1945.

———. "The Evolution of Culture," *International Journal of Psychoanalysis*, XV (1934), pp. 387–418.

———. "Heiliges Geld in Melanesien," *Internationale Zeitschrift für Psychoanalyse*, IX (1923), pp. 384–401.

———. *The Origin and Function of Culture*. (Nervous and Mental Disease Monograph no. 69.) New York: Nervous & Mental Disease Monographs, 1943.

———. *War, Crime and the Covenant*. (Journal of Clinical Psychopathology Monograph Series no. 1.) Monticello, N. Y.: Medical Journal Press, 1945.

Rudwin, M. J. *The Devil in Legend and Literature*. Chicago: Open Court Publishing Co., 1931.

———. *Les écrivains diaboliques de France*. Paris: Figuière, 1937.

———. *Die Teufelszenen im geistlichen Drama des deutschen Mittelalters*. Baltimore: The Johns Hopkins Press, 1914.

Ruskin, J. *Works of John Ruskin*, ed. E. T. Cook and A. Wedderburn, 39 vols. London: G. Allen & Unwin, 1903–12.

Russell, B. *Philosophical Essays*. London: Longmans, Green, 1910.
Sartre, J. P. *Being and Nothingness: An Essay on Phenomenological Ontology*, tr. H. E. Barnes. New York: Philosophical Library, 1956.
Savage, D. S. "Jung, Alchemy and Self," in *Explorations: Studies in Culture and Communication, no. 2*. Toronto: University of Toronto, 1954.
Scheler, M. *The Nature of Sympathy*. London: Routledge & Kegan Paul, 1954.
Schilder, P. *The Image and Appearance of the Human Body*. London: Kegan Paul, Trench, Trübner, 1935.
Schiller, F. C. S. *Humanism*. London: Macmillan, 1912.
———. *Riddles of the Sphinx*. London: S. Sonnenschein, 1910.
Schiller, J. C. F. *Essays Aesthetical and Philosophical*. London: G. Bell, 1884.
Scholem, G. G. *Major Trends in Jewish Mysticism*. New York: Schocken Books, 1941.
Schopenhauer, A. *The World as Will and Idea*, tr. R. B. Haldane and J. Kemp. London: Kegan Paul, Trench, Trübner, 1896.
Schumpeter, J. A. *Capitalism, Socialism and Democracy*. New York: Harper, 1942.
———. *Theory of Economic Development*. Cambridge: Harvard University Press, 1934.
Simenauer, E. "Pregnancy Envy in Rainer Maria Rilke," *American Imago*, XI (1954), pp. 235–48.
Simmel, G. *Philosophie des Geldes*. Munich: Duncker & Humblot, 1922.
———. *The Sociology of Georg Simmel*, tr. and ed. K. H. Wolff, Glencoe: Free Press [1950].
Smith, A. *Wealth of Nations*. London: J. F. Dove, 1826.
Sombart, W. *Der moderne Kapitalismus*. Leipzig: Duncker & Humblot, 1902.
Sorel, G. *Réflexions sur la violence*. Paris: M. Rivière, 1925.
Spengler, O. *The Decline of the West*. London: G. Allen & Unwin, 1932; (New York: Knopf).
Swift, J. *Prose Works of Jonathan Swift*, ed. H. Davis. Oxford: B. Blackwell, 1939–57.
———. *Prose Works of Jonathan Swift*, ed. T. Scott. London: G. Bell, 1897–1908.
Taylor, G. R. *Sex in History*. New York: Vanguard Press, 1954.
Tawney, R. H. *Religion and the Rise of Capitalism*. London: J. Murray, 1926.
Thiel, R. *Luther*. Vienna: P. Neff, 1952.
Tillich, P. *The Interpretation of History*. New York: Scribner's, 1936.

Tillich, P. *The Protestant Era.* Chicago: University of Chicago Press, 1948.

Trilling, L. *The Liberal Imagination.* Garden City: Doubleday, 1953.

Troeltsch, E. *The Social Teaching of the Christian Churches.* London: G. Allen & Unwin, 1931.

Tunnard, C. *The City of Man.* New York: Scribner's, 1953.

Turner, R. *The Great Cultural Traditions.* New York: McGraw-Hill, 1941.

Unamuno y Jugo, M. de. *Tragic Sense of Life,* tr. J. E. Crawford Flitch. New York: Dover, 1954.

Underhill, E. *Mysticism.* New York: Noonday, 1955.

Valabrega, J. P. "L'anthropologie psychanalytique," *La Psychanalyse,* III (1957), pp. 221-45.

Veblen, T. *The Instinct of Workmanship.* New York: Macmillan, 1914.

———. *The Theory of the Leisure Class.* New York: Modern Library, 1934.

Von Neumann, J. and Morgenstern, O. *Theory of Games and Economic Behavior.* Princeton: Princeton University Press, 1944.

Watts, A. W. "Asian Psychology and Modern Psychiatry," *American Journal of Psychoanalysis,* XIII (1953), pp. 25-30.

Weber, M. *Gesammelte Aufsätze zur Religions-sociologie.* Tübingen: Mohr, 1920.

Whitehead, A. N. *Adventures of Ideas.* New York: Macmillan, 1954.

———. *The Aims of Education, and Other Essays.* New York: New American Library, 1949.

———. *Science and the Modern World.* Cambridge: Cambridge University Press, 1927.

Whorf, B. L. *Collected Papers on Metalinguistics.* Washington: Dept. of State, Foreign Service Institute, 1952.

Wilbur, G. B. "Freud's Life-Death Instinct Theory," *American Imago,* II (1941), pp. 134-96, 209-65.

Wisdom, J. O. *Philosophy and Psycho-Analysis.* Oxford: B. Blackwell, 1953.

———. *The Unconscious Origin of Berkeley's Philosophy.* London: Hogarth Press, 1953.

Wittgenstein, L. *Philosophical Investigations,* tr. G. E. M. Anscombe. Oxford: B. Blackwell, 1953

———. *Tractatus Logico-Philosophicus.* London: Kegan Paul, Trench, Trübner, 1922.

Index

of Authorities and Works Referred to and Quoted in the Text

(References in *italics* indicate quoted matter.)

Index